Reclaiming Islamic Tradition

Modern Interpretations of the Classical Heritage

Edited by
Elisabeth Kendall and Ahmad Khan

EDINBURGH
University Press

Edinburgh University Press is one of the leading university presses in the UK. We publish academic books and journals in our selected subject areas across the humanities and social sciences, combining cutting-edge scholarship with high editorial and production values to produce academic works of lasting importance. For more information visit our website: edinburghuniversitypress.com

Edinburgh University Press Ltd
The Tun – Holyrood Road
12 (2f) Jackson's Entry
Edinburgh EH8 8PJ

Typeset in 11/13 Adobe Garamond by
Servis Filmsetting Ltd, Stockport, Cheshire

A CIP record for this book is available from the British Library

ISBN 978 1 4744 0311 5 (hardback)
ISBN 978 1 4744 0312 2 (webready PDF)
ISBN 978 1 4744 1515 6 (epub)

Contents

Acknowledgements v

About the Contributors vi

Introduction 1
Elisabeth Kendall and Ahmad Khan

1 Modern Shiᶜite Legal Theory and the Classical Tradition 12
Robert Gleave

2 Muḥammad Nāṣīr al-Dīn al-Albānī and Traditional Hadith Criticism 33
Christopher Melchert

3 Islamic Tradition in an Age of Print: Editing, Printing and Publishing the Classical Heritage 52
Ahmad Khan

4 Reaching into the Obscure Past: The Islamic Legal Heritage and Reform in the Modern Period 100
Jonathan A. C. Brown

5 Reading Sūrat al-Anᶜām with Muḥammad Rashīd Riḍā and Sayyid Quṭb 136
Nicolai Sinai

6 Contemporary Iranian Interpretations of the Qurʾan and Tradition on Women's Testimony 160
Karen Bauer

7 Ibn Taymiyya between Moderation and Radicalism 177
Jon Hoover

8 The Impact of a Sixteenth-Century Jihad Treatise on Colonial and Modern India 204
Carole Hillenbrand

9 Jihadist Propaganda and its Exploitation of the Arab Poetic Tradition 223
Elisabeth Kendall

10 Contemporary Salafi Literature on Paradise and Hell: The Case of ᶜUmar Sulaymān al-Ashqar 247
Christian Lange

Index 263

Acknowledgements

We would like to thank our home institution, Pembroke College, University of Oxford, for its strong commitment to bringing cross-disciplinary, historical and linguistic depth to the field of Islamic and Middle Eastern Studies. We especially wish to thank Mr Brian Wilson, an alumnus of Pembroke, for his generous support for the ongoing cycle of academic symposia and collaborations out of which this book project developed.

About the Contributors

Karen Bauer is a Research Associate in the Qur'anic Studies Unit of the Institute of Ismaili Studies in London. She received her PhD from Princeton and specialises in Islamic social and intellectual history. Her specific interests include the Qur'an and its interpretation (*tafsīr*), gender in Islamic history and thought, genre and its effect on discourse, and the transition from medieval to modern in Islamic thought. Much of her work is motivated by the question of how social and intellectual context affect the content of texts. Her publications include *Gender Hierarchy in the Qur'an: Medieval Interpretations, Modern Responses* (2015) and *Aims, Methods, and Contexts of Qur'anic Exegesis* (ed. 2013).

Jonathan A. C. Brown is the Alwaleed bin Talal Chair of Islamic Civilization at Georgetown University. His book publications include *The Canonization of al-Bukhari and Muslim: The Formation and Function of the Sunni Hadith Canon* (2007), *Hadith: Muhammad's Legacy in the Medieval and Modern World* (2009) and *Muhammad: A Very Short Introduction* (2011), which was selected for the National Endowment for the Humanities' Bridging Cultures Muslim Journeys Bookshelf. His most recent book, *Misquoting Muhammad: The Challenges and Choices of Interpreting the Prophet's Legacy* (2014), was named one of the top books on religion in 2014 by the *Independent*.

Robert Gleave is Professor of Arabic Studies in the Institute of Arab and Islamic Studies at the University of Exeter. His research focuses on Islamic law and legal theory, with a particular emphasis on the history of Shiʿi jurisprudence. He is director of the Islamic Reformulations project, funded by the UK's Economic and Social Research Council, which aims to map and understand the transition from classical to contemporary Islamic thought.

He is the author of *Islam and Literalism: Literal Meaning and Interpretation in Islamic Legal Theory* (2012) and co-editor of *Violence in Islamic Thought: from the Qur'an to the Mongols* (2014).

Carole Hillenbrand is Professorial Fellow in History at the University of St Andrews and Professor Emerita at the University of Edinburgh. She was educated at the Universities of Cambridge, Oxford and Edinburgh and held the post of Professor of Islamic History at Edinburgh University between 2000 and 2008. She has published widely on medieval Islamic history and political thought. Her best-known book is *The Crusades: Islamic Perspectives* (1999) for which she was awarded The King Faisal International Prize in Islamic Studies in 2005. This was the first time this prize had been awarded to a non-Muslim. She is a Fellow of the British Academy, a Corresponding Fellow of the Medieval Academy of America, an Honorary Fellow of Somerville College, Oxford, and was awarded the Order of the British Empire for Services to Higher Education in 2009. She has held visiting professorships at Dartmouth College and St Louis University in the USA and Groningen University in the Netherlands.

Jon Hoover is Associate Professor of Islamic Studies at the University of Nottingham. He is the author of *Ibn Taymiyya's Theodicy of Perpetual Optimism* (2007). He has also published articles and edited volumes on Christian–Muslim relations and various studies on creation, theodicy, and the duration of hell-fire in the thought of the medieval traditionalist theologians Ibn Taymiyya, Ibn Qayyim al-Jawziyya and Ibn al-Wazir. His current work focuses on God's attributes in medieval Islamic theology.

Elisabeth Kendall is Senior Research Fellow in Arabic and Islamic Studies at Pembroke College, University of Oxford. Her current research focuses on how Arabic cultural production both reflects and fuels political and militant movements. She spends significant time researching in the field, particularly in Yemen and Egypt. Her publications include *Twenty-First Century Jihad* (co-edited with Ewan Stein, 2015), *Literature, Journalism and the Avant-Garde: Intersection in Egypt* (2006), *Media Arabic* (2nd ed. 2012), as well as several articles on aspects of modern Arab culture and its relationship to political landscapes in the Middle East today. She studied Arabic, Islamic Studies and Turkish at the Universities of Oxford and Harvard and served as Director of the Centre for the Advanced Study of the Arab World (CASAW) at the University of Edinburgh before returning to Oxford in 2010.

Ahmad Khan is Postdoctoral Researcher in the Asien-Afrika-Institut at Universität Hamburg. In 2014–15, he was Lecturer in Islamic Studies and History in the Faculty of Oriental Studies at the University of Oxford. His

DPhil thesis examined discourses of heresy and the formation of medieval Sunni orthodoxy between the eighth and eleventh centuries. His current research at Universität Hamburg focuses on the social, political, and religious history of medieval Iran during the seventh to tenth centuries. He has a second research specialism in the field of modern Islamic history and thought, particularly the emergence of publishing houses and editors in the Middle East and Indian subcontinent.

Christian Lange is Professor of Arabic and Islamic Studies at Utrecht University. He is the author of *Justice, Punishment and the Medieval Muslim Imagination* (2008), a study of notions of justice in late-medieval Islam, both in this world and the next. His most recent book is *Paradise and Hell in Islamic Traditions* (2015), a cultural history of the otherworld from the beginnings of Islam to the eve of modernity. He has also edited several scholarly volumes, including *Locating Hell in Islamic Traditions* (2016). From 2011 to 2015, he was the Principal Investigator of the research project 'The here and the hereafter in Islamic traditions', funded by the European Research Council and hosted at Utrecht University.

Christopher Melchert is Professor of Arabic and Islamic Studies at the University of Oxford where he is a Fellow of Pembroke College. He is the author of *The Formation of the Sunni Schools of Law* (1997) and *Ahmad ibn Hanbal* (2006) and has also published over fifty articles on Islamic movements and institutions, mostly of the eighth to eleventh centuries CE. His next book will deal with renunciant piety before Sufism.

Nicolai Sinai is Sheikh Zayed Associate Professor of Islamic Studies at Pembroke College, University of Oxford. He is the author of *Fortschreibung und Auslegung: Studien zur frühen Koraninterpretation* (2009), *Die heilige Schrift des Islams: Die wichtigsten Fakten zum Koran* (2012) and co-editor (with Angelika Neuwirth and Michael Marx) of *The Qurʾān in Context: Historical and Literary Investigations into the Qurʾānic Milieu* (2010). He has produced a German translation of and commentary on the Persian philosopher Shihāb ad-Dīn as-Suhrawardī's (d. 1191) greatest work, *Ḥikmat al-ishrāq: Die Philosophie der Erleuchtung* (2011). He is the author of numerous articles and book chapters on topics such as the Qurʾan's literary features, its engagement with earlier (Christian, Rabbinic, Arabian) traditions, and Islamic scriptural exegesis.

Introduction

Elisabeth Kendall and Ahmad Khan

> Men make their own history, but they do not make it as they please; they do not make it under self-selected circumstances, but under circumstances existing already, given and transmitted from the past. The tradition of all dead generations weighs like a nightmare on the brains of the living. And just as they seem to be occupied with revolutionizing themselves and things, creating something that did not exist before, precisely in such epochs of revolutionary crisis they anxiously conjure up the spirits of the past to their service, borrowing from them names, battle slogans, and costumes in order to present this new scene in world history in time-honored disguise and borrowed language. Thus Luther put on the mask of the Apostle Paul …
>
> Karl Marx (1954)[1]

The notion of tradition is a powerful one for historians of Islam and Islamic societies, although they probably would not describe its burden in such morbid terms as does Marx. Events in the modern period have catapulted the Islamic tradition well beyond the confines of academic scholarship and into the public sphere, where aspects of the Islamic tradition have acquired a new potency in political, social, economic and religious life. Recent events in the Islamic world have also provoked new interpretations of the Islamic tradition by movements and intellectuals in countries as diverse as Iran, India, Saudi Arabia, Egypt and Yemen, all of which feature in this volume. A fascinating range of modern Islamic movements and intellectuals has sought to reinterpret certain rulings, inherited texts, concepts, ideas, genres, persons, events and trends from the Islamic tradition.

Despite this contemporary alacrity over the Islamic tradition, careful treatments of the Islamic tradition in its *longue durée* perspective have been few and far between. There is good reason for this tardiness. The Islamic tradition represents a vast corpus of texts, ideas and practices expressed in a variety of languages and whose geographical range is limited neither to the Middle East nor to the Global South. No one book can encompass the complex diversity that constitutes the Islamic tradition and no one scholar can survey its entire literary heritage. Yet, its very breadth demands a careful examination of how modern thinkers, scholars and movements have navigated the contours of the Islamic tradition in the modern period. The challenge with the Islamic tradition, and indeed with any tradition in the modern period (as Marx's memorable indictment of tradition shows), is how to examine it without boxing it into reductive ideological categories that establish immutable and simplistic spectrums running from 'Islamism' to 'modernism', degeneration to progress, stagnation to innovation. Recent scholarship has attempted to move beyond this to delineate the strategies and mechanisms by which modern movements, intellectuals, scholars and societies reinterpret the Islamic tradition.[2] Despite the impressive contributions made in this direction, the old historiography continues to find new supporters, and nowhere is this more obvious than in the vocabulary of impotence that dominates the titles of such works.[3]

There are other challenges scholars must confront when studying the Islamic tradition. There is the problem of defining tradition. Tradition can convey a myriad of terms, concepts and histories in Islam, and it is entirely reasonable that a tradition whose participants expressed themselves in Arabic, Persian, Ottoman Turkish, Urdu and Hindi (to name just a few) did not employ one all-encompassing Islamicate word for 'tradition', even if some terms appear more frequently than others in the primary sources (*āthār*, *turāth*, *sunan*). If single terms do not convey the breadth of what the Islamic tradition entails, then we must turn to broader definitions.

In his brilliant conceptual history of tradition, Edward Shils offered a definition of tradition capacious enough to accommodate the way in which the Islamic tradition is understood in this volume. For Shils, a tradition is

> anything which is transmitted or handed down from the past to the present. It makes no statement about what is handed down or in what particular combination or whether it is a physical object or a cultural construction; it says nothing about how long it has been handed down or in what manner, whether orally or in written form … The decisive criterion is that, having been created through human actions, through thought and imagination, it is handed down from one generation to the next … Tradition – that which is handed down – includes material objects, beliefs about all sorts of things, images of persons and events, practices and institutions. It includes buildings, monuments, landscapes, sculptures, paintings, books, tools, machines.[4]

Narrowing Shils' definition of tradition, this volume provides a survey of the modern reception history of the Islamic tradition as it appears not in buildings and paintings, but as it has been articulated in books and journals.

Even with this contraction in definition, the study of Islamic tradition is beset with further methodological difficulties. Within the field of Islamic intellectual history, it is easy to succumb to the temptation to concentrate one's analytical efforts mainly on the specifically 'modern' aspects of the thinkers and texts which one is studying. In part, this may simply result from identifying one's subject as modern Islamic thought. This bold act of periodisation from European patterns of history serves to invite scholars to think primarily about the novel themes, ideas and modes of communication that distinguish the intellectual production of the nineteenth to twenty-first centuries from earlier ages.[5]

In addition, apologetic presentations of modern values and ideas as already enshrined in the canonical sources of Islam often trigger predictable interventions by Western scholars insisting, for example, that the Qurʾanic reference to *shūrā* (consultation) cannot really be equated with a call for democratic participation. However, to position writers of the colonial and postcolonial periods primarily against the background of contemporary events and modern Western thought entails the risk of viewing their moorings in the pre-modern tradition as superficial and rhetorical or as precluding the exercise of any agency over it. In such a framework, modern writers emerge either as strategically employing traditional concepts and ideas in order to serve as transparent guises for what are 'really' imported Western notions, or as compulsively, and sometimes aggressively, parroting ancient traditions in an act of intellectual resistance.

This book aims to move beyond the tacit assumption that modern Muslims are subconsciously steered by the Islamic tradition, without exerting any sort of agency or control over it. It interrogates simplistic suggestions that modern Muslim thinkers arbitrarily distort elements of the tradition to which they lay claim. Studying the intellectual history of the modern Islamic world therefore requires a difficult hermeneutical balancing act. Whilst taking account of contemporary references, it is imperative also to accord appropriate weight to the manifold and often complex ways in which Islam's canonical texts and the pre-modern interpretive tradition (both of which exhibit a diversity that one volume cannot survey) are invoked, redirected and reconfigured. It is nevertheless worth stating explicitly that this kind of historically nuanced evaluation need not result in locating an author on an ideal spectrum running from 'modernism to Islamism'. This spectrum is itself a modern construction and using it to explain how pre-modern ideas evolve in the modern period can result in anachronisms and/or reductive teleological approaches to the classical Islamic heritage.

This book profiles some of the most important debates, figures and contestations that have defined the conversation between the past and the present in the Islamic world. Qurʾanic exegesis, Islamic law, gender and women, violence and extremism, and Islamic eschatology are just some of the key themes that are treated in this study of the Islamic tradition's vitality in the modern Islamic world. It does not pretend to offer an overarching theory of the Islamic tradition. In our view, the diversity and sophistication of such a voluminous tradition renders any meta-theory of Islamic tradition premature. The field of Islamic studies requires deliberate and focused investigations into the functioning of Islamic traditions, and this volume represents an important step in this direction. Rather than forcing one single theoretical model upon the Islamic tradition, this volume provides a scholarly platform for different hypotheses and conclusions about how the classical Islamic tradition has been interpreted in the modern period. Above all, this book will allow readers to situate modern developments in the Islamic world within the longer contours of Islamic thought.

Robert Gleave's chapter begins by acknowledging the tendency of both intellectuals in the Islamic world and modern academics to characterise the scholarly traditions of pre-modern Islam as archaic and inconsequential to contemporary issues. This rhetoric against classical intellectual forms of thought may be loud and widespread, but, according to Gleave, modern Shiʿi scholars in the seminaries of Iran and Iraq exhibit a very different trend. The institutional structures of the *ḥawza*s, their curricula, intellectual practices and literary production point to a conscious effort to establish continuities between past achievements and ongoing scholarly practices and contributions. Gleave's point is not that scholars are in complete harmony with aspects of the pre-modern intellectual tradition, but rather that any dissatisfaction with the scholarly heritage rarely expresses itself in a jettisoning of the classical tradition. In order to illustrate this relationship, Gleave examines modern discussions about a delicate subject in classical Islamic legal theory (*uṣūl al-fiqh*); namely, how the meanings of words in revelatory texts evolve and acquire literal or non-literal meanings and whether the acquisition of new meanings could institute new legal-literal interpretations (*al-ḥaqāʾiq al-sharʿiyya*). Gleave undertakes a close reading of the works of Shiʿi scholars such as al-Ākhūnd al-Khurāsānī (d. 1911), the latter's pupil Muḥammad al-Ḥusayn al-Nāʾīnī (d. 1936), Muḥammad Bāqir al-Ṣadr (d. 1980), Rūḥallāh al-Khumaynī (d. 1989) and Abū al-Qāsim al-Khūʾī (d. 1991), among others. This debate has important consequences for Islamic law, and Gleave sets out to examine how the interaction between contemporary jurists in the Shiʿi tradition and their classical heritage produces new developments, debates and criticisms without undermining the classical tradition of Shiʿi legal scholarship.

The subject of **Christopher Melchert**'s chapter is one of the most influential figures of Salafism in the modern period, Muḥammad Nāṣir al-Dīn al-Albānī (d. 1999). Despite a number of surveys of his life and work in Arabophone scholarship, detailed analysis of his scholarly contribution in European languages is almost non-existent. Melchert is interested al-Albānī's influence as a hadith critic. A major advocate of Salafism, al-Albānī proposed to infer rules directly from hadith, bypassing the historic Sunni schools of law. He taught in Saudi Arabia 1961–3 but was forced to leave owing to his allegedly aberrant legal opinions; for example, he considered it unnecessary to remove one's footwear to pray, or to fast in Ramadan if one could not see daylight, as in a house with the windows blocked. Melchert argues that al-Albānī's method of hadith criticism appears to rely heavily on evaluations of men's characters by the most prominent medieval critics. Melchert's assessment of al-Albānī's intellectual contributions goes against a number of characterisations of al-Albānī as an iconoclastic figure who sought to bypass the scholarly legacy of the Middle Ages and return to the programme of the early pious ancestors and hadith critics. Although Melchert's main objective is to analyse al-Albānī's methods against those of his predecessors, he also provides some fascinating insights into scholarly developments in the Islamic world that al-Albānī seems inadvertently to have provoked. Melchert highlights works in Arabophone scholarship in the field of hadith criticism that re-examine medieval methods of hadith criticism. As such, his chapter fills an important gap in our understanding of hadith criticism in the modern Islamic world.

Ahmad Khan's chapter argues that the technology of print and the business of publishing houses provided new opportunities for religious scholars and students to advocate alternative conceptions of the pre-modern, textual canon. Khan focuses on the paramount role played by a new professional class, scholars-cum-editors, in the twentieth and twenty-first centuries, and highlights the impact that contestations on the margins, in footnotes and introductions to modern editions of medieval texts had on religious debate among Sunni movements. Khan argues that the technical and professional apparatus of producing modern editions of medieval texts – discovering manuscripts, editing them, writing introductions to the editions, commenting in the footnotes, and then eventually printing and publishing them – renewed medieval controversies over Abū Ḥanīfa's (d. 767) scholarly credentials. Khan demonstrates how debates over publishing the medieval tradition contributed to new contestations between Salafi traditionalists and late Sunni traditionalists over how the classical heritage of pre-modern Islam ought to function in the modern world.

Jonathan Brown's chapter stresses the increasing importance of obscure legal opinions from the early period of Islamic history to projects for Islamic reform in the modern period. Brown observes that Muslim scholars, in their debates over doctrine and authority, have long accused opposing schools of thought of basing their stances on obscure and errant statements by early Muslim authorities, whose proximity to the Prophet lends them credence. Yet some of the most important and widely accepted reforms implemented by Muslim scholars in the modern period depend on just such isolated opinions. Brown finds that this is the case for the two very important issues of instituting restrictions on marriage age and permitting lending for mortgages and finance. Both of these positions rely on the unique opinions of an obscure eighth-century scholar from Kufa named Ibn Shubruma (d. 761). Brown analyses the tension over reaching back into the obscure past to legitimate present legal reform. He explores this tension not in terms of whether or not one can access the distant past but rather in terms of who is qualified to access it. His chapter addresses such issues in the course of examining how modern Muslim scholars have excavated obscure opinions and figures when rethinking the application of Islamic law in the modern world with respect to underage marriage and modern finance.

While the chapters by Gleave, Melchert, Khan and Brown concentrate on modern developments in the disciplines of hadith criticism, Islamic law and legal theory, **Nicolai Sinai**'s chapter brings the volume on to the study of contemporary Qurʾanic exegesis. Sinai analyses the phenomenon of exegetical holism: the emphasis on the literary and thematic coherence of Qurʾanic suras. His chapter compares the treatment of Sura 6 in two twentieth-century Egyptian commentaries, the famous *Tafsīr al-manār* compiled by Rashīd Riḍā (d. 1935) and Sayyid Quṭb's (d. 1966) *Fī ẓilāl al-Qurʾān*. Sinai traces the deployment of exegetical holism in Qurʾanic commentaries in the pre-modern period and argues that Riḍā's and Quṭb's hermeneutical techniques signal their participation in a centuries-long exegetical conversation. Sinai's careful examination of the delicate exegetical manoeuvers of these modern thinkers suggests that modern scholarship can risk misreading developments in modern exegesis if it fails to study these against the pre-modern backdrop. Moreover, Sinai's comparison of Quṭb's and Riḍā's relationship with pre-modern Qurʾanic exegesis allows him to detect sufficient differences in their level of participation with the longer tradition. He argues that their exegetical activities demand greater sophistication of analysis from modern scholars of Qurʾanic exegesis. Sinai's chapter makes a compelling case for why scholarship on modern *tafsīr* must resist the temptation to focus on sources exclusively or even primarily in terms of their response to modern Western values, concepts and ideas.

With **Karen Bauer**, the book stays with the subject of Qurʾanic exegesis (and Islamic law) in the modern Islamic world, but returns to Iran, the region with which this book begins. Bauer explores how contemporary Iranian *ᶜulamāʾ* resolve the tension between the words of the Qurʾan and modern ideas of intellectual equality between the sexes. Qurʾan 2:282 reads: 'if there are not two men [to testify] then a man and two women, so that if one of the two women errs, the other can remind her'. Though medieval interpretations of this verse varied in important ways, on the whole exegetes understood it to be proof of women's intellectual deficiency. They supported their interpretations with a hadith stating that women are deficient in reason and religion. Bauer examines the way in which modern Iranian *ᶜulamāʾ* interpret this verse, and how they reconcile their interpretation with both the words of the Qurʾan and the history of interpretation. Some modern Iranian *ᶜulamāʾ* uphold pre-modern legal rulings that prevent women from testifying equally with men. However, they justify their interpretation using modern rationales, including scientific research. They generally discount the 'deficiency' hadith. Others believe that interpretation is culturally mandated. Therefore, while it is appropriate for women's testimony to be less than men's in some cultural settings, in others women's testimony should equal men's. Ayatollah Saanei interprets this verse through the lens of history: it reflects the Qurʾan's time and place, when women and men were not equally educated. Today, when women can achieve as well as men academically and professionally, women's testimony is equal to men's in all areas. Some modern *ᶜulamāʾ* seek to reinterpret the actual words of the verse, but Ayatollah Saanei admits the plain sense of the Arabic, which for him is no barrier to reinterpretation. Bauer's chapter argues that both conservative and reformist readings of the Qurʾan exhibit shared hermeneutical strategies which exemplify their engagement with the classical tradition. She suggests that it is mistaken to assume that conservatives are less responsive to contemporary circumstances and debates than reformists. Both classes of scholars are involved in reinterpreting classical Qurʾanic exegesis and Islamic law in an effort to tackle new and changing social realities in the modern period.

Bauer's chapter raises the problem of the spectrums that scholars employ when trying to locate figures or ideas as expressions of a particular and rigid ideological category. **Jon Hoover** addresses this very problem in relation to the prolific fourteenth-century Muslim scholar, Ibn Taymiyya (d. 1328). Hoover analyses the ways in which Ibn Taymiyya's writings have been read and marshalled to diverse ends in the modern period. His chapter begins with a survey of modern interpreters of Ibn Taymiyya in the Islamic world. Hoover notes that extensive use of Ibn Taymiyya for radical jihadist purposes goes back to ᶜAbd al-Salām Faraj's *The Neglected Duty* (*Al-Farīda al-ghāʾiba*), which served to justify Islamic Jihad's assassination of Egyptian President Anwar Sadat in 1981. Quoting several of Ibn Taymiyya's anti-Mongol fatwas and his fatwa on the legal status of Mardin at length, Faraj analogises from Ibn Taymiyya's response to the Muslim Mongol invaders of Syria to his own contemporary Egyptian rulers. Just as Ibn Taymiyya ruled that the Mongols had apostatised by failing to uphold Islamic law and must be fought, so also the rulers of this age had likewise apostatised and must be opposed with militant jihad. According to Hoover, a great many scholars and analysts – both Muslim and non-Muslim – are happy to allow that Faraj has interpreted Ibn Taymiyya accurately and then lay the blame for modern Muslim terrorism at his feet. However, the contemporary Muslim theologian Yahya Michot, currently a professor at Hartford Seminary in the USA, vigorously contests this interpretation arguing that it is unfaithful to Ibn Taymiyya's intention. Hoover moves between Ibn Taymiyya's writings and two of Michot's books, *Muslims under non-Muslim Rule* (2006) and *Against Extremisms* (2012), as well as his 2011 article 'Ibn Taymiyya's "New Mardin Fatwa"', to show how Michot reads Ibn Taymiyya instead to be a moderate and pragmatic scholar of piety who offers a vision for Muslims seeking to live constructive and engaged lives, especially in minority situations in the West. He examines Michot's use of philology, historical contextualisation and ethical reframing to undermine the radical jihadist reading of Ibn Taymiyya and provide a counter interpretation of the fourteenth-century Damascene scholar as an inspiring guide for moderate Muslim life today. At the core of Michot's strategy for interpreting Ibn Taymiyya is translating selected texts and situating them in historical and intellectual context in ways that highlight the tolerant and pragmatic aspects of his ethics and spirituality. Hoover's chapter highlights the contestations over the hermeneutical appropriation of Ibn Taymiyya's texts, insights and authority in the modern period. It raises a number of questions as to why Ibn Taymiyya's voice commands so much attention in the contemporary period and what it is about the character of his writings and thought that lend themselves to such divergent interpretations.

The themes of violence and moderation are also at the centre of **Carole Hillenbrand**'s chapter. Hillenbrand presents a wide-ranging analysis of the legacy of a sixteenth-century jihad treatise in colonial India written by Sheikh Zainuddin Makhdum (d. 1583). Hillenbrand begins by analysing how medieval concepts of jihad, developed and refined during the Crusades, are revived in Makhdum's *Tuḥfat al-mujāhidīn fī baᶜḍ aḥwāl al-Burtugāliyyīn*. This text acquired an unexpected relevance in nineteenth-century India, when the region was under the control of another set of foreign invaders, with the decision of an early Orientalist scholar and serving British army officer, Michael John Rowlandson (d. 1894), to translate the work from Arabic in 1833. Hillenbrand's chapter reveals the complicated and conflicting interpretive layers of Rowlandson's translation. She demonstrates that Rowlandson's efforts served an apparently innocuous purpose as a teaching tool for both Europeans and Indians interested in the study of the Arabic language. Her careful reading also reveals the missionary and evangelical purposes of Rowlandson's work, which were directed not just against the Muslims of India but against the Catholic Portuguese, the latter being Britain's main rivals in India. Finally, Hillenbrand observes Rowlandson's admiration for the armed struggle of the Malabri Muslims in the sixteenth century against the Portuguese and his acknowledgement of the historical accuracy of Makhdum's account. Hillenbrand's chapter underscores the necessity of avoiding simplistic assumptions about how controversial pre-modern concepts are interpreted by particular figures. Her investigation demonstrates that the process of reinterpreting the Islamic tradition in the modern period extended to a diverse range of persons. This exposes the risks attached to making assumptions about such efforts based solely on an individual's confessional or political loyalties. Hillenbrand's chapter provides a fascinating illustration of how Muslims and non-Muslims, Orientalists and government officials, were all involved in debating and publishing the classical heritage.

With **Elisabeth Kendall**, the book shifts focus from the expressly Islamic textual tradition to the Arab classical poetic tradition. However, it still looks at this tradition in terms of its reconfiguration by contemporary religious thinkers and groups, in this case, specifically militant jihadist groups. Kendall focuses on how and why groups like al-Qāᶜida in the Arabian Peninsula exploit the classical poetic tradition as a propaganda tool. The incorporation of canonical texts from the classical poetic tradition into today's jihadist narratives mirrors their use of canonical religious texts. Both categories of text are 'claimed' and reinterpreted within contexts that buttress the ideals of modern militant jihad. Jihadist use of poetry has received little attention from scholars, analysts and translators. This may in part be because the poetry has been considered peripheral in comparison with pronouncements on religious doctrine or military tactics. Kendall seeks to address this gap in understanding by investigating the ways in which the Arab poetic tradition is being appropriated, reconfigured, redeployed and even reinvented by contemporary jihadists. More specifically, Kendall investigates which elements of the poetic heritage have been resurrected and what this can tell us. To establish firm evidence for the kind of poetry that jihadists favour in their propaganda, Kendall has undertaken a basic content analysis of the main Arabic magazine of al-Qāᶜida in the Arabian Peninsula, which is generally considered to be the most active, entrenched and aggressive branch of al-Qāᶜida today. She then looks at how the poetic tradition is selectively reconstructed by jihadists and explores issues of both plagiarism and modern simulation. Kendall also discusses the possible motivations behind and effects of this reclamation of the poetic tradition, particularly in terms of bolstering jihadist legitimacy and providing alternative claims to authority. This chapter demonstrates how exploring the deeper historical and traditional roots of contemporary cultural activities can illuminate aspects of the contemporary political landscape to both complement and challenge mainstream counter-terrorism analysis.

The book concludes with **Christian Lange**'s study of writings on paradise and hell by contemporary traditionalists. Lange takes as his case study the writings of the late ʿUmar Sulaymān al-Ashqar (d. 2012), a prolific former professor at the Faculty of Shariʿa at Amman University and student of Muḥammad Nāṣir al-Dīn al-Albānī who features prominently in the chapters by Melchert and Khan. Al-Ashqar was the author-compiler of several handbooks on eschatology, most notably perhaps *al-Yawm al-ākhir* (1986), written when al-Ashqar was still professor at the University of Kuwait, a position he held until 1990. *Al-Yawm al-ākhir* is divided into three sections on the life in the grave (*al-qiyāma al-sughrā*), resurrection (*al-qiyāma al-kubrā*), and paradise and hell (*al-janna wa-l-nār*). The final section of this trilogy was translated into English and published by the Riyadh-based International Islamic Publishing House in 1999; it has subsequently seen several new editions. Lange compares al-Ashqar's arrangement of topics, choice of emphases, as well as his criteria for admissibility of hadith (which in the field of eschatological traditions, are traditionally lower than in other areas) to some of his 'classical' forerunners. His chapter provides a fascinating insight into how a prolific, yet understudied, modern scholar interprets the classical eschatological tradition in a modern age, whose defining intellectual orientation, according to Karl Jaspers, is that 'there is no longer anything outside. The world is closed. The unity of the earth has arrived.'[6]

This introduction opened with Marx's moribund assessment of tradition. The very diversity of the persons, events, concepts, disciplines and traditions examined in this volume, from the eve of modernity to the present day, suggests that now is no time for obituaries of tradition. The Islamic tradition is constantly being reinterpreted, reconfigured, recast and, in some cases, wilfully manipulated to address the complexities of modern social, cultural, economic and political landscapes. In order to understand the Islamic world today, scholars must explore how and why centuries of tradition are transformed in the modern period and marshalled to new and diverse ends. We hope that this volume will encourage new investigations into the rich and variegated interpretation of the classical Islamic heritage in the modern world.

Notes

1. Karl Marx, *The Eighteenth Brumaire of Louis Bonaparte* (Moscow: Progress Publishers, 1954), 10.
2. Muhammad Qasim Zaman, *The Ulama in Contemporary Islam: Custodians of Change* (Princeton: Princeton University Press, 2002).
3. For example, Dan Diner, *Lost in the Sacred: Why the Muslim World Stood Still* (Princeton: Princeton University Press, 2009); S. Frederick Starr, *Lost Enlightenment: Central Asia's Golden Age from the Arab Conquest to Tamerlane* (Princeton: Princeton University Press, 2013).
4. Edward Shils, *Tradition* (Chicago: University of Chicago Press, 1981), 12.
5. This is at least one reason why intellectuals and scholars in the Islamic world who contested the rhetoric of reform in the nineteenth to twenty-first centuries have received such little attention. The secondary literature on reformists, on the other hand, is vast. For the relationship between periodisation and the genesis of concepts, see Reinhart Koselleck, *Futures Past: On the Semantics of Historical Time* (New York: Columbia University Press, 2004), 222–54. See also Dipesh Chakrabarty, *Provincializing Europe: Postcolonial Thought and Historical Difference* (Princeton: Princeton University Press, 2000); Kathleen Davis, *Periodization and Sovereignty: How Ideas of Feudalism and Secularization Govern the Politics of Time* (Philadelphia: University of Pennsylvania Press, 2008).
6. Karl Jaspers, *The Origin and Goal of History* (New Haven: Yale University Press, 1953), 127.

1

Modern Shi^c^ite Legal Theory and the Classical Tradition

Robert Gleave

Many Muslim reform thinkers are frustrated with the classical tradition. The arcane and rather obscure discussions of past scholars are often viewed as at best irrelevant, focusing on hypothetical and unreal cases, or being overly theoretical and impractical.[1] At worst, these discussions are pointless distractions, sapping the intellectual talent of the Muslim community, making Islam dangerously out of touch with the needs of the modern age. At best, they are frivolous intellectual games.[2] To be fair, this is not a purely modern critique. The frustration with tradition expressed by many modern reform intellectuals echoes that of numerous past Muslim thinkers.[3] There is, then, a long tradition of rejecting tradition in Islamic thought. Dissatisfaction with pre-modern ('classical') intellectual forms of thought is also expressed occasionally in the secondary literature on modern Islam.[4] This sometimes extends to academics who focus on the pre-modern period, viewed as unreconstructed Orientalists. They are, in the view of some, as bad as the hidebound classical *ᶜulamāʾ*; they too cannot come to terms with the new paradigms of knowledge which modernity brings.[5] There is then an oft-cited assessment that the classical tradition is unable to withstand the challenges brought by the modern world.[6]

The discussions and debates of modern Shiᶜi scholars, working primarily in the seminaries (*ḥawza*s) of Iran and Iraq, are counterexamples to this. These scholars, generally speaking, have a strong sense of the continuity between their activities today (teaching, writing, debating) and those of their fellow *ᶜulamāʾ* of the past generations. They perceive an ongoing need to maintain the longstanding position of the current intellectual structures of Shiᶜism. These include the *marjaᶜiyya* system (in which the leading scholars – the *marājiᶜ* – are recognised as the ultimate authorities in law), the ever-growing stratum of Ayatollahs (particularly in Iran, where their number has increased significantly since the Revolution), the *ḥawza* study method and the seminary curricula. These structures also preserve the primacy of Najaf and Qum as the powerhouses of Shiᶜi theological, legal and philosophical development.[7] This position is sustained through the promotion of the institutions' history and an intimate connection with its past achievements. There is, to be sure, an emerging dissatisfaction with the current *ᶜulamāᵓ* leadership from within the *ḥawza*, but this rarely expresses itself in a rejection of the classical tradition.[8] Rather, this defiant voice normally expresses itself in a reassertion of this connection: the renegades often self-declare themselves as Ayatollahs or *marājiᶜ*, claiming their own position as the rightful heirs to the classical tradition. Whilst the traditional structures are not without their challenges, the persistent respect for the 'classical tradition' in contemporary Shiᶜi religious circles indicates that traditional structures of thought and the educational structures around them can not only survive, but may (with some modification) thrive in the modern period.

The internal discussions of the top-rank Shiᶜi scholars are rarely the subject of research and analysis in the secondary literature.[9] This is surprising considering the important political and societal role played by the *ᶜulamāᵓ* in modern Shiᶜism.[10] In this chapter, I illustrate how these scholars continue the classical topics of debate, the established genres of literature and the traditional educational structures, through the detailed examination of a single topic encountered in the many texts of Shiᶜi legal theory produced in the last 150 years. Within the *ḥawza* system, the classical tradition is most obviously represented by the many pre-modern authors and their texts which form the focus of study and commentary. Reading and showing command of these texts is the hallmark of an accomplished scholar, one who has progressed through the ranks.[11] This scholarly accomplishment results in respect from those with influence within the institution. Many works produced today within the *ḥawza* bear no marks of a revolutionary paradigm shift between the classical and the modern. They are written with a conscious effort to establish continuity between the past accomplishments and the current scholarly activity. This is particularly evident in modern works of Islamic legal theory (*uṣūl al-fiqh*) produced by seminarians, where the precise relevance of the topic for the practical application of the law is often obscure; as we shall see below, the topic is even explicitly described as irrelevant, though it remains much discussed and debated. This occasional irrelevance does not, however, prevent such works being seen as the highest achievement of Shiᶜi learning.[12]

Law and Legal Theory in the Modern *Ḥawza*

Modarressi has offered a periodisation of Shiᶜi legal learning in which he does indicate a break, or at least the emergence of new schools in the modern period.[13] The first new school he mentions appeared in the late eighteenth/early nineteenth century under the leadership of Muḥammad Bāqir al-Bihbihānī (d. 1791),[14] and the second was in the late nineteenth century under the leadership of al-Shaykh Murtaḍā al-Ansārī (d. 1864).[15] Al-Bihbihānī is normally credited with ending a period of dominance by the anti-*uṣūlī* scripturalist Akhbārī school.[16] Put briefly, the Akhbārīs considered the sayings of the Shiᶜi Imams (the *akhbār*) as sufficient to provide legal knowledge. The *mujtahids* (or *uṣūlīs* as they are often called) considered the *akhbār* as needing explanation by the qualified jurist (the *mujtahid*). Until this explanation has been produced, the ordinary follower of the *mujtahid*'s judgement (the *muqallid*) cannot understand the intended meaning in the sources. For *mutjahids*, the content of the law is, effectively, unavailable, and only those qualified to interpret these sources can create an estimation of the law's contents. For Akhbārīs, the law is generally available and can be known with certainty – the scholar is needed only to transmit this knowledge, and to facilitate a resolution if there are any apparent contradictions in the sources.[17] The Shiᶜi traditional sources describe al-Bihbihānī as having being the reviver (*murawwij*) of the *mujtahid* position by his active promotion of the probative force (*ḥujjiyya*) of a qualified jurist's opinion. Though this opinion falls short of certain knowledge, it is nonetheless legally authoritative. This is termed *ẓann*, and the history of Shiᶜi *uṣūl al-fiqh* since al-Bihbihānī is, in the main, the elaboration of *ẓann* as an epistemological category.[18] It is in the modalities of how this *ẓann* might produce valid legal rulings whilst remaining in itself less than certain that al-Shaykh al-Anṣārī, the founder of the second school outlined by Modarressi, made his contribution.

Modarressi states that, 'The contemporary scholars of the Shīᶜa … are followers of al-Anṣārī's school.'[19] Much research remains to be done here, and it is debatable whether al-Shaykh al-Anṣārī's school is best seen as a 'new' school or as a continuation and elaboration of the ideas of al-Bihbihānī. Be that as it may, al-Anṣārī's collected *uṣūl* writings (normally referred to as *al-Rasāʾil*) and his important work of Islamic substantive law, *Kitāb al-Makāsib*, certainly injected a new impetus into the study of law in the Shiᶜi seminaries at the turn of the twentieth century. Of particular note was his structuring of *uṣūl* composition around three epistemological categories: certainty (*qaṭᶜ*), opinion (*ẓann*) and doubt (*shakk*).[20] Information about the law, as it can be deduced from the sources, falls into one of these categories. The work of *uṣūl al-fiqh* is to determine which category legal information falls into, and how this information might then be used in the derivation of the law. Whilst his work became central to the advanced *ḥawza* curriculum, his ideas inspired a number of abbreviated and integrated *uṣūl* works, the most important of which was *Kifāyat al-uṣūl* by al-Ākhund al-Khurāsānī

(d. 1911).[21] The *Kifāya* was taught, studied, and the subject of many commentaries in the twentieth century, and remains a key *uṣūl* text in today's seminary curriculum. Even when disagreeing with the formulation of the issue in the *Kifāya*, it is this text which subsequent Shiᶜi *uṣūl* authors usually cite first and in reference to which they develop their own ideas. This dynamic, in which classical problems of *uṣūl* are summarised by Ākhund and then commented on by subsequent writers, is one manifestation of continuity in Shiᶜi *uṣūl al-fiqh*.

Discussion of Legal-Literal Meaning

In what follows, I aim to demonstrate how classical *uṣūl* topics structure the debates in modern Shiᶜi works of legal theory. This is best illustrated through a detailed elaboration of a single issue (*masʾala*) which can be found in premodern works of *uṣūl al-fiqh*, both Sunni and Shiᶜi. The issue I have selected concerns whether God or the Prophet (usually referred to as the 'Lawgiver' *al-Shāriᶜ* in works of legal theory), when revealing the Shariᶜa, can institute new meanings for existing words, and in doing so establishes these new meanings as 'literal'.[22] In order to understand why this might be a problem worth discussing, a little background on classical Muslim theories of language is necessary.

Elsewhere, I have explored the utility of the term 'literal' when describing the linguistic theory of the *uṣūlīs*.[23] If we are to retain it in our English language analysis, then the most obvious 'literal' element of the *uṣūlī* linguistic system is the meaning 'instituted' for a particular sound. Nearly all medieval *uṣūl al-fiqh* writers elaborate a linguistic theory in which meanings and sounds become associated with each other through an act of 'designation' or 'coining' (literally 'placing' – *al-waḍᶜ*). At some point in the past, and by an agent or set of agents unknown (around this there is dispute), the meaning of a word (say, the idea of a lion) became associated with a particular sound (namely, *asad* in Arabic). This established association means that when the word *asad* is used the idea of a lion appears in the language-speaker's mind. This is called *ḥaqīqa* ('true') usage, and the meaning is termed *al-maᶜnā al-waḍᶜī* ('the coined meaning', or later *al-maᶜnā al-ḥaqīqī*, 'the true/literal meaning'). This, as I have already argued, is the most natural fit for the English term literal.[24]

According to this model, the institution of meaning–sound relationships was how communication between language speakers became possible. As language skills developed, however, words began to be used for other things – a person who is brave in battle, for example, might be called an *asad* in Arabic, but this is a derived, secondary use of the term. This type of usage is termed *majāz*, and it is not impossible for speakers to use these words and convey meaning, but there must be indicators (*qarāʾin*) which justify us assuming that a usage other than the *ḥaqīqa* is being used.[25] The *ḥaqīqa* has, then, a priority over the *majāz* because, so the *uṣūlī*s argued, the *ḥaqīqa* is what appears first in the mind of the speaker (a phenomenon known as *tabādur*).

Classical *uṣūl al-fiqh* works contain a canon of questions around which there was always debate, and the debate around the meanings instituted by the Lawgiver was no exception. Who was the agent who instituted the coining of meaning for words, or who designated the meaning to the sound (i.e. the *wāḍiʿ*)? How does this system accommodate homonymity? A word may have two meanings which are both considered 'literal' in the sense that both are the designated meaning for that word: the Arabic term *ʿayn* means 'eye' but it also means 'water spring' – one can see how these two might be seen as linked, but they are two different meanings, and normally thought of as both *ḥaqīqī* or literal. How does one choose between two literal meanings? Which one can be considered the 'apparent' intended meaning (the *ẓāhir*) in a given context? Sometimes a word is used so often in its derived (*majāz*) meaning that the original meaning is forgotten. The great Arabic linguist Murtaḍā al-Zabīdī (d. 1791) refers to how one of the words for the firearm 'rifle' in the Arabic of his day (*mukḥula*) actually means 'kohl pot', coming from an association of the blackness of both the kohl pot and the rifle's barrel. However, when anyone hears the word *mukḥula*, he thinks immediately of the rifle, not the kohl pot. Something that was a non-literal usage (*majāz*) has now become the most immediate meaning of the word through continuous employment, and immediacy (*tabādur*) is an indication of the literal (*ḥaqīqa*). This new literal usage is called *ḥaqīqa ʿurfiyya* (customary literal usage) in classical works of *uṣūl al-fiqh*.[26]

The issue that concerns us here is yet another sub-question in the topic of how words come to have particular meanings. When the Lawgiver institutes a new meaning for a word which already has an established meaning, is this new meaning a literal or a non-literal meaning? The common example used by *uṣūlī*s is the word for prayer (*ṣalāh*) which originally meant supplication, but after the Islamic revelation, was used by God and the Prophet to mean the ritual prayer of the Muslims (*al-ṣalāh al-maktūba*). Expressed in the technical terminology of the *uṣūlī*s, the word *ṣalāh* can be used with a linguistic-literal meaning (*al-ḥaqīqa al-lughawiyya*) to mean supplication, but after revelation, for some *uṣūlī*s, it acquired a new literal meaning and can now be used in a 'legal-literal' way (*al-ḥaqīqa al-sharʿiyya*) to mean the ritual, prescribed Muslim prayer.[27] Other *uṣūlī*s disagreed and considered this new meaning to be a non-literal extension (*majāz*) of the original meaning by the Lawgiver. Over time, the word has acquired the appearance of a literal meaning by language users after the Lawgiver (i.e. it is a case of non-divine *al-ḥaqīqa al-ᶜurfiyya* following a case of divine *majāz* usage), but the Lawgiver himself did not institute a new literal meaning. This was a much-discussed question in pre-modern *uṣūl* works, and a number of complex positions emerged amongst those writing legal theory.[28]

To summarise, nearly all classical works of legal theory describe three ways in which words acquire literal meanings (that is, meanings which are immediate in the mind of the language user), and when they are used in this way, it constitutes *ḥaqīqa* usage. First, the meaning assigned through the original act of designation, or coining, envisaged by classical writers is intended by the speaker (linguistic-literal usage: *al-ḥaqīqa al-lughawiyya*). Second, the speaker intends meaning acquired through continuous use which has become immediate and therefore literal (customary-literal usage: *al-ḥaqīqa al-ᶜurfiyya*). Finally, the speaker may intend the meaning given to the word by the Lawgiver at the time of revelation (divinely-instituted legal-literal usage: *al-ḥaqīqa al-sharᶜiyya*). My focus here is on the question raised by some later Shiᶜi writers: does it make any difference to the actual interpretation of revelatory texts whether the meaning–word relationship in cases of *al-ḥaqīqa al-sharᶜiyya* is literal or non-literal?

In the central Shiᶜi *uṣūl* work of the pre-modern period, *Maᶜālim al-dīn* of al-Shaykh Ḥasan b. al-Shahīd al-Thānī (d. 1602), the discussion of *al-ḥaqīqa al-sharᶜiyya* extends over six pages in one printed edition.[29] In a short work such as the *Maᶜālim*, this represents quite a lengthy discussion. Al-Shaykh Ḥasan explains that there has been dispute (*khilāf*) over *al-ḥaqīqa al-sharᶜiyya* between two sets of jurists (though he mentions no specific names). Some jurists considered the Lawgiver to have instituted a new meaning for words like *ṣalāh* in a divine act of designation. Others consider *al-ḥaqīqa al-sharᶜiyya* to be merely a case of divine *majāz* usage which had become so common in the discourse of the jurists that it had become *al-ḥaqīqa al-ᶜurfiyya* (not *al-sharᶜiyya*). Al-Shaykh Ḥasan himself considers those who deny the real existence of *al-ḥaqīqa al-sharᶜiyya* as a category of word use to be most likely correct:

> There is no doubt that these words [like *ṣalāh*] were coined for their linguistic meaning [i.e. supplication], and at that point they were *ḥaqīqa* in terms of language (*lughatan*). All that is known of the situation of the Lawgiver is that he used these words with the [new] meanings. It could have been that this usage was by way of transferring [the word from having one meaning to another] or it could have been that it had become so common in his time, and so well-known that it did not need any contextual indicator (*qarīna*) to understand it. Which of these is not known because understanding what was meant may have come about through contextual indicators specific to

> that particular time and environment. There are no texts to help us here at all, and without these texts, the thing which [they] seek to demonstrate [i.e. *al-ḥaqīqa al-sharᶜiyya*] is left unproven. The preference is therefore with the position of those who deny [*al-ḥaqīqa al-sharᶜiyya*], even though what is reported of their proofs share some of the weaknesses of those who wish to establish [*al-ḥaqīqa al-sharᶜiyya*].[30]

The point being made by al-Shaykh Ḥasan here is that those who wish to establish that God does establish new meanings for words need evidence that this act of coining has taken place. There is no evidence, and hence the preference (though not necessarily a definitive judgement) favours those who deny the existence of *al-ḥaqīqa al-sharᶜiyya*. As I have discussed elsewhere, not all Shiᶜi jurists agreed.[31] This debate spawned another: is there any point in arguing over this issue?

Al-Shaykh Ḥasan clearly did think there was a point to these discussions – for him there were real hermeneutic implications:

> There is no debate that words current amongst the people of the Law [i.e. the legal scholars] are used in ways at variance with their linguistic meanings, and that these [meanings] have become 'literal' with regard to these meanings – such as the use of the word *ṣalāh* to mean specific actions after it was originally coined in language for the [idea of] 'supplication' … There is only debate over how this meaning came about:
>
> [1] Was it by an act of coining by the Lawgiver, whereby he specifically assigned it to [this meaning], such that the word [*ṣalāh*] indicates [the meaning of specific actions] without the need for contextual evidence [*bi-ghayr qarīna*]? If so, this becomes 'legal-literal'.
>
> [2] Or, [did the literal association] come about through the extensive usage of these words with these meanings by the legal scholars, and the Lawgiver only used this word in a non-literal manner which required contextual evidence [to be understood]? If so, then these are [examples] of customary literal meanings, not legal-literal ones.
>
> The outcome of the debate [or its 'effect' – *thamarat al-khilāf*] here is that if a word occurs in the speech of the Lawgiver without any contextual evidence, then it can be interpreted as having the aforementioned meaning, according to position [1] above. For position [2] above, it would have to be interpreted as having a linguistic meaning. When it is used by the Legal scholars, then it is understood to have its legal meaning – on that there is no dispute.[32]

A debate ensued over whether or not the question of *al-ḥaqīqa al-sharᶜiyya* had any practical effect and brings any benefit to the process of deriving the law. The discussion around the implications and the result of the discussion (the *thamarat al-khilāf* as al-Shaykh Ḥasan describes it) is important because it brings into sharp relief whether *uṣūl al-fiqh* was to be assessed by its ability to be applied to the law or is a purely scholastic discipline. As we shall see, some writers felt that discussing *how* a word came to have a meaning (i.e. whether it was by original coining, or by customary usage, or by divine designation) was, in the end, a purely academic question (*ᶜilmī*) with no practical relevance. If all actually agree on the meaning of the utterance in which the word appears, the discussion over whether the Lawgiver has instituted a new literal meaning or is just using the word in a non-literal meaning becomes irrelevant. This is not quite the same as pronouncing the discussion a waste of time, but this is clearly a pointed description.

Al-Ākhund al-Khurāsānī and the Epistemological Problems of Legal-Literal Meanings

After al-Shaykh Ḥasan's treatment in his *Maᶜālim al-dīn*, there were, then, two questions which emerged from the above-cited passages. First, was the Lawgiver's use of words like *ṣalāh* an example of *ḥaqiqah* or *majāz*? Second, would finding an answer to this question make any practical difference? Discussions of these issues in the twentieth and twenty-first centuries are primarily framed as a reaction to the formulation of the problem found in al-Ākhund al-Khurāsānī's *Kifāyat al-uṣūl*. The *Kifāya* became the standard text book in the *ḥawzas* of Najaf and Qum,[33] and al-Ākhund's description of the issue is expressed in the usual compressed manner of a short *uṣūl al-fiqh* handbook. Such formulations, almost intentionally, require explanation, providing another example of continuity between the classical and the modern.[34] In this section, then, I offer a translation of the *Kifāya*'s passage on the issue, followed by a more extended explication.

On the issue of the debate over the Lawgiver's use (or otherwise) of legal-literal meaning, al-Ākhund writes:

> [1] Concerning the effect of [opting] for one of the two positions (*al-thamara bayn al-qawlayn*);
> [1.1] [The effect] becomes obvious in that, if [*al-ḥaqīqa al-sharᶜiyya*] is not established, then, in the absence of contextual evidence, one is forced to interpret the words in the speech of the Lawgiver according to their linguistic meanings.
> [1.2] If, on the other hand, [*al-ḥaqīqa al-sharᶜiyya*] is established, then [one must interpret them] according to their legal-literal meanings,
> [1.3] providing that it is known that there was a delay in usage (*taᵓakhkhur al-istiᶜmāl*).[35]

Al-Ākhund is here arguing that any choice between the two positions (i.e. between legal-literal meanings being established or not) will affect interpretive practice; it is not simply a theoretical or academic question with no practical consequences. For him, affirming or denying *al-ḥaqīqa al-sharᶜiyya* affects the exegete's assumed literal meaning of the text (i.e. the 'base' (*aṣl*) meaning before any contextual evidence is considered). Identifying the base meaning is important because it can only be set aside when there is sufficient contextual evidence (i.e. *qarīna*). When the contextual evidence is deemed sufficient, then the Lawgiver's intended meaning shifts from a literal to a non-literal meaning. The evidence required to justify this shift is, inevitably, itself a matter of debate: one theorist's 'justified' transfer of meaning, may be, for another, wild speculation. Nevertheless, the system is built around the principle that the literal meaning has a hermeneutical pole position as the assumed meaning. It is, if you like, the linguistic equivalent of the principle that the burden of proof lies with the claimant arguing against the status quo (in *fiqh* terms, *al-bayyina ᶜalā al-muddaᶜī*). For al-Ākhund, it matters whether the literal meaning is linguistic-legal or legal-literal. If *al-ḥaqīqa al-sharᶜiyya* is established (1.2 above), then the default meaning becomes the legal-literal meaning; if it is not established (1.1), the linguistic-literal meaning becomes the default. If the question over *al-ḥaqīqa al-sharᶜiyya* is answered one way, legal-literal meanings form the initially presumed meaning when they are not the intended one. Answered another way, another set of presumptions will kick in. In this way, the question is of fundamental importance for al-Ākhund's procedure of interpreting scripture.

Al-Ākhund's final caveat in the above passage (1.3) concerning a delay in usage (*taᵓakhkhur al-istiᶜmāl*) also requires some explication. He states that the proposed legal-literal meaning only becomes, for the exegete, the new literal (i.e. assumed) meaning if it is known that there has been a 'delay in usage'. He means here that the use of the word with the new meaning must have occurred after the designation of this new meaning by the Lawgiver. The exegete needs to know, then, that the particular use of *ṣalāh* to mean the prescribed Muslim ritual prayers postdates the time when the Lawgiver decided that *ṣalāh* now would refer not to supplication generally (*duᶜāᵓ*) but specifically to Muslim prescribed prayer (*al-ṣalāh al-maktūba*). If usage predates designation, then the linguistic-literal meaning is assumed. This is what is meant by the stipulation that a 'delay in usage' has occurred, and this must be known to have taken place. Establishing a time lapse between the point of designation and the point of use is a prerequisite for the exegete to assume the legal-literal meaning before considering any contextual evidence.[36]

Disputes about the word meaning should no longer play a decisive part in legal debate as the jurist now has procedures whereby the meaning of words can be determined and a potential element of ambiguity in the interpretive process is, if not eliminated, then much reduced. What the Lawgiver is assumed to mean by his usage of individual words may be fixed; what the legal implications of the whole text might be is left undetermined. Dispute is not eliminated, but it is restricted and controlled within a traditional framework.

This, in a sense, is one of al-Ākhund's major accomplishments in his *Kifāyat al-uṣūl*. He managed to strike a balance between the arena of legal dispute and the maintenance of juristic tradition. It was this balance which was to be challenged by more maverick figures, in subsequent Shiᶜi discussions.

Rejecting the Debate's Effect

Al-Ākhund's argument that the *al-ḥaqīqa al-sharᶜiyya* debate had real effects on the interpretation of the Shariᶜa was not universally accepted in subsequent Shiᶜi *usūl* writings. The most vigorous response to this formulation came from al-Ākhund's own star pupil, Muḥammad al-Ḥusayn al-Nāʾīnī (d. 1936). In his classes of *uṣūl al-fiqh*, al-Nāʾīnī argued that 'the discussion in this area has no effect at all' (*al-baḥth fī hādhihi al-masʾala lā yatarattab ᶜalay-hi thamara aṣlan*).[37] Al-Nāʾīnī's position is nicely summarised by a more recent opponent, Ayatallāh Jawād al-Tibrīzī (sometimes al-Tabrīzī, d. 2006) in his book entitled *Kifāyat al-uṣūl: Durūs fī masāʾil ᶜilm al-uṣūl*, which as the title indicates discusses *uṣūlī* issues prompted by the study of al-Ākhund's *Kifāya*. After summarizing al-Ākhund's position, al-Tibrīzī says:

> According to al-Muḥaqqiq al-Nāʾīnī, one would never find one of these words in the speech of the Lawgiver with there being an issue over whether to interpret it according to its linguistic or its literal meaning, such that one does not know the Lawgiver's intended meaning (*murād al-shāriᶜ*). So for [al-Nāʾīnī], the discussion over *al-ḥaqīqa al-sharᶜiyya* is a purely academic discussion (*baḥthan ᶜilmiyyan maḥḍan*).[38]

Al-Nāʾīnī's own expression of the argument (as found recorded by Abū al-Qāsim al-Khūʾī in his published *taqrīrāt* or lecture notes) is considerably more involved. Basically, if the Lawgiver's intended meaning is known in each case of these words' usage, then it does not really matter if that meaning came about through a new act of *waḍᶜ* or it began as a *majāz* usage becoming *ᶜurfī* gradually under the usage of the jurists after the Lawgiver. It makes no difference, al-Nāʾīnī argues, to the exegetical procedure or ultimately the derivation of meaning from the revelatory statement.

In order for this argument to work, of course, al-Nāʾīnī has to demonstrate that the intended meaning of a word, as used by the Lawgiver (which he terms *al-murād al-istiᶜmālī* – the 'practical/usage meaning') is never in doubt. This he does through an examination of the *waḍ*ᶜ mechanisms by which words are designated meaning, showing at each point how the literal meaning (be it linguistic or legal) is established and known in each case. Rather than run through all of al-Nāʾīnī's arguments, one can gain the flavour of his presentation through an examination of his treatment of a single *waḍ*ᶜ mechanism. Al-Shaykh Ḥasan argued in his *Ma*ᶜ*ālim al-uṣūl* that the evidence does not support there having been any new acts of *waḍ*ᶜ by the Lawgiver – his use of terms like *ṣalāh* to mean the regulation prayer was more likely *majāz* rather than *ḥaqīqa*. Given the respect with which the *Ma*ᶜ*ālim* was held generally, this argument undermined the category of *al-ḥaqīqa al-shar*ᶜ*iyya*. Words such as *ṣalāh*, which had been considered as having new legal-literal meanings, were in fact simply customary-literal meanings accrued through the repeated use by the jurists after the Lawgiver's revelatory episode. The Lawgiver's own use was a straightforward case of *majāz*.

Shiᶜi jurists tried to salvage the category of legal-literal meaning by an involved typology of *al-waḍ*ᶜ in which coining a meaning for a word can be shown to have taken place, even if there is no direct evidence that the Lawgiver explicitly said 'X now means Y'. Both al-Ākhund and al-Nāʾīnī worked within this new typology, notwithstanding their differences as to how it might operate. One of the ways in which *al-waḍ*ᶜ can take place, so they argue, is through 'self-specifying designation' (*al-waḍ*ᶜ *al-ta*ᶜ*ayyunī*).[39] This refers to a word acquiring a new designation by continuous use such that the connection between the sound (*lafẓ*) and the new (*shar*ᶜ*ī*) meaning is established. It differs from the abovementioned 'customary-literal usage' (*al-ḥaqīqa al-*ᶜ*urfiyya*) in that the Lawgiver himself is one of the language community using the word in this manner, which is evidence that he has designated a new meaning for the word. It is argued, then, that the continued usage creates a designation-*waḍ*ᶜ*ī* link and given that the Lawgiver participates, so to speak, in a discourse and is part of a community of discussants, the new word-meaning connection (e.g. *ṣalāh* meaning the designated Muslim prayer) is established alongside any original meaning (e.g. *ṣalāh* meaning 'supplication'). The result is a divinely generated meaning that can legitimately claim to be the default meaning of that word when it appears in a revelatory text.

Al-Nāʾīnī contemplates whether it is possible for anyone to know when (and whether) this *ta*ᶜ*ayyunī* connection might have occurred such that *al-ḥaqīqa al-shar*ᶜ*iyya* can be established. He argues that this could not have happened during the time of the Prophet:

> There is no way for us to establish it having occurred in the time of the Prophet in such a way that it proves *al-ḥaqīqa al-shar*ᶜ*iyya*. On the basis of this, the words at the time of the Prophet are *mujmal* (ambiguous).[40]

Taᶜyyunī (self-specifying) designation can only be located with any certainty from the time of Imams al-Bāqir and al-Ṣādiq, a century after the Prophet's death.

It transpires, then, that this form of *waḍᶜ* requires the Lawgiver's participation in a discourse over an extended period of time to the point where the meaning-word linkage becomes as established as that achieved through an explicit act of coinage. In texts from the time of the Prophet, words which later had technical legal meaning (e.g. *ṣalāh*) are unclear or ambiguous (*mujmal* – they could mean ritual prayer, or they could refer to general supplication). By this, al-Nāʾīnī is not arguing that the intended meaning of the Prophet's utterance is unknown, but rather that one cannot, with any certainty, categorise the Prophet's own usage as *al-ḥaqīqa al-lughwiyya*, *al-ḥaqīqa al-sharᶜiyya*, *majāz* or some other category through *al-waḍᶜ al-taᶜayyunī*. A century later (that is by the time of Imams Muḥammad al-Bāqir and Jaᶜfar al-Ṣādiq), there is sufficient evidence to establish with certainty that *al-waḍᶜ al-taᶜayyunī* has taken place. The Imams themselves – who are as reliable conveyors of the content of the Shariᶜa as the Prophet himself – participated in exchanges in which words were used with legal meanings with such frequency that their legal-literal meaning was established.[41] In such instances, we are dealing with *al-ḥaqīqa al-sharᶜiyya* usage of a word as firmly established as if the Lawgiver had made an explicit designation (i.e. if he has said 'X means Y'). This form of designation, then, requires a longer involvement of the Lawgiver in the life of the community than the Prophet's mission, and this condition is satisfied by the time period up to the two named Imams. It is the Imams, rather than the Prophet, who confirm *al-waḍᶜ al-taᶜayyunī* to have taken place, and their legal-literal meaning to be the meaning the Prophet intended to use when he uttered words such as *ṣalāh* in the first place. Al-Nāʾīnī's argumentation here makes the Imams the true conveyors of the original Lawgiver's (i.e. God's and the Prophet's) intended meaning. At the time of the original Lawgiver, an expression's meaning was *mujmal*; the Imams establish the legal-literal meaning of the expression's individual words and determine its intended meaning.[42] This, then, is a specifically Shiᶜi form of argumentation; the limited exposure of the community to the Lawgiver in Sunni Islam (the Prophet's availability ending with his death) would prevent this form of designation coming about. Because of the Imams laying down the legal-literal meaning of words in the Qurʾan and the Prophet's hadith, one can be certain as to the Lawgiver's intended meaning (that is, *al-murād al-istiᶜmālī*) when using that word. When this is the case, the debate over whether the Prophet used *ṣalāh* in a *ḥaqīqa* or *majāz* manner becomes purely academic.

The 'self-specifying designation' is not the only mechanism whereby *waḍᶜ* was established, and elsewhere I have described al-Nāʾīnī's argumentation around the other main form of *waḍ*ᶜ developed by the Shiᶜi *uṣūlī*s (namely *al-waḍ*ᶜ *al-ta*ᶜ*yīnī* – specifying designation).[43] Al-Nāʾīnī argues generally that one can have certainty of the Lawgiver's intended meaning in using these words, but one need not know how the *waḍ*ᶜ designation took place. His arguments here were persuasive for some, though not all, of the subsequent Shiᶜi scholars of *uṣūl al-fiqh*.

The *al-Ḥaqīqa al-Shar*ᶜ*iyya* Dispute after al-Nāʾīnī

The disagreement between al-Ākhund and al-Nāʾīnī, two great modern scholars of *uṣūl al-fiqh*, was not limited to *al-ḥaqīqa al-shar*ᶜ*iyya*. Indeed, it might be said that much of modern Shiᶜi *uṣūl* is a struggle between the versions of legal theory propounded by these giants of early twentieth-century Shiᶜi learning. On the question of whether or not the *al-ḥaqīqa al-shar*ᶜ*iyya* debate was purely academic, there were impressive voices on either side. There were also those who avoided an explicit declaration, such as the Grand Ayatollah and leader of the Seminary in Qum, Ḥusayn al-Burūjirdī (d. 1961), who appears to avoid the debate by not addressing it, even in his commentary (taken from lecture notes) on the *Kifāya*.

In the reiteration of al-Ākhund's view, the position is modified by some later supporters defending his position against al-Naʾīnī's attack. At first, the account follows al-Ākhund's description closely. ᶜAbd al-Karīm al-Ḥāʾirī (d. 1937), the reviver of the *ḥawza* in Qum in the early twentieth century, explains, along the lines of al-Ākhund's argumentation, why the debate has a real effect.[44] Ḍiyāʾ al-Dīn al-ᶜArāqī (sometimes al-ᶜIrāqī, d. 1942) writes, 'the effect of the two positions is only in those words which were used by [the Prophet] without relying on circumstantial evidence',[45] which is a roundabout way of saying the Prophet could have used these words and intended a meaning other than the legal-literal meaning, but if (and when) he did, he always provided evidence of this non-linguistic-literal usage.

Some thirty years later, Muḥammad Bāqir al-Ṣadr (d. 1980) rejected the views of what he called 'the Nāʾīnī School' (*madrasat al-muḥaqqiq al-Nāʾīnī*) arguing that whilst it is valid to say that the Imams themselves use words such as *ṣalāh* according to a legal-literal meaning, one cannot say this of these words when used in the Qurʾan. The implication is that for the Nāʾīnī School, the Qurʾan cannot be understood directly when it uses these words, and this, surely, has real exegetical implications.[46] Bāqir al-Ṣadr mentions another objection to the Nāʾīnī School's position here: what of Prophetic statements which are transmitted through chains which do not include the Imams? How are we to interpret these words in these reports? Jawād al-Tibrīzī, whose summary of al-Nāʾīnī's position was cited above, goes on to take, in effect, al-Ākhund's side, with some interesting elaborations:

> It is possible that the debate here is around the meaning of *ṣalāh* in the words of the Sublime One [for example]: 'He who purifies himself and mentions the name of his Lord and prays (*fa-yuṣallī*), will certainly prosper.' [Q87/al-Aʿlā.14] which is ambiguous between supplication and the legal meaning [of ritual prayer] … In the same way, there are words which come from the Prophet but not via our Imams. Most of what [the Prophet] said comes to us by way of the Imams, and they had to transmit it because his meaning is understood through the transmission [of his words] and [the Imams] hold the role of explaining the legal rulings (*bayān al-aḥkām al-sharʿiyya*). However, some of it comes via some other means. Explicating what he meant in [these statements] is based on the discussion concerning *al-ḥaqīqa al-sharʿiyya*.[47]

This later elaboration of al-Ākhund's discussion restricts the effect of the debate first, to instances in the Qurʾan where the word could be being used in one of the two ways (linguistic- and legal-literal, such as in the example cited in the quote above) and second, to reports from the Prophet not transmitted through an *isnād* which includes the Shiʿi Imams. The latter category is interesting in that if a report is transmitted by the Imams, they would have transmitted it in a manner which perfectly reflected the Prophet's intended meaning. This makes them different to other transmitters (*muḥaddiths*). Unlike other transmitters, they are privy to the Prophet's intended meaning, and hence the Imams are not under an obligation to transmit the meaning (*maʿnā*) rather than the words.[48]

Notwithstanding the popularity of al-Ākhund's *Kifāyat al-uṣūl* within the *ḥawza* curriculum, recent scholars have taken the position of the Nāʾīnī School more frequently. A famous pupil of al-Ākhund, Muḥammad Ḥusayn al-Iṣfahānī (d. 1942), in his commentary on the *Kifāya*, gives ground to al-Nāʾīnī's position by saying that he suspends decision on the dispute itself (*tawaqquf*). With regard to the effect of the dispute, he accepts that the Lawgiver's usages here may be referred to as *al-ḥaqīqa al-sharʿiyya*, but equally could be viewed as non-literal (*majāz*). However, even if they are non-literal, they are 'preferred non-literal usages' (*min al-majāzāt al-rājiḥa*) which have, it appears, the same exegetical force as literal meanings in the exegetical process, and thereby extinguishing the debate's effect.[49] The *marjiʿ* recognised after al-Burūjirdī, the Najaf-based Muḥsin al-Ḥakīm (d. 1970), also appears to follow al-Nāʾīnī. In his *Ḥaqāʾiq al-uṣūl*, a commentary on the *Kifāya*, he argues that for legal-literal meanings to be the default meaning in textual exegesis, it would require not only that they come into being through an act of designation (*al-waḍʿ*), but that this designation supplant the linguistic-literal meaning. If it does not supplant it, then this is a case of homonymity (*ishtirāk*), and contextual evidence (*qarīna*) would be required to decide which literal meaning was the intended one, 'making the effect [of the dispute] an academic rather than a practical matter.' If they do not need a *qarīna*, then 'these meanings are the type for which we know the intended meanings of Lawgiver in each case of usage.'[50] For Muḥsin al-Ḥakīm, the debate between whether the Lawgiver employs legal-literal or *majāz* meanings for words such as *ṣalāh* has no real exegetical implications. Rūḥallāh al-Khumaynī (d. 1989)[51] and Abū al-Qāsim al-Khūʾī (d. 1991) argue that the intended meaning of these words when spoken by the Lawgiver are never in doubt. 'There is no point at which we doubt the intended usage meaning' (*lā yabqā mawrid nashakku fī-hi fī al-murād al-istiᶜmālī*),[52] al-Khūʾī declares uncompromisingly. Amongst the living *mujtahids*, one finds Muḥammad Isḥāq al-Fayyād[53] in Najaf, and the controversial Iranian Ayatallāh Muḥammad Ṣādiq al-Rūḥānī[54] adopting al-Nāʾīnī's position explicitly in their works of *uṣūl*, namely that 'the debate has no practical effect' (*thamara ᶜamaliyya*), though with no new argumentation as such. These references could be replicated, but even from this brief survey it appears that the dispute being of academic interest only is currently the dominant position amongst Shiᶜi jurists.

Conclusions

These debates, and the positions adopted by the modern Shiᶜi jurists, clearly owe more to the classical tradition than they do to any imperative to answer a pressing contemporary question. The arguments use the classical understanding of the origins and functions of language, and the authors, without exception, employ the technical terminology inherited from the history of Muslim legal theory. This reflects a general characteristic of seminary Shiᶜi scholarship: the current *ᶜulamāʾ* are the successors of the previous generations, and this generation's debates are but a continuation of the established tradition of scholastic enquiry. This is not to say that there is no innovation: al-Ākhund's formulation of the debate around the effect of the different views on *al-ḥaqīqa al-sharᶜiyya* was novel; al-Nāʾīnī's response was equally original. The accretions to the arguments and the modifications of the various positions also show development and creativity. The continuity with pre-modern tradition does not mean that these works are somehow 'timeless' with no signs of development, but it does not mean they are rooted in modern concerns either. They are recognisable as products of the contemporary period as they assume the recent developments of the Shiᶜi *uṣūl* discipline. They are not really concerned with the epistemological challenges supposedly posed by 'modernity'.

It could be argued that the discussion over whether the views on *al-ḥaqīqa al-sharᶜiyya* have any effect might be the result of a modern demand for practical applicability and a rejection of obscurantism. For the Nāʾīnī School, the different positions have no exegetical effect; by implication, there is little point in the discussion since legal theory is supposed to inform the derivation of rules. Is al-Nāʾīnī's position an expression of frustration with the impracticality of the discipline of *uṣūl al-fiqh* in the face of modern challenges? Tempting as it may be to come to this conclusion, a few caveats are in order. First, the discussion over the relationship between legal theory and the derivation of the law in Islamic jurisprudence is not peculiarly modern. It recurs again and again in the discipline's history. It may have been given an added piquancy in the modern era, with the frustration of some contemporary scholars with the abstract nature of the traditional disciplines. However, discussions around the effect (*thamara*) of a debate do not necessarily indicate any pressure from a new epistemological paradigm demanding practicality. Second, al-Nāʾīnī's demonstration that there is no effect is, itself, achieved through argumentation techniques which are thoroughly traditional and scholastic. His intervention is a critique, rather than a debunking of the achievements of the traditional sciences. Just because, on this particular point, the discussions of *uṣūl* have no effect on legal exegesis does not mean either that these are not interesting matters to discuss, or that the position of legal theory generally is fundamentally undermined. For all of his originality, al-Nāᶜīnī's thinking (on this point and on others) represents a development of the classical tradition rather than a radical break with it.

Finally, there have been more radical challenges to the traditional epistemological framework of Shiᶜi legal thought in the *ḥawza*, and these have often explicitly referenced external philosophical traditions. Some of these have been the focus of extensive research within the secondary literature.[55] Nonetheless, their influence has not yet transformed the way *uṣūl* is written; nor has it overturned the prestige of a *ḥawza* education and its role as a passport to religious and political authority in modern Shiᶜism. The continuity of that tradition of learning is expressed not through an absence of intellectual development or the unthinking preservation of past orthodoxies. Rather the back and forth of dispute within the *ḥawza* creates new positions which are then tested by a new cadre of scholars, and modified or discarded in response to criticism, continuing a debating style with a long history. The vibrancy of the internal discussions over *al-ḥaqīqa al-sharᶜiyya* exemplifies the debt of contemporary jurists to the classical tradition of Shiᶜi legal scholarship.

Notes

1. See Norman Calder, 'The limits of Islamic orthodoxy', in Farhad Daftary (ed.) *Intellectual Traditions in Islam* (London: I. B. Tauris, 2000), 67–86 and N. Calder, 'Law', in Seyyed Hossein Nasr and Oliver Leaman (eds), *History of Islamic Philosophy* (London: Routledge, 1996), 979–98.

2. In the modern period, the rejection of traditional methods of intellectual enquiry was most forcefully expressed by Jamāl al-Dīn al-Afghānī's (d. 1897) barrage of rhetorical questions to the *ᶜulamāᵓ* of India: 'Why do you not raise your eyes from those defective books and why do you not cast your glance on this wide world? Why do you not employ your reflection and thought on events and their causes without the veils of those works? Why do you always utilize those exalted minds on trifling problems?', cited in Nikki Keddie, *An Islamic Response to Imperialism: Political and Religious Writings of Sayyid Jamal al-Din 'al-Afghani'* (Berkeley: University of California Press, 1983), 120.
3. See, for example, Konrad Hirschler, 'Pre-eighteenth-century traditions of revivalism: Damascus in the thirteenth century', *Bulletin of the School of Oriental and African Studies* 68 (2005), 195–214.
4. The *ᶜulamāᵓ* are often portrayed in the secondary literature as lost in the past, their '"Islamic political imagination" has endeavored to ignore or disqualify anything new ... The atemporality of the mullahs' and ulamas' discourse is striking to this day. History is something that must be endured; whatever is new is contingent and merits only a *fatwa* from time to time.' Olivier Roy, *The Failure of Political Islam* (Cambridge, MA: Harvard University Press, 1994), 20. These stereotypes are masterfully tackled in Muhammad Qasim Zaman's *The Ulama in Contemporary Islam: Custodians of Change* (Princeton: Princeton University Press, 2002), particularly the introduction, 1–16.
5. That early (and some modern) European studies of the pre-modern (classical) period contributed to an 'essentialising' of the Muslim tradition is relatively uncontroversial, and creates the methodological issue of how the 'classical', 'pre-modern' or 'medieval period' might be characterised in relation to Islam. See Daniel Varisco, 'Making "Medieval" Islam meaningful', *Medieval Encounters* 13 (2007), 385–412.
6. Numerous citations would evidence this, but perhaps the most pithy expression of this modernism is the unsourced quote from Sayyid Aḥmad Khān (d. 1898): 'Look forward, learn modern knowledge, and do not waste time in studies of old subjects of no value'.
7. The most commonly cited anthropological and semi-autobiographical accounts of the traditional *ḥawza* system are those of R. Mottahedeh, *The Mantle of the Prophet* (Oxford: Oneworld Publications, 2002; a republication of the 1985 original) and Michael M. J. Fischer, *Iran: From Religious Dispute to Revolution* (Wisconsin: University of Wisconsin Press, 2003).
8. The names of these *ḥawza* reformers are increasingly the subject of research, in part because they are viewed as having an influence on internal reform in the Islamic Republic of Iran; the extensive secondary literature includes examinations and translations of the works of individual thinkers (for example, Ziba Mir-Hosseini and Richard Tapper, *Islam and Democracy in Iran: Eshkevari and the Quest for Reform* (London: I. B. Tauris, 2006); Behrooz Ghamari-Tabrizi, *Islam and Dissent in Postrevolutionary Iran: Abdolkarim Soroush, Religious Politics and Democratic Reform* (London: I. B. Tauris, 2008) and more general accounts

such as M. Kamrava, *Iran's Intellectual Revolution* (Cambridge: Cambridge University Press, 2008). Secondary literature is mainly focused on intellectual developments in Iran, is usually linked to matters of political reform, and rarely engages with the intellectual pursuits of what has been termed 'traditional' Shiᶜi *ᶜulamāʾ*. Norman Calder links Ayatollah al-Khumaynī's ideas with the classical tradition in his 'Accommodation and revolution in Imami Shiᶜi jurisprudence: Khumayni and the Classical Tradition', *Middle Eastern Studies* 18:1 (1982), 3–20.

9. Exceptions to this general characterisation include A. P. Dahlén, *Islamic Law, Epistemology and Modernity: Legal Philosophy in Contemporary Iran* (London: Routledge, 2003), though the more traditional approach of Ayatollah Jawādi-al-Āmulī is a counterpoint for the positions of reforms such as Muḥammad Mujtahid-Shabistārī and ᶜAbd al-Karīm Surūsh. I have tried to engage with the elements of religious learning which receive less attention in my 'Modern Šīᶜī discussions of Khabar al-wāḥid: Ṣadr, Ḫumaynī and Ḫūʾī', *Oriente Moderno* 21 (2002), 189–205, and 'Continuity and originality in Shiᶜi thought: the relationship between the Akhbariyya and the Maktab-i Tafkik', in S. Mervin and D. Hermann (eds), *Shiite Streams and Dynamics (1800–1925)* (Beirut: Orient-Institut, 2010), 71–94.
10. The role of the Shiᶜi *ᶜulamāʾ* in Iran since 1979, and more recently in Iraq, is the subject of extensive study. A controversial attempt to link up the various Shiᶜi movements is V. Nasr, *The Shia Revival* (New York: Norton, 2006), and examining Shiᶜi leadership generally, we now have O. Goldberg and S. Mishal, *Understanding Shiite Leadership: The Art of the Middle Ground in Iran and Lebanon* (Cambridge: Cambridge University Press, 2015).
11. Mottahedeh, *The Mantle of the Prophet*, 71–88.
12. Ibid. 198–219. The relationship between legal theory and jurisprudence, and beyond that to the actual application of the law, is not a peculiarly modern obsession, though it has been the subject of a number of scholarly studies in the recent past. I summarise the modern scholarly debate in my 'Deriving rules of law', in Rudolph Peters and Peri Bearman (eds), *The Ashgate Research Companion to Islamic Law* (Farnham: Ashgate, 2014), 57–72.
13. Hossein Modarressi Tabātabāʾi, *An Introduction to Shīᶜī Law: A Bibliographical Study* (London: Ithaca Press, 1984), 23–58 (Introduction).
14. Ibid. 55–7.
15. Ibid. 57–8.
16. For an account of Bihbihānī's influence, see my *Inevitable Doubt: Two Theories of Shīᶜī Jurisprudence* (Leiden: Brill, 2000), 1–15, and in greater detail, the recently published monograph by Z. Heern, *The Emergence of Modern Shīᶜism: Islamic Reform in Iraq and Iran* (Oxford: Oneworld, 2015), chs 4, 5 and 6.
17. See my *Scripturalist Islam: The History and Doctrines of the Akhbārī Shīᶜī School* (Leiden: Brill, 2007), 177–216, for how the Akhbārī position was defined against the *uṣūlī*s.
18. *Ẓann* is, of course, not an exclusively Shiᶜi epistemological category: indeed,

Sunni *uṣūl al-fiqh* detailed the employment of *ẓann* extensively (on this see A. Zysow, *The Economy of Certainty* (Atlanta: Lockwood Press, 2013)). However, modern Shiᶜi jurisprudence has elaborated on the category and created an impressive epistemological structure supporting its legal validity.

19. Modarressi, *An Introduction to Shīᶜī Law*, 58.
20. The effects of al-Anṣārī's epistemological framework within Shiᶜi thinking are now explored by Ali-Reza Bhojani in his monograph *Moral Rationalism and Sharīᶜa: Independent Rationality in Modern Shīᶜī uṣūl al-fiqh* (New York: Routledge, 2015), 117–42.
21. Al-Ākhund Muḥammad Kāẓim al-Khurāsānī, *Kifāyat al-uṣūl* (Qum: Muᵓassasat al-Nashr al-Islāmī, 1415/1994).
22. On the issue of these new literal meanings, termed *al-ḥaqīqa al-sharᶜiyya*, see B. Weiss, *The Search for God's Law: Islamic Jurisprudence in the Writings of Sayf al-Dīn al-Āmidī* (Salt Lake City: Utah University Press, 2010), 142–7.
23. Robert Gleave, *Islam and Literalism: Literal Meaning and Interpretation in Islamic Legal Theory* (Edinburgh: Edinburgh University Press, 2012), 1–25.
24. Ibid. passim and especially 29–35.
25. See Wael Hallaq, 'Notes on the term *Qarīna* in Islamic legal discourse', *Journal of the American Oriental Society* 108:3 (1988), 475–83.
26. Stephan Reichmuth, *The World of Murtada al-Zabidi (1732–91): Life, Networks and Writings* (Cambridge: E. J. W. Gibb Memorial Trust, 2009), 243–4.
27. This categorisation differs slightly from that espoused by al-Āmidī and other Sunni *uṣūlī*s where *lughawī* covers *waḍᶜ* and *ᶜurfī* meanings, which are both contrasted with *sharᶜī*. I suppose this is due to the Shiᶜi tradition wishing to stress that *lughawī*, *ᶜurfī* and *sharᶜī* are themselves all forms of *waḍᶜ*. See Weiss, *The Search for God's Law*, 147.
28. See Gleave, *Islam and Literalism*, 175–96.
29. Al-Shaykh Ḥasan b. al-Shahīd al-Thānī, *Maᶜālim al-uṣūl* (Qum: Dār al-Fikr, 1374 AH), 45–51.
30. Al-Shaykh Ḥasan, *Maᶜālim al-uṣūl*, 50–1.
31. Gleave, *Islam and Literalism*, 184–94.
32. Al-Shaykh Ḥasan, *Maᶜālim al-uṣūl*, 46.
33. Meir Litvak, *Shiᶜi Scholars of Nineteenth-Century Iraq: The ᶜUlamaᵓ of Najaf and Karbalaᵓ* (Cambridge: Cambridge University Press, 1998), 92.
34. The dynamics of legal text and commentary are nicely demonstrated by Norman Calder in his analysis of Ḥanafī law, *Islamic Jurisprudence in the Classical Era* (Cambridge: Cambridge University Press, 2010), 21–63.
35. Al-Ākhund, *Kifāyat al-uṣūl*, 37.
36. There is, following this discussion, a detailed account of when one can rationally assume that designation came before usage (or vice versa). The intense debate around this will be the subject of a forthcoming study on the effect of al-Ākhund's linguistic philosophy on subsequent Twelver *uṣūlī* discussions.
37. The transcripts of these lessons were compiled by al-Nāᵓīnī's pupil, Abū

al-Qāsim al-Khū'ī (d. 1992), *Ajwad al-taqrīrāt* (Qum: Manshūrāt-e Mustafawī, 1368 SH). This passage is found on 33.

38. Jawād al-Tibrīzī, *Kifāyat al-uṣūl: Durūs fī masā'il ᶜilm al-uṣūl* (Qum: Dār al-Ṣiddiqa al-Shahīdah, 1429 AH), 1: 98.
39. The translation is from R. Mottahedeh, *Lessons in Islamic Jurisprudence* (Oxford: Oneworld, 2003), 73. I think, on balance, I prefer this translation in this context to my own, 'required' designation, *Islam and Literalism*, 190.
40. al-Khū'ī, *Ajwad al-taqrīrāt*, 1, 34.
41. The argument here is similar to Shiᶜi arguments around consensus (*ijmāᶜ*) which is validated by the Imam's presence in amongst those agreeing (*al-mujmiᶜīn alay-hi*). See Gleave, *Inevitable Doubt*, 55–60, 75–81.
42. The essential role of the Imams here in determining the meaning of the original revelation is reminiscent of the famous Akhbārī argument that the Imams are the only *tafsīr* of the Qur'an. See Todd Lawson, 'Akhbari Shiᶜi approaches to tafsir', in G. R. Hawting and Abdul-Kader Shareef (eds), *Approaches to the Qur'an* (London: Routledge, 1993), 173–210.
43. Gleave, *Islam and Literalism*, 188–9.
44. ᶜAbd al-Karīm al-Ḥā'irī, *Durar al-fawā'id* (Qum: Mu'assasat al-Nashr al-Islāmī, 1408 AH), 1: 46.
45. Ḍiyā' al-Dīn al-ᶜArāqī, *Nihāyat al-afkār: Taqrīr Baḥth Āqā Ḍiyā' al-dīn al-Burūjirdī* (Qum: Mu'assasat al-Nashr al-Islāmī, 1405 AH), 1–2: 72.
46. This is reminiscent of the Akhbārī position where the Qur'an can only be understood through the *tafsīr* (see Gleave, *Scripturalist Islam*, 216–44).
47. al-Tibrīzī, *Kifāyat al-uṣūl: Durūs fī masā'il ᶜilm al-uṣūl*, 1: 98.
48. This is not a new notion in Imāmī thinking, as it echoes the early Imāmī notions of how God and the Prophet made the message unavailable to the general populous. That message is only generally available because the Imams are, in a sense, bilingual in the language of revelation and the ordinary language of the people. See R. Gleave, 'Literal meaning and interpretation in early Imāmī law', in A. K. Reinhart and R. Gleave (eds). *Islamic Law in Theory: Studies on Jurisprudence in Honor of Bernard Weiss* (Leiden: Brill, 2014), 231–55.
49. Muḥammad Ḥusayn al-Iṣfahānī, *Nihāyat al-dirāya fī sharḥ al-kifāya* (Qum: Intishārāt Sayyid al-Shuhadā', 1374 SH), 1: 5.
50. Muḥsin al-Ḥakīm, *Ḥaqā'iq al-uṣūl* (Qum: Maktabat-i Baṣīratī, 1408 AH), 1: 51.
51. Rūḥallāh al-Khumaynī, *Manāhij al-wuṣūl ilā ᶜilm al-uṣūl* (Mu'assasat tanẓīm wa-nashr āthār al-Imām al-Khumaynī, 1414 AH), 1: 137–9.
52. Abū al-Qāsim al-Khū'ī, *Muḥāḍarāt fī uṣūl al-fiqh: taqrīr al-baḥth li-l-Sayyid al-Khū'ī li-l-Fayyāḍ* (Qum: Mu'assasat al-Nashr al-Islāmī, 1419 AH), 1: 42.
53. Muḥammad Isḥāq al-Fayyāḍ, *al-Mabāḥith al-uṣūliyya* (n.p. (Najaf?): Maktab Āyatallāh al-ᶜUẓmā Muḥammad Isḥāq al-Fayyād, n.d.), 101.
54. Muḥammad Ṣādiq al-Rūḥānī, *Zubdat al-uṣūl* (Qum: Madrasat al-Imām al-Ṣādiq, 1412 AH), 1: 75.
55. See above, note 6, and amongst others: E. Sadeghi-Boroujerdi, 'Mostafa

Malekian: spirituality, Siyasat-Zadegi and (a)political self-improvement', *Digest of Middle East Studies* 23 (2014), 279–311; Yasuyuki Matsunaga, 'Mohsen Kadivar, an advocate of postrevivalist Islam in Iran', *British Journal of Middle Eastern Studies* 34:3 (2007), 317–29.

2

Muḥammad Nāṣir al-Dīn al-Albānī and Traditional Hadith Criticism

Christopher Melchert

Muḥammad Nāṣir al-Dīn al-Albānī was a prolific and influential Salafi writer. He was born in Albania in 1914. His family emigrated to Damascus, where he grew up to be a tradesman and an informally-trained *ᶜālim*, expert in hadith and Ḥanafī law. He taught in Saudi Arabia 1961–3, having to leave because of aberrant legal opinions; for example, that it was unnecessary to fast in Ramadan if one could not see daylight, as in a house with the windows blocked; that it was unnecessary to remove one's footwear to pray; and that the full-face veil was unnecessary. He was invited back to Mecca for a brief period in the 1970s but spent most of the rest of his life in Jordan. He died in Amman in 1999.[1]

To me as a student of hadith, he is interesting first of all for his fearless criticism of the traditional canon. What first caught my eye were things like *Ṣaḥīḥ* Sunan *Ibn Māja* (1986), followed two years later by *Ḍaᶜīf* Sunan *Ibn Māja* (1988), the sound and the weak of Ibn Māja (d. 887?), one of the Six Books, the most prestigious Sunni collections of hadith (although admittedly Ibn Māja's was the last to be added to the list and never enjoyed the same prestige as the rest). These were shortly followed by similar volumes identifying the strong and weak of the collections of Tirmidhī (d. 892?) and Nasāʾī (d. 915?), two others of the Six Books (and both less obvious targets). The earliest book of his that I have come across is *Ḥijāb al-marʾa al-muslima*, dated on the cover 1374/1954–5, completed according to a note at the end in Damascus, 7/5/1371; that is, 3 February 1952.[2] Its bibliography seems to indicate an earlier publication (probably no more than a pamphlet), *Takhrīj aḥādīth kitābi-hi* Ṣifat ṣalāt al-nabī, I take it as an extract from the *Sunan* of Abū Dāwūd with commentary. Already at this point, he seems to have projected an abridgement of one of the Six Books comprising only its sound hadith.[3] I am a student of medieval hadith criticism. I have written about

Abū Nuᶜaym al-Iṣbahānī (d. 1038), al-Nasāʾī, al-Bukhārī (d. 870), and other early-medieval collectors and critics. Naturally, my first question with regard to Albānī is whether he uses the same methods as medieval hadith critics or only thinks he does.

Salafism

Albānī identified his own position as Salafism. For example, he says he had the idea for an abridgement with commentary of a thirteenth-century book on pious works 25 years earlier (in the early 1950s) when he was teaching this book to a group of Salafi brothers in Syria.[4] It was notably opposed to organised Sufism and the schools of law. 'Salafism' refers to a movement begun in the late nineteenth century by Jamāl al-Dīn al-Afghānī (d. 1897) and Muḥammad ᶜAbduh (d. 1905), who briefly published together a newspaper, *al-ᶜUrwa al-wuthqā* ('the firmest handle', with allusion to Q. 2:256 and 31:22). Albānī himself pointed to a polemic against Ghazālī's defence of Sufism and use of weak hadith reports in the journal *al-Manār*, founded by ᶜAbduh, as a formative influence (although also a detailed list of weak hadith in Ghazālī's *Iḥyāʾ ᶜulūm al-dīn* by Zayn al-Dīn al-ᶜIrāqī (d. 1414)).[5] It is named for the *salaf*, those who went before, as opposed to the *khalaf*, those who came after them. *Salaf* usually refers more specifically to the Companions of the Prophet and the first generation or two after them. There is Prophetic hadith declaring that the best of his community was the generation amongst whom he was sent, then the next one or two generations, uncertainty as to what he said expressed by the Companion himself.[6] *Salaf* itself is a rare word in both Qurʾan and hadith. The noun occurs just once in the former, and not with an encouraging meaning: speaking of Pharaoh and his people, 'We took vengeance on them and drowned them all. We made them *a thing of the past* and an example for those of later times' (Q. 43:55–6, Jones trans., emphasis added). In Bukhārī's collection of hadith, it occurs once, in a topic heading, 'How far the *salaf* would store up food and other things in their houses'. The following hadith report stresses how long the Prophet would keep food, since his family had so little to eat. Bukhārī evidently uses *salaf*, then, to indicate the generation of the Companions.[7] Early uses of *salafī* that I have come across are unspecific as to how early the *salaf* are taken to be, and refer to theological orthodoxy rather than law; for example, of Abū Ḥanīfa's grandson Ismāᶜīl ibn Ḥammād (d. 827–8), 'They said he was a sound *salafī*.'[8]

Albānī himself used a somewhat flexible definition of the *salaf*. He comments thus on the hadith report, 'God (blessèd and exalted be he), when it is the Day of the Resurrection, will descend to his servants':

> I say this is a real descent (*nuzūl ḥaqīqī*), as befits his exaltedness and perfection. It is a character of action belonging to God (alternatively: it describes an action of God's). Beware of interpreting it figuratively (*an tata'awwala-hu*), as do some of the recent ones (*khalaf*) and so go astray.[9]

Here is an example of traditionalist theology, accepting whatever revelation says without applying rationalist interpretation. (At that, the distinction between characters of action and characters of essence apparently betrays some rationalist theological reflection.) He says of an opinion from Ibn Ḥajar (against invoking the Prophet as *sayyida-nā*), 'This is an important *fatwā* in which the Ḥāfiẓ pursued the way of the *salaf* in following (*ittibā*ᶜ) and leaving innovations.'[10] It would be hard to say that the *salaf* and *khalaf* here are anything more than (respectively) modest early authorities who let hadith be their opinions and immodest later authorities who wanted to elaborate on the early tradition, with relevance to both law and theology.

As for law in particular, the Salafi idea has been to get behind the schools, named for jurisprudents of the later eighth to earlier ninth centuries, back to the material of revelation, Qurᵓan and hadith. The tradition often opposes *ijtihād* to *taqlīd*. The former term refers literally to effort, technically (in jurisprudence) the effort of examining the evidence and coming up with one's own answer to a legal question. The latter term refers literally to putting a collar on someone, technically to bestowing authority on someone to answer a legal question without troubling to examine the evidence for oneself. Medieval jurisprudents came up with hierarchies of *ijtihād*, some persons being allowed more scope for their scholarly effort than others. In the late 1950s, Albānī edited a book by the Ḥanbalī Aḥmad ibn Ḥamdān (d. Cairo, 1295) that posits a hierarchy and, unsurprisingly (since it comes from an authority of one of the recognised guild schools), calls for a layman to stay within the schools, not presuming to choose any of the *salaf* to follow in preference to Abū Ḥanīfa, Mālik, al-Shāfiᶜī, Aḥmad, and their like. Albānī protests in a note,[11]

> Do not be misled by this here, for to take as one's school the doctrine of any of the Companions, especially the Rightly-Guided Caliphs (assuming it is soundly transmitted), is the worthiest way for a Muslim after the Book of God and the *sunna* of his Messenger …

Apparently, Albānī does not reject *taqlīd* altogether in favour of going directly to Qurᵓan and hadith for rules. Rather, he expressly allows one to invest authority in Companions as well, especially the first four caliphs. This is reminiscent of Aḥmad ibn Ḥanbal's reported definition of *sunna*, meaning authoritative precedent:

> I more than once heard Aḥmad when he had been asked whether the practice of Abū Bakr, ᶜUmar, ᶜUthmān, and ᶜAlī was *sunna*. He said, 'Yes.' Once he said, 'On account of the hadith report of the Messenger of God: "Incumbent on you is my *sunna* and the *sunna* of the Rightly Guided Caliphs."' He thus named it *sunna*.

When someone asked whether the dicta of such persons as Abū Muᶜādh and Ibn Masᶜūd (other Companions) equally constituted *sunna*, he said, 'I will not deny it, for I dislike to disagree with any of them.'[12]

His professed disdain for relying on the *khalaf* notwithstanding, Albānī in practice does cite jurisprudents from throughout the long tradition. Here for example are the legal authorities he cites in his early work on the veil (*Ḥijāb al-marʾa*; not just relating hadith) in descending order of frequency.

eight times:

- Ibn Taymiyya (d. Damascus, 1328), Ḥanbalī

three times:

- Ibn Ḥazm (d. Majorca, 1064), Ẓāhirī
- al-Qurṭubī (d. Munyat Banī Khaṣīb, Upper Egypt, 1273?), Mālikī
- Ibn Ḥajar al-Haythamī (d. Cairo, 1405), Shāfiᶜī

twice:

- al-Nawawī (d. Nawā, 1271), Shāfiᶜī
- Ibn Kathīr (d. Damascus, 1373), Shāfiᶜī

once:

- al-Shāfiᶜī (d. Old Cairo, 820), independent
- Aḥmad ibn Ḥanbal (d. Baghdad, 855), independent
- al-Bayhaqī (d. Nishapur, 1066), Shāfiᶜī
- Ibn ᶜAbd al-Barr (d. Jativa, 1071), Mālikī
- Ibn Rushd (d. Marrakech, 1198), Mālikī (but the book cited, *al-Bidāya*, purports to cover all schools)
- al-Rāfiᶜī (d. Qazvin, 1226), Shāfiᶜī
- Abū Muḥammad ibn Abī Jamra (d. Cairo, bef. 1300–1), Mālikī
- Ibn Daqīq al-ᶜĪd (d. Cairo, 1302), Mālikī and Shāfiᶜī
- Abū Ḥayyān al-Andalusī (d. Cairo, 1344), Ẓāhirī and Shāfiᶜī
- al-Dhahabī (d. Damascus, 1348?), Shāfiᶜī
- Ibn Ḥajar al-ᶜAsqalānī (d. Cairo, 1449), Shāfiᶜī
- al-Shawkānī (d. Sanaa, 1834), independent
- Anwar al-Kashmīrī (d. Deoband, 1933), independent

These are mostly the sort of authorities one would expect a writer to cite who has a high regard for hadith but a low one for scholastic law. It is not surprising that Ibn Taymiyya is cited more often than anyone else, since he famously stood for his own prerogative of going back to original sources as a *mujtahid muṭlaq*, while Ibn Kathīr and al-Dhahabī were both close to him. Al-Shawkānī and Anwar al-Kashmīrī were notable later advocates of going back to original sources. The rest are predominantly Shāfiʿī, probably reflecting some of that school's strong preference for hadith-based jurisprudence (or at least the appearance of it). It is a minor puzzle why Ibn Taymiyya should be the only Ḥanbalī on the list, since the Ḥanbalī school was even more strongly characterised by a preference for hadith-based jurisprudence, often to the point of taking aberrant positions. (For example, when I looked into the question of women's attendance in the mosque, I found that the Ḥanbalī school was more permissive than any other of women going to the mosque without their husbands' permission, in line with hadith, and also of women leading prayers.[13] When I looked into the question of using public baths, I found the Ḥanbalī school was the only one to maintain a strong, restrictive position, again in line with hadith.[14]) Part of the reason is probably the history of legal publication up to the early 1950s: there were simply few Ḥanbalī books in print for Albānī to become familiar with. It is also a minor puzzle why there are no Companions on the list. At that, Albānī professed himself to be highly respectful of past juristic activity. Establishing the legal categories (*aḥkām*) to which different things are assigned, even things merely recommended or discouraged (not absolutely required or forbidden), requires sound hadith as evidence, he says in a book of the late 1970s – just what we expect him to say. Surprising is his justification: less than this 'detracts from what the *ʿulamāʾ* have established.'[15] The prevailing idea is apparently not that Islamic jurisprudence at one time took a wrong turn and became an irrelevance, rather that properly hadith-based law has always had its followers, within and without the schools, in whose tradition Albānī places himself at this end.

Albānī's Hadith Criticism

It may seem conceptually easy to shove aside the schools of law. There are some precedents for it; for example, the Almohads seem to have shoved aside Mālikī law in the twelfth century, and Ibn Rushd's survey of the different schools may have been planned as a prelude to writing a single code for them to impose.[16] But the project of getting behind the learning of the eighth and ninth centuries in order to work directly from revelation runs into a greater difficulty when it comes to hadith, for our major collections of hadith date from the time of the schools of law, not before. Can a Salafi dismiss Shaybānī and Shāfiʿī as fallible individuals, creatures of their time, but treat Bukhārī and Muslim as impeccable scholars who transcended the limitations of their time? Albānī is notable for questioning their impeccability, which has made him highly controversial among Sunni Muslims. How do his methods compare with those of the major collectors?

Hadith is basically the body of quotations of the Prophet and descriptions of his actions that constitutes the principal basis of Islamic law. A major question in modern hadith studies is how our medieval collectors and critics went about sorting the sound from the weak; that is, the more reliably attributed from the less. Most twentieth-century scholarship has concentrated on the terms used by early critics, following the example above all of Ibn al-Ṣalāḥ al-Shahrazūrī (d. 1245), whose textbook on hadith science comprises a series of chapters each explaining one evaluation: sound hadith, fair hadith, and so on.[17] This stress on understanding what early critics meant by various expressions was dictated partly by the crystallisation of a hadith canon, so that scholars got their hadith mainly from recognised collections of the (mostly) ninth and tenth centuries. It was presumably reinforced by the feeling that they were all epigones who should not presume to come up with better evaluations than the great collectors and critics of the ninth and tenth centuries, just as they should not presume to come up with better rules than the pioneers of their schools of law.

To the contrary, Eerik Dickinson read early hadith criticism directly and stressed rather *isnād* (chain of transmission) comparison. If a hadith report was supported by multiple, mutually corroborative *isnād*s, it must be sound. If a particular link was without parallels, one investigated whether the transmitter's hadith were usually corroborated or not. If they were, he got the benefit of the doubt in this case; if not, then this uncorroborated report must be considered weak and the transmitter became suspect.[18] Similar reliance on *isnād* comparison is attributed to Bukhārī (correctly, I believe) in a 2007 biography and has moved into the textbooks with Jonathan Brown's *Hadith*.[19] In the late 1970s, Albānī himself said that he thought to identify the weak hadith in the book at hand 'depending in that on hadith terminology, *al-jarḥ wa-al-taᶜdīl* (the aspersion and pronouncing just of individual traditionists), and looking up what the careful *ᶜulamāᵓ* had said about each hadith in it.'[20] That is to say, he will rely on the opinions of past experts without presuming to redo their work.

Examples of early hadith criticism I take from a book by al-Tirmidhī, *al-ᶜIlal al-kabīr*, supplementary to his great hadith collection, in which he quotes the most revered Sunni hadith collector of all, Muḥammad ibn Ismāᶜīl al-Bukhārī (d. 870). Asked about the hadith report < Muḥammad ibn al-Muthannā < Muḥammad ibn Bakr al-Bursānī < Yūnus ibn Yazīd < al-Zuhrī < Anas ibn Mālik, that the Messenger of God walked before funeral processions, likewise Abū Bakr, ᶜUmar and ᶜUthmān, Bukhārī said, 'Muḥammad ibn Bakr was mistaken about this. It is related only < Yūnus < al-Zuhrī < Sālim < Ibn ᶜUmar.'[21] Muḥammad ibn Bakr (Basran, d. 818–19?) had evidently substituted Anas ibn Mālik for Sālim and Ibn ᶜUmar, he being the only one who related it this way. He was also asked about the hadith report related by Abū Kurayb < Isḥāq ibn Sulaymān al-Rāzī < Mughīra ibn Muslim < Yūnus < al-Ḥasan < Abū Hurayra < Messenger of God: 'God likes forbearance in selling, forbearance in buying, and forbearance in judgement', to which Bukhārī said, 'This hadith report is a mistake. Ismāᶜīl ibn ᶜUlayya related this hadith report < Yūnus < Saᶜīd al-Maqburī < Abū Hurayra.' Someone had substituted al-Ḥasan's name for Saᶜīd al-Maqburī's.[22] In fact, the rejected version is in Tirmidhī's major hadith collection (no. 1319) with the comment *gharīb* (meaning uncorroborated). Both of these examples are of hadith criticism by *isnād* comparison, with the discrepant version discarded. In both cases, Tirmidhī relies on his teacher Bukhārī's expertise, but he gives us Bukhārī's reasoning, not just Bukhārī's one-word characterisation.

For comparison, here are a few examples of Albānī's hadith criticism. I start with one from his earliest work, a collection of what he considers the sound hadith pertaining to women's veiling:[23]

> Abū Dāwūd related it with full *isnād* (2:182–183) and al-Bayhaqī (2:226 and 7:87) by way of Saᶜīd ibn Bashīr < Qatāda < Khālid ibn Durayk < ᶜĀᵓisha. Abū Dāwūd said immediately afterwards, 'This is *mursal* [lacking one link]. Khālid ibn Durayk never met ᶜĀᵓisha.' I say that Saᶜīd ibn Bashīr is weak, as in *al-Taqrīb* by the *ḥāfiẓ* Ibn Ḥajar. However, the hadith report has come by other ways by which it is strengthened.

The first two references are to hadith collections of the ninth and eleventh centuries, respectively.[24] Ibn Ḥajar (d. 1449), *al-Taqrīb*, is a succinct biographical dictionary of all the men in the Six Books.[25] Next, Albānī offers another hadith report from Abū Dāwūd (related by Qatāda directly from the Prophet) and another from Bayhaqī, of which, as he says, Bayhaqī himself commented, 'Its *isnād* is weak.' Then Albānī defends it:[26]

> I say that its weakness is this Ibn Lahīᶜa. His name is ᶜAbd Allāh al-Ḥaḍramī, Abū ᶜAbd al-Raḥmān the Egyptian qāḍī. He is trustworthy and virtuous. However, he used to relate hadith from his notebooks, then they were burnt so he related hadith by memory and became confused. Some late critics have pronounced his hadith good, others sound … What I do not doubt is that his hadith, when corroborated by additional witnesses, do not go below the level of 'good', this being an example.

> Al-Bayhaqī strengthened the hadith report from another direction, for after he had related the report of ᶜĀᵓisha, also from Ibn ᶜAbbās and others in explaining *illā mā ẓahara min-hā* (Q. 24:31), he said, 'Along with this *mursal* is the pronouncement of those who have passed of the Companions (may God be pleased with them) in clarifying what God has permitted by way of external adornment.' With this, the position becomes strong.

A *mursal* hadith report is one whose *isnād* has a gap, as between Qatāda (d. 735–6?) and the Prophet. The position in question is whether a woman's whole face need be covered. Albānī thinks not, in line with the position of the traditional schools of law. Albānī's method here is mainly to see what earlier critics said, then to look for corroboration in parallel reports. He seems remarkably complacent about defective chains of transmission, also deferential to earlier hadith critics and even jurists, as by not testing Bayhaqī's investigation of Companion opinion.

Here is another example from the same early work:[27]

> Al-Ḥākim brought it out … saying, 'a sound hadith report by the criterion of the two shaykhs.' Al-Dhahabī agreed with him. However, it is so by the criterion of Muslim alone, for Zakarīyā [*sic*] ibn ᶜAdī is in its *isnād*, and al-Bukhārī related from him only elsewhere than in *al-Jāmiᶜ al-ṣaḥīḥ*, as (is said) in *al-Tahdhīb*.

Albānī refers to al-Ḥākim al-Naysābūrī (d. 1014), *al-Mustadrak ᶜalā al-ṣaḥīḥayn*, Bukhārī and Muslim ('the two shaykhs'), Dhahabī (d. 1348?), and Ibn Ḥajar, *Tahdhīb* al-Tahdhīb, the work of which *al-Taqrīb* is an abridgement. Here is another example of Albānī's reliance on critics of the High Middle Ages. Al-Ḥākim al-Naysābūrī invented the idea of 'the criterion of Bukhārī' and 'the criterion of Muslim' (*sharṭ al-Bukhārī, sharṭ Muslim*). Muslim hadith critics across the centuries have written extensively to define these criteria. The most popular definition in modern times is a distinction proposed by Ibn Ḥajar: that Muslim wanted uninterrupted chains of transmitters of known probity who might have met each other, whereas Bukhārī would accept only uninterrupted chains of transmitters of known probity who demonstrably did meet each other. Muslim's introduction to his *Ṣaḥīḥ* does defend the *isnād* in which direct audition is not asserted at every link, but it seems to be unsupportable speculation that Bukhārī excluded such hadith.[28] It is to Albānī's credit that he here accepts the evidence of Bukhārī's including a hadith report in his *Ṣaḥīḥ* as sufficient to establish that it met his criterion, since further evidence cannot be found. Again, however, he relies implicitly on the judgement of medieval critics, especially (here) Muslim.

Here is an example from the early 1960s:[29]

> An excellent hadith report. Al-ᶜAṭṭār is not celebrated for his *isnād* (chain of authorities), but Qabīṣa corroborated his transmission from Sufyān. Al-Tirmidhī brought it out and said, 'a good sound hadith report.'

Al-Tirmidhī has a longer version of this hadith report < Hannād < Qabīṣa < Sufyān, of which he comments *ḥasan* ('good') or, according to one manuscript, *ḥasan ṣaḥīḥ* ('good and sound').[30] Here then from the later 1960s:[31]

> Sound, short of his saying 'above seven heavens.' Thus it is in the *Ṣaḥīḥayn* and the *Musnad*. As for this addition, Muḥammad ibn Ṣāliḥ al-Tammār alone related it, as in *al-ᶜUlūw*, 162, saying 'He being *ṣadūq*.' In the *Taqrīb*, he says, '*Ṣadūq*, making mistakes.' I say that from the like of him is not accepted single narration (*tafarrud*), even if the author pronounces it sound. So likewise (says) al-Dhahabī. In affirmation of his (God's) being above are sound hadith reports that make us not need this one.

Al-ᶜUlūw probably refers to a collection of hadith by al-Dhahabī (d. 1348?).[32] For Albānī, again, a medieval critic's evaluation of a traditionist is decisive.

Here is Albānī's comment on the well-attested hadith report, 'Do not write from me. Whoever writes anything from him besides the Qurᵓan, let him erase it': 'This is abrogated by the many hadith reports in which is the command to write Prophet hadith.'[33] There is no attempt here to show that the hadith report in question was inaccurately transmitted; rather, Albānī resorts to the legal concept of abrogation. Elsewhere, he does resort to hadith criticism to discredit another on the topic. Yaḥyā ibn Jaᶜda (Ḥijāzī Follower): 'ᶜUmar wished the *sunna* to be written, then he wrote to the people, "Whoever has any of that written, let him erase it."' Of this, Albānī says, 'Its *isnād* is interrupted, for Yaḥyā ibn Jaᶜda did not meet ᶜUmar ibn al-Khaṭṭāb. They mentioned that he did not meet Ibn Masᶜūd, who died after ᶜUmar by about twenty years.'[34] Two early critics are quoted as saying that Yaḥyā ibn Jaᶜda did not meet Ibn Masᶜūd, although 'twenty years' is an odd estimate: ᶜUmar is universally said to have died in 23/644, while Ibn Masᶜūd is said to have died in 32 or 33/*ca.* 653.[35] Albānī goes on to acknowledge that there was a controversy among the *salaf* over the permissibility of writing hadith (the term expressly indicates an oral report), with permissibility, even obligation, becoming established over time. This seems to be true.[36] I just observe that hadith on the topic going back to Companions and the Prophet seem to an outsider patent back-projections of current opinion, whereas Albānī strongly resists finding back-projection.

Another example: the collection he is evaluating includes the hadith report,

> Fasting and the Qurʾan will intercede for the servant on the Day of the Resurrection. Fasting will say, 'O Lord, I forbade him food and desires, so make me an intercessor for him.' The Qurʾan will say, 'I forbade him to sleep by night, so make me an intercessor for him.' Then they will be made intercessors.

Al-Mundhirī comments, 'Aḥmad related it, also al-Ṭabarānī in *al-Kabīr*. Its men are argued by in the *Ṣaḥīḥ*. Ibn Abī al-Dunyā related it in *Kitāb al-Jūʿ* and elsewhere with a good *isnād*. Al-Ḥākim said, "Sound by the criterion of Muslim."' In the margin, Albānī comments *ṣaḥīḥ* (sound).[37] In his note, Albānī first quotes the Egyptian al-Munāwī (d. 1621?): 'This saying may be interpreted literally, such that the reward for the two of them is incarnated and God created for them a voice, "God being capable of anything" [Q. 2:284, 3:29, etc.]. It may also be interpreted as a kind of figurative case and allegory.' Albānī then comments,

> The first is correct, the one that must be firmly endorsed here and in similar cases of hadith in which works are incarnated; for example, the incarnation of one's treasure as a spotted serpent.[38] There are many others like it. The allegorical interpretation (*taʾwīl*) of such texts as these is not the way of the *salaf* (God be pleased with them); rather, it is the way of the Muʿtazila and those who followed the way of the *khalaf*. This is one of the things that contradict the first condition of faith, 'those who believe in the unseen' (Q. 2:3). Beware of taking after them, lest you go astray and be hapless. Our refuge is with God (be He exalted).

The assumption here that the *salaf* who disbelieved in allegorical interpretation came earlier than the *khalaf* who accepted it seems likely to be correct, but it would be difficult to prove, since assertions that such hadith reports are to be taken literally could only appear in response to proposals to interpret them figuratively. *Salaf* and *khalaf* practically stand for 'the orthodox' and 'unorthodox' anyway. This seems to be exactly the way the Ḥanbalī writer Ibn Rajab (d. 1393), among others, uses the terms in *Faḍl ʿilm al-salaf ʿalā ʿilm al-khalaf*, 'The superiority of the knowledge of the *salaf* to that of the *khalaf*', which warns against theological discussion and indeed most of the sciences as distracting from what is necessary, mainly knowledge of what is required and forbidden, without attempting to demonstrate that the *salaf* discussed only this.[39]

What I conclude from this survey is that Albānī does not offer new methods of hadith criticism. On the face of it, Albānī seems to have combined reliance on medieval critics to have identified strong and weak traditionists with reliance on multiple lines of transmission to confirm authenticity in difficult cases. This is to stress corroboration, as our medieval critics did. He does not particularly favour early collectors or critics over later. He does not point to the phenomenon of 'partial common links' like Juynboll or labour to identify variant wordings with particular transmitters like Motzki and his students.[40] My conclusion is similar to that of Kamaruddin Amin, which he based on a more extensive analysis of a smaller number of hadith reports: that Albānī's method was thoroughly traditional, with stress on the evaluations of particular traditionists by medieval critics but apparently applied more systematically than by medieval collectors such as Muslim.[41] (The chief weakness of Amin's analysis, I would say, is his reluctance to acknowledge either that later theories of hadith criticism, as from Ibn al-Ṣalāḥ, might not agree perfectly with early practice, or that a collector like Muslim might have been inconsistent.)

An Example of Albānī's Legal Reasoning

Hadith is important to Albānī mainly because it tells us our obligations; that is, because of its implications for Islamic law. He started with a book on women's veiling that is mostly a collection of what he considers the relevant sound hadith reports, but it is organised to make a systematic argument and every now and then interrupts the series of hadith reports for an extended legal discussion. I provide here one example of Albānī's legal reasoning. The subject is saluting non-Muslims. Some well-attested hadith discourages saluting them first; for example, from Muslim,[42]

> < Qutayba ibn Saʿīd < ʿAbd al-Raḥmān (i.e. al-Darāwardī) < Suhayl < his father < Abū Hurayra < the Messenger of God: 'Do not take the initiative in saluting the Jews and Nazarenes. When you meet one of them on the road, force him onto its narrowest part.' Variants come < Muḥammad ibn al-Muthannā < Muḥammad ibn Jaʿfar < Shuʿba; < Abū Bakr ibn Abī Shayba and Abū Kurayb < Wakīʿ < Sufyān; < Zuhayr ibn Ḥarb < Jarīr, all of them < Suhayl with this *isnād*. In Wakīʿ's version, 'When you meet the Jews.' In Ibn Jaʿfar's version < Shuʿba concerning the People of the Book. In Jarīr's version, 'When you meet them' without naming the polytheists.

Very typically, Muslim presents several alternative *isnād*s one after another, so that we can see the evidence for ourselves. Albāni says,[43]

> It is established by these reports that saluting a *kitābī* first is not permitted at all, whether on the way, in a house, or elsewhere. If it is asked, 'Is it permissible to say first something other than saluting, such as saying "How are you this morning?" or "This evening?" or "How are you?"' and the like of that, then I say: what appears to me (and God knows better) is

> permissibility, for the prohibition mentioned in the hadith report is only the salutation …
>
> What is intended is only the Islamic salutation that includes the name of God (mighty and glorious is he), as in his saying … 'Peace is one of the names of God that he put on the earth, so spread peace amongst you …' Ibn Masᶜūd permitted saluting them first with a gesture, for it is not the salutation peculiar to the Muslims. Likewise they may be saluted by such words as we have mentioned.
>
> As for what has been brought up in some of the books of the Ḥanābila such as *al-Dalīl*, that it is also forbidden to say first to them the like of 'How are you this morning?' or 'this evening?' or 'how are you?' or 'what is your condition?' I know of no evidence from the *sunna*. Rather, he declares in his commentary *Manār al-sabīl* that it is by analogy with the salutation. I say it cannot be concealed that it is an analogy despite a difference; that 'peace' is a distinction that does not come up in the mentioned expressions. God knows best.

Albānī does permit *wa-ᶜalaykum al-salām* in reply, pointing to the hadith report commanding a like or better reply.

The first thing that strikes me about this discussion is how traditional it seems. The argument is about the operation of analogy, a normal recourse in the jurisprudence of the schools. Classically, analogy is a means to extend the rulings of Qurᵓan and hadith. To see whether two cases are analogous, one looks for a common property (*ᶜilla*). A standard example is date wine. The Qurᵓan forbids *khamr*, meaning grape wine. For a time, a party of Muslim jurisprudents held out for *nabīdh*, date wine, on the ground that it was not *khamr* and therefore not forbidden. Hadith could be found on both sides. The argument that won the day was that *khamr* was forbidden because of its property of intoxicating, hence *nabīdh* also was forbidden, since it shared this property (their common *ᶜilla*). Albānī argues that saying *al-salāmu ᶜalaykum* to non-Muslims is forbidden because *al-salām*, one of the names of God, is reserved for Muslims. Saying 'How are you this morning?' does not have the property of including this word; therefore, it must be permissible. It seems as though it should have been easy to argue the other way around: that putting non-Muslims in their proper, subordinate place is the common property, neither saluting them nor offering them other pleasantries. But this apparent opportunism is a prominent feature of traditional Islamic jurisprudence.[44]

Also notable is Albānī's arguing against a twentieth-century Ḥanbalī commentary on a seventeenth-century Ḥanbalī epitome (*Manār al-sabīl* and *al-Dalīl*, respectively).[45] This also seems remarkably traditional. He has learnt

Islamic law as it was expounded by the generation before him. He has not leapt back to the High Middle Ages, as to Ibn Qudāma, nor even the Early Middle Ages, as to al-Shāfiᶜī. Rather, again, he apparently puts himself at the near end of a long tradition.

Conclusion

Muḥammad Nāṣir al-Dīn al-Albānī turns out to be more a traditionalist than an innovator. He is willing to cast out hadith from revered collections, but with notable reluctance when it comes to Bukhārī and Muslim, the most revered of all. He often goes to lengths to defend hadith in the revered collections with obvious defects in their *isnāds*. His inconsistency is itself fairly traditional. Likewise his legal reasoning: it turns out that hadith do not provide an obvious answer to every question, so he resorts to analogy, just as medieval jurisprudents did (and not, as pre-classical jurisprudents did, to Companion and Follower opinions, even though his professed theory of Salafism seems to allow it). Like those medieval jurisprudents, he purports to control the operation of analogy so as to stay loyal to revelation, not presuming to arrive at norms by reason; yet, like them, he often gives the appearance of actually starting with desirable rules, then finding ways to justify them from revelation.

Willy-nilly, Albānī does seem to have provoked progress in hadith studies by Muslims. In Europe and North America, the authenticity question has tended to dominate hadith studies.[46] Among the very few writers about the Islamic tradition of hadith criticism, James Robson was typical in stressing the definitions of terms such as *ṣaḥīḥ* and *ḥasan* and categories of men such as *thiqa* and *ṣadūq* (*ṣaḥīḥ* and *thiqa* indicating high degrees of reliability, *ḥasan* and *ṣadūq* middling).[47] The same emphasis on terminology and upright transmitters pervades accounts by Muslims.[48] It was thought that sound hadith reports were such as had only upright men in their *isnāds*. Albānī similarly looks first to terms such as *ṣaḥīḥ* and categories of men but approximates the actual earliest method when he says that a formally defective hadith report is strengthened by parallels, although he does not stress particular links in need of corroboration.

When I started to read modern hadith scholarship in Arabic, it seemed as though it was all stuck in the same rut as Robson and others, relying heavily on later synthetic treatments by writers like al-Khaṭīb al-Baghdādī (d. 1071) and Ibn al-Ṣalāḥ, scarcely paying attention to what the important early collectors wrote. For example, I recall a book by two professors at the University of Kuwait, ᶜAbd al-Razzāq ibn Khalīfa al-Shāyajī and al-Sayyid Muḥammad al-Sayyid Nūḥ about hadith transmission by paraphrase (*al-riwāya bi-l-maᶜnā*).[49] The authors review in chronological order arguments allowing traditionists to paraphrase, then in chronological order arguments forbidding paraphrase in favour of verbatim transmission alone, drawing mainly on a handbook by al-Khaṭīb al-Baghdādī.[50] The authors add their own hypothetical rebuttals to the major arguments in favour of paraphrase. Their final conclusion is that the Companions were too careful about exact transmission, too skilled at memorisation, for similar but distinct wordings credited to different Companions to reflect anything but hearing from the Prophet on different occasions, so that the differences in wording go back all the way to the Prophet himself. As for the transmission of hadith after the Companions, widespread and early written transmission of hadith must have meant that in practice, only rarely, as for long stories, would traditionists resort to paraphrase, even those traditionists such as Sufyān al-Thawrī (d. 778?) who argued strongly that paraphrase was permissible. Their interpretation is clearly driven heavily by dogmatic certainty that Sunnis know what the Prophet said, uninformed by examination of actual collections of hadith.

Perhaps a fairer test is something by a more industrious researcher, Zuhayr ᶜUthmān ᶜAlī Nūr, a study of a tenth-century biographical dictionary of weak traditionists.[51] He directly compares a number of works on weak traditionists and supplies many interesting figures. However, he tends to assume that later writers always understood exactly what earlier writers had meant. For example, his discussion of the term *munkar* ('disreputable') includes many interesting quotations, but he explains Bukhārī's use of it by quoting someone else from over a century later, not (failing an explanation by Bukhārī himself) by deduction from where Bukhārī applies it. Contrast Eerik Dickinson's concern to identify changing usage over time.[52]

Recently, however, more imaginative treatments have begun to appear; for example, surveys of Aḥmad ibn Ḥanbal's *rijāl* criticism from Bashīr ᶜAlī ᶜUmar and Abū Bakr ibn Laṭīf Kāfī, both of whom try to make out how he assessed hadith directly from the earliest Ḥanbalī literature, not later synthetic treatments, and both of whom stress the comparison of *isnāds*.[53] Neither ᶜUmar nor Kāfī is so fully free from the influence of later developments in hadith study as I should like. For example, ᶜUmar is justified in investigating Aḥmad's attention to who had actually met whom, but he frames it in terms of whether Aḥmad shared Bukhārī's criterion or Muslim's, as identified (dubiously, I would say) long after their deaths. (It appears that Aḥmad was inconsistent about accepting or rejecting hadith by the criterion of whether some link in the *isnād* could or could not be shown to come of a face-to-face encounter.) Kāfī spends a great deal of time trying to figure out the precise definitions of various terms that Aḥmad used to characterise hadith reports and their transmitters (e.g. *munkar* and *lā yathbut*), obviously starting from the list of technical terms that is so prominent in later exposés of hadith criticism rather than from categories strongly suggested by quotations of Aḥmad. (Both ᶜUmar and Kāfī conclude, sensibly, that Aḥmad's terminology was loose with much overlapping.) Still, both are extraordinarily good, since they overwhelmingly reconstruct Aḥmad's method from ninth-century sources. In the context of the present study, most important is Kāfī's stress on *isnād* comparison as the fundamental technique of the early hadith critics:[54]

> Yes, the *ᶜilla* is a hidden matter but the way to realizing it is not to investigate the conditions of the narrators only, for the conditions of the narrators are in actuality (known) as a result of the investigation of what they relate. A narrator's being *a liar* or *suspect* or *left* [i.e. his hadith ignored] is verified only as a result of probing his narrations and comparing them with those of others.

Partly stimulated by polemics against Albānī and his followers, who simplistically look up evaluations of men in references like Ibn Ḥajar, *al-Tahdhīb*, these new studies point out how characterisations of men in late compilations such as Ibn Ḥajar's are the end product of much *isnād* comparison, not the original basis for evaluating hadith. Albānī's reliance on *isnād* comparison seldom goes beyond piling up alternatives, the more that can be found, the better for the reliability of whatever quotation of the Prophet is in question. Ninth-century scholars actually had somewhat more subtle methods than his, and Muslim scholars have recently been rediscovering them, in part because of Albānī's prodding.

Notes

1. A good short survey of his life and especially the controversy he aroused by his hadith criticism can be found in Jonathan Brown, *The Canonization of al-Bukhārī and Muslim: the Formation and Function of the Sunnī Ḥadīth Canon*, Islam [*sic*] History and Civilization, Studies and Texts 69 (Leiden: Brill, 2007), 321–34. A survey of his hadith criticism is in Abū al-Ḥasan ᶜAbd al-Raḥmān ibn Muḥammad al-ᶜAyzarī, *Juhūd al-shaykh al-Albānī fī al-ḥadīth* (Riyadh: Maktabat al-Rushd, 1427/2006), which see especially for his biography and lists of works written or edited by him, 33–90. See also Kamaruddin Amin, 'Nāṣiruddīn al-Albānī on Muslim's *Ṣaḥīḥ*: a critical study of his method', *Islamic Law and Society* 11 (2004), 149–76, on which more below. The context and effects of his teaching in Saudi Arabia are developed in Stéphane Lacroix, 'Between revolution and apoliticism: Nasir al-Din al-Albani and his impact on the shaping of contemporary Salafism', in Thomas Hegghammer and Stéphane Lacroix, *The Meccan Rebellion: the Story of Juhayman al-ᶜUtaybi Revisited* (Bristol: Amal Press, 2011), 31–54, 66–71, and Stéphane Lacroix, *Awakening Islam: the Politics of Religious Dissent in Contemporary Saudi Arabia*, trans. George Holoch (Cambridge, MA: Harvard University Press, 2011).

2. Muḥammad Nāṣir al-Dīn al-Albānī, *Ḥijāb al-marʾa al-muslima fī al-Kitāb wa-l-sunna* (Cairo: Lajnat al-Shabāb al-Muslim, 1374), 89.
3. Albānī, *Ḥijāb*, 102.
4. Al-Mundhirī (d. 1258), *Ṣaḥīḥ* al-Targhīb wa-l-tarhīb, ed. Muḥammad Nāṣir al-Dīn al-Albānī (Damascus: al-Maktab al-Islāmī, 1402/1982). The title page says 'volume 1', but I am not aware that a second volume was ever published. There has also appeared a three-volume edition (Riyadh: Maktabat al-Maʿārif li-l-Nashr wa-l-Tawzīʿ, 2000), along with a two-volume edition of *Ḍaʿīf* al-Targhīb wa-l-tarhīb, ed. Muḥammad Nāṣir al-Dīn al-Albānī (Riyadh: Maktabat al-Maʿārif li-l-Nashr wa-l-Tawzīʿ, 2000), neither seen by me.
5. Brown, *Canonization*, 321–2. The book by al-ʿIrāqī is *al-Mughnī ʿan ḥaml al-asfār fī al-asfār fī takhrīj mā fī* al-Iḥyāʾ *min al-akhbār*, published with Ghazālī, *Iḥyāʾ ʿulūm al-dīn*, 4 vols (Cairo: Muṣṭafā al-Bābī al-Ḥalabī wa-Awlādu-hu, 1346). The connection between Afghānī and ʿAbduh on the one hand and Salafism on the other has been questioned by Henri Lauzière, 'The construction of *salafiyya*: reconsidering Salafism from the perspective of Conceptual History', *International Journal of Middle East Studies* 42 (2010), 369–89. The crux of the issue seems to be how strictly one defines 'Salafism'.
6. E.g. Bukhārī, *Kitāb al-shahādāt 9, bāb lā tashhadu ʿalā shahāda jawr*, no. 2651; *Kitāb faḍāʾil aṣḥāb al-nabī* 1, *bāb faḍāʾil aṣḥāb al-nabī*, no. 3650; *Kitāb al-riqāq* 7, *bāb mā yuḥdharu min zahrat al-dunyā*, no. 6428; *Kitāb al-aymān wa-l-nudhūr* 27, *bāb ithm man lā yafī bi-l-nadhr*, no. 6695; *Kitāb faḍāʾil al-ṣaḥāba* 52, *bāb faḍl al-ṣaḥāba, thumma alladhīna yalūnahum*, no. 2535 (multiple versions). Cf. G. H. A. Juynboll, *Encyclopedia of Canonical Ḥadīth* (Leiden: Brill, 2007), 542, ascribing it in its present form to a Basran of the mid-eighth century CE but supposing that the idea of ranking the generations so went back to the seventh century CE.
7. Bukhārī, *atʿima 27, bāb mā kāna al-salaf yaddakhirūna fī buyūti-him wa-asfāri-him min al-ṭaʿām wa-l-laḥm wa-ghayrih*, followed by no. 5423.
8. Wakīʿ (d. 918), *Akhbār al-quḍā*, ed. ʿAbd al-ʿAzīz Muṣṭafā al-Marāghī, 3 vols (Cairo: Maṭbaʿat al-Istiqāma, 1366–9/1947–50), 2: 167.
9. Mundhirī, *Ṣaḥīḥ*, 14 and fn.
10. Ismāʿīl ibn Isḥāq, *Faḍl al-ṣalāh ʿalā al-nabī*, ed. Muḥammad Nāṣir al-Dīn al-Albānī (Damascus: al-Maktab al-Islāmī, 1383/1963), fn. 36.
11. Ibn Ḥamdān, *Ṣifat al-fatwā wa-l-muftī wa-l-mustaftī*, ed. Muḥammad Nāṣir al-Dīn al-Albānī (Damascus: al-Maktab al-Islāmī, 1380), fn. 73.
12. Abū Dāwūd, *Masāʾil al-imām Aḥmad*, ed. Muḥammad Bahja al-Bayṭār (Cairo: Dār al-Manār, 1353/1934; reprint Beirut: Muḥammad Amīn Damj, n.d.), 277. See further Christopher Melchert, *Ahmad ibn Hanbal*, Makers of the Muslim World (Oxford: Oneworld, 2006), 70–9.
13. Christopher Melchert, 'Whether to keep women out of the mosque', *Authority, Privacy and Public Order in Islam*, eds B. Michalak-Pikulska and A. Pikulski, Orientalia Lovaniensia Analecta 148 (Leuven: Peeters, 2006), 59–69.
14. Christopher Melchert, 'Public baths in Islamic law', forthcoming in a collection of essays edited by Thibaud Fournet *et al.*

15. Albānī, introduction to Mundhirī, *Ṣaḥīḥ*, 33.
16. Maribel Fierro, 'The legal policies of the Almohad caliphs and Ibn Rushd's *Bidāyat al-mujtahid*', *Journal of Islamic Studies* 10 (1999), 226–48.
17. Now conveniently available in translation: Ibn al-Ṣalāḥ, *An Introduction to the Science of the Ḥadīth*, trans. Eerik Dickinson with Muneer Fareed (Reading: Garnet, 2005).
18. Eerik Dickinson, *The Development of Early Sunnite Ḥadīth Criticism: The Taqdima of Ibn Abī Ḥātim al-Rāzī (240/854–327/938)*, Islamic History and Civilization, Studies and Texts, 38 (Leiden: Brill, 2001), ch. 6.
19. Ghassan Abdul-Jabbar, *Bukhari*, Makers of Islamic Civilization (London: I. B. Tauris, 2007); Jonathan A. C. Brown, *Hadith: Muhammad's Legacy in the Medieval and Modern World*, Foundations of Islam (Oxford: Oneworld, 2009). See also Christopher Melchert, 'Bukhārī and early hadith criticism', *Journal of the American Oriental Society* 121 (2001), 7–19.
20. Albānī, introduction to Mundhirī, *Ṣaḥīḥ*, 37.
21. Tirmidhī, *ᶜIlal al-Tirmidhī al-kabīr*, eds Abū Ṭālib al-Qāḍī, Ṣubḥī al-Sāmarrāʾī, Abū al-Maᶜāṭī al-Nūrī and Maḥmūd Muḥammad Khalīl al-Ṣaᶜīdī (Beirut: ᶜĀlam al-Kutub, 1409/1989), 144, no. 248.
22. Ibid. 196, no. 349.
23. Muḥammad Nāṣir al-Dīn al-Albānī, *Ḥijāb al-marʾa al-muslima fī al-kitāb wa-l-sunna* (Cairo: Lajnat al-Shabāb al-Muslim, 1374), 8.
24. For the hadith report in question, see Abū Dāwūd (d. 889), *Sunan*, *Kitāb al-libās* 31, *bāb fīmā tubdī al-marʾa min zīnati-hā*, no. 4104. Albāni cites the edition Abū Dāwūd, *al-Sunan* (al-Maṭbaᶜa al-Tāziya, 1348), of which I have otherwise seen no record, let alone the work itself. Albānī also cites Bayhaqī (d. 1066), *al-Sunan al-kubrā*, 10 vols (Ḥyderabad: Maṭbaᶜat Majlis Dāʾirat al-Maᶜārif al-Niẓāmiyya, 1316; reprint 1352). Ibn Ḥajar quotes two authorities as saying that Khālid ibn Durayk never met ᶜĀʾisha: Ibn Ḥajar, *Kitāb Tahdhīb* al-Tahdhīb, 12 vols (Hyderabad: Majlis Dāʾirat al-Maᶜārif al-Niẓāmiyya, 1325–7; reprint Beirut: Dār Ṣādir, n.d.), 3: 86–7.
25. See Ibn Ḥajar, *Taqrīb* al-Tahdhīb, ed. ᶜAbd al-Wahhāb ᶜAbd al-Laṭīf, 2 vols (Medina: Muḥammad Sulṭān al-N*m*n*kānī, 1961), but at this point Albānī was probably using an earlier Indian edition such as the Lucknow printing of 1937.
26. Albānī, *Ḥijāb*, 9.
27. Ibid. 29.
28. For attempts to define the criteria of Bukhārī and Muslim, see Brown, *Canonization*, 162–70. For a test of Ibn Ḥajar's version of Bukhārī's criterion, see Christopher Melchert, 'Bukhārī and his *Ṣaḥīḥ*', *Le Muséon* 123 (2010), 425–54, at 437–40.
29. Ismāᶜīl ibn Isḥāq, *Faḍl al-ṣalāh ᶜalā al-nabī*, ed. Muḥammad Nāṣir al-Dīn al-Albānī (Damascus: al-Maktab al-Islāmī, 1383/1963), n. 8.
30. Tirmidhī, *Jāmiᶜ*, *abwāb al-ruʾyā* 88, no. 2457.
31. Anon., *Mukhtaṣar sharḥ al-ᶜaqīda al-ṭaḥāwiyya*, nn. by Muḥammad Nāṣir

al-Dīn al-Albānī, Manshūrāt Kulliyyat al-dirāsāt al-islāmiyya (Baghdad: Dār al-Nadhīr, 1388/1969), n. 151. The commentary here abridged is evidently that of Ibn Abī al-ᶜIzz (d. 1390).

32. Dhahabī, *al-ᶜUlūw li-l-ᶜAlī al-Ghaffār fī ṣaḥīḥ al-akhbār wa-saqīmihā*, ed. ᶜAbd al-Razzāq ᶜAfīfī and Zakariyyāᵓ ᶜAlī Yūsuf (ᶜĀbidīn [Cairo]: Maṭbaᶜat Jamāᶜat Anṣār al-Sunna, 1938), not seen by me.
33. ᶜAbd al-ᶜAẓīm al-Mundhirī, *Mukhtaṣar Ṣaḥīḥ Muslim*, ed. Muḥammad Nāṣir al-Dīn al-Albānī (Damascus: al-Maktab al-Islāmī; and Beirut: Dār al-ᶜArabiyya, 1388, repr. 1393), 492 and n. The same hadith report in Muslim, *Ṣaḥīḥ*, *Kitāb al-zuhd wa-l-raqāᵓiq* 16, *bāb al-tathabbut fī al-ḥadīth wa-ḥukm kitābat al-ᶜilm*, no. 3004.
34. Abu Khaythama, *Kitāb al-ᶜIlm*, ed. Muḥammad Nāṣir al-Dīn al-Albānī (Beirut: al-Maktab al-Islāmī, 1403/1983), 11 and n.
35. Ibn Ḥajar mentions from two authorities that he did not meet Ibn Masᶜūd, although one of them, Abū Ḥātim al-Rāzī, is not so quoted by his son, the usual source for his criticism: Ibn Ḥajar, *Tahdhīb*, 11: 193; Ibn Abī Ḥātim, *Kitāb al-jarḥ wa-l-taᶜdīl*, 9 vols (Hyderabad: Jamᶜiyyat Dāᵓirat al-Maᶜārif al-ᶜUthmāniyya, 1360–71; reprint Beirut: Dār Iḥyāᵓ al-Turāth al-ᶜArabī, n.d.), 9: 133. Mizzī mentions Ibn Masᶜūd among those from whom he related hadith but no one who questioned this link: *Tahdhīb* al-Kamāl, ed. Bashshār ᶜAwwād Maᶜrūf, 35 vols (Beirut: Muᵓassasat al-Risāla, 1413/1992), 31: 253–4. No such source that I have checked does list ᶜUmar among those from whom Yāḥyā ibn Jaᶜda related hadith. For ᶜUmar and Ibn Masᶜūd's dates of death, see Ibn Ḥajar, *Tahdhīb*, 6: 28, 7: 441.
36. See Michael Cook, 'The opponents of the writing of tradition in early Islam', *Arabica* 44 (1997), 437–530.
37. Mundhirī, *Ṣaḥīḥ*, 411. Aḥmad, *Musnad imām al-muḥaddithīn*, 6 vols (Cairo: al-Maṭbaᶜa al-Maymaniyya, 1313/1895), 2: 174 = *Musnad al-imām Aḥmad*, ed. Shuᶜayb al-Arnaᵓūṭ *et al.*, 50 vols (Beirut: Muᵓassasat al-Risāla, 1413–21/1993–2001), 11: 199–200. Al_Ḥākim al-Naysābūrī, *al-Mustadrak ᶜalā al-ṣaḥīḥayn*, 4 vols (Hyderabad: Maṭbaᶜat Majlis Dāᵓirat al-Maᶜārif al-ᶜUthmāniyya, 1334–42), 1: 554. I have been unable to locate this hadith report in Ṭabarānī, *al-Muᶜjam al-kabīr*, ed. Ḥamdī ᶜAbd al-Majīd Salafī, Iḥyāᵓ al-turāth al-Islāmī 31, 25 vols, 2nd edn (n.p.: al-Jumhūriyya al-ᶜIrāqiyya, Wizārat al-Awqāf wa-l-Shuᵓūn al-Dīniyya, 1984–90), likewise in Ibn Abī al-Dunyā, *al-Jūᶜ*, ed. Muḥammad Khayr Ramaḍān Yūsuf (Beirut: Dār Ibn Ḥazm, 1417/1997).
38. Someone who withholds payment of the alms tax will have his treasure made into a spotted serpent on the Day of the Resurrection to encircle and bite him. See, among other places, Bukhārī, *Kitāb al-zakāh* 3, *bāb ithm mānīᶜ al-zakāh*, no. 1403, *Kitāb al-tafsīr ad* Q. 3:180 and 9:12, no. 4565 and 4659, and *Kitāb al-ḥiyal* 3, *bāb fī al-zakāh*, no. 6957.
39. Ibn Rajab, *Faḍl ᶜilm al-salaf ᶜalā ᶜilm al-khalaf*, ed. Yaḥyā Mukhtār Ghazzāwī (n.p.: Dār al-Bashāᵓir li-l-Malāyīn, 1403/1983).
40. See Juynboll, *Encyclopedia of Canonical Ḥadīth*, 'General introduction', esp.

xx–xxii; Harald Motzki, 'Dating Muslim traditions: a survey', *Arabica* 52 (2005), 204–53; Harold Motzki with Nicolet Boekhoff-van der Voort and Sean Anthony, *Analysing Muslim Traditions*, Islamic History and Civilization, Studies and Texts, 78 (Leiden: Brill, 2010).

41. Amin, 'Nāṣiruddīn al-Albānī', esp. 171–2.
42. Muslim, *Ṣaḥīḥ*, *Kitāb al-salām* 4, *bāb al-nahy ᶜan ibtidāʾ ahl al-kitāb bi-l-salām*, no. 2167.
43. Muḥammad Nāṣir al-Dīn al-Albānī, *Silsilat al-aḥādīth al-ṣaḥīḥa wa-shayʾ min fiqhi-hā wa-fawāʾidi-hā*, 6 vols in 8, 2nd edn (Riyadh: Maktabat al-Maᶜārif, 1415–17/1995–6), 2: 320–1.
44. See Behnam Sadeghi, *The Logic of Law Making in Islam*, Cambridge Studies in Islamic Civilization (Cambridge: Cambridge University Press, 2013).
45. Ibrāhīm ibn Muḥammad ibn Ḍūyān (d. 1934–5), *Manār al-sabīl fī sharḥ* al-Dalīl, 2 vols (n.p.: al-Maktab al-Islāmī, 1378), a commentary on Marᶜī al-Karmī (d. Cairo, 1623–4?), *Dalīl al-ṭālib li-nayl al-maṭālib* (many editions).
46. Two good surveys of the controversy are Harald Motzki, *The Origins of Islamic Jurisprudence*, trans. Marion H. Katz, Islamic History and Civilization, Studies and Texts 41 (Leiden: Brill, 2002), ch. 1, and Herbert Berg, *The Development of Exegesis in Early Islam*, Curzon Studies in the Qurʾān (Richmond: Curzon, 2000), ch. 2.
47. For example, *The Encyclopaedia of Islam*, new edn, s.v. 'ḥadīth', by J. Robson.
48. For example, Muhammad Zubair Siddiqi, *Ḥadīth Literature: Its Origin, Development and Special Features*, ed. and rev. Abdal Hakim Murad (Cambridge: Islamic Texts Society, 1993).
49. ᶜAbd al-Razzāq ibn Khalīfa al-Shāyajī and al-Sayyid Muḥammad al-Sayyid Nūḥ, *Manāhij al-muḥaddithīn fī riwāyat al-ḥadīth bi-l-maᶜnā* (Beirut: Dār Ibn Ḥazm, 1998).
50. ᶜAlī al-Khaṭīb al-Baghdādī, *Kitāb al-kifāya fī ᶜilm al-riwāya* (Hyderabad: Dāʾirat al-Maᶜārif al-ᶜUthmāniyya, 1357 AH).
51. Zuhayr ᶜUthmān ᶜAlī Nūr, *Ibn ᶜAdī wa-manhaju-hu fī kitāb* al-Kāmil fī ḍuᶜafāʾ al-rijāl, 2 vols (Riyadh: Maktabat al-Rushd and Sharikat al-Riyāḍ, 1997), originally a 1990 doctoral dissertation at the University of Umm al-Qurā, Mecca.
52. Ibn al-Ṣalāḥ, *An Introduction*, fn. 59.
53. Bashīr ᶜAlī ᶜUmar, *Manhaj al-imām Aḥmad fī iᶜlāl al-ḥadīth*, Silsilat al-iṣdārāt al-ᶜilmiyya 2, 2 vols (Riyadh: Waqf al-Salām al-Khayrī, 2005); Abū Bakr ibn Laṭīf Kāfī, *Manhaj al-imām Aḥmad fī al-taᶜlīl wa-atharu-hu fī al-jarḥ wa-l-taᶜdīl*, sup'd Muḥammad ᶜAbd al-Nabī (Beirut: Dār Ibn Ḥazm, 2005), originally a doctoral dissertation at Jāmiᶜat al-Amīr ᶜAbd al-Qādir, Constantine, Algeria.
54. Kāfī, *Manhaj*, 155.

3

Islamic Tradition in an Age of Print: Editing, Printing and Publishing the Classical Heritage[1]

Ahmad Khan

For many historians of medieval Islamic history, Marshall G. S. Hodgson's magisterial synthesis of Islamicate societies provides an initiation into the complex and diverse contours of a sprawling medieval civilisation. His sensitivities to intellectual, social, political and military history in *The Venture of Islam* are precisely what allow for such a wide-ranging engagement with his work. This wide sense of historical ambition helps to explain the work's unparalleled durability. It is also the work's historical ingenuity that makes Hodgson's account of Islamicate societies so difficult to replicate. Hodgson's panoptic approach enables him to move beyond conventional parameters of analysis in which politics and religion feature as the only driving historical forces, to consider the historical peculiarities of an arid-zone cultural civilisation and what that means for trade, economic productivity, labour and social relations.[2] At the same time, Hodgson was able to adumbrate carefully the many features of 'the great western transformation', which with some intent he renamed 'the great western *transmutation*', a phenomenon recently popularised by global historians such as Kenneth Pomeranz and Christopher Bayly.[3] Hodgson's own venture into the impact that the great western transmutation had on the Islamic world has been one of the underappreciated aspects of his scholarship. Scholars also seem to have glossed over the fact that many of Hodgson's posthumously published essays explicitly address the role of tradition in the modern Islamic world.

The notion of tradition in Islamic Studies has become synonymous with Talal Asad's insightful 1986 essay, *The Idea of an Anthropology of Islam*. Tradition is not the focus of Asad's otherwise brilliant extended essay, and his disquisition on the Islamic tradition as a discursive tradition occupies no more than a few pages.[4] Still, Asad's brief remarks have been transformed into a theory of Islamic tradition.[5] Meanwhile, it is often overlooked that Norman

Calder, a historian of Islamic law and legal literature, explained the activity of jurists writing within the *madhhab* tradition as a form of discursive tradition; and, apparently, his formulation of discursive tradition was independent of Asad's published work.[6] It is noteworthy that Asad's discrete theoretical discussion has evolved into a scholarly consensus about how to understand tradition in Islam. The subsequent theoretical literature on tradition in Islam continues to appeal to Asad and Alisdair MacIntyre (Asad expressed his indebtedness to the latter in formulating the notion of discursive tradition in Islam).[7] Subsequent scholarship on tradition has not enagaged with Hodgson's incisive formulation of questions and issues about the function of the Islamic tradition and classical heritage in the modern world.

Hodgson was a medievalist, and the medieval sections of *The Venture* form its strongest part. The strength of his account begins to wane as he moves closer to the modern period, and nowhere is this better exemplified than when Hodgson, like many a classical historian before him, commits the historiographical sin of decline and fall history.[8] Nevertheless, one may disagree with Hodgson's conclusions but still be motivated by the perspicacity of the questions he posed. One development to which Hodgson was especially alert was that of 'technicalism'. He patiently describes in unmistakably Weberian terms the transformations brought about by technicalism and its fundamental effect on the rationalisation of society.[9] Similarly, in a number of writings Hodgson sought to understand the irruptive, interactive and evolutional aspects of the reception of the classical tradition in the modern period.[10] It is in light of this acute sensitivity that Hodgson had for the potential of technology and its apparatus of rationalisation to affect the pre-modern Islamic tradition that one struggles to understand why Hodgson failed to appreciate the potent role that printing presses and publishing houses played in the acceleration and increasingly transregional character of Islamic scholarship which, among other things, resulted in dramatic reappraisals of the classical Islamic canon.

In this chapter, my aim is to present the first instalment of a longer project dedicated to writing the history of how the medieval textual tradition was edited, printed and published in the modern Islamic world. In this contribution, it is not my objective to perpetuate a theory of Islam as a discursive tradition; nor do I attempt to articulate a new theory of tradition. Work on theory can begin in earnest only when more history has been written; and even then, historians of the Islamic tradition will have to address some of the more rigorous conceptual histories of tradition produced in neighbouring fields.[11] This chapter attempts to say more about the relationship between technicalisation and the function of the medieval tradition in the modern world by examining the work of scholars-cum-editors (*muṣaḥḥiḥūn* and *muḥaqqiqūn*) of medieval religious texts. I argue that the rise of a new professional class of scholars-cum-editors had important implications for the reception of the classical tradition in the modern period. Printing presses, publishing houses and editors became embroiled in debates over the production of the pre-modern textual tradition. Examining some of these contestations allows us to see just how diverse conceptions of the pre-modern tradition could be. In the process, scholars-cum-editors assumed a pivotal role in determining the form in which medieval debates and ideas would evolve in the modern period.

The contestations studied in this chapter centered on the religious credibility of the eponymous founder of the Ḥanafī *madhhab*, Abū Ḥanīfa (d. 767). Although attacks on Abū Ḥanīfa were by no means *terra incognita* in the history of Muslim scholarship, the use of print technology in the twentieth and twenty-first centuries facilitated the wide circulation of early classics from the ninth and tenth centuries that hosted deprecations of Abū Ḥanīfa. The most crucial difference between pre-modern and modern attacks on Abū Ḥanīfa was that the editing and publishing of these texts was taking place in a period when *madhhab* loyalties were dissipating. Criticisms of Abū Ḥanīfa gained particular momentum because they tapped into a resounding sense of discomfort with the *madhhabs*' institutional edifice and dominance in the modern Muslim world; a discomfort that constituted an integral characteristic of Salafi and *Ahl-i Ḥadīth* reform movements in the nineteenth and twentieth centuries.

Islamic Reform and Modern Contestations

Modern contestations over the religious credibility of Abū Ḥanīfa arose out of the repertoire of eighteenth- and nineteenth-century reformist tendencies made familiar to us in the secondary literature by scholars such as John Voll, Basheer Nafi, Muhammad Qasim Zaman, Bernard Haykel, Henri Lauzière, and many others. The scholarly consensus still identifies the beginnings of these reformist tendencies with circles of scholarship in the Ḥijāz between the eighteenth and nineteenth centuries. As such, most of the focus has zoomed in on the contributions of Muḥammad Ḥayāt al-Sindī (d. 1751), Shāh Walī Allāh al-Dihlawī (d. 1762) and Muḥammad b. ᶜAbd al-Wahhāb (d. 1792).[12]

Indeed, any discussion of subsequent reform movements in the Muslim world has to grapple to some degree with their legacy. I would like to identify four essential components of this legacy. These are noteworthy not just for their overwhelming concentration in reformist scholarship of the period, but also for their centrality to debates between late Sunni traditionalists and Salafis over Abū Ḥanīfa's legacy. The first is the energetic renewal of the study of hadith and its corollary sub-disciplines. The second is an intense discomfort with the *madhhabs*' institutional grip on Muslim thought, practice and scholarship. A third legacy, which tends to find less attention in the secondary literature, is a renewed emphasis on minimalist and stripped-down formulations of Islamic creed and theology, in order to jettison – what to Salafi reformers amounted to – the sophisticated accretions and foreign, hermeneutical layers that characterised Islamic scholarship in the High Middle Ages. Equally neglected, but of no less significance as a reformist legacy, is a distaste for polyvalence in Islamic thought and practice.[13]

The role of early modern and modern reformers in loosening the ties of *madhhab* loyalty is visible to varying degrees in the works of Muḥammad Ḥayāt al-Sindī, Shāh Walī Allāh and Jamāl al-Dīn al-Qāsimī.[14] Al-Qāsimī's efforts are manifested in his influential *Qawāᶜid al-taḥdīth min funūn muṣṭalaḥ al-ḥadīth*. Al-Qāsimī's provocative essay on the science of hadith is a Salafi reformist manifesto, which lifts large chunks, with attribution, straight from Shāh Walī Allāh's magnum opus, *al-Ḥujja al-bāligha*, which included the latter's *al-Inṣāf*. Written in 1907, the book describes the discipline of hadith and celebrates the pioneering role that the *aṣḥāb al-ḥadīth* played in securing, and thereafter carrying forward, the Prophetic legacy.[15] His praise for the *aṣḥāb al-ḥadīth* is supplemented with a sleight against the *madhhab*s, whose proponents are charged with confusing others and plotting against the religion.[16]

Now that we have rehearsed some of the key reformist trends that the subject of this paper will refer back and forth to, let us turn to our contestations to understand why Abū Ḥanīfa's legacy, in particular, became a battleground for contestations between late Sunni traditionalists and Salafis. The ninth to tenth centuries witnessed a relentless campaign by a group of influential proto-Sunni traditionalists to cast Abū Ḥanīfa as a heretical figure. These proto-Sunni traditionalists came to identify Abū Ḥanīfa with theological heresies, serious breaches in jurisprudence, a supercilious attitude, contempt for the hadith, support for rebellions and uprisings, and a poor record of personal and devotional piety. All of these criticisms of Abū Ḥanīfa were part of the stockpile of invective directed against modern Ḥanafīs and late Sunni traditionalists, but it is worth noting that three of these became cornerstones of traditionalist Salafi attacks on Abū Ḥanīfa and his followers: (1) Abū Ḥanīfa's legal approach; (2) his theological leanings; and (3) his attitude towards the hadith. Abū Ḥanīfa's jurisprudential legacy was, for his opponents, one that was underscored by an irresponsible commitment to polyvalence. His legal views and the school that they spawned constituted a highly speculative system that was rooted in a supra-scriptural reading of Islamic law, one which found little room and respect for the hadith of the Prophet. The Ḥanafī *madhhab*, and indeed all the *madhāhib*, perhaps with the exception of the Ḥanbalī school, came to represent precisely what modern reformers found so disconcerting in their appraisal of the condition of Muslim thought and scholarship. Abū Ḥanīfa's legal casuistry was seen to have resulted from his deprecation of Prophetic hadith. For traditionalist Salafis, Abū Ḥanīfa's legacy represented the very opposite of the trend that energised their intellectual efforts, the discipline (and sub-disciplines) of hadith. Traditionalist Salafis were well aware that a large gamut of hadith criticism in the formative period of Islamic history not infrequently indicted Abū Ḥanīfa for his alleged poor grasp of hadith. Al-Bukhārī's (d. 870) two *tārīkh* works speak scathingly of Abū Ḥanīfa. Other works such as Ibn ʿAdī's (d. 970–1?) *al-Kāmil fī ḍuʿafāʾ al-rijāl*, Ibn Ḥibbān al-Bustī's (d. 965) *Kitāb al-thiqāt* and *Kitāb al-majrūḥīn min al-muḥaddithīn*, and many others make space for long invective against Abū Ḥanīfa.[17]

Beyond hadith and law, these texts, which traditionalist Salafis were intent on reviving, attacked Abū Ḥanīfa for his association with certain theological heresies. This dovetailed with a renewed puritanism in matters of creed and theology visible not only in the patterns of the publication of classical theological creeds, but also in the kinds of dissertations and monographs that were being produced in Saudi Arabia, the seat of much traditionalist Salafi literature, in the mid-late twentieth century on ninth-century theological movements. Safar b. ʿAbd al-Raḥmān al-Ḥawālī's PhD dissertation submitted to the Umm al-Qurā University in Mecca, *Ẓāhirat al-irjāʾ fi-l-fikr al-islāmī*, among other things, was part of a trend to explain deviant practices and notions in the contemporary period by linking them to medieval heresies and heresiarchs.[18] For Salafi reformers, Abū Ḥanīfa's legacy and the Ḥanafī *madhhab* constituted convenient whipping boys for reformist agitations against the *madhhabs* and theological 'deviancy'.

Traditionalist Salafis and Late Sunni Traditionalists

My work will narrow the discussion to two groups in the modern period: late Sunni *madhhab* traditionalists, who were dedicated to the perpetuation of an institutional conception of Islam embodied in a commitment to sufism, dialectic theology and *madhhab* polyvalency; and traditionalist Salafis, who sought to rejuvenate the Muslim community by reviving the study of hadith and rooting all Islamic practice and belief in the hadith and Sunna, whilst insisting on a complete break from the moribund *madhhabs* and the anomic development generated by intellectual polyvalence and elaborate hermeneutics.[19] To talk about the Salafi reform movement in general is to cast an irresponsibly wide net. The term Salafiyya has, historically, invoked such a wide spectrum of ideological strands, often in direct contradistinction to one another, that one's identification of a Salafi reform movement has to be qualified, if not isolated, to its particular regional or historical context. For example, the Salafiyya of the late nineteenth and early twentieth centuries can denote a 'modernist' reform movement associated with the efforts of Jamāl al-Dīn al-Afghānī (d. 1897), Rashīd Riḍā (d. 1935) and Muḥammad ᶜAbduh (d. 1905).[20] Contemporary Salafism since the mid-late twentieth century, however, denotes a different ideological programme.[21]

Traditionalist Salafis, diagnosing what they saw to be the deep malaise of the Muslim world, identified excessive loyalty to the *madhhabs*, along with popular religious practices legitimised by the *madhhabs*, as the primary ailments. Traditionalist Salafis ranging from Muḥammad b. Ismāᶜīl al-Ṣanᶜānī (d. 1768) to Muḥammad Nāṣir al-Dīn al-Albānī (d. 1999) routinely decried the aberration of the *madhhabs*, describing the corrosive effect of '*madhhab* fanaticism' (*taᶜaṣṣub al-madhhabī*) and the 'heretical innovation of adhering to the *madhhabs*' (*bidᶜat al-tamadhhub*).[22] The programme of traditionalist Salafis prioritised uprooting affiliation to the *madhhabs* to make way for a pure Islam predicated on scripture but spearheaded by a renewed reification of the hadith and Sunna. Their scholarship and instruction set in motion a shift away from *madhhab* loyalty, which had traditionally enjoyed a special status in a broader hermeneutical and hierarchical structure.[23] The same anti-*madhhab* rhetoric defined the reformist agenda advanced by scholars belonging to the *Ahl-i Ḥadīth* movement in the Indian subcontinent.[24] Very soon, transnational alliances were formed between Middle Eastern and Indian subcontinent scholars, institutions and publishing houses in an effort to double up, as it were, against late Sunni traditionalists, and communicate their ideas in both the language of scholarship, Arabic, and local vernacular, Urdu.[25]

The contestations that we are concerned with sharpened as traditionalist Salafis came to assess how best to undermine the institutional hold that the *madhhabs* had on many facets of Muslim social and religious life. In both the Indian subcontinent and the Middle East, for different reasons, Abū Ḥanīfa's legacy and reputation became a key battleground for these contestations. In the Indian subcontinent, Ḥanafism and its eponymous founder somewhat predictably became targets of reformist opposition. Indian subcontinent Islam was, after all, dominated by Ḥanafism. Inevitably, any attempt to unsettle the religious establishment would require bringing into focus (and disrepute) the existing supremacy of the Ḥanafī *madhhab*.[26]

Their interlocutors were late Sunni traditionalists. Following Jonathan Brown, I identify late Sunni traditionalists as scholars who championed an understanding of Islam in the late-modern period that was characterised by a commitment to mystical, theological and legal hermeneutical systems.[27] In some ways, we can see their project as being committed to an institutional reading of Islamic civilisation and scholarship. Islamic institutions of higher learning in the Middle Ages celebrated the sophistication of legal, theological and mystical disciplines. These disciplines carried through to affect popular culture, too, as Muslims came to identify with ritual practices negotiated by jurists; theological axioms expounded by dialectic-theologians; and devotional acts inspired by sufi masters and the brotherhoods that emerged from their following. These were, of course, the very features of the Islamicate heritage that traditionalist Salafis identified as being the core culprits, responsible for the 'decay' and 'decline' of the Muslim world. Their disdain for the late Sunni traditionalist conception of Islamic history was not simply a rhetorical device. As we shall now see, Salafis went beyond telescoping the Islamic Middle Ages as a history of decline to challenging their interlocutors on many platforms.

Publishing the Tradition

There can be little doubt that the history of the production of modern editions of classical texts constitutes a massive scholarly blindspot in our understanding of how contemporary scholars have engaged with the pre-modern Islamic heritage.[28] The history of publishing houses, patterns of publishing, and tracking ideological shifts through inspecting dissertation topics in Middle Eastern and Indian subcontinent universities and seminaries are all elementary avenues of inquiry that remain to be pursued.[29]

Analysing reformist texts of the nineteenth and twentieth centuries certainly provides unequalled insight into the historical provenance of reform movements and their programmes. Yet, in the process of studying these texts carefully, scholars have underestimated the ideological prowess that informs the decision to privilege the publication of one pre-modern text over another. In the Middle East and the Indian subcontinent, many publishing houses were pioneered by traditionalist Salafis like Zuhayr al-Shāwīsh, whose al-Maktab al-Islāmī became the publishing headquarters for traditionalist Salafism in the Middle East.[30]

The first printing presses in Istanbul and Cairo published works from the early modern and modern periods on mysticism, hadith and legal commentaries, and logic.[31] This first phase in the history of print represents a continuation of the pre-print manuscript production of post-classical texts and commentaries. There was a shift in the second half of the nineteenth century with many publishing houses in the Middle East and Indian subcontinent committing themselves to editing and publishing classical texts from the formative period of Islamic history, paying special attention to those concerning the study of hadith and its corollary sciences. Publishing efforts, therefore, were geared towards hadith works, early creeds, texts critical of *madhhab* hermeneutics, and works broadly connected to the hadith literature. As editors came to assess these manuscripts with a fresh, reformist zeal, they capitalised on some of the withering attacks against Abū Ḥanīfa found in many of the books on *rijāl* criticism, hadith criticism and heresiographical works (*firaq*). But there was something even more consequential about the relationship between reformist impulses and the process of editing and publishing medieval texts. Salafi reformers were sensitive to the fact that, beyond simply recovering the antiquity of their tradition, they would have to communicate this process of recovery to diverse audiences. This realisation required subtle innovations in style and substance in order to attract wider audiences. The impact that this had on popular and elite conceptions of the classical Islamicate heritage deserves closer scrutiny. Elizabeth Eisenstein, in her pathbreaking study of the printing revolution in early modern Europe, argued that the advent of printing facilitated new conceptions of antiquity.[32] The evidence for print culture stimulating new conceptions of antiquity is slim, for now. As I have suggested, it seems more likely that this was a later development. Contestations between late Sunni traditionalists and traditionalist Salafis should be understood in light of this development, where publishing houses and editors selected, edited and published editions of medieval texts and, in doing so, articulated competing conceptions of the classical Sunni canon. For traditionalist Salafis, reinventing the classical canon meant prioritising the editing of hadith and theological texts, whilst leaving pre-modern works on the *madhhab*s and legal theory to acquire more dust in manuscript libraries. They commissioned the former manuscripts to mass publication and directed them to both the scholarly community and popular laity. Salafis were thus redefining the classical Islamicate heritage as one wholly dedicated to the recovery of antiquity, the generation of the pious ancestors (*salaf al-ṣāliḥ*). In this way, they positioned themselves as modern guardians of the 'correct' pre-modern canon and presented their interlocutors, late Sunni traditionalists, as representatives of aberrant post-formative traditions such as the *madhhab*s and legal theory.

Late Sunni traditionalists responded to this attack on their conception of the classical Islamicate heritage in different ways. For example, they displayed an impressive capacity for dexterity by contesting Salafi *ᶜulamāᵓ* over the very discipline which the latter had come to privilege and champion, the discipline of hadith. As impressive as this was, it was, nevertheless, still a concession to the reinvention of a particularly seductive version of the classical religious canon, as engineered by Salafis. This intense relationship between ideas, texts, publishers and printing meant that contestations over the religious credibility of Abū Ḥanīfa became a consistent fixture in the skirmishes between traditionalist Salafis and late Sunni traditionalists in the twentieth century, and to examine these we must turn to publishing houses and their editions of pre-modern texts.

Editing the Tradition

Publishing houses in the late-nineteenth to early-twentieth centuries were popular career destinations for graduates of religious seminaries and universities. Graduates from Al-Azhar, seminaries in the Indian subcontinent and religious institutions would secure employment at publishing houses and dedicate themselves to analysing, editing and publishing pre-modern religious manuscripts. This kind of career move had obvious incentives for recent graduates. It provided them with an opportunity to become acquainted with manuscript libraries and the vast treasure trove of the pre-modern Islamic heritage. The art of producing modern editions and learning the craft of editing provided graduates with a set of professional and employable skills. But, above all, these publishing houses provided early-career scholars with an important bridge of continuity that connected particular scholarly outlooks in pre-modern Islam with contemporary institutions that shared, perpetuated and chanelled these very outlooks. What this meant was that the decision to work with a particular publishing house was the first step in marking one's commitment to steering the classical heritage in a particular ideological direction. Immediately, this would limit one's horizons as to the kinds of genres and manuscripts that one would take to the task of editing, so that when it came to the task of producing an edition of a pre-modern text, the scholar-cum-editor (*muṣaḥḥiḥ, muḥaqqiq*) would have already betrayed an allegiance to a particular interpretation of what constitutes the correct canon of medieval, religious texts. This process usually would result in the scholar-cum-editor producing editions of texts that spoke to his religious orientation. On occasions, though, the more ambitious and enterprising of the scholars-cum-editors would engage in preemptive techniques, whereby they might produce an edition of a medieval text that would ostensibly challenge their own religious orientation in an effort to undermine it, or at least mitigate its potential to do so, in the introduction or footnotes.[33]

Both the introduction and footnotes afforded the authors an opportunity to steer the classical heritage in a direction that would (1) boost the veritableness of their ideological programme or (2) undermine the legitimacy of their opponents' reading of the classical heritage. Authors from both camps were extremely sensitive to this capacity that modern editions had to orient a pre-modern text in one direction or another.[34] Late Sunni traditionalists and Salafi scholars commonly engaged in post-edition polemics, accusing the other camp of tampering with texts or distorting the classical heritage. An excellent example of this is Muḥammad Nāṣir al-Dīn al-Albānī's and Zuhayr al-Shāwīsh's edition of Ibn Abī al-ᶜIzz al-Ḥanafī's (d. 1389) commentary on Abū Jaᶜfar Aḥmad b. Muḥammad al-Ṭaḥāwī's (d. 933) *al-ᶜAqīda al-Ṭaḥāwiyya*.[35]

Al-Ṭaḥāwī was a tenth-century Ḥanafī scholar who had a paramount role in a process that Christopher Melchert has termed the 'traditionalisation' of the Ḥanafī school.[36] This process involved a realigning of Ḥanafī jurisprudence with hadith reports in a nod, as it were, to the ascendancy of the proto-Sunni traditionalist camp.[37] Al-Ṭaḥāwī's contribution to the traditionalisation of Ḥanafism went beyond jurisprudential scaffolding. Al-Ṭaḥāwī was, after all, perhaps best known for his creed, which became known simply as *al-ᶜAqīda al-Ṭaḥāwiyya*.[38] The creed was reconciliatory. It negotiated the speculative theological trends that percolated during his career with the more anthropomorphic postulations often associated with followers of Aḥmad b. Ḥanbal.[39] Ibn Abī al-ᶜIzz al-Ḥanafī's commentary espoused a number of anthropomorphic doctrines. The discovery of an intensely anthropomorphic commentary by a Ḥanafī from the High Middle Ages on the work of a prominent tenth-century Ḥanafī was a great scoop for traditionalist Salafis, and one that al-Albānī and his partner Zuhayr al-Shāwīsh wasted no time in turning to their advantage.

Al-Albānī certainly seemed to be cognisant of the opportunity that this sort of work provided to undermine advocates of late Sunni traditionalism, the Ḥanafī *madhhab* and speculative theology (*ᶜilm al-kalām*). His introduction, which runs into forty pages in the published edition, is an acutely severe indictment, probably the most vehement one we have from al-Albānī, against late Sunni traditionalism, its *éminence grise*, al-Kawtharī, and the latter's staunchest supporter, Abū Ghudda.[40]

Al-Albānī's introduction furnishes little of value as to the text in question or its author. It is, instead, a lengthy, dyspeptic response to the 'wicked, fanatic, Ḥanafī deviant (*al-khabīth al-mutaᶜaṣṣib al-ḥanafī al-jāᵓir*), who is renowned for his extreme animosity towards the *ahl al-sunna* and *ahl al-ḥadīth* (*al-maᶜrūf bi shiddati ᶜadāᵓihi li ahl al-sunna wa-l-ḥadīth*), ᶜAbd al-Fattāḥ Abū Ghudda.' Muḥammad Zāhid al-Kawtharī (d. 1951) does not escape al-Albānī's obloquy. According to al-Albānī,

> Al-Kawtharī, in all frankness, was profusely well-endowed with the knowledge of hadith and its practitioners (*rijāl*); except that, tragically, his knowledge was a proof against him and a curse because it increased him neither in guidance nor illumination, not in the knowledge of particulars nor of the critical foundations. He was an obstinate jahmī, Ḥanafī, who was destroyed by fanaticism.[41]

Al-Albānī details his other frustrations with al-Kawtharī and Abū Ghudda. He finds unacceptable al-Kawtharī's and Abū Ghudda's hostility towards the *ahl al-ḥadīth* and the gatekeepers of the medieval Salafi canon: the *ruwāt, thiqāt* and *ḥuffāẓ*. He refers to al-Kawtharī's slander of al-Khaṭīb al-Baghdādī, ᶜAbd Allāh b. Aḥmad b. Ḥanbal, al-ᶜUqaylī, and another three-hundred or so 'trustworthy transmitters'. Al-Albānī also highlights al-Kawtharī's assertion that Ibn Khuzayma's *Kitāb al-Tawḥīd* was nothing but the book of idolatory (*Kitāb al-Shirk*).[42] Al-Albānī's motives for mentioning these particular scholars are not arbitrary. These were all notable scholars of the ninth to eleventh centuries who charged Abū Ḥanīfa with a range of religious, theological and jurisprudential improprieties. For late Sunni traditionalists, al-Kawtharī's slander (*ṭaᶜn*) of these scholars was an act of defence, a show of reciprocity, a condign response to the large tome of anti-Abū Ḥanīfa material that these scholars helped to promulgate. Al-Albānī devotes the mainstay of his introduction to challenging the *madhhab*-inspired principles that underpin the intellectual leanings and scholarship of late Sunni traditionalists.[43] He also finds time to write off the teachers of Abū Ḥanīfa and the very many *masānīd* that are attributed to him. He does this by highlighting critical appraisals of the compilers of these *masānīd* by medieval Sunni hadith critics.[44]

In this way, al-Albānī is able to use the apparatus of the modern edition to transform a pre-modern manuscript into a coherent rebuttal of late Sunni traditionalism, its doctrines and its representatives. Al-Kawtharī, a prolific scholar and editor of pre-modern manuscripts, responded mildy to the publication. In a footnote in his monograph on the life and writings of al-Ṭahāwī, al-Kawtharī called into question Ibn Abī al-ᶜIzz's affiliation to the Ḥanafī *madhhab*, dismissed the commentator as an ignorant anthropomorphist who lost his way, and directed readers to more reputable commentaries on al-Ṭaḥāwī's creed.[45] Footnotes were to play a much more central role in contestations between late Sunni traditionalists and traditionalist Salafis over Abū Ḥanīfa. The meteoric rise of the foonote in disputes over the editions of medieval texts is nowhere better illustrated than in the history of the publication of al-Khaṭīb al-Baghdādī's *Tārīkh Baghdād*.

In the 1930s, a group of Egyptian-based editors were working on the publication of al-Khaṭīb's voluminous history.[46] One of the editors, Muḥammad Amīn al-Khānjī (d. 1939), approached Muḥammad Zāhid al-Kawtharī expressing his consternation about the longest biographical entry contained in this history.[47] Muḥammad Amīn al-Khānjī had discovered an unrelenting and garrulous attack on Abū Ḥanīfa in what was scheduled to be the thirteenth volume of the publication. Al-Kawtharī was well aware of al-Khaṭīb's notorious entry on Abū Ḥanīfa. He urged al-Khānjī to publish a condensed version of a manuscript housed in Dār al-Kutub al-Miṣriyya authored by the Ayyūbid ruler of Damascus, al-Malik al-Muᶜaẓẓam ᶜĪsā b. Abī Bakr al-Ayyūbī (r. 1218–27). This manuscript, entitled *al-Sahm al-muṣīb fi kabid al-Khaṭīb*, was a rebuttal of al-Khaṭīb's entry on Abū Ḥanīfa.[48]

The editors were not amenable to al-Kawtharī's suggestion of incorporating the Ayyūbid ruler's rejoinder into the published edition. Al-Khānjī again solicited al-Kawtharī's advice. In response, al-Kawtharī penned a short and rushed rejoinder to al-Khaṭīb's entry that would be incorporated into the footnotes of the edition without attribution to al-Kawtharī. According to al-Kawtharī, his notes were grossly mishandled and reproduced in a most truncated fashion. Al-Kawtharī laid the blame at the feet of Muḥammad Ḥāmid al-Fiqī (d. 1959).

Muḥammad Ḥāmid al-Fiqī was a monumental figure in the diffusion of Salafism in Egypt. He is well known to academics today as the editor of Ibn Abī Yaᶜlā b. al-Farrā's (d. 1065) *Ṭabaqāt al-Ḥanābila*, Ibn Rajab's (d. 1393) *Kitāb dhayl ᶜalā ṭabaqāt al-Ḥanābila* and many of Ibn Taymiyya's (d. 1328) works. The Cairene publishing house, Maṭbaᶜat al-Sunna al-Muḥammadiyya, published most of his editorial work. Al-Fiqī, the founder of the influential, Cairo-based Salafi organisation, Anṣār al-Sunna al-Muḥammadiyya, also arranged for the preparation of a single-volume publication reproducing al-Khaṭīb's entry on Abū Ḥanīfa as a book.[49] This was published and sent by al-Fiqī to the Indian subcontinent where it was swiftly translated into Urdu.[50] In the end, the thirteenth volume was published without a defence of Abū Ḥanīfa. After the ensuing outrage in response to the publication, al-Kawtharī and others lobbied the relevant authorities and demanded a reissuing of the thirteenth volume. The authorities relented and pushed through a revised publication that incorporated a defence of Abū Ḥanīfa. Still, al-Kawtharī was dissatisfied. In 1941, he published a larger refutation: *Taʾnīb al-Khaṭīb ᶜalā mā sāqa-hu fi tarjamat Abī Ḥanīfa min al-abāṭīl*. This work tackles in some detail one hundred and fifty scandalous reports contained in al-Khaṭīb's history. Al-Kawtharī, *matn*-by-*matn*, *isnād*-by-*isnād*, tries to pick apart al-Khaṭīb's material. Before getting to the material, he prefaces this section – the mainstay of the work – with an essay on the unrivalled primacy of the eponymous founders of the *madhhab*s, singling out, of course, Abū Ḥanīfa. Next comes a methodological statement about how one should understand the friction between the *muḥaddithūn* and *fuqahāʾ*, which is mixed with an exercise in historical interpretation to account for the rise of animosity towards the eponymous founders of the *madhhab*s. For good measure, he also gathers a range of adversarial and captious biographies of al-Khaṭīb.[51]

The saga over al-Khaṭīb's entry on Abū Ḥanīfa did not end there. For reasons not immediately obvious, Salafi scholars were incensed by al-Kawtharī's book. Al-Khaṭīb was a marginal figure if we consider the nexus of scholars and texts that came to constitute a classical, pre-modern canon to which

Salafis hearkened back. Moreover, he had a more than checkered history with the Ḥanbalī school to which many Salafis in Saudi Arabia, though not all, expressed some fealty. Al-Khaṭīb famously turned his back on the Ḥanbalīs, embraced the Shāfiʿī school of law, and his entry on Aḥmad b. Ḥanbal was partly the catalyst for his exile from Baghdad.[52]

In order to appreciate why Salafi scholars reacted so sharply to al-Kawtharī's book, we must return to the person of Abū Ḥanīfa. Abū Ḥanīfa had come to represent much of what, to Salafis, was institutionally decrepit about the development of Islam since the High Middle Ages. Although many Salafis shied away from habitually reproducing some of the fiercest polemics against Abū Ḥanīfa located in their classical canon, it was more astute a strategy to simply draw attention to the medieval controversy surrounding Abū Ḥanīfa.

It is for this reason that al-Kawtharī's rejoinder resulted in the publication of one of the most popular and readily available manifestos of Salafism and its contestations with late Sunni traditionalists. *Al-Tankīl bi-mā fī taʾnīb al-Kawtharī min al-abāṭīl* is a sweeping two-volume critique of late Sunni traditionalism and its staunchest spokesperson, Muḥammad Zāhid al-Kawtharī. It is a pellucid setting down of the main contours of the contestations between the two camps, with contributions from two of the most prolific advocates of Salafism in the twentieth century: ʿAbd al-Raḥmān b. Yaḥyā al-Muʿallimī al-Yamānī, the author of the book, and Muḥammad Nāṣir al-Dīn al-Albānī, the book's editor and author of the book's introduction. In al-Albānī's words:[53]

> This book is a refutation of some of the fanatics who oppose the book and the *sunna*. In it, the author demonstrates beyond any doubt and with demonstrable proofs the incriminations and slander of al-Kawtharī upon the imams of hadith and its transmission, and his accusing them of anthropomorphism (*al-radd ʿalā baʿḍ al-mutaʿaṣṣiba, al-mukhālifīn li-l-kitāb wa-l-sunna; bayyana fīhi bi-l-adilla al-qāṭiʿa wa-l-barāhīn al-sāṭiʿa tajannī al-Kawtharī ʿalā aʾimmat al-ḥadīth wa-riwāyatihī wa-ramyihi iyyāhum bi-l-tajsīm wa-l-tashbīh*).

We see here that the authors avoid bringing Abū Ḥanīfa directly into disrepute. Al-Muʿallimī falls short of explicitly supporting the content and purport of anti-Abū Ḥanīfa material, but painstakingly defends the authenticity of the *isnāds* in reports labelling Abū Ḥanīfa a heretic.[54] Interacting with the classical heritage in the way that al-Muʿallimī did allowed one a certain degree of scholarly cover. Al-Muʿallimī does not explicitly endorse the anti-Abū Ḥanīfa material located in al-Khaṭīb's entry, but by providing a lengthy defence of al-Khaṭīb's entry, he contests Abū Ḥanīfa's religious credibility against late Sunni traditionalists in less provocative fashion. Al-Kawtharī was now dedicated to issuing rejoinders in response to the publication of classical texts vehement in their criticism of Abū Ḥanīfa and their appropriation of such texts by Salafi scholars.[55]

The publication of Ibn Abī Shayba's (d. 849) *al-Kitāb al-muṣannaf fī-l-aḥādīth wa-l-āthār* is another illustration of al-Kawtharī's tremendous zeal in defending Abū Ḥanīfa.[56] Ibn Abī Shayba was a ninth-century hadith scholar whose lasting legacy is a multi-volume collection of hadith and *āthār*. One of the volumes contains a small chapter entitled *Radd ᶜalā Abī Ḥanīfa*, wherein Ibn Abī Shayba lists no less than 485 hadith and *āthār* reports that Abū Ḥanīfa is said to have contravened or contradicted.[57]

Its publication sparked a refutation by the erstwhile defender of the Ḥanafī *madhhab*, al-Kawtharī, entitled *al-Nukat al-ṭarīfa fī-l-taḥadduth ᶜan rudūd Ibn Abī Shayba ᶜalā Abī Ḥanīfa*.[58] True to his past form, al-Kawtharī produces a point-by-point riposte to all 485 hadith and *āthār* reports that Abū Ḥanīfa is alleged to have contravened. That the most accomplished edition of Ibn Abī Shayba's *al-Muṣannaf* contains a substantial part of al-Kawtharī's rebuttal is a testament to the intrusive nature of modern contestations, their longevity beyond the lifespan of Salafi and late Sunni traditionalist protagonists, and to the fact that the painstaking efforts of late Sunni traditionalists, al-Kawtharī in particular, would sometimes pay off. Here, the capacity to steer the classical tradition, even posthumously, could not be clearer. Moreover, the fact that one of the main contestations between late Sunni traditionalists and Salafi traditionalists was sparked by one scholar-cum-editor's indefatigable determination to insist on the right to defence through something so technical and marginal as a footnote should alert us to the critical opportunities opened by the publishing of classics and its attendant technical apparatus in the Islamic world.

Scholars-cum-Editors (*Muṣaḥḥiḥūn* and *Muḥaqqiqūn*)

Nevertheless, contestations on the margins, in the form of introductions to editions or footnotes, did have their limitations: scholars-cum-editors were limited somewhat as to how directly or how widely they could contest ideas and persons not directly relevant to the manuscript in question. Editions of medieval texts were also bespoke products, designed with a specific readership in mind. Traditionalist Salafis and late Sunni traditionalists, conscious of these limitations, became embroiled in polemical refutations against one another in an arena other than the constricted space of classical editions. These works were dedicated to post-edition polemics. Traditionalist Salafis came to dominate this genre, where they hosted fiery deprecations of the pillars of late Sunni traditionalism and its spokepersons. Late Sunni traditionalists were criticised for allegedly tampering with medieval texts, dishonouring the companions of the Prophet and formative members of the *aṣḥāb al-ḥadīth*, and displaying a divisive partisanship to the Ḥanafī *madhhab* and Abū Ḥanīfa. Above all, these works served to crystallise the animosity between these two groups and the scholars most deeply entrenched in these polemics. On the Salafi side, we shall draw attention to some of the most important works of this kind. We will have occasion to highlight how the controversy over Abū Ḥanīfa featured in these works. In the process, we will gain an insight into the corporate nature of traditionalist Salafism and the close connections between its leading protagonists. More than the publication of classical texts, we will see that direct refutations contributed to the vernacularisation of controversies over Abū Ḥanīfa's religious pedigree.

Bakr Abū Zayd

Bakr Abū Zayd was one of the most influential traditionalist Salafi scholars of the twentieth century.[59] He was born in 1944 in Najd, Saudi Arabia. His religious orientation formed during his studies at the Faculty of Sharīᶜa in Riyadh, Mecca, where he graduated in 1996–7. During his studies there, Bakr Abū Zayd studied with ᶜAbd al-ᶜAzīz ᶜAbd Allāh b. Bāz (d. 1999). With ᶜAbd Allāh b. Bāz, he covered a wide range of medieval texts which included *Fatḥ al-bārī*, *Bulūgh al-marām*, and works of jurisprudence (*fiqh*), doctrine (*tawḥīd*) and hadith. Another formative influence upon him was the ten years of instruction he received under Muḥammad al-Amīn al-Shinqīṭī (d. 1973). By 1979, Bakr Abū Zayd had successfuly obtained both his masters and doctorate degrees. For both degrees, he successfully defended dissertations on the religious thought of Ibn al-Qayyim al-Jawziyya (d. 1350). Upon graduating, Bakr Abū Zayd received various teaching appointments in Saudi Arabia, but his official appointments as a judge (*qāḍī*) in the Public Courts of Medina and as a member of The Permanent Committe for Issuing Legal Edicts and The Committee of Senior Scholars in the Kingdom of Saudi Arabia secured his national and international reputation among the *ᶜulamāᵓ*. It was only with an upsurge in his scholarly activities that Bakr Abū Zayd gradually began to gain recognition as a leading advocate of traditionalist Salafis. He had authored fifty-nine books and edited close to ten medieval texts. These works included careful monographs on the Ḥanbalī school of law, Aḥmad b. Ḥanbal, and the *aṣḥāb al-ḥadīth*.[60]

But it was his venture into more polemical and popular religious subjects that gained him a place alongside notable scions of traditionalist Salafism of the twentieth century, such as al-Albānī and al-Muᶜallimī al-Yamānī. These popular books were his *Ḥukm al-intimāᵓ ilā al-firaq wa-l-aḥzāb wa-l-jamāᶜāt al-Islāmiyya*, *Darᵓ al-fitna ᶜan ahl al-sunna*,[61] *Barāᵓat ahl al-sunna min al-waqīʿa fī ʿulamāʾ al-umma*,[62] and *al-Rudūd*. It is to the content of the two books *al-Rudūd* and *Barāʾat ahl al-sunna*, and their discussion of Abū Ḥanīfa and his modern-day advocates, to which I should now like to turn. *Al-Rudūd* consists of six of Bakr Abū Zayd's writings. The second and third books, *Taḥrīf al-nuṣūṣ min maʾākhidh ahl al-ahwāʾ fī-l-istidlāl* and *Barāʾat ahl al-sunna*, are wholly devoted to singling out the gross distortions that were produced by 'some extremists among the people of heresy in our time', the three leading representatives of late Sunni traditionalism in the twentieth century: al-Kawtharī, ʿAbd al-Ḥayy al-Laknawī and Abū Ghudda.[63]

Bakr Abū Zayd introduces his first victim, al-Kawtharī, in a deceptively grandiloquent manner:[64]

> Indeed, the fourteenth century has not witnessed a Muslim devoted so tirelessly to sacred knowledge but whose understanding was so blinkered by reprehensible fanaticism ... than this creature. You see him standing, waiting to ambush any medieval text that opposes the view of his reprehensible fanaticism.

Abū Ghudda receives a less emphatic introduction, being introduced disparagingly as the 'little al-Kawtharī' (*al-Kawtharī al-ṣaghīr*).[65] Bakr Abū Zayd then draws attention to three particularly egregious aspects of al-Kawtharī's and Abū Ghudda's writings: (1) their slander of Ibn al-Qayyim and Ibn Taymiyya, which, Bakr Abū Zayd insists, extends to their charging them with unbelief (*al-kufr*) and heresy (*zandaqa*); (2) dishonouring the scholars of hadith (*ʿulamāʾ al-ḥadīth*) and upholders of the Sunna (*anṣār al-sunna*), scholars like Mālik b. Anas (d. 795), al-Shāfiʿī (d. 820), al-Khaṭīb, and many others; and (3) attacking approximately 280 scholars from the formative period of Islam who are guilty of no other crime but that they hold views opposing the Ḥanafī *madhhab*.[66] The jobation continues. Al-Kawtharī is characterised as someone who mastered the art of distorting medieval texts. These distortions are not evidenced by Bakr Abū Zayd himself; rather, he quotes from al-Muʿallimī al-Yamānī's *al-Tankīl* eight gross distortions produced by al-Kawtharī in his refutation of al-Khaṭīb's biographical entry on Abū Ḥanīfa.[67] In addition, Abū Ghudda is criticised for his transgressions in producing al-Laknawī's *al-Rafʿ wa-l-takmīl*. The book is chided for criticising 300 scholars of the Sunna and espousing spurious doctrines (*ʿaqāʾid zāʾifa*), which squarely contradict the doctrine of the *salaf*. Bakr Abū Zayd highlights al-Laknawī's negative assessment of al-Bukhārī, which is offered in the context of the latter's caustic remarks about Abū Ḥanīfa in *al-Tārīkh al-kabīr*, *al-Tārīkh al-awsaṭ* and *Kitāb rafʿ al-yadayn*.[68] Ashraf ʿAlī al-Tahānawī's (d. 1943) acerbic take on al-Bukhārī in the former's *Qawāʿid fī ʿulūm al-ḥadīth* is also cited by Bakr Abū Zayd.[69]

Bakr Abū Zayd's antipathy towards the *madhhabs*, which is scattered across his *oeuvre*, is characteristically mediated through scornful, polemical attacks upon its modern-day representatives. This technique of not attacking Abū Ḥanīfa directly, but engaging proxies to undermine the underlying principles that define the *madhhab*, is consistently invoked by traditionalist Salafis. Occasionally, however, Salafis like Bakr Abū Zayd were tenacious enough to engage in charientisms and veiled barbs directed towards Abū Ḥanīfa and his supporters. This was executed with some caution, and traditionalist Salafis usually resorted to simply reproducing vitriol directly from ninth- and tenth-century proto-Sunni traditionalist texts. Bakr Abū Zayd's *al-Rudūd* is no different in this respect. In a short essay on the Murjiʾa, a heretical group according to our author, Bakr Abū Zayd diligently identifies the roots of this heresy with a group of jurists from Iraq.[70] Bakr Abū Zayd does not, of course, name Abū Ḥanīfa. But any discerning reader, aware of the ninth-century sources identifying Abū Ḥanīfa as Murjiʾī, coupled with the most elementary knowledge about Abū Ḥanīfa's activities as an Iraqi jurist, will not fail to notice the slight.[71]

In any case, Bakr Abū Zayd soon drops the equivocating style, and his attack upon Abū Ḥanīfa strengthens with the insertion of more targeted comments about him. He begins on a sardonic note with a passage taken from al-Laknawī's *al-Rafᶜ wa-l-takmīl* in a section which describes al-Tahānawī's (and Abū Ghudda's and al-Laknawī's) unrestrained display of *madhhab* fanaticism (*ghāriq fi-l-taᶜaṣṣub al-madhhabī*).[72] The passage from al-Tahānawī's work that Bakr Abū Zayd quotes reads:

> By God, no one has been born in Islam after the Prophet more trustworthy and blissful than al-Nuᶜmān Abū Hanīfa. And the proof of this lies in what is visible from the effacement of the *madhhabs* of [his] slanderers; while his *madhhab* became widespread, and his increase in fame by day and by night. Indeed, God and the believers willed this for Abū Ḥanīfa.

Bakr Abū Zayd then proceeds to pick apart countless passages from al-Laknawī's *al-Rafᶜ wa-l-takmīl* and *al-Ajwiba al-fāḍila*, and al-Tahānawī's *Qawāʾid fi ᶜulūm al-ḥadīth*, where the authors attempt to discredit scholars who produced or hosted anti-Abū Ḥanīfa material.[73]

Muḥammad ᶜAbd al-Razzāq Ḥamza

Muḥammad ᶜAbd al-Razzāq Ḥamza was an Egyptian-born Salafi scholar of the mid-late twentieth century. His career resembles the professional trajectory of many of Egypt's most prodiguous Salafi *ᶜulamāʾ*. Upon graduating from Al-Azhar, ᶜAbd al-Razzāq Ḥamza took up employment at, what was then, Rashīd Riḍā's recently established institute, *Dār al-daᶜwa wa-l-irshād*.

Rashīd Riḍā made him responsible for producing modern editions of classical texts. He continued his active involement with Salafi organisations and publishing houses through his work as a senior deputy to Muḥammad Ḥāmid al-Fiqī at the latter's Jamāᶜat Anṣār al-Sunna al-Muḥammadiyya. In 1924, he set out for the Ḥijāz, where he took up employment as the imam of the Prophet's mosque in Medina. In 1929, he transferred to Mecca as an assistant to his erstwhile Egyptian comrade, ᶜAbd al-Ẓāhir Muḥammad Abī al-Samḥ. Both helped to establish Dār al-Ḥadīth in Mecca in 1931. He died in 1972.[74]

ᶜAbd al-Razzāq Ḥamza's contribution to the vernacularisation of debates over Abū Ḥanīfa can be seen in his influential book, entitled *al-Muqābala bayna al-hudā wa-l-ḍalāl: Ḥawla tarḥīb al-Kawtharī bi-naqd taᵓnīb.*[75] Despite the book's brevity (ninety pages), ᶜAbd al-Razzāq manages to squeeze in large passages from medieval writings that heap opprobrium upon Abū Ḥanīfa. We are introduced to reports stating that Abū Ḥanīfa was a polytheist (*mushrik*);[76] no birth was more harmful to Islam than Abū Ḥanīfa's;[77] Abū Ḥanīfa was the incurable disease (*dāᵓ ᶜuḍāl*);[78] the scholars had doubts about his Islam;[79] and that Abū Ḥanīfa was made to repent from heresy twice.[80] The vitriol against Abū Ḥanīfa, extracted from medieval writings, continues for twenty pages. Admittedly, ᶜAbd al-Razzāq Ḥamza's refutation is bolder than Bakr Abū Zayd's. The former still marshals and reproduces medieval invective against Abū Ḥanīfa, but he leaves little room for doubt as to how important it was for some Salafi scholars to discredit Abū Ḥanīfa in an effort to debilitate late Sunni traditionalism.

Muḥammad ᶜĪd ᶜAbbāsī

Muḥammad ᶜĪd ᶜAbbāsī was born in Damascus in 1938.[81] In 1954, ᶜAbbāsī was introduced to al-Albānī, and the latter had a formative and lasting influence upon ᶜAbbāsī's religious orientation. Thereafter, ᶜAbbāsī devoted himself to studying with al-Albānī, and by the end of his career he was deputising for al-Albānī in the latter's absence.[82]

Like many Salafi scholars, Muḥammad ᶜĪd ᶜAbbāsī pursued a multi-track professional career. He worked as a professional preacher and imam in a local mosque in Damascus; he worked in the publishing house, al-Maktab al-Islāmī, owned by his friend, Zuhayr al-Shāwīsh; he also established a journal, '*al-Salafiyya*'; and he published and edited numerous books. In short, ᶜAbbāsī cottoned on to one of the most potent secrets that contributed to the mass penetration of Salafism in the Middle East: professional dexterity and the pursuit of various channels of communication, not a scholastic mastery of a single discipline, had become the currency of popular religious legitimacy. His book, The Heresy of *Madhhab* Fanaticism (*Bidᶜat al-taᶜaṣṣub al-madhhabī*) spoke to this popular appeal. Like all popular writers, ᶜAbbāsī had overcome the first hurdle that any writer seeking wide appeal must. He managed to capture his thesis in the book's title: *madhhab* affiliation, particularly of a fanatic kind expressed by modern-day Ḥanafīs, was a heretical innovation. ᶜAbbāsī is perfectly comfortable, however, with innovations of a different kind: innovations in literary techniques. The work opens with a *précis* of the entire book, encapsulated by one Qurᵓanic verse and four statements from medieval scholars.[83] It is worth quoting the passage in full:

> * God the exalted said: And if you disagree on a matter, return it to God and His messenger if you are believers in God and the last day.
> * Imam Mālik, may God have mercy upon him, said: I am only a man. Some things I get right, others I get wrong. So look carefully at my opinions, and take only that which is in agreement with the book and the *sunna*. And leave that which is not in agreement with the book and the *sunna*.
> * Imam al-Shāfiᶜī, may God have mercy upon him, said: The Muslims have agreed that for him to whom the *sunna* of the Prophet has been made explicitly clear, it is impermissible for him to call to it [the *sunna*] on the basis of the opinion of any individual.
> * Imam Abū Jaᶜfar al-Ṭaḥāwī the Ḥanafī said: no one practises blind imitation (*taqlīd*) except that he is an ignoramus or a fanatic.
> * Imam Ibn al-Jawzī al-Ḥanbalī said: The performance of blind imitation (*taqlīd*) is nothing but the obliteration of the benefits of one's intellect, because one was created to exercise one's intellect and ponder over things. Ignominy be to the one who has been given a candle with which to obtain enlightenment, yet he blows it out and proceeds to walk in darkness.

These five, carefully chosen, programmatic statements against conformity to the *madhhabs* neatly illustrate the hypothesis of the book. Two of these statements are attributed to the eponyms of the *madhhabs*, and one goes back to a prominent medieval Ḥanafī. The next page of the book opens with a common trope in contemporary reformist writings: the social and political deterioration of the Muslim world is reduced to the moribund influence of astray doctrines. 'The true Islam,' our author states, 'has been veiled by heresies. This book is devoted to one particular, but very significant and dangerous, heresy that has befallen the Muslims for many generations: the heresy of *madhhab* fanaticism.'[84] ᶜAbbāsī is scathing in his attack on the *madhhabs*. He is particularly concerned with refuting the criticisms levelled at Salafi scholars by Ramaḍān al-Būṭī in the latter's *al-Lā madhhabiyya akhṭar bidᶜa tuhaddid al-Sharīᶜa al-Islāmiyya*.[85]

At the same time, however, ᶜAbbāsī's views on Abū Ḥanīfa represent a trend that began to emerge among Salafis of softening direct attacks on Abū Ḥanīfa. He clarifies his position on Abū Ḥanīfa and the eponymous founders of the *madhhabs*, insisting that a commitment to scriptural sources, not fallible human beings, is what is demanded by the religion. The imams, often unwittingly, end up flagrantly opposing the book and the Sunna.[86] This climb down in anti-Abū Ḥanīfa polemic may represent two things: firstly, it could represent a softening of attitudes in response to the success of late Sunni traditionalists in demonstrating what to them is Abū Ḥanīfa's unimpeachable orthodox credentials as a scholar of hadith and an exceptional jurist; alternatively, it could reflect a reappraisal of the tenor of Salafi contestations against late Sunni traditionalists over Abū Ḥanifa's religious pedigree. Without a forthcoming confession, we cannot categorically pinpoint which late Sunni traditionalist texts, if any, effected a change in Salafi discourses about Abū Ḥanīfa. However, as we shall see in our discussion of late Sunni traditionalist works on hadith criticism, there seems to have been some correlation between the two.

Corporate Salafi Publications

As we have seen in the preceding section, the dialogue between late Sunni traditionalists and Salafis resulted in some very particular innovations of both style and substance. I have already indicated that Salafis appeared more enterprising in their attempts to dislodge late Sunni traditionalism. I would now like to suggest that the transnational and corporate nature of traditionalist Salafism was an important factor in the introduction of further innovations to authorial conventions otherwise uncommon to Islamic scholarship. The publication of the book by 'Al-Kawtharī and his attack on the classical heritage and an illustration of this in his writings and editorial notes' best illustrates this.[87] For one thing, the work has no single author. It is ascribed, rather, to five different scholars, all of whom constitute nothing short of a stellar line-up of Salafi scholars: Muḥammad Bahjat al-Bīṭār, al-Muᶜallimī al-Yamānī, Muḥammad b. ᶜAbd al-Razzāq Ḥamza, Ḥusām al-Dīn al-Qudsī and al-Albānī.[88] Secondly, the book is a hodgepodge of short and long refutations of al-Kawtharī. Some of these refutations are taken from the published works of our five authors; others are unique to this publication. The book is divided into ten different treatises. It includes the influential *al-Tankīl bi-mā fī taᵓnīb al-Kawtharī min al-abāṭīl.* The author of this work has featured elsewhere in this paper, but we have not had occasion to introduce his biography and contribution to contestations between late Sunni traditionalists and Salafis.

ᶜAbd al-Raḥmān b. Yaḥyā al-Muᶜallimī al-Yamānī was born in 1895. He was appointed as the Amīr of the Southern provinces of modern-day Saudi Arabia, Jizan and Asir. He departed for India, where he was appointed as an editor at the publishing house, Dāᵓirat al-Maᶜārif al-ᶜUthmānīyya in Hyderabad, Dakkan. He served in this position for thirty years. Upon returning to Mecca, he was appointed over the Maktabat al-Ḥaram al-Makkī in Saudi Arabia. Beyond these appointments, al-Muᶜallimī al-Yamānī was an indefatigable scholar. Until recently, only some of his books were available to scholars. Earlier this year, however, Bakr Abū Zayd, another Salafi whom we have profiled in this paper, spearheaded a twenty-five-volume posthumous publication containing al-Muᶜallimī's entire corpus of writings.[89] Al-Muᶜallimī received a ringing endorsement from al-Albānī, who confirmed to some who were sceptical of al-Muᶜallimī's Salafi pedigree 'that the man was a Salafi in theology, Salafi in his school of thought and methodology.'[90]

To return to his *al-Tankīl bi-mā fī taʾnīb al-Kawtharī min al-abāṭīl*, it is useful to look at al-Yamānī's driving motivation behind the work, which he describes in the following passage:

> I saw that the *ustādh* [al-Kawtharī] went beyond that which people of knowledge agree about with him with regards to Abū Ḥanīfa's honour and defending him. So much so, in fact, that it does not befit a serious, established scholar to [engage in] falsifications and contradictions, [which undermine] the sacred duty of intellectual honesty due to sacred knowledge. [He also engages in] mixing up the principles, insulting the imams of the *sunna* and its transmitters, such that [this defamation] extends to the noble companions, successors, three imams, Mālik, al-Shāfiᶜī, and Aḥmad and their ilk, and the esteemed imams of hadith, and the trustworthy transmitters of hadith. He also opposes confirmed authentic traditions and denounces the doctrine of the Salafiyya.

The treatise is divided into four parts: part I aims to clarify the principles which al-Kawtharī is said to have abused; part II serves to correct the biographies of the scholars and transmitters whom al-Kawtharī is alleged to have defamed, and they amount to around three hundred. These include: Anas b. Mālik, Hishām b. ᶜUrwa b. Zubayr b. al-ᶜAwwām, Mālik b. Anas, al-Shāfiᶜī, Aḥmad b. Ḥanbal, and al-Khaṭīb. Part III tackles legal issues for which Abū Ḥanīfa and his disciples were criticised. The final part relates to doctrinal matters, in which the author champions the correctness of the doctrines of the hadith scholars against the jurists. In al-Yamānī's own words:

> I have mentioned the indisputable proofs for the correctness of the doctrines of the imams of hadith. Here, I have enumerated the doctrines which the *ustādh* has attacked, and I have not been lenient in pursuing my investigation. Rather, I have striven for this book to be a comprehensive repository for the mighty virtues of the knowledge of the *sunna*, which will be distinguished for its expansiveness and the diligent research therein.[91]

ᶜAbd al-Fattāḥ Abū Ghudda

Late Sunni traditionalists were less prolific in their engagement with these contestations; or at least, we can say, their engagement was not as diverse as that of their Salafi peers. Whereas Salafis commanded the full value of publication houses, polemical refutations and popular treatises, late Sunni traditionalists tended to respond in very specialised genres. These scenes of contestations shall be discussed below. But we can note here that there were some exceptions to this otherwise selective choice of output. ᶜAbd al-Fattāḥ Abū Ghudda's *Kalimāt fi kashf abāṭīl wa-iftirāʾāt* is one such exception. Born in Ḥalab in 1917, Abū Ghudda rose to prominence as a leading member of the Syrian Muslim Brotherhood, but his scholarly credentials were equally impressive. He is best known for his works on hadith and his scholarly editions of medieval texts. Altogether, he authored and edited over seventy publications. His formative education took place in Egypt at al-Azhar, where he graduated from the Faculty of Shariᶜa in 1948. He continued his studies for a further two years before returning to his native country. Among his teachers was Muḥammad Zāhid al-Kawtharī, who encouraged him to develop an acquaintance with scholarship in the Indian subcontinent. This he did, and his travels to India and Pakistan seemed to have had a lasting impression upon his scholarly outlook. In the Indian subcontinent he was introduced to the region's leading representatives of late Sunni traditionalism, among them Muḥammad Zakariyyā al-Kāndahlawī (d. 1982), Abū al-Wafāʾ al-Afghānī (d. 1975) and Muḥammad Yūsuf al-Banūrī.[92]

He taught Ḥanafī jurisprudence, jurisprudential theory and comparative jurisprudence for three years at the Faculty of Shariᶜa, University of Damascus. His prominent role within the Muslim Brotherhood prompted a long exile in Saudi Arabia. He took teaching appointments at the Faculty of Theology, at Jāmiᶜ al-Imām Muḥammad b. Saᶜūd al-Islāmiyya and Jāmiᶜ al-Malik Saᶜūd in Riyadh. He died in 1997. The *Kalimāt fi kashf abāṭīl wa-iftirāʾāt* is a targeted response to the wide-ranging attacks by Salafi scholars such as al-Albānī, Zuhayr al-Shāwīsh, Muḥammad ᶜĪd ᶜAbbāsī and ᶜAbd al-Razzāq Ḥamza on late Sunni traditionalists like al-Kawtharī and its principle doctrines and beliefs. The book responds to a number of publications which singled out Abū Ghudda for withering critique. In particular, Abū Ghudda responds at length to the vapid denigration of himself and al-Kawtharī by al-Albānī and Zuhayr al-Shāwīsh in their edition of *Sharḥ ᶜAqīdat al-Ṭaḥāwī*. He turns his attention to ᶜAbd al-Razzāq Ḥamza, criticising him for his decision to include in his *al-Muqābala bayna al-hudā wa-l-ḍalāl: Ḥawla tarḥīb al-Kawtharī bi-naqd taʾnīb* reports stating that Abū Ḥanīfa was a heretic and polytheist.[93]

It is not immediately clear why late Sunni traditionalists were reluctant to engage in these direct refutations. I have not scanned the full range of material that might hint at a more active trend among late Sunni traditionalists to debate Salafis on such a platform. Having said that, it is difficult to overlook the hesitancy of late Sunni traditionalists in this arena of polemic, particularly when there may be good reason for this low level of activity. It is likely that late Sunni traditionalists realised that their objective of defending Abū Ḥanīfa may not be well served in the ambiguous setting that direct refutations provided. As we have seen, this very ambiguity, on the other hand, seems to have been a convenient home for a wide range of Salafi criticisms of Abū Ḥanīfa and late Sunni traditionalists designed to undermine the authority of the *madhhabs*. But late Sunni traditionalists seem to have channelled their responses to Salafis by revisiting one of the major occupations of eighteenth- to twentieth-century reform movements, the discipline of hadith. In the next two sections, we shall see how late Sunni traditionalists, not for the first time, produced a sizable body of specialised texts that spoke not only to Abū Ḥanīfa's expertise in hadith and its associated disciplines, but to their own mastery over a field of study that, until only very recently, had been used by traditionalist Salafis and eighteenth- to twentieth-century reform movements to mobilise support against late Sunni traditionalists and Abū Ḥanīfa.[94]

Monographs

Monographs represented a more sober, academic setting for late Sunni traditionalists to defend Abū Ḥanīfa against criticisms of his disregard for hadith, a medieval criticism rehabilitated by Salafi scholars in the twentieth century. Although this genre was represented in Salafi discourse in the Middle East, it is clear that scholars from the Indian subcontinent came to dominate this genre of writing.[95]

Foremost among them is ʿAbd al-Rashīd al-Nuʿmānī.[96] His scholarship is well known in the Indian subcontinent. But it was Abū Ghudda's commitment to importing hadith scholarship from the Indian subcontinent into the Middle East that secured al-Nuʿmānī, and others such as al-Laknawī, Anwarshāh Kashmīrī (d. 1933), pride of place among Middle Eastern *ʿulamāʾ*.[97] In the case of al-Nuʿmānī's *Makānat Abī Ḥanīfa fī-l-ḥadīth*, Abū Ghudda saw through its publication in the Middle East. He writes in the foreword to the work:[98]

> I saw to the publication of this book in the Arab lands after it had been published many times in India and Pakistan, because of the spread of a sickness that resulted in people belittling the status of Abū Ḥanīfa with regards to the field of hadith.

Al-Nuᶜmānī's monograph is a thoroughly well-researched presentation of Abū Ḥanīfa as a hadith master *par excellence*. Drawing almost entirely from medieval hadith critics of the early medieval and higher middle periods, al-Nuᶜmānī argues that Abū Ḥanīfa was considered a pioneer in the science of hadith, and was recognised as such by hadith masters.[99] He patiently makes his case for Abū Ḥanīfa being a distinguished practitioner of hadith criticism (*al-jarḥ wa-l-taᶜdīl*).[100] Al-Nuᶜmānī then details Abū Ḥanīfa's conditions (*shurūṭ*) for establishing the authenticity of a hadith.[101]

What al-Nuᶜmānī is attempting here is nothing short of a difficult *volte-face* with regards to Abū Ḥanīfa's image in both medieval texts and as portrayed by traditionalist Salafis. It is difficult to determine precisely what effect these focused monographs had on the wider contestations between the two groups over Abū Ḥanifa's religious standing. The contestations, as we have shown, were acutely fierce. We cannot expect, therefore, a forthcoming confession such that Salafis acknowledge that al-Nuᶜmānī's monograph treatment of the subject was convincing enough for them to retract their views. However, it is worth considering whether the softening of anti-Abū Ḥanifa sentiment, which we noted in the writings of traditionalist Salafis, was related to the rise of monograph treatments devoted to this particular criticism of Abū Ḥanīfa. It is possible that these focused works, which avoided the virulence that characterised direct refutations between Salafis and late Sunni traditionalists, mitigated, or compelled Salafis to compromise on, contestations over Abū Ḥanīfa.

Late Sunni traditionalists seeking to defend Abū Ḥanīfa went beyond penning single monographs on Abū Ḥanīfa to turning to a genre with a long and rich history in the pre-modern scholastic disciplines, primers on hadith and transmitter (*rijāl*) criticism.[102] For late Sunni traditionalists, this was a smart, tactical move. Firstly, this genre was a favourite for traditionalist Salafis, whose reformist enterprise gravitated toward hadith scholarship. As a genre that featured the mainstay of anti-Abū Ḥanīfa material, it was pregnant with ideological significance for Salafis in their conversation with late Sunni traditionalists. By taking up this genre, late Sunni traditionalists were able to reduce the subject's predisposition to be employed against Abū Ḥanīfa. Muḥammad ᶜAbd al-Ḥayy al-Laknawī's (d. 1886–7) *al-Rafᶜ wa-l-takmīl* is a skilful manifestation of how late Sunni traditionalists drew on the genre to thwart attacks on their eponymous founder.

Muḥammad ᶜAbd al-Ḥayy al-Laknawī was born in India in 1847. His religious learning took place under the tutelage of his father. Despite a very brief career – al-Laknawī was forty years old at the time of his death – al-Laknawī wrote over one hundred books. His *al-Rafᶜ wa-l-takmīl* bears a deep imprint of the contestations between late Sunni traditionalists and Salafi scholars. The book was edited by Abū Ghudda and opened with a dedication to al-Kawtharī. Al-Laknawī's work is a specialist primer on the discipline of hadith criticism. That al-Laknawī chose this medium for defending Abū Ḥanīfa is doubly significant. First, it provided him with an opportunity to demonstrate his mastery, as a late Sunni-Ḥanafī traditionalist, of hadith criticism. This served to undermine criticisms of late Sunni-Ḥanafī traditionalists by Salafi scholars that the former's poor grasp of the hadith tradition was a reflection of the legacy of Ḥanafism, reaching far back to its eponymous founder. Second, he drew on the genre which most frequently hosted vehement statements about Abū Ḥanīfa to push back and insist that Abū Ḥanīfa had an exceptional grasp of hadith and its corollary sciences. Al-Laknawī's primer tackles some very thorny issues about Abū Ḥanīfa's legacy. He mentions the stir that the Indian publication of Ibn Abī Shayba's chapter, *al-Radd ᶜalā Abī Ḥanīfa*, from his multi-volume *al-Muṣannaf*, caused, but swiftly points to Muḥammad Zāhid al-Kawtharī's rebuttal of the work.[103] He also invokes the watchword of Salafi rhetoric against Abū Ḥanīfa and late Sunni traditionalists, fanaticism (*taᶜaṣṣub*), and cleverly points to the *taᶜaṣṣub* of Abū Ḥanīfa's detractors as a motivating factor in attacks on Abū Ḥanīfa.[104] Al-Laknawī displays an impressive knowledge of the classical Islamic heritage which allows him, for example, to cite two Ḥanbalī refutations of al-Khaṭīb al-Baghdādī's entry on Abū Ḥanīfa.[105] The issue of Irjāᵓ, which featured prominently in Bakr Abū Zayd's, Muḥammad ᶜĪd ᶜAbbāsī's and ᶜAbd al-Razzāq Ḥamza's writings, is tackled by al-Laknawī: he points to two developments in the history of Irjāᵓ. There existed, al-Laknawī writes, the Murjiᵓa who belonged to Sunni orthodoxy (*ahl al-sunna wa-l-jamāᶜa*) and a heretical wing of the Murjiᵓa. Contrary to Bakr Abū Zayd's findings, Abū Ḥanīfa was of the orthodox Sunni Murjiᵓites (*murjiᵓat ahl al-sunna*).[106] A whole host of other medieval critics are challenged on their views about Abū Ḥanīfa: figures such as al-Nasāᵓī, al-Dhahabī, Ibn ᶜAdī and al-ᶜUqaylī.[107]

We should consider here, too, a complimentary work that we have only cursorily reviewed: Ẓafar Aḥmad al-ᶜUthmānī's (d. 1974) one-volume introduction to his monumental twenty-volume commentary on hadith supporting Ḥanafī positions.[108] Although I have introduced it here as a primer on hadith criticism and Abū Ḥanīfa's unrivalled mastery over it, it is important to note that the work is a little more than that. As well as detailing Abū Ḥanīfa's definitive qualification as a Successor (*tābiᶜī*) and his being a hadith critic, the author adds a very important prosopographical history of early Ḥanafī hadith scholars amounting to 264 persons.[109] To understand why al-ᶜUthmānī went to such lengths in this short, but rich work, it is helpful to quote his motivation for composing the work:[110]

> Whoever arrogantly pours scorn upon Abū Ḥanīfa, he becomes an exemplary punishment for the world, and his knowledge becomes a curse upon him (*wa-kāna ᶜilmu-hu wabālan*). We see in our times the emergence of a group completely ignorant of his esteemed status, who have tried to extinguish his heavenly light, diminish his status, deride him, seeking to honour others whilst belittling him. The group made it their trademark to defame him, and they covered themselves in abusing and reviling his followers. They also accuse him of not transmitting hadith and having a poor grasp of its science; they also declare him to be unreliable because of his deficient memory and mastery of the discipline; that he opposed the hadith with his personal opinions. So I was gripped by a divine, religious zeal and a fanatical Ḥanafite-Nuᶜmānite fervour, and so I set out to gather the sayings of the scholars of hadith in praise of this imam and the words of the hadith critics affirming his qualifications, probity, and precedence in this science over and above the other famous imams. After this, I go on to mention the biographical details of some of his esteemed students and followers who were of the most noble and learned hadith scholars. All of this in order to manifest his elevated status in the science of hadith, and in order to decisively refute the views of this most wicked group (*yandaḥiḍu raʾy hādhihi al-ṭāʾifa al-khabītha*).

This is an impassioned elucidation of precisely how high the stakes were for late Sunni traditionalists to defend Abū Ḥanīfa against traditionalist Salafi deprecations. Al-Kawtharī frames the contestations over Abū Ḥanīfa in equally stark fashion. Discussing the dangers of criticising scholars like Abū Ḥanīfa, he writes that critics:[111]

> Declare [early scholars] to be deficient and slander the jurists with accusations of being reckless. [Instead], they should do their utmost to remove the road blocks that separate the Muslims; yet their recklessness is what will lead to grave sin, and will open the door to plotting between the Muslims; setting this course of action in motion is nothing short of inducing the gravity of the verdict of apostasy in an age in which the apostate does not fear His punishment. It is obligatory, therefore, upon the people of knowledge that they guard the entry point of corruption and exert all their effort in fortifying the fences and blocking the gaps [to this danger]. [They must] not construct roads leading to heresy.

For al-Kawtharī, the consequences of traditionalist Salafi slights against Abū Ḥanīfa and the Ḥanafī *madhhab* were by no means trivial. Though his interlocutors regularly assailed him for being a fanatical Ḥanafī, al-Kawtharī's main concerns seem to be anything but tribal and trivial. Al-Kawtharī was aware of how central the theory of great men was to Sunnism. If patron saints like Abū Ḥanīfa continued to be attacked in editions and polemical works, almost any of the great epigones of the Islamic tradition could be subject to similar criticisms. For al-Kawtharī, this insouciance towards medieval Sunnism's orthodox heroes threatened to unravel the achievements of medieval Sunnism. It is this broader concern, expressed here by al-Kawtharī, that we should keep in mind whilst studying his incessant defence of Abū Ḥanīfa in modern editions and post-edition polemics. For late Sunni traditionalists, the contestations over Abū Ḥanīfa were anything but trivial. It required, in this case, late Sunni traditionalists to marshal a wide range of skill and evidence. Of these, the most impressive seems to have been their creative undertaking of the discipline of hadith to counter more or less pervasive views as to Abū Ḥanīfa's lack of expertise in hadith.[112]

In the tradition of their tenth-century intellectual ancestors, late Sunni-Ḥanafī traditionalists showed that they were equally able to engender a creative and dynamic reworking of a hadith-related genre to defend and rehabilitate Abū Ḥanīfa. Al-Kawtharī's plea in the passage above also hints at another explanation for the occasional reduction in anti-Abū Ḥanīfa sentiment. To pose the question directly, why did some traditionalist Salafis shirk from communicating the full range of anti-Abū Ḥanīfa material that figured so prominently in the writings of their intellectual ancestors? Indeed, contestations over Abū Ḥanīfa's religious pedigree were real and animated, but only on some occasions did traditionalist Salafis charge Abū Ḥanīfa with heresy or launch invective upon him in a way that would recall the vitriol of ninth- and tenth-century proto-Sunni traditionalists against Abū Ḥanīfa. Yes, traditionalist Salafis were intensely uncomfortable with the overarching presence of the *madhhab* in the social and religious life of Muslims; they were equally perturbed by the degree of reverence afforded to the eponymous founders of the *madhhab*s. If undermining the authority of the *madhhab*s was a cornerstone of reform projects during the nineteenth and twentieth centuries, and if questioning the revered status of the eponymous founders was an accompanying feature of the Salafi reform enterprise, why, then, did some of them avoid directly engaging anti-Abū Ḥanīfa material as some of their alleged intellectual ancestors had done in the formative period of Islamic history?

The answer, I propose, lies in coming to terms with the salience of collective memory in Islamicate societies. Efforts to pluck out the deep connections that Muslims shared with the *madhhab*s required displacing a core characteristic of the collective memory of Muslims. The task that confronted traditionalist Salafis was not simply to undermine the legitimacy of the *madhhab*s; or to call into question the relevance of medieval formulations of ritual, commercial or criminal law; nor to dispute the genealogy of the *madhhabs* as legitimate carriers of the Prophetic intent, however that might be construed. Rather, the challenge was to disabuse Muslims of a collective memory that, since the late-tenth to early-eleventh centuries, possessed and generated a connective, bonding memory-identity. This process is neatly summarised by the leading theorist of memory studies, Jan Assmann:[113]

> Wherever people join together in larger groups they generate a connective semantics, thereby producing forms of memory that are designed to stabilize a common identity and point of view that span several generations.

Some aspects of this deposit of collective memory were indeed susceptible to the criticisms put forth by Salafi scholars. As a rule of thumb, these tended to be features that attracted the scorn of Muslim scholars in the High Middle Ages, too.[114] The reputation and patron saint status of Abū Ḥanīfa, however, was too firmly entrenched in the collective memory of Muslims to permit a rehearsal of the anti-Abū Ḥanīfa trends that were prominent amongst proto-Sunni traditionalists in the ninth and tenth centuries. It was a feature of the homeostatic edifice of Sunnism that, if jettisoned, might threaten irreparable damage to that homeostatic balance. In many ways, Sunnism prized the great man narrative of history. As such, Abū Ḥanīfa, in spite of the resistance across the ninth-century of certain proto-Sunni traditionalists, had acquired a distinguished role in the collective memory of Muslims. Just as certain memories can be manufactured and refashioned so can others be forgotten and relegated to the margins of history. Perhaps traditionalist Salafis decided that, as useful as a repeat of ninth–tenth century attacks upon Abū Ḥanīfa might have been towards debilitating the grip of the *madhhabs*, attacking Abū Ḥanīfa directly in a spirit akin to the ninth–tenth centuries would do more harm than good to their reformist efforts. Seen in this light, we can appreciate the pragmatism that might have defined the approach of some traditionalist Salafis who, as we have seen in this case study, picked their battles very carefully and sometimes resorted to the art of compromise. In a nod to al-Kawtharī's logic – if Abū Ḥanīfa could become a target, who else might be next – Salafi scholars seem to have satisfied themselves with the understanding that Abū Ḥanīfa was too big to fail.

Conclusion

This chapter has examined a number of contestations between late Sunni traditionalists and traditionalist Salafis over Abū Ḥanīfa's reputation. I have drawn attention to the emergence of a professional class in the twenty-first century that was actively involved in debates about reshaping tradition. They had different and conflicting ideas about the modern legacy of medieval tradition, and they employed the new economy, technology and industry of printing to assert different conceptions of religious tradition in the modern period. Moreover, both late Sunni traditionalists and traditionalist Salafis utilised features of the modern edition to advocate for their particular interpretations of tradition. Introductions, prefaces, footnotes, post-edition polemics, manuals on the craft of editing religious texts were all part of this new enterprise to steer the medieval tradition in different directions. And the *muṣaḥḥiḥūn* and *muḥaqqiqūn* were cognisant of the powerful tripartite relationship between *taḥqīq*, *ṭibāᶜa*, and *turāth*.[115]

The rise of publishing houses and printing presses in the Middle East and Indian subcontinent, and its relevance to understanding the nature of contestations over Abū Ḥanīfa, was an epochal moment in the conversation between modern Islamic movements and scholars and the medieval Islamicate heritage. These scenes of contestations, particularly editions of classical texts, demonstrate a new kind of interpretive agency over the classical tradition. In his influential essay, 'Islam and the impact of print in South Asia', Francis Robinson remarks:[116]

> By printing the Islamic classics ... they undermined their authority; they were no longer necessarily around when the book was read to make up for the absence of the author in the text; their precious *ijazas*, which brought the authority of the past of their learning in the present, were made less significant; their monopoly over the transmission of knowledge was broken. As a consequence, as Akbar Ahmad so often says, no one knows nowadays who speaks for Islam. In fact, the twentieth century has witnessed a steady decline in the authority of the ulema.

Notwithstanding the uncertainty over the connection between the proliferation of print and the decline of *ijāzas*, Robinson's assessment of the impact that printing Islamic classics had on the transmission of knowledge and decline in the authority of the *ulamāᵓ* seems too emphatic. What the printing of Islamic classics did allow for was a different kind of opportunity to exercise authority over medieval texts and debates. And the *ᶜulamāᵓ* utilised this and expanded their professional skills to include the craft of editing and publishing medieval manuscripts.

In a similar vein, some scholars have overlooked the agency of scholars-cum-editors. This approach can reflect a technological determinism reminiscent of earlier scholarship on print and religious reformation in Europe that asserts a simplistic relationship between the printing of early Islamic 'classics' and the 'democratisation' of religious learning. In this view, print culture in the Islamic world allowed the public to access texts directly without such texts being mediated or interpreted.[117] As I have tried to show, this is not entirely accurate. These texts were appropriated, steered and coloured with the ideological biases of editors and publishing houses. The presence of the scholar-cum-editor was, in many cases, overwhelming. Editions of classical texts could often contain an excessive amount of editorial intrusions before and throughout the text, and many times a manuscript containing a dozen or so folios would be transformed into a thick volume on the basis of the editor's interventions in the introduction and footnotes. The monopoly over the transmission of knowledge was not broken, but rather exercised and extended in dramatically significant (and different) ways. Transregional alliances were formed between publishing houses, editors and scholars across the Middle East and Indian subcontinent. Publishing houses in Saudi Arabia, Egypt and the Indian subcontinent encouraged cross-cultural exchanges to enhance their transnational appeal and scholarly credentials.

These are new techniques, but they bear some resemblance to a scholarly tradition that has been out of vogue for decades and was subject to fierce denigration by reformers of different ideological stripes: the medieval commentary tradition. The history of the functions and techniques of medieval commentaries has yet to be written, and there is much work to be done on modern printing, publishing and editing in the Islamic world. Ideally, whoever ends up writing on this should be trained to pursue the *longue durée* study of concepts, practices and techniques in the Islamic tradition.[118] Such a study will yield important insights into competing attempts in the modern period to adjust the medieval Sunni canon.

Notes

1. Versions of this chapter were presented at seminars in Oxford, Princeton and Berlin. The author would like to thank Christopher Melchert, Talal al-Azem and Harry Munt for commenting on earlier drafts of this chapter.
2. Marshall G. S. Hodgson, *The Venture of Islam: Conscience and History in a World Civilization, The Expansion of Islam in the Middle Periods* (Chicago: University of Chicago Press, 1974), 387–91.
3. Hodgson, *The Venture of Islam: Conscience and History in a World Civilization, The Gunpowder Empires and Modern Times* (Chicago: University of Chicago Press, 1974), 176–223; Hodgson, *Rethinking World History: Essays on Europe, Islam, and World History* (Cambridge: Cambridge University Press, 1993), 44–72, 213–24; Kenneth Pomeranz, *The Great Divergence: China, Europe, and the Making of the Modern World Economy* (Princeton: Princeton University Press, 2001); Christopher Bayly, *The Birth of the Modern World 1780–1914. Global Connections and Comparisons* (Oxford: Oxford University Press, 2003); Ian Morris, *Why the West Rules for Now: The Patterns of History and What They Reveal About the Future* (London: Profile Books, 2011). This is a theme that has its origins, of course, in scholarship produced in the second half of the

twentieth century. See Karl Polanyi, *The Great Transformation: The Political and Economic Origins of Our Time* (Boston: Beacon Press, 1957); Norbert Elias, *The Civilizing Process: The History of Manners and State Formation and Civilization* (Oxford; Blackwell, 1982); Patricia Crone, *Pre-Industrial Societies: Anatomy of the Pre-Modern World* (Oxford: Oneworld, 2003), 146–75, although this was first published in 1989; Ernest Gellner, *Sword, Plough, and Book: The Structure of Human History* (Chicago: University of Chicago Press, 1989), esp. 154–70; Alan Macfarlane, *The Origins of English Individualism: The Family, Property, and Social Transition* (Cambridge: Cambridge University Press, 1979); William H. McNeill, *The Pursuit of Power: Technology, Armed Force, and Society since A.D. 1000* (Chicago: University of Chicago Press, 1982); McNeill, *The Rise of the West: A History of the Human Community* (Chicago: Chicago University Press, 1963); Immanuel Wallerstein, *The Modern World-System, vol. 1: Capitalist Agriculture and the Origins of European World-Economy in the Sixteenth Century* (New York: Academic Press, 1974); E. L. Jones, *The European Miracle. Environments, Economies, and Geopolitics in the History of Europe and Asia* (Cambridge: Cambridge University Press, 1981); Krishan Kumar, *Prophecy and Progress: The Sociology of Industrial and Post-Industrial Society* (London: Allen Lane, 1978).

4. Talal Asad, *The Idea of an Anthropology of Islam* (Washington, DC: Center for Contemporary Arab Studies, 1986), 14–17.
5. Fareeha Khan, 'Traditionalist approaches to Sharīᶜah reform: Mawlana Ashraf ᶜAlī Thānawī's fatwa on women's right to divorce', PhD dissertation, University of Michigan, 2008, 20–2; Ovamir Anjum, 'Islamic as a discursive tradition: Talal Asad and his interlocutors', *Comparative Studies of South Asia, Africa and the Middle East*, 27:3 (2007), 656–72; Samira Haj, *Reconfiguring Islamic Tradition: Reform, Rationality, and Modernity* (Stanford: Stanford University Press, 2009), 4–5.
6. Norman Calder, 'Law', in Seyyed Hossein Nasr and Oliver Leaman (eds), *History of Islamic Philosophy*, 2 vols (London: Routledge, 1996), 2: 979–98; Calder, 'The limits of Islamic orthodoxy', in Farhad Daftary (ed.), *Intellectual Traditions in Islam* (London: I. B. Tauris, 2000), 60–86, esp. 84–5.
7. Talal Asad, *The Idea of an Anthropology of Islam*, 14. MacIntyre provides an exceptionally clear account of his conception of tradition in Alisdair MacIntyre, *After Virtue: A Study in Moral Theory* (Notre Dame, IN: University of Notre Dame Press, 2007), 204–225, but esp. 221–5.
8. For examples, see Hodgson, *The Gunpowder Empires*, 134–223, 136, 142, 161, 272, 333–41; Hodgson, *Rethinking*, 204–43. It should be borne in mind that Hogdson's analyses appear in posthumous publications: both *Rethinking World History* and *The Gunpowder Empires* were not subject to the revisions that Hodgson had intended to make. See Hodgson, *The Venture of Islam: Conscience and History in a World Civilization, The Classical Age of Islam* (Chicago: University of Chicago Press, 1974), viii–xi; and Hodgson, *Rethinking*, vii–viii. Given Hodgson's important contribution towards chal-

lenging characterisations of post-Mongol Islamdom as a time of prolonged cultural stagnation, we might well entertain the possibility that Hodgson's revisions would have included a more careful treatment of the Islamic world from the 1700s onwards. See Hodgson, *Conscience and History in a World Civilization*, 372–85. On decline and fall history, see Owen Chadwick, *The Secularization of the European Mind in the Nineteenth Century* (Cambridge: Cambridge University Press, 1975), 3; and Herbert Butterfield, *The Origins of History* (London: Eyre Methuen, 1981), 211–13. It is possible that Hodgson inherited this acutely bleak vision of the Islamic world in the post-1700s from his mentor, Gustave E. von Grunebaum. See von Grunebaum, 'Fall and rise of Islam: a self-view', in von Grunebaum (ed.), *Modern Islam: The Search for Cultural Identity* (Berkeley: University of California Press, 1962), 180–90. Fazlur Rahman, who arrived in Chicago a year after Hodgson's untimely death, also endorsed this decline and fall narrative. See Rahman, *Islam*, 2nd edn (Chicago: University of Chicago Press, 2002), 196–206. By the 1960s, Fernand Braudel had adopted this narrative and, thereby, contributed to its wider dissemination among non-Islamicists. See Fernand Braudel, *A History of Civilizations* (New York: Penguin, 1993), 69–114. Thomas Bauer's searching essay, wherein he connects the tendency to invoke decline and fall models to the field's lack of appreciation for the dynamic nature of post-classical Arabic literature, furnishes an excellent critique of decline narratives with respect to Arabic literature: Thomas Bauer, 'In search of 'post-classical literature': a review article', *Mamluk Studies Review* XI:2 (2007), 137–67, esp. 141. Peter Burke has scrutinised this historiographical trope and identified a six-tier typology of decline and fall models: Burke, 'Tradition and experience: the idea of decline from Bruni to Gibbon', *Daedalus* 105:3 (1976), 137–52. See also Randolph Starn, 'Meaning-levels in the theme of historical decline', *History and Theory* 14:1 (1975), 1–31, esp. 28–31. Recent studies have attempted to push back against the decline paradigm. See Wael Hallaq, *Sharīᶜa: Theory, Practice, Transformations* (Cambridge: Cambridge University Press, 2009), 355–550; Khaled El-Rouayheb, 'Opening the gate of verification: intellectual trends in the 17th century Arab-Islamic world', *Comparative Intellectual Histories of Early Modern Asia*, 43 (2007); El-Rouayheb, 'Was there a revival of logical studies in eighteenth-century Egypt?', *Die Welt Des Islams* 45:1 (2005), 1–19; El-Rouayheb, 'Opening the gate of verification: the forgotten Arab-Islamic florescence of the 17th century', *International Journal of Middle Eastern Studies* 38 (2006), 263–81; Asad Q. Ahmed and Margaret Larkin, 'The Ḥāshiya and Islamic intellectual history', *Oriens* 41 (2013), 213–6; A. Q. Ahmed, 'Post-classical philosophical commentaries/glosses: innovation in the margins', *Oriens* 41 (2013), 317–48, 319. A slightly different, but related, approach is advanced by Jack Goody in two thought-provoking publications: Goody, *Renaissances: The One or the Many* (Cambridge: Cambridge University Press, 2009); Goody, *The Theft of History* (Cambridge: Cambridge University Press, 2012).

9. Hodgson, *Rethinking*, 181. For Hodgson's indebtedness to Max Weber, see Hodgson, *Rethinking*, 179–96.
10. Ibid. 214–31.
11. For example, Edwards Shils' conceptual history of tradition: Shils, *Tradition* (Chicago: University of Chicago Press, 1981). It is a striking fact that modern treatments of the Islamic tradition have ignored the work of Shils, one of the most influential sociologists of the twentieth century.
12. See John O. Voll, 'Muḥammad Ḥayyāt al-Sindī and Muḥammad ibn ᶜAbd al-Wahhāb: an analysis of an intellectual group in eighteenth-century Madina', *Bulletin of the School of Oriental and African Studies*, 38:1 (1974), 32–39; Voll, 'Hadith scholars and Tariqas: an ulama group in the 18th century Haramayn and their impact in the Islamic World', *Journal of Asian and African Studies* 15:3–4 (1980), 264–73; Muhammad Qasim Zaman, *The Ulama in Contemporary Islam: Custodians of Change* (Princeton: Princeton University Press, 2002); Bernard Haykel, *Revival and Reform in Islam: The Legacy of Muḥammad al-Shawkānī* (Cambridge: Cambridge University Press, 2003); Haykel, 'On the nature of Salafi thought and action', in R. Meijer (ed.) *Global Salafism: Islam's New Religious Movement* (London: Hurst, 2009), 33–57; Henri Lauzière, 'The construction of Salafiyya: reconsidering Salafism from the perspective of conceptual history', *International Journal of Middle East Studies* 42:3 (2010), 369–89; Lauzière, 'The evolution of the Salafiyya in the twentieth century through the life and thought of Taqi al-Din al-Hilali', PhD dissertation, Georgetown University, 2008; Basheer Nafi, 'A teacher of Ibn ᶜAbd al-Wahhāb: Muḥammad Ḥayāt al-Sindī and the revival of Aṣḥāb al-Ḥadīth's methodology', *Islamic Law and Society* 13:2 (2006), 208–41; Nafi, 'The rise of Islamist reformist thought and its challenge to traditional Islam', in S. Taji-Farouki and B. Nafi (eds), *Islamic Thought in the Twentieth Century* (London: I. B. Tauris, 2004), 28–60; David Commins, 'Social criticism and reformist Ulama of Damascus', *Studia Islamica* 78 (1993), 169–80; Commins, *Islamic Reform: Politics and Social Change in Late Ottoman Syria* (Oxford: Oxford University Press, 1990); John M. S. Baljon, *Religion and Thought of Shah Wali Allah of Delhi* (Leiden: Brill, 1986); Ahmad Dallal, 'The origins and objectives of Islamic revivalist thought, 1750–1850', *Journal of the American Oriental Society* 113:3 (1993), 341–59; Dallal, 'Appropriating the past: twentieth-century reconstruction of pre-modern Islamic thought', *Islamic Law and Society* 7:3 (2000), 325–58; Reinhard Schulze, 'Das islamische achtzehnte Jahrhundert: Versuch einer historiographischen Kritik', *Die Welt des Islams* 30 (1990), 140–9; Schulze, 'Was ist de islamische Aufklärung?' *Die Welt des Islams* 36:3 (1996), 276–325. Schulze's optimistic account has received wide criticism from scholars. See Gottfried Hagen and Tilman Seidensticker, 'Reinhard Schulzes Hypothese einer islamischen Aufklärung', *Zeitschrift der Deutschen Morgenländischen Gesellschaft* 148 (1998), 83–110; Ruud Peters, 'Reinhard Schulze's quest for an Islamic Enlightenment', *Des Welt des Islams* 30 (1990), 160–2; and most severely, Bernd Radtke, *Authochthone islamische Aufklärung*

im 18. Jahrhundert (Utrecht: Houutsma Stichting, 2000); Michael Cook, 'On the origins of Wahhabism', *Journal of the Royal Asiatic Society* 2:2 (1992), 191–202; Esther Peskes, *Muhammad b. ᶜAbdwahhāb (1703–92) im Widerstreit: Untersuchungen zur Rekonstruktion der Frühgeschichte der Wahhābīya* (Beirut: In Kommission bei Franz Steiner, 1993); Barbara Daly Metcalf, *Islamic Revival in British India: Deoband, 1860–1900* (Princeton: Princeton University Press, 1982); Francis Robinson, *Islam and Muslim History in South Asia* (Oxford: Oxford University Press, 2000); Robinson, *The ᶜUlama of Farangi Mahall and Islamic Culture in South Asia* (London: Hurst, 2001); Jan-Peter Hartung, *Viele Wege und ein Ziel. Leben und Wirken von Sayyid Abu l-Hasan ᶜAli al-Hasani Nadwi (1914–1999)* (Würzburg: Ergon, 2004); Daniel Brown, *Rethinking Tradition in Modern Islamic Thought* (Cambridge: Cambridge University Press, 1996); Yohanan Friedmann, *Shaykh Aḥmad Sirhindī: an outline of his thought and a study of his image in the eyes of posterity* (Montreal: McGill-Queen's University Press, 1971); Rudolph Peters, 'Idjtihād and Taqlīd in 18th and 19th century Islam', *Die Welt des Islams* 20:3–4 (1980), 131–45; Usha Sanyal, *Devotional Islam and Politics in British India: Ahmad Riza Khan Barelwi and His Movement, 1870–1920* (New York: Oxford University Press, 1999); Thomas Bauer, *Die Kultur der Ambiguität. Eine andere Geschichte des Islams* (Berlin: Verlag der Religionen im Insel Verlag, 2011); Konrad Hirschler, 'Pre-eighteenth-century traditions of revivalism: Damascus in the thirteenth century', *Bulletin of the School of Oriental and African Studies* 68:2 (2005), 195–214; Stefan Reichmuth, 'Murtada az-Zabidi (d. 1732–91) in biographical and autobiographical accounts: glimpses of Islamic scholarship in the 18th century', *Die Welt des Islams* 39:1 (1999), 64–102; Nehemia Levtzion and John O. Voll (eds), *Eighteenth-Century Renewal and Reform in Islam* (Syracuse: Syracuse University Press, 1987); Martin Riexinger, *Ṣanāᵓullāh Amritsarī (1868–1948) und die Ahl-i Ḥadīs im Punjab unter britischer Herrschaft* (Wurzburg: n.p., 2004); Butrus Abu-Manneh, 'Salafiyya and the rise of the Khālidiyya in Baghdad in the early nineteenth century', *Die Welt des Islams* 43:3 (2003), 349–72; Thomas Eich, 'The forgotten Salafī – Abū al-Hudā As-Sayyadī', *Die Welt des Islams* 43:1 (2003), 61–87; Claudia Preckel, 'Screening Ṣiddīq Ḥasan Khān's library: the use of Ḥanbalī literature in 19th-century Bhopal' and Martin Riexinger, 'Ibn Taymiyya's worldview and the challenge of modernity: a conflict among the Ahl-i Ḥadīth in British India', in Birgit Krawietz and Georges Tamer (eds), *Islamic Theology, Philosophy, and Law: Debating Ibn Taymiyya and Ibn Qayyim al-Jawziyya* (Berlin: Walter de Gruyter, 2013), 162–219 and 493–517. See also Preckel's very comprehensive dissertation on the life and thought of Ṣiddīq Ḥasan Khan: Preckel, 'Islamische Bildungnetzwerke und Gelehrtenkultur im Indien des 19. Jahrhunderts. Muḥammad Ṣiddīq Ḥasan Ḫān (st. 1890) und die Entstehung der Ahl-e ḥadīth-Bewegung in Bhopal', PhD dissertation, Ruhr Universität Bochum, 2005.

13. Besides hadith, law and theology, an antipathy towards Sufism is another important feature of reformist tendencies. However, only the first three are relevant

to our appraisal of modern contestations over Abū Ḥanīfa, and, for this reason, I have omitted mention of Sufism. For a thorough treatment of this subject, see Itzchak Weismann, *Taste of Modernity: Sufism, Salafiyya, and Arabism in Late Ottoman Damascus* (Leiden: Brill, 2001). It seems to me that the relationship between Islamic reform and Sufism is more complicated. Consider the case of al-Qāsimī, often described as an Islamic reformer, but whose relationship with Akbarī Sufism certainly brings into question the notion of a hostile reception of Sufism by Islamic reformers. I am indebted to Norman Calder's insightful discussion of the concept of polyvalence in the Islamic tradition: Calder, 'Tafṣīr from Ṭabarī to Ibn Kathīr: problems in the description of a genre, illustrated with reference to the story of Abraham', in Gerald Hawting and Abdul-Kader A. Shareef (eds), *Approaches to the Qurʾān* (Oxford: Routledge, 1993), 101–40, esp. 103–4; Calder, 'Law', 2: 979–98; Calder, *Islamic Jurisprudence in the Classical Era* (Cambridge: Cambridge University Press, 2010), 74–115, esp. 115; Calder, 'The limits of Islamic orthodoxy', 60–86.

14. Muḥammad Jamāl al-Dīn al-Qāsimī, *Qawāʾid al-taḥdīth min funūn muṣṭalaḥ al-ḥadīth*, ed. Muḥammad Bahjat al-Bīṭār, 2nd edn (Damascus: Dār Iḥyāʾ al-Kutub al-ʿArabiyya, 1961), 330–57, esp. 344–5; Shāh Walī Allāh al-Dihlawī, *al-Inṣāf fī bayān asbāb al-ikhtilāf*, ed. ʿAbd al-Fattāḥ Abū Ghudda (Beirut: Dār al-Nafāʾis, 1997), 94–8; Muḥammad Ḥayāt al-Sindī, *al-Īqāf ʿalā sabab al-ikhtilāf*, ed. Abī Humām Muḥammad b. ʿAlī al-Ṣūmaʿī al-Bayḍānī (Beirut: Dār al-Istiqāma, 2013), 105–42, esp. 141. In *Tuḥfat al-anām fī-l-ʿamal bi-l-ḥadīth al-nabī ʿalay-hi al-ṣalāt al-salām*, ed. Abū ʿAlī Ṭāha Bū Surīḥ (Beirut: Dār Ibn Ḥazm, 1993), 31, Muḥammad Ḥayāt al-Sindī suggests that partisan *madhhab*ism was the cause for the subjugation of the Muslims by the Crusaders and the Mongols. On Muḥammad Ḥayāt al-Sindī's life and legacy, see ʿAbd al-Ḥayy b. ʿAbd al-Kabīr al-Kattānī, *Fihras al-fahāris wa-l-athbāt wa-muʿjam al-maʿājim wa-l-mashīkhāt wa-musalsalāt*, ed. Iḥsān ʿAbbās (Beirut: Dār al-Gharb al-Islāmī, 1982), i: 356–7; Siddīq Ḥasan Khān, *Ithāf al-nubalāʾ al-muttaqīn bi-Iḥyāʾ al-fuqahāʾ al-muḥaddithīn* (Kanpur: Maṭbaʿ Niẓamī, 1871), 2: 403–4; Ṣiddīq Ḥasan Khān, *Abjad al-ʿulūm* (Beirut: Dār al-Kutub al-ʿIlmiyya, 1999), 3: 138–9; ʿAbd al-Ḥayy al-Ḥasanī al-Nadwī, *Nuzhat al-khawāṭir wa-bahjat al-masāmiʿ wa-l-nawāẓir* (Rāʾī Bareylī: Dār ʿArafāt, 1991), 6: 309–10; Ṣāliḥ b. Muḥammad al-ʿUmarī al-Fulānī, *Īqāẓ himam ulī al-abṣār li-l-iqtidāʾ bi-Sayyid al-muhājirīn wa-l-anṣār*, ed. Abī ʿImād al-Sakhāwī (Sharjah: Dār al-Fatḥ, 1997), 192. For Western scholarship on al-Sindī, see Nafi, 'A teacher of Ibn ʿAbd al-Wahhāb: Muḥammad Ḥayāt al-Sindī', 208–41; on Shāh Walī Allāh, see Marcia Hermansen's introduction to Shāh Walī Allāh, *The Conclusive Argument from God: Shāh Walī Allāh of Delhi's Ḥujjat Allāh al-Bāligha*, trans. Marcia K. Hermansen (Leiden: Brill, 1995); John Baljon's treatment in Baljon, *Religion and Thought of Shāh Walī Allāh*, 166–70; and Saiyid Athar Abbas Rizvī, *Shāh Walī-Allāh and His Times: A Study of Eighteenth Century Islām, Politics and Society in India* (Canberra: Maʿrifat Publishing House, 1980).
15. On al-Qāsimī, see the following: Commins, *Islamic Reform*, 45–6, 65–88;

Mun'im Sirry, 'Jamāl al-Dīn al-Qāsimī and the Salafi approach to Sufism', *Die Welt des Islams* 51 (2011), 75–108; Ẓāfir al-Qāsimī, *Jamāl al-Dīn al-Qāsimī wa-ʿaṣruhu* (Damascus: Maṭbaʿat al-Ḥāshimiyya, 1965).

16. Al-Qāsimī, *Qawāʾid al-taḥdīth*, 60.
17. These have been studied in the author's DPhil dissertation: Ahmad Khan, 'Heresy and the formation of medieval Sunnī orthdoxy: making and unmaking heretics', DPhil dissertation, University of Oxford, 2016. See Muḥammad b. Ismāʿīl al-Bukhārī, *al-Tārīkh al-kabīr*, 4 vols in 8 (Hyderabad: Maṭbaʿat Jamʿiyyat Dāʾirat al-Maʿārif al-ʿUthmāniyya, 1943), 4.2: 81; al-Bukhārī, *al-Tārīkh al-kabīr*, 2.4: 397; al-Bukhārī, *Kitāb al-Mukhtaṣar min tārīkh hijrat Rasūl Allāh wa-l-muhājirīn wa-l-anṣār wa-ṭabaqāt al-tābiʿīn bi-iḥsān wa-man baʿda-hum wa-wafāti-him wa-baʿḍ nasabi-him wa-kunā-hum, wa-man yurghabu ʿan ḥadīthi-hi al-mashhūr bi-l-tārīkh al-awsaṭ*, ed. Taysīr ibn Saʿd Abū Ḥaymad (Riyadh: Maktabat al-Rushd, 2005), 3: 382–3; al-Bukhārī, *al-Awsaṭ*, 3: 503; al-Bukhārī, *Kitāb Rafʿ al-yadayn fī-l-ṣalāt*, ed. Badī al-Dīn al-Rāshidī (Beirut: Dār Ibn Ḥazm, 1996), 17–18 and taken up again at 107; Ibn Ḥibbān, *Kitāb al-thiqāt* (Hyderabad: Maṭbaʿat Majlis Dāʾirat al-Maʿārif al-ʿUthmāniyya, 1981), 7: 645–6; Ibn Ḥibbān, *al-Majrūḥīn min al-muḥaddithīn wa-l-ḍuʿafāʾ wa-l-matrūkīn*, ed. Maḥmūd Ibrāhīm Zāyid (Ḥalab: Dār al-Waʿī, 1976), 3: 61–73; Ibn ʿAdī, *al-Kāmil fī ḍuʿafāʾ al-rijāl*, 7 vols (Beirut: Dār al-Fikr, 1984), 7: 2476.
18. This polemical technique has been analysed with respect to debates over political quietism among Salafis by Johannes J. G. Jansen, 'The early Islamic movement of the Kharidjites and modern Moslem extremism: similarities and differences', *Orient: Deutsche Zeitschrift für den moderner Orient* 27:1 (1986), 127–35; Daniel Lav, *Radical Islam and the Revival of Medieval Theology* (Cambridge: Cambridge University Press, 2012), ch. 1, 3 and 4; and Joas Wagemakers, '"Seceders" and "Postponers"? An analysis of the "Khawarij" and "Murjiʾa" labels in polemical debates between Quietist and Jihadi Salafis', in Jeevan Deol and Zaheer Kazmi (eds), *Contextualising Jihadi Thought* (New York: Columbia University Press, 2011), 145–65. On al-Ḥawālī, see Zaman, *The Ulama in Contemporary Islam*, 155–9.
19. I should point out that these preoccupations were not exclusive to traditionalist Salafis, and late Sunni traditionalists took them up, too, as I demonstrate later in this chapter.
20. For the complex relationship between these Egyptian reformers and traditionalist Salafism, see Dallal, 'Appropriating the past,' and Lauzière, 'The construction of Salafiyya'. The standard accounts for what some have termed 'Modernist Salafism' are: Malcolm Kerr, *Islamic Reform: The Political and Legal Theories of Muhammad ʿAbduh and Rashid Rida* (Berkeley: University of California Press, 1966); Aziz Ahmad, *Islamic Modernism in India and Pakistan, 1857–1964* (London: Oxford University Press, 1967). See also Aziz Al-Azmeh's piercing analysis of Islamic modernism in the Arab world in Al-Azmeh, *Islams and Modernities*, 2nd edn (London: Verso, 1996), 80–127.

21. Very little scholarship exists on traditionalist Salafism and, for many of the Salafi scholars under discussion in this chapter, no secondary scholarship is available, as far as I am aware. The following works discuss different aspects of contemporary traditionalist Salafism: Haykel, 'On the nature of Salafi thought and action'; Lauzière, 'The evolution of the Salafiyya'; Thomas Hegghammer, 'Violent Islamism in Saudi Arabia, 1979–2006', PhD dissertation, Institut d'Etudes Politiques de Paris, 2007; Stéphane Lacroix, *Awakening Islam: The Politics of Religious Dissent in Contemporary Saudi Arabia* (Harvard: Harvard University Press, 2011), 81–9; Lacroix, 'Between revolution and apoliticism: Nasir al-Din al-Albani and his impact on the shaping of contemporary Salafism', in Meijer (ed.), *Global Salafism*, 58–81; Jonathan A. C. Brown, *Hadith: Muhammad's Legacy in the Medieval and Modern World* (Oxford: Oneworld, 2009), 256–61; Brown, *The Canonization of al-Bukhārī and Muslim: The Formation and Function of the Sunnī Ḥadīth Canon* (Leiden: Brill, 2007), 309–34; Kamaruddin Amin, 'Nāṣiruddīn al-Albānī on Muslim's Ṣaḥīḥ: a critical study of his method', *Islamic Law and Society* 11:2 (2004), 149–76. M. Q. Zaman's *Modern Islamic Thought in a Radical Age: Religious Authority and Internal Criticism* (Cambridge: Cambridge University Press, 2012) provides an important window onto twentieth-century developments, but neither traditionalist Salafis nor late Sunni traditionalists are the focus of his study.
22. Muḥammad b. Ismāᶜīl al-Ṣanᶜānī, *Kitāb īqāẓ al-fikra li-murājaᶜat al-fiṭra*, ed. Muḥammad Ṣubḥī b. Ḥasan al-Ḥallāq (Beirut: Dār Ibn Ḥazm, 1999), 52; Ibn al-ᶜIzz, *Sharḥ ᶜAqīdat al-Ṭaḥāwī*, eds Muḥammad Nāṣir al-Dīn al-Albānī and Zuhayr al-Shāwīsh (Beirut: al-Maktab al-Islāmī, 2006), 26–62.
23. Late Sunni traditionalism is a very green field of study in modern scholarship. See Brown, *Hadith*, 261–5; Zaman, *The Ulama in Contemporary Islam*, 38–59.
24. Metcalf, *Islamic Revival*, 268–96.
25. Al-Kawtharī's and Abū Ghudda's relationship with scholarly networks in the Indian subcontinent was extremely significant. Saud al-Sarhan has informed me that he has just published an edition of Muḥammad Zāhid al-Kawtharī's correspondences with Muḥammad Yūsuf al-Banūrī (d. 1977), which I have not been able to consult: Muḥammad Zāhid al-Kawtharī, *Rasāʾil al-imām Muḥammad Zāhid al-Kawtharī ilā al-ᶜallāma Muḥammad Yūsuf al-Binnūrī*, ed. Saᶜūd al-Sarḥān (Saudi Arabia: Dār al-Fatḥ li-l-Dirāsāt wa-l-Nashr, 2013). For now, see Muḥammad Yūsuf al-Banūrī's encomium to al-Kawtharī in al-Kawtharī, *Maqālāt al-Kawtharī* (Cairo: Maktabat al-Tawfīqiyya, n.d.), 3–13. Abū Ghudda's role in importing ideas, texts and debates from Indian subcontinent scholarship into the Middle East seems to me the most prominent and understudied example of this phenomenon. For Abū Ghudda's relationship with late Sunni traditionalists in the Indian subcontinent, see Muḥammad b. ᶜAbd Allāh al-Rashīd, *Imdād al-fattāḥ bi-asānīd wa-marwiyyāt al-shaykh ᶜAbd al-Fattāḥ* (Riyadh: Maktabat al-Imām al-Shāfiᶜī, 1999), 34–55, 59 and 60–2. Zaman has highlighted the role of the Nadwat al-ᶜUlamāʾ in Lucknow in

bridging the gap between scholarship in the Indian subcontinent and the Arab world. Zaman, *Modern Islamic Thought in a Radical Age*, 4–5.

26. For specific socio-legal case studies of where an indigenous Ḥanafism became the target of reformist opposition, see Zaman, *Modern Islamic Thought in a Radical Age*, ch. 6 and 7; Zaman, *The Ulama in Contemporary Islam*, ch. 1; F. Khan, 'Traditionalist approaches to Sharīᶜah reform'.
27. Brown, *Hadith*, 262, 264.
28. Gautier Juynboll's early works addressed this gap in scholarship: G. H. A. Juybnoll, *The Authenticity of the Tradition Literature: Discussions in Modern Egypt* (Leiden: Brill, 1969) and Juynboll, 'Aḥmad Muḥammad Shākir [1892–1958] and his edition of Ibn Ḥanbal's *Musnad*', *Der Islam* XLIX (1972), 221–47.
29. The relationship between print and the 'Arab Renaissance' (*nahḍa*) has received considerable attention: see Ami Ayalon, *Reading Palestine: Printing and Literacy, 1900–1948* (Austin: University of Texas Press, 2004), esp. ch. 2 and 3; Robin Ostle, 'The Printing press and the renaissance of modern Arabic literature', *Culture and History* 16 (1997), 145–57; for the most recent contribution to this field, see Hala Auji, 'Between script and print: exploring publications of the American Syria Mission and the Nascent Press in the Arab world, 1834–1860', PhD dissertation, Binghamton University State University of New York, 2013. Lauzière has tracked the influence of Salafi journals in the twentieth century, 'The construction of Salafiyya', 376–81. See also Zaman, 'Commentaries, print, and patronage: Ḥadīth and the Madrasas in modern South Asia', *Bulletin of the School of Oriental and African Studies* 62:1 (1999), 60–81. Scholars have pursued some important lines of inquiry outside the scope of our investigation into how modern scholars came to interact with printing presses and publishing houses. For this body of literature, see Francis Robinson, 'Technology and religious change: Islam and the impact of print', *Modern Asian Studies* 27 (1993), 229–51; R. Schulze, 'Mass culture and Islamic cultural production in 19th-century Middle East', in George Stauth and Sami Zubaida (eds), *Mass Culture, Popular Culture, and Social Life in the Middle East* (Frankfurt am Main: Campus Verlag, 1987), 194–202; Schulze, 'The birth of tradition and modernity in 18th- and 19th-century Islamic culture: the case of printing', 29–71; Geoffrey Roper, 'Arabic printing in Malta 1825–1845: its history and its place in the development of print culture in the Arab Middle East', PhD dissertation, University of Durham, 1988; Roper, 'The printing press and change in the Arabic world', in Sabrina Alcorn Baron, Eric N. Lindquist and Eleanor F. Shevlin (eds), *Agent of Change: Print Culture Studies After Elizabeth L. Eisenstein* (Massachusetts: University of Massachusetts Press, 2007), 250–67; Jakob Skovgaard-Petersen, *Defining Islam for the Egyptian State: Muftis and Fatwas of the Dār al-Iftā* (Leiden: Brill, 1997); Metcalf, *Islamic revival*, 198–215, though she does not consider the significance of editors and editions; Brinkley Messick, *The Calligraphic State: Textual Domination and History in a Muslim Society* (Berkeley: University of

California Press, 1993), 115–31; Adeeb Khalid, 'Printing, publishing, and reform in Tsarist Central Asia', *International Journal of Middle East Studies* 26 (1994), 187–200; Muhsin Mahdi, 'From the Manuscript Age to the Age of Printed Books', in George N. Atiyeh (ed.), *The Book in the Islamic World: The Written Word and Communication in the Middle East* (Albany: State University of New York Press, 1995), 1–15, which shares Robinson's insistence on the adverse impact of the printing press upon the religious authority of the *ᶜulamāᵓ*; Nile Green, 'Journeymen, middlemen: travel, transculture, and technology in the origins of the Muslim printing', *International Journal of Middle Eastern Studies* 41 (2009), 203–24; James Clyde Allen Redman, 'The evolution of Ottoman printing technologies: from scribal authority to print-capitalism', in Seyfi Kenan (ed.), *The Ottomans and Europe: Travel, Encounter, and Interaction: from the Early Classical Period until the End of the 18th Century* (Istanbul: ISAM, 2010), 495–512. Arabophone scholarship has been more diligent in tracing the history of publishing. See ᶜĀᵓida Ibrāhīm Nuṣayr, *Ḥarakat nashr al-kutub fī Miṣr fī-l-qarn al-tāsiᶜ ᶜashar* (Cairo: al-Hayᵓa al-Miṣriyya al-ᶜĀmma li-l-Kutub, 1994); Abū al-Futūḥ Muḥammad al-Riḍwān, *Tārīkh maṭbaᶜat Būlāq* (Cairo: al-Maṭbaᶜa al-ᶜĀmiriyya, 1953); Khalīl Ṣābāt, *Tārīkh al-ṭibāᶜa fī al-Sharq al-ᶜArabī* (Cairo: Dār al-Maᶜārif, 1958); Bihnām Faḍīl ᶜAffāṣ, *Tārīkh al-ṭibāᶜa wa-l-maṭbūᶜāt al-ᶜIrāqiyya* (Baghdad: Maṭbaᶜat al-Adīb al-Baghdādiyya, 1992). For more on the publications of the Būlāq Press, see N. Verdery, 'The publication of the Būlāq Press under Muḥammad ᶜAlī of Egypt', *Journal of the American Oriental Society* 91 (1971), 129–32.

30. I am not aware of any secondary scholarship on this publishing house. Some information is available in al-Albānī (ed.), *Sharḥ*, 62.
31. Reinhard Schulze, 'The birth of tradition and modernity in 18th- and 19th-century Islamic culture: the case of printing', *Culture & History* 16 (1997), 29–71.
32. Elizabeth L. Eisenstein, *The Printing Press as an Agent of Change: Communications and Cultural Transformations in early-modern Europe, Vols I and II* (Cambridge: Cambridge University Press, 1979), 3–43, 1834. On Eisenstein's thesis, see Baron *et al.*, *Agent of Change.*
33. For example, see al-Kawtharī's edition of Ibn Qutayba, *al-Ikhtilāf fī-l-lafẓ wa-l-radd ᶜalā al-jahmiyya wa-l-mushabbaha*, ed. Muḥammad Zāhid al-Kawtharī (Cairo: al-Maktaba al-Azhariyya li-l-Turāth, 2001).
34. This can be gleaned from the frequency with which scholars from both camps would accuse each other of violating the scholarly integrity (*ikhlāl li-l-amāna al-ᶜilmiyya*) that was demanded of them. Accusations of tampering with and distorting medieval texts were never distant. Bakr Abū Zayd's *al-Rudūd* serves as an excellent illustration of this. His treatise, *Taḥrīf al-nuṣūṣ*, opens with this description of the scholarly transgressions that characterise al-Kawtharī's and Abū Ghudda's works: '*ikhḍāᶜ al-nuṣūṣ wa-ḍaghṭu-hā li-l-muᶜtaqadāt al-bāṭila wa-l-madhāhib al-fāsida wa-l-ārāᵓ al-shādhdha, faḍlan ᶜan taᵓwīlāt al-bāṭiniyya al-fajja al-kāfira … wa-jināyati-him ᶜalāᵓ al-nuṣūṣ … taḥrīf mabānī-hā bi-l-*

ziyāda wa-l-naqṣ wa-l-taḥwīr wa-l-talfīq.' See Bakr Abū Zayd, *al-Rudūd* (Riyadh: Dār al-ᶜĀṣima, 1993), 177, 191–7.

35. For disputes over its attribution, see al-Albānī (ed.), *Sharḥ*, 21–2, 38; Abū Ghudda, *Kalimāt fī kashf abāṭīl wa-iftirāʾāt* (Ḥalab: Maktab al-Maṭbūᶜāt al-Islāmiyya, 1394), 11–13. On al-Albānī, see Muḥammad ᶜĪd ᶜAbbāsī, *Fatāwā al-shaykh al-Albānī wa-muqāranatu-hā fī fatāwā al-ᶜulamāʾ*, 1st edn (Cairo: Maktabat al-Turāth al-Islāmī, 2002), 2: 3–20; Muḥammad Ibrāhīm al-Shaybānī, *Ḥayāt al-Albānī wa-āthāru-hu wa-thanāʾ al-ᶜulamāʾ ᶜalay-hi* (n.p.: Maktabat al-Sadāwī, 1987); and the recently published *Festschrift*: Abū Usāma Salīm b. ᶜĪd al-Hilālī, *al-Imām al-Albānī: Shaykh al-Islām wa-imām ahl al-sunna wa-l-jamāᶜa fī ᶜuyūn al-aᶜlām al-ᶜulamāʾ wa-fuḥūl al-udabāʾ* (Cairo: Dār al-Imām Aḥmad, 2012); and Christopher Melchert's chapter in this volume on al-Albānī.
36. Christopher Melchert, *The Formation of the Sunnī Schools of Law, 9th–10th Centuries* C.E. (Leiden: Brill, 1997), 116–23.
37. On proto-Sunni traditionalists, see Eerik Dickinson, *The Development of Early Sunnite Hadith Criticism: the Taqdima of Ibn Abī Ḥātim al-Rāzī (240/854–327/938)* (Leiden: Brill, 2001); Melchert, *The Formation of the Sunni Schools of Law*; Melchert, 'Traditionist-jurisprudents and the framing of Islamic law', *Islamic Law and Society* 8:3 (2001), 383–406; Scott Lucas, *Constructive Critics, Hadith Literature, and the Articulation of Sunni Islam: the Legacy of the Generation of Ibn Saᶜd, Ibn Maᶜīn, and Ibn Ḥanbal* (Leiden: Brill, 2004); Zaman, *Religion and Politics under the Early Abbasids: the Emergence of the proto-Sunni Elite* (Leiden: Brill, 1997).
38. Al-Ṭaḥāwī, *al-ᶜAqīda al-Ṭaḥāwiyya* (Riyadh: Maktabat Dār Ṭabariyya, 1995). Al-Ṭaḥāwī has another short creed, entitled *Fuṣūl fī uṣūl al-dīn*, ms. Princeton, Arabic, Third Series, 288.
39. On this association, see Daniel Gimaret, *Dieu à l'image de l'homme: les anthropomorphismes de la sunna et leur interprétation par les théologiens* (Paris: Patrimoines, 1997); Melchert, *Ahmad ibn Hanbal* (Oxford: Oneworld, 2006), ch. 4; Wesley Williams, 'Aspects of the creed of Imam Ahmed ibn Hanbal: a study of anthropomorphism in early Islamic discourse', *International Journal of Middle Eastern Studies* 34 (2002), 441–63; Josef van Ess, *Theologie und Gesellschaft im 2. und 3. Jahrhundert Hidschra. Eine Geschichte des religiosen Denkens im frühen Islam*, 6 vols (Berlin: Walter de Gruyter, 1991–5), III: 142–7; Saud al-Sarhan, 'Early Muslim traditionalism: a critical study of the works and political theology of Aḥmad Ibn Ḥanbal', PhD dissertation, University of Exeter, 2011, 32–8.
40. For al-Albānī's attack on the methodology of late Sunni traditionalists, see al-Albānī (ed.), *Sharḥ*, 45–6; for his characterisation of late Sunni traditionalists and their Ḥanafī antecedents as being opposed to the *aʾimmat al-ḥadīth*, see al-Albānī (ed.), *Sharḥ*, 45.
41. Al-Albānī (ed.), *Sharḥ*, 52: '*Zāhid al-Kawtharī alladhī kāna – wa-l-ḥaqq an yuqāl – ᶜalā ḥaẓẓ wāfir min ᶜilm al-ḥadīth wa-rijāli-hi wa-lākinna-hu, maᶜa-l-*

asaf, kāna ᶜilmu-hu ḥujjatan ᶜalay-hi wa-wabālan. Li-anna-hu lam yazdud bi-hi hudan wa-nūran, lā fī-l-furūᶜ wa-lā fī-l-ᶜuṣūl, fa-huwa jahmī muᶜaṭṭal, ḥanafī hālik fī-l-taᶜaṣṣub.' On Jahm b. Ṣafwān, see van Ess, *Theologie und Gesellschaft*, II: 493–506; on Jahm b. Ṣafwān and Abū Ḥanīfa, see Khan, 'Heresy and the formation of medieval Sunnī orthodoxy', 54–6 and al-Bukhārī, *al-Awsaṭ*, 2: 37. On the Jahmiyya, see van Ess, *Theologie und Gesellschaft*, II: 700–2.

42. Al-Albānī (ed.), *Sharḥ*, 52.
43. Ibid. 44–6.
44. Ibid. 49–50. On the *masānīd* of Abū Ḥanīfa, see Abū al-Muᵓayyad al-Khwārizmī, *Jāmiᶜ masānīd al-imām al-aᶜẓam* (Hyderabad: Dāᵓirat al-Maᶜārif, 1913), 4–6; Khan, 'Heresy and the formation of medieval Sunnī orthodoxy', 95–104; Kātib Çelebī, *Kashf al-ẓunūn ᶜan asāmī al-kutub wa-l-funūn*, eds Şerefettin Yaltkaya and Rifat Bilge (Istanbul: Maarif Matbasi, 1941), 2: 1680–2; Fuat Sezgin, *Geschichte des arabischen Schrifttums* (Leiden: Brill, 1967), i: 414–6; Sezgin's record must be supplemented with the following manuscripts located at Dār al-Kutub al-Ẓāhiriyya manuscript library, for which see al-Albānī, *Fihras makhṭūṭāt dār al-kutub al-ẓāhiriyya: al-muntakhab min makhṭūṭāt al-ḥadīth* (Riyadh: Maktabat al-Maᶜārif li-l-nashr wa-l-tawzīᶜ, 2001), 169–70 for Abū ᶜAbd Allāh Muḥammad b. Isḥāq Ibn Manda (d. 1005), *Qawl al-thiqāt fī Abī Ḥanīfa wa-shihādati-him ᶜalay-hi wa-l-kashf ᶜan masāwī-hi*; 103 for Yūsuf b. Ḥasan b. Aḥmad Jamāl al-Dīn al-Ṣāliḥī al-Ḥanbalī (d. 1503), *al-Arbaᶜīn al-mukhtāra min ḥadīth al-imām Abī Ḥanīfa*; 76–7 for ᶜAfīf al-Dīn Abū al-Maᶜālī ᶜAlī b. ᶜAbd al-Ḥasan al-Baghdādī al-Shāmī (d. 1454), *Sittūn ḥadīth ᶜan Abī Ḥanīfa*; 38 and 404 for ᶜAbd Allāh b. Muḥammad b. Aḥmad b. Yaḥyā b. al-Hārith Abū al-Qāsim al-Saᶜdī (d. 946), *Faḍāᵓil al-imām Abī Hanīfa wa-akhbāru-hu wa-manāqibu-hu*; al-Kattānī, *Fihras al-fahāris*, I: 99, 473, II: 721, 972, 990, 1091; ᶜAbd Allāh Muḥammad al-Ḥibshī, *Jāmiᶜ al-shurūḥ wa-l-ḥawāshī: muᶜjam shāmil li-asmāᵓ al-kutub al-mashrūḥa fī-l-turāth al-Islāmī wa-bayān shurūḥi-hā*, 3rd edn (Abu Dhabi: al-Majmaᶜ al-Thaqāfī, 2004), 3: 1980–2.
45. Muḥammad Zāhid al-Kawtharī, *al-Ḥāwī fī sīrat al-imām Abī Jaᶜfar al-Ṭaḥāwī* (Cairo: al-Maktaba al-Azhariyya li-l-Turāth, 1995), 38–9. The book was authored in 1948.
46. Al-Kawtharī, *Taᵓnīb al-Khaṭīb ᶜalā mā sāqa-hu fī tarjamat Abī Ḥanīfa min al-akādhīb* (Beirut: n.p., 1990), 28–30. These controversies are omitted in the most recent edition of al-Khaṭīb's history. The editor does quip, however, that whatever exchange took place between al-Kawtharī and al-Muᶜallimī al-Yamānī was completely unbefitting of the community of scholars. See al-Khaṭīb, *Tārīkh Baghdād*, ed. Bashshār ᶜAwwād Maᶜrūf (Beirut: Dār al-Gharb al-Islāmī, 2001), 15: 444–5. I have written about the medieval and modern reception of al-Khaṭīb al-Baghdādī's *Tārīkh Baghdād*, forthcoming as a journal article: 'Publish or perish: the publication history of al-Khaṭīb al-Baghdādī's *Tārīkh Baghdād* and technologies of reform in the twentieth century.'

47. Khayr al-Dīn al-Ziriklī, *al-A^clām qāmūs tarājim li-ashhar al-rijāl wa-l-nisā^ᵓ min al-^carab wa-l-musta^cribīn wa-l-mustashriqīn*, 15th edn (Beirut: Dār al-^cIlm li-l-Malayīn, 2002), 6: 44. See also Maḥmūd Muḥammad al-Ṭanāḥī, *Madkhal ilā tārīkh nashr al-turāth al-^carabī ma^c muḥāḍara ^can al-taṣḥīf wa-l-taḥrīf* (Cairo: Maktabat al-Khānjī, 1984), 59–62, where al-Ṭanāḥī describes al-Khānjī's publishing and editing activities.
48. *Kitāb al-Radd ^calā Abī Bakr al-Khaṭīb al-Baghdādī* (Cairo: n.p., 1932). See Sezgin, *Geschichte des arabischen Schrifttums*, i: 411; Ibn Quṭlūbughā, *Tāj al-tarājim*, ed. Muḥammad Khayr Ramaḍān Yūsuf (Damascus: Dār al-Qalam, 1992), 225–6. Ibn Quṭlūbughā prefers the attribution of this work to Hunād b. Ibrāhīm al-Nasafī. See Ibn Quṭlūbughā, *Tāj al-tarājim*, 226 and 314. On Hunād b. Ibrāhīm, see Abū Ghudda, *al-^cUlamā^ᵓ al-^cuzzāb alladhīna ātharū al-^cilm ^calā al-zawāj* (Ḥalab: Maktab al-Maṭbū^cāt al-Islāmiyya, 1982), 36–51.
49. Muḥammad Ḥāmid al-Fiqī was an instrumental Salafi scholar of the twentieth century. A founding member of Anṣār al-Sunna al-Muḥammadiyya, al-Fiqī and his organisation attracted some of the most talented Salafi scholars. As with most of the Salafi scholars examined in this article, there is often little to no published material detailing their careers. I have been able to consult Muwaffaq b. ^cAbd Allāh ^cAlī, 'Juhūd al-shaykh Muḥammad Ḥāmid al-Fiqī fī nashr al-^caqīdat al-salafiyya', MA. dissertation, Umm al-Qurā University, Saudi Arabia, 2002. On Anṣār al-Sunna al-Muḥammadiyya, see Aḥmad Muḥammad Ṭāhir ^cUmar, 'Jamā^cat anṣār al-sunna al-muḥammadiyya wa-juhūdu-hā fī nashr ^caqīdat al-salaf', PhD dissertation, Umm al-Qurā University, Saudi Arabia, 2001. The dissertation is disappointing in the lack of detail it furnishes, but it is the only secondary source I am aware of wholly devoted to the organisation. See Aḥmad Muḥammad Ṭāhir ^cUmar, 'Jamā^cat anṣār al-sunna al-muḥammadiyya', 55–78 and 94–107 for an overview of the history of its establishment, and 106–7 for a succint summary of its publication wing, Maṭba^cat al-Sunna al-Muḥammadiyya. Al-Ṭanāḥī devotes a page to al-Fiqī's contributions as an editor and publisher in al-Ṭanāḥī, *Madkhal ilā tārīkh nashr al-turāth al-^carabī*, 69–70.
50. Al-Kawthari, *Ta^ᵓnīb al-Khaṭīb*, 28–30.
51. Ibid. 1–27.
52. See Fedwa Malti Douglas, 'Controversy and its effects in the biographical tradition of al-Khaṭīb Al-Baghdādī', *Studia Islamica* 46 (1997), 115–31, esp. 121. Despite this tension, as the author of two seminal monographs celebrating the achievements of the *aṣḥāb al-ḥadīth* and other works profiling the science of hadith, al-Khaṭīb was a figure worth laying claim to for Salafis. The two mongraphs are: al-Khaṭīb, *Sharaf aṣḥāb al-ḥadīth*, ed. Mehmet Saîd Khaṭīboğlu (Ankara: Maṭba^cat Jāmi^cāt Ankara, 1971) and al-Khaṭīb, *Naṣīḥat ahl al-ḥadīth*, ed. ^cAbd al-Karīm Aḥmad Warīkāt (Jordan: Maktabat al-Manār, 1988). Among his many works on the science of hadith are al-Khaṭīb, *al-Jāmi^c li-akhlāq al-rāwī wa-adāb al-sāmi^c*, ed. Maḥmūd Ṭaḥḥān (Riyadh: Maktabat

al-Maᶜārif, 1983); al-Khaṭīb, *Kitāb al-kifāya fī ᶜilm al-riwāya* (Beirut: Dār al-Kutub al-ᶜIlmiyya, 1988).

53. ᶜAbd al-Raḥmān b. Yaḥyā al-Muᶜallimī al-Yamānī, *al-Tankīl bi-mā fī taᵓnīb al-Kawtharī min al-abāṭīl* (Riyadh: Maktabat al-Maᶜārif, 1985), 1–2.
54. Al-Muᶜallimī al-Yamānī, *al-Tankīl*, 246–7.
55. On al-Kawtharī, see Khayr al-Dīn al-Ziriklī, *al-Aᶜlām*, 6: 129.
56. Ibn Abī Shayba, *al-Muṣannaf fi-l-aḥādīth wa-l-āthār*, ed. Muḥammad ᶜAwwāma, 20 vols (Jeddah: Dār al-Qibla, 2006), 20: 14–34. The edition reproduces the introduction and conclusion of Muḥammad Zāhid al-Kawtharī's riposte to Ibn Abī Shayba's attack on Abū Ḥanīfa; Sezgin, *Geschichte des arabischen Schrifttums*, i: 109. We are told that Ibn Abī Wafā al-Qurashī (d. 1373) authored *al-Durar al-munīfa fī al-radd ᶜalā Ibn Abī Shayba ᶜan al-imām Abī Hanīfa*. See Ibn Quṭlūbughā, *Tāj al-tarājim*, 196. Ibn Quṭlūbughā is also reported to have authored a rebuttal, *al-Ajwiba ᶜan iᶜtirāḍāt Ibn Abī Shayba ᶜalā Abī Ḥanīfa*. See Ibn Quṭlūbughā, *Tāj al-tarājim*, 16 (editor's introduction).
57. On Ibn Abī Shayba, see Carl Brockelmann, *Geschichte der arabischen Litteratur* (Leiden: Brill, 1937), supp. 1, 215; Sezgin, *Geschichte des arabischen Schrifttums*, i: 108–9; Ibn Abī Ḥātim al-Rāzī, *Kitāb al-Jarḥ wa-l-taᶜdīl*, ed. ᶜAbd al-Raḥmān al-Muᶜallimī al-Yamānī, 9 vols (Beirut: Dār al-Fikr, reprint of the 1951 Hyderabad edition), 5: 160; al-Dhahabī, *Siyar aᶜlām al-nubalāᵓ*, ed. Shuᶜayb al-Arnaᶜūṭ, 28 vols (Beirut: Muᵓassasat al-Risāla, 2001), 11: 122–7; al-Dhahabī, *Tadhkirat al-ḥuffāẓ*, ed. Zakariyyā ᶜUmayrāt, 4 vols in 2 (Beirut: Dār al-Kutub al-ᶜIlmiyya, 1998), 2: 16–17; Ibn al-Nadīm, *Kitāb al-fihrist li-l-Nadīm*, ed. Reza Tajaddod (Tehran: n.p., n.d.), 286; al-Khaṭīb, *Tārīkh madīnat al-salām*, 11: 259–67. For modern scholarship on Ibn Abī Shayba's career, see Scott Lucas, 'Where are the Legal Ḥadīth? A study of the Muṣannaf of Ibn Abī Shayba', *Islamic Law and Society* 15 (2008), 283–314; Heinrich Schützinger, 'Ibn Abī Šaiba und sein Taᵓrīx. Eine Untersuchung an Hand des Ms. Berlin 9409', *Oriens* 23 (1974), 134–46. For more on Ibn Abī Shayba's attitudes towards Abū Ḥanīfa, see Khan, 'Heresy and the formation of medieval Sunnī orthodoxy', 18–21. For the manuscript, see Walter Ahlwardt, *Verzeichniss der arabischen Handschriften der Konylichen Bibliothek zu Berlin* (Berlin: n.p., 1887–99), 9: 568–9. On the organisation of the *Muṣannaf*, see al-Rāmahurmuzī, *al-Muḥaddith al-fāṣil bayna al-rāwī wa-l-wāᶜī*, ed. Muḥammad ᶜAjjāj al-Khaṭīb (Beirut: Dār al-Fikr, 1991), 614. It is worth noting, too, that the work was first published in 1966 by a publisher in Hyderabad: Ibn Abī Shayba, *Muṣannaf Ibn Abī Shayba fi-l-aḥādīth wa-l-āthār wa-istinbāṭ aᵓimmat al-tābiᶜīn* (Hyderabad: al-Maṭbaᶜa al-ᶜAzīziyya, 1966).
58. Al-Kawtharī, *al-Nukat al-ṭarīfa fi-l-taḥadduth ᶜan rudūd Ibn Abī Shayba ᶜalā Abī Ḥanīfa* (Islamabad: Idārat al-Qurᵓān wa-l-ᶜUlūm al-Islāmiyya, 1987). Muḥammad ᶜAwwāma, the editor of Ibn Abi Shayba's *al-Muṣannaf li-Ibn Shayba*, 20: 14–34, reproduces al-Kawtharī's introduction and conclusion from *al-Nukat*.

59. I have not come across any secondary literature on him. I have benefitted from ᶜUmar b. ᶜĀmir b. ᶜUmar al-Khirmānī, 'Juhūd al-shaykh al-ᶜallāma Bakr Abū Zayd fī daᶜwā ilā Allāh taᶜālā᾽', MA dissertation, Islamic University Medina, Saudi Arabia, 2009.
60. Bakr Abū Zayd, *al-Madkhal al-mufaṣṣal ilā fiqh al-imām Aḥmad b. Ḥanbal* (Riyadh: Dār al-ᶜĀṣima, 1997); Bakr Abū Zayd, *Tashīl al-sābila li-murīd maᶜrifat al-ḥanābila* (Beirut: Mu᾽assasat al-Risāla, 2001); Bakr Abū Zayd, *ᶜUlamā᾽ al-Ḥanābila* (Dammam: Dār Ibn al-Jawziyya, 2001), which is a biographical dictionary of Ḥanbalīs from Aḥmad b. Ḥanbal to the modern period, 1999.
61. Bakr Abū Zayd, *Ḥukm al-intimā᾽ ilā al-firaq wa-l-aḥzāb wa-l-jamāᶜāt al-Islāmiyya* (Dammām: Dār Ibn al-Jawzī, 1993).
62. Bakr Abū Zayd, *Dar᾽ al-fitna ᶜan ahl al-sunna* (Riyadh: Dār al-ᶜĀṣima, 1998).
63. Bakr Abū Zayd, *al-Rudūd*, 101.
64. Ibid. 185.
65. Ibid. 186.
66. Ibid. 186–7.
67. Ibid. 191–3.
68. Ibid. 195–223, esp. 204–6.
69. Ibid. 206. On al-Tahānawī, see Zaman, *Ashraf ᶜAli Thanawi* (Oxford: Oneworld, 2007).
70. Bakr Abū Zayd, *al-Rudūd*, 201 (*wa-hunā yanbaghī al-tanbīh ᶜalā amr muhimm, wa-huwa anna mā wurida ᶜan kathīr min al-tābiᶜīn wa-talāmidhati-him fī dhamm al-irjā᾽ wa-ahli-hi wa-l-taḥdhīr min bidᶜati-him innamā al-maqṣūd bi-hi hā᾽ulā᾽ al-murji᾽a al-fuqahā᾽*). For modern treatments of the Murji᾽a, see van Ess, *Theologie und Gesellschaft*, i: 152–233, II: 164–86, 493–544, 659–63; Cook, *Early Muslim Dogma: a source-critical study* (Cambridge: Cambridge University Press, 1981), esp. 23–50; Cook, 'Activism and quietism in Islam: the case of the early Murji᾽a', in A. S. Cudsi and A. E. H. Dessouki (eds), *Islam and Power* (Baltimore: Johns Hopkins University Press, 1981), 15–23; A. J. Wensinck, *The Muslim Creed: Its Genesis and Historical Development* (New York: Barnes and Noble, 1932), 131–9; J. Meric Pessagno, 'The Murji᾽a, Īmān and Abū ᶜUbayd', *Journal of the American Oriental Society* 953 (1975), 382–94; Saleh Said Agha, 'A viewpoint of the Murji᾽a in the Umayyad period: evolution through application', *Journal of Islamic Studies* 8:1 (1997), 1–42; Joseph Schacht, 'An early Murci᾽ite treatise: the Kitāb al-ᶜĀlim wal-Mutaᶜallim', *Oriens* 17 (1964), 96–117; Gerlof van Vloten, 'Irdja', *Zeitschrift der Deutschen Morgenlädischen Gesellschaft* 45:2 (1891), 161–71; Wilferd Madelung, 'The early Murji᾽a in Khurasān and Tranoxania and the spread of Hanafism', *Der Islam* LIX (1982), 32–9; Khalil Athamina, 'The early Murji᾽a: some notes', *Journal of Semitic Studies* XXXV (1990), 109–30, Zaman, *Religion and Politics under the early Abbasids*, 59–60.
71. Ninth- and tenth-century sources identifying Abū Ḥanīfa as a Murji᾽ī are plentiful. For a small sample, see al-Bukhārī, *al-Tārīkh al-kabīr*, 4.2: 81; al-Fasawī,

Kitāb al-maʿrifa wa-l-tārīkh, ed. Akram Ḍiyāʾ al-ʿUmarī, 4 vols (Baghdad: Maṭbaʿat al-Irshād, 1975), 2: 782; Ibn Qutayba, *al-Maʿārif li-Ibn Qutayba*, ed. Tharwat ʿUkāsha (Cairo: Dār al-Maʿārif, 1969), 625.

72. Bakr Abū Zayd, *al-Rudūd*, 208 (*fa wa-Allāhi lam yūlad fī-l-islām baʿd al-nabī ayman wa-asʿad min al-Nuʿmān Abī Ḥanīfa. Wa-dalīl dhālik mā huwa mushāhad min indirās madhāhib al-ṭāʿinīn ʿalay-hi, wa-intishār madhhab Abī Ḥanīfa, wa-izdiyādi-hi ishtihāran laylan wa-nahāran. Wa-yaʾba Allāh wa-l-muʾminūn illā Abā Ḥanīfa*). To the untrained eye, the sardonicism might go unnoticed. The more alert of Bakr Abū Zayd's readership, and most certainly late Sunni traditionalists, would be expected to note al-Tahānawī's conspicuous turnaround of disparaging reports, widespread in ninth-century sources, to the effect that 'no birth was more accursed than Abū Ḥanīfa's (*mā wulida fī-l-islām ashʾam min-hu*). See al-Bukhārī, *al-Awsaṭ*, 3: 382–3. See Ẓafar Aḥmad al-ʿUthmānī, *Muqaddimat iʿlā al-sunan: Abū Ḥanīfa wa-aṣḥābu-hu al-muḥaddithūn* (Karachi: Idārat al-Qurʾān wa-l-ʿUlūm al-Islāmiyya, 1994), 33.

73. Bakr Abū Zayd, *al-Rudūd*, 208–9, 214–23 (where Bakr Abū Zayd gives nineteen instances of editorial tampering (*taḥrīf*) in *al-Rafʿ wa-l-takmīl*), 250–1, 269–302 (for Bakr Abū Zayd's *Barāʾat ahl al-sunna min al-waqīʿa fī ʿulamāʾ al-umma*, wherein he seeks to discredit three texts devoted to vindicating Abū Ḥanīfa and the Ḥanafī *madhhab*. This section hosts some of the fiercest attacks on late Sunni traditionalism).

74. See http://www.ahlalhdeeth.com/vb/showthread.php?t=33746 (accessed 1 December 2013; http://www.saaid.net/Doat/gamdi/11.html (accessed 1 December 2013).

75. Muḥammad ʿAbd al-Razzāq Ḥamza, *al-Muqābala bayna al-hudā wa-l-ḍalāl: Ḥawla tarḥīb al-Kawtharī bi-naqd taʾnīb* (Egypt: Maṭbaʿat al-Imām, n.d).

76. Ibid. 39.

77. Ibid. 51.

78. Ibid. 52.

79. Ibid.

80. Ibid. 58.

81. http://www.alukah.net/culture/0/28931 (accessed 1 December 2013).

82. ʿAbbāsī wrote one of the most authoritative works on al-Albānī: Muḥammad ʿĪd ʿAbbāsī, *Fatāwā al-shaykh al-Albānī*.

83. Muḥammad ʿĪd ʿAbbāsī, *Bidʿat al-taʿaṣṣub al-madhhabī wa-āthāru-hā al-khaṭīra fī jumūd al-fikr wa-inḥiṭāṭ al-muslimīn* (Amman: al-Maktaba al-Islāmiyya, n.d.), 2.

84. Ibid. 3–5.

85. Saʿīd Ramaḍān al-Būṭī, *al-Lā madhhabiyya akhṭar bidʿa tuhaddid al-sharīʿa al-islāmiyya* (Damascus: Dār al-Farābī, n.d).

86. Muḥammad ʿĪd ʿAbbāsī, *Bidʿat al-taʿaṣṣub al-madhhabī*, 48.

87. *Al-Kawtharī wa-taʿaddī-hi ʿalā turāth wa-bayān ḥāli-hi fī muʾallafāti-hi wa-taʿlīqāti-hi.*

88. A good illustration of this corporate dimension to traditionalist Salafism can be found in the *Festschrift* for al-Albānī, where Muḥammad Ḥāmid al-Fiqī, al-Muᶜallimī al-Yamānī and Bakr Abū Zayd all furnish sterling encomiums: Abū Usāma Salīm b. ᶜĪd al-Hilālī, *al-Imām al-Albānī*, 49–55, 56–59, 183–6.
89. Al-Muᶜallimī al-Yamānī, *Āthār al-shaykh al-ᶜallāma ᶜAbd al-Raḥmān b. Yaḥyā al-Muᶜallimī al-Yamānī*, ed. Bakr Abū Zayd, 25 vols (Mecca: Dār al-ᶜĀlam al-Fawāʾid, 2013). I have not been able to consult this work. Some of his writings on the discipline of hadith have been gathered in al-Muᶜallimī al-Yamānī, *Mawsūᶜat al-Muᶜallimī al-Yamānī wa-āthāru-hu fī ᶜilm ḥadīth: al-musammā al-nukat al-jiyād al-muntakhaba min kalām shaykh al-nuqqād* (Riyadh: Dār Ṭayba, 2010). Al-Muᶜallimī al-Yamānī's *ᶜIlm al-rijāl wa-ahammiyyatu-hu* (Riyadh: Dār al-Rāya, 1997) is particularly noteworthy on account of its brevity and clarity as a primer on hadith criticism as conceived of by Salafis.
90. Abū Usāma Salīm b. ᶜĪd al-Hilālī, *al-Imām al-Albānī*, 58.
91. Al-Albānī *et al.*, *al-Kawtharī wa-taᶜaddīhi ᶜalā turāth*, 35.
92. Muḥammad b. ᶜAbd Allāh al-Rashīd, *Imdād al-fattāḥ*, 139–241. For al-Banūrī, see above note 25. On al-Kāndahlawī, see Abū al-Ḥasan Nadwī, *Imām al-muḥaddith al-shaykh Muḥammad Zakariyyā al-Kāndahlawī wa-maʾāthiru-hu al-ᶜilmiyya* (Damascus: Dār al-Qalam, 2012). On Abū al-Wafāʾ, see Abū Ghudda, *al-ᶜUlamāʾ al-ᶜuzzāb*, 113–25.
93. Abū Ghudda, *Kalimāt fī kashf abāṭīl wa-iftirāʾāt*, 3rd edn (Ḥalab: Maktab al-Maṭbūᶜāt al-Islāmiyya, 1990), 16.
94. The emergence of the *masānīd Abī Ḥanīfa* genre in the tenth century and its role in unmaking Abū Ḥanīfa as a heretic in the eyes of a significant group of proto-Sunni traditionalists, I argue, was a forerunner to the manner in which late Sunni traditionalists defended Abū Ḥanīfa. See Khan, 'Heresy and the formation of medieval Sunnī orthodoxy', 95–104.
95. Al-Nuᶜmānī's important role in attempting to establish Abū Ḥanīfa's and his students' firm grounding in the discipline of hadith is visible in his other writings. See Muḥammad ᶜAbd al-Rashīd al-Nuᶜmānī, *al-Imām Ibn Māja wa-kitābu-hu al-sunan*, ed. ᶜAbd al-Fattāḥ Abū Ghudda, 6th edn (Beirut: Maktab Maṭbūᶜāt al-Islāmiyya, 1998), 50, 60, 67–74, 76, 92–93, 105, 131–228; al-Nuᶜmānī, *Tārīkh-i tadwīn-i ḥadīth* (in Urdu) (Rāʾī Baraylī: Dār ᶜArafāt, 2002), 63–125. I have largely avoided incorporating Urdu sources into this study. Although the Urdu sources would undoubtedly add much to our understanding of the variety of modern responses to contestations over Abū Ḥanīfa, doing so would also mean that the study would extend well beyond what one chapter can hope to survey. This does not mean, of course, that Indian subcontinent scholarship has been sidelined in this study. Many of the most important sources used in this study are, after all, Arabic sources produced by scholars from the Indian subcontinent, sources that Arabists have tended to neglect.
96. A biography is available in al-Nuᶜmānī, *al-Imām Ibn Māja*, 15–19.
97. For Anwarshāh Kashmīrī, see Abū Ghudda, *Tarājim sitta min fuqahāʾ al-ᶜālam al-islāmī fī al-qarn al-rābiᶜ ᶜashar wa-āthāru-hum al-fiqhiyya* (Beirut: Maktab

al-Maṭbūʿāt al-Islāmiyya, 1997), 13–81. Abū Ghudda's contribution to forming transnational links and alliances between late Sunni traditionalists from the Middle East and the Indian subcontinent was immensely important for the fortification of late Sunni traditionalism in the modern period. On the importance of these transnational links, see Zaman, *The Ulama in Contemporary Islam*, 53–4.

98. ʿAbd al-Rashīd al-Nuʿmānī, *Makānat Abī Ḥanīfa fi-l-ḥadīth*, ed. Abū Ghudda (Beirut: Maktab al-Maṭbūʿāt al-Islāmiyya, 2007), 6.
99. Ibid. 21–68.
100. Ibid. 68–80.
101. Ibid. 81–6. There is little available, to the best of my knowledge, on the subject of *shurūṭ al-ḥadīth*. Goldziher has an excellent discussion of *shurūṭ* in I. Goldziher, *Muslim Studies*: (*Muhammedanische Studien*), ed. S. M. Stern and trans. C. R. Barber and S. M. Stern (London: Allen & Unwin, 1967–71), I: 226–44; see also Brown, *The Canonization of al-Bukhārī and Muslim*, 118–20, 170–2.
102. On hadith criticism, see Eerik Dickinson, *The Development of Early Sunnite Hadith Criticism*; Leonard Librande, 'Contrasts in the two earliest manuals of ʿulūm al-ḥadīth: the beginnings of a genre', PhD dissertation, McGill University, 1976; Librande, 'The scholars of ḥadīth and the retentive memory', *Cahiers d'onomastique arabe*, 1998–1992 (1993), 39–48; Librande, 'The supposed homogeneity of technical terms in ḥadīth study', *Muslim World* LXXII (1982), 34–50; Librande, 'A reconsideration of Ibn Khallād's place in the Buwayhid Lands', *Der Islam* 57 (1980), 1–8; J. A. C. Brown, 'Criticism of the proto-hadith canon: Al-Dāraquṭnī's adjustment of the Ṣaḥīḥayn', *Journal of Islamic Studies* 15:1 (2004), 1–37; Brown, 'How do we know early hadith critics did *matn* criticism and why it's so hard to find', *Islamic Law and Society* 15 (2008), 143–84; Lucas, *Constructive Critics*; Melchert, 'Bukhārī and early hadith criticism', *Journal of the American Oriental Society* 121 (2001), 7–19; Asma Hilali, 'ʿAbd al-Raḥmān al-Rāmahurmuzī (m. 360/971) à l'origine de la réflexion sur l'authenticité du hadith', *Annales Islamologiques* 39 (2005), 131–47; Gautier Juynboll, *Muslim Tradition: Studies in Chronology, Provenance, and Authorship of Early Ḥadīth* (Cambridge: Cambridge University Press, 1983), 134–60.
103. Abū Ḥasanāt Muḥammad ʿAbd al-Ḥayy al-Laknawī, *al-Rafʿ wa-l-takmīl fi-l-jarḥ wa-taʿdīl*, ed. ʿAbd al-Fattāḥ Abū Ghudda (n.p.: Maktabat Ibn Taymiyya, n.d), 22.
104. Ibid. 24.
105. Ibid. 25.
106. Ibid. 29.
107. Ibid. 60–1, 142 and 184.
108. The work should be seen as a joint effort between Ẓafar Aḥmad al-ʿUthmānī and his uncle Ashraf ʿAlī al-Tahānawī. The title page does, after all, state that the work was composed by Ẓafar on the basis of what he acquired from al-Tahānawī (*ʿalā ḍawʾ mā afāda-hu*). The background to its publication is

detailed in Ẓafar Aḥmad al-ʿUthmānī, *Iʿlā al-sunan*, 21 vols (Beirut: Dār al-Fikr, 2001), I: 29–32.

109. See Ẓafar Aḥmad al-ʿUthmānī, *Muqaddimat iʿlā al-sunan*, 6–11, 45–51 and 82–211 for the prosopographical summaries of 264 Ḥanafī hadith scholars.

110. Ẓafar Aḥmad al-ʿUthmānī, *Muqaddimat iʿlā al-sunan*, 4 (*jaʿalat al-ṭaʿn ʿalay-hi shiʿāra-hu wa-l-sabb wa-l-shatm li-itbāʿi-hi dithāra-hu … fa-laḥiqatnī ḥamiyyatun dīniyyatun rabbāniyyatun wa-ʿaṣabiyyatun ḥanafiyyatun nuʿmāniyyatun, fa-aradtu an ajmaʿa aqwāl al-aʾimmat al-muḥaddithīn fī-l-thanāʾ ʿalā hādha al-imām wa-kalimāt ahl al-naqd fī tawthīqi-hi wa-taʿdīli-hi wa-taqdīmi-hi fī-l-ʿilm ʿalā aʾimmat al-aʿlām …*).

111. Al-Kawtharī, *Maqālāt al-Kawtharī*, 226 (*wa-l-iftāʾ bi-l-aqwāl al-ḍaʿīfa, wa-ittihām al-fuqahāʾ bi-l-mujāzafa, wa-l-saʿy fī izālat al-ḥawājiz bayn al-muslimīn; wa-ghirru-hum mimmā yajrī ilā istifḥāl al-sharr wa-fatḥ bāb al-dass bayn al-muslimīn, fa-l-ijtirāʾ ʿalā mithl dhālik lā yaqill khūṭūra ʿan al-tasarruʿ fī-l-ḥukm bi-l-ridda fī zaman lā yakhāf al-murtadd fīhi min ḍarb raqabati-hi, fa-l-wājib ʿalā ahl al-ʿilm an yasharū ʿalā madākhil al-fasād wa-yasʿaw juhda-hum fī tarṣīn al-siyāj wa-sadd al-khilal lā taʿbīd al-ṭarīq ilā-l-murūq*).

112. Another important and effective tool for defending Abū Ḥanīfa against the opprobrium heaped upon him (and the Ḥanafī *madhhab*) by traditionalist Salafis was modern commentaries on hadith works. The genre is too vast to permit a detailed survey, but the main works in this field are: Ẓafar Aḥmad al-ʿUthmānī's (d. 1974) *Iʿlā al-sunan*, Shabbīr Aḥmad al-ʿUthmānī's (d. 1949) *Fatḥ al-mulhim*, Rashīd Aḥmad Gangohī's (d. 1905) *Lāmiʿ al-dararī*, Anwarshāh Kashmīrī's (d. 1933) *Fayḍ al-bārī*, among others.

113. Jan Assmann, *Religion and Cultural Memory* (Stanford: Stanford University Press, 2006), 11.

114. I have in mind here certain elements of institutionalised Sufi practice or theological positing that flourished during the High Middle Ages. For example, see Ibn Qudāma, *Ibn Qudāma's Censure of Speculative Theology: An edition and translation of Ibn Qudāma's Taḥrīm an-nazar fī kutub ahl al-kalām, with introduction and notes; a contribution to the study of Islamic religious history*, ed. and trans. George Makdisi (Oxford: E. J. W. Gibb Memorial Trust, 1962), xi–xxiii.

115. I hope to address elsewhere the vast body of literature produced in the twentieth century on the craft of editing religious texts. Examples include: Aḥmad Shākir, *Taṣḥīḥ al-kutub wa ṣunʿ al-fahāris al-muʿjama wa kayfa ḍabṭ al-kitāb wa sabaq al-muslimīn al-afrang fī dhālik*, ed. ʿAbd al-Fattāḥ Abū Ghudda (Beirut: Maktabat al-Maṭbūʿāt al-Islāmiyya, 1993); ʿAbd al-Majīd Diyāb, *Taḥqīq al-turāth al-ʿarabī* (Cairo: Dār al-Maʿārif, 1993).

116. Francis Robinson, 'Islam and the impact of print in South Asia', 80–1.

117. Samira Haj, *Reconfiguring Islamic Tradition*, 11.

118. See Marc Bloch, *The Historian's Craft* (New York: Vintage Books, 1953), 46: 'Now, more often than is generally supposed, it happens that, in order to find daylight, the historian may have to pursue his subject right up to the present.'

4

Reaching into the Obscure Past: The Islamic Legal Heritage and Reform in the Modern Period

Jonathan A. C. Brown

In a scandalous story reported about the caliph al-Ma᾿mūn (r. 813–33 CE), the opinionated dynast does the unthinkable. He decides to declare permissible that most controversial of unions: 'pleasure' (*mutᶜa*) marriage, by which a man and woman were joined in wedlock only temporarily for some preset period of time. As remembered in Sunni sources, scholars in the caliph's court act quickly to correct the edict. They vociferously remind him that the Qur᾿an and the Prophet's Sunna had made clear that *mutᶜa* (also known as temporary marriage) was strictly prohibited.[1] Some eight centuries later in India, during a meeting of his famed interfaith salon, the Mughal Emperor Akbar the Great (r. 1556–1605 CE) discovered to his chagrin that he had far, far exceeded a Muslim man's Shariᶜa limit of only four wives at any one time. Tasking his thought, the emperor recalled that his shaykh, the staunch Sunni revivalist ᶜAbd al-Nabī al-Gangūhī (d. 1583–4), had once remarked that an early Muslim scholar in Kufa had held that a Muslim could marry up to nine women. In response to a hasty correspondence sent by Akbar, ᶜAbd al-Nabī clarified to his former charge and current sovereign that he had only noted this unusual opinion as an example of early juristic disagreement. No scholar could now actually give a ruling to that effect. Fortunately, the emperor's courtiers proved more pliant. One noted that Imāmī Shiᶜites (true) and the Mālikī school of law (untrue) allowed a limitless number of wives if they were by *mutᶜa* marriages. Akbar immediately appointed a presumably ill-informed Mālikī judge to declare all his marriages legal, with the emperor's advisors explaining (somewhat correctly) that all other judges in the realm would have to respect this ruling.[2]

In recent decades, some Muslim intellectuals have revived al-Ma᾿mūn's and Akbar's call. In countries like Egypt, the occasional advocate of temporary marriage has argued for its suitability as a solution to the dire challenges facing Muslim youth, who find the socio-economic demands of normal marriage unmanageable. Books like *Temporary Marriage is Permitted in the Qurʾan and the Sunna* (2009) present evidence such as the Companion Ibn ᶜAbbās' acceptance of *mutᶜa* and a ruling on the permissibility of *pro tempore* marriage (*zawāj muwaqqat*) issued by Zufar (d. 775), an early pillar of the Ḥanafī school of law.[3] Just as in al-Maʾmūn's day, rebuttals have been swift and sure. In a widely published booklet entitled *Temporary Marriage is Prohibited in Islam*, the Syrian shaykh Muḥammad Ḥāmid (d. 1969) retorted that Ibn ᶜAbbās recanted his opinion and that, anyway, it was not permissible to act on such faulty and superseded rulings. Asked about Zufar's opinion, Ḥāmid replied, 'He alone held this opinion, none of the other Ḥanafī scholars (*aṣḥāb*), and his opinion is not relied upon (*ghayr muᶜtamad*) according to the jurists.'[4]

Along with questions of sex, those of finance are perennially relevant. Modern debates over Islamic alternatives to conventional interest (*riban* or *al-ribā*) often rehash those of past centuries. By the mid sixteenth century, the Ottoman economy and its religious infrastructure of mosques and charitable institutions had come to rely on pious endowments (*waqf*) made in cash (*naqd*) as opposed to real property. Many leading Ḥanafī jurists in the empire objected to this practice and urged the Ottoman sultan to ban it. Not only did cash *waqf*s violate the established position of the Ḥanafī school, which prohibited endowments of gold, silver and other currency, but also it had paved the way for the vile sin of *al-ribā*, the interest collected on this cash. But jurists affiliated with the Ottoman state, like Shaykh al-Islam Ebūsuᶜūd Efendi (d. 1574), defended the cash *waqf* as essential. It was a cornerstone for basic religious functions in the realm. Without it, mosques could not even be maintained. Furthermore, scholars like Ebūsuᶜūd justified the cash endowment by reaching far back to the great founding fathers of their Ḥanafī tradition. Indeed, one (if only one) of the early masters had allowed the cash *waqf*: Zufar.[5]

The selective use and abuse of Zufar in debates over legal reform offer a glimpse at a crucial and enduring tension in the discourse tradition of Islamic law. For the *ᶜulamāʾ*, in their capacity as the guardians of the faith, the diversity of the Islamic legal tradition has always been a blessing and curse, a trove to be utilised and a force to be managed. Produced by varied interpretive methods applied to sources of often-disputed authenticity, the Shariᶜa tradition was inevitably pluralistic. On the one hand, the resulting legal heritage provided a rich resource for adapting the law to meet legitimately the changing needs of the Muslim community. On the other, it could also be taken advantage of to legitimise misguided desires, indulge laziness and excuse surrendering to fads. Muslim scholars have therefore tried to limit access to this diversity through restrictive procedures and by requiring sound intentions and high qualifications for those who sought to draw on it.

A major question was whether and when a scholar could cross the boundaries between the four schools of law within Sunni Islam to mine diverse legal rulings. As we shall see, this was primarily restricted by limiting it to situational necessity and by urging those involved to double-check their intentions in doing so. The main subject of this chapter, however, lies even further out in the terrain of diversity: the question of whether and when scholars could reach back to the ancient, pre-*madhhab* legal landscape. Here we will show that this was either prohibited or limited to senior scholars whose intentions were sound. Of course, determining intention and gauging necessity are subjective calls. Within the Sunni tradition, so is judging scholarly qualifications. As a result, there is no objective rule for determining the legitimacy of a particular instance of a scholar drawing on the full diversity of the Shariᶜa tradition. Ideally, this determination should hinge on a scholar presenting a sound Shariᶜa argument for his or her choice. But both in the pre-modern and modern periods, accepting or rejecting such a ruling could just as much turn on political power or the normative power of culture.

This is clearly illustrated in the case of Ibn Shubruma (d. 761), a relatively obscure eighth-century jurist who has proven surprisingly essential in modern legal reforms. On two controversial and crucial issues, restrictions on marriage age and Islamic finance, Ibn Shubruma's opinions have been indispensible for Shariᶜa legitimation. As in the case of Zufar and temporary marriage, opposing camps have in turn affirmed and decried drawing on this ancient authority. The scholastic volleys they have traded with each other have aimed at bolstering or undermining the opponent's Shariᶜa evidence and inferences, but they have also gestured with admiration, resignation or outrage at the looming forces of cultural and political expectation in the eras of colonialism and globalisation.

Routinising Adjudication, Tailoring to Piety

For centuries, the *ᶜulamāᵓ* were both the elaborators and appliers of Islamic law. They felt the pull to routinise and delimit the diversity of the Shariᶜa tradition in their capacity as judges and agents responsible for bringing normative order to their communities. Yet the bulk of the Shariᶜa consisted of matters of ritual and etiquette, which would never see the inside of a court. Whether acting as judges or pastors, the *ᶜulamāᵓ* understood keenly the varied needs, capacities and inclinations of their flocks. Allowing flexibility in the expression of God's law was thus essential.[6]

As an applied legal system, the Shariᶜa had achieved impressive success by the ninth century.[7] By the thirteenth century, Muslim jurists had developed sophisticated models for the stable and routinised forms into which the Shari^ca had settled. As Mohammed Fadel, Yossef Rapoport and Ruud Peters have demonstrated, in areas where one *madhhab* prevailed, like Mālikī North Africa or the Ḥanafī heartland of the Ottoman Empire, judges either tended to restrain themselves to the primary ruling of the *madhhab* or received instructions from state authorities to do so (the primary ruling was known as the *mashhūr* in the Mālikī school, the *mu^ctamad* in the Shāfi^cī and Ḥanbalī schools, and the *aṣaḥḥ* or *ẓāhir al-riwāya* in the Ḥanafī school).[8]

The diversity of Islamic law remained valuable, however, since judges would rule by minority positions within the monopoly *madhhab* if regional practice or some sultanic decree specified this. Thus the Mughal Empire's seventeenth-century promulgation of the *Fatāwā ^cĀlamgīrī* codified the primary rulings of the Ḥanafī school, unless a non-primary ruling had become preferred (*al-fatwā*) in the school's Central and South Asian traditions.[9] The Ottoman Shaykh al-Islam decreed that Zufar's minority opinion would carry the day in the question of cash *waqf*s. Similarly, the Ottoman state instructed judges to require the permission of a woman's guardian (*walī*) for her to marry, taking the early Ḥanafī authority Muḥammad b. Ḥasan al-Shaybānī's (d. 804) minority opinion on this issue over the school's well-known position to the contrary.[10]

Moreover, Muslim judges felt the very common tension between the need to provide a predictable rule of law on the one hand and ensuring equitable rulings on the other. An eleventh-century judge's manual therefore acknowledged the 'political (*siyāsa*)' urge for judges to rule predictably by their school of law even while insisting on their right to follow their best judgement.[11] Senior scholars serving as judges often felt more flexibility in selecting rulings when they deemed it necessary, and inequitable rulings could be appealed to more senior judges or respected jurisprudents.[12] Based on local patterns of divorce, Mālikī scholars in Fez in the nineteenth century thus deviated from the primary ruling of their school in cases in which irate husbands had told their wives 'You are forbidden (*ḥarām*) to me!', treating their outburst as a revocable single divorce declaration instead of the irrevocable final one.[13]

In regions where numerous *madhhab*s coexisted, like Mamlūk Egypt and Syria, litigants took advantage of the courts of one *madhhab* rather than another when it favoured them, often with the judges' encouragement.[14] Thus, while in any one region at any one time judges and lay litigants might work with a legal platform that was cobbled together, it was a stable and routine platform nonetheless.

Outside of the courts, many of the questions posed to Muslim scholars concerned matters of private religious practice or supererogatory piety, brought by lay Muslims to the *ᶜulamāʾ* in their capacity as muftis providing non-binding *responsa*. A common scholarly dictum held that 'the layperson (*ᶜāmmī*) has no *madhhab*.' First and foremost, this meant that the laity had no involvement in the byzantine disputes among *madhhab*s and no capacity to evaluate their evidence. They followed whatever local scholars told them. A mufti's response to a lay questioner lay entirely within his scholarly discretion – or in some cases within the range of accepted opinions for his *madhhab*. But this principle also reflected an opposing consequence: the layperson posing the question was not bound to follow any particular *madhhab* or even any one mufti. In effect, he or she had only to follow the mufti of his or her choosing on that occasion.[15]

Of course, there was obvious danger inherent in this flexibility. The leading Sufi of Baghdad, Abū Ḥafṣ al-Suhrawardī (d. 1234), complained about the lazy Qalandar Sufis, whom he describes as habitually taking advantage of licences in practice (*rukhṣa*)[16] and lolling about in the realm of the permissible (*mubāḥ*) instead of conscientiously abiding by the Shariᶜa.[17] An even more perilous possibility was that a Muslim would try to 'pursue licences habitually (*tatabbuᶜ al-rukhaṣ*)', either shopping between muftis or picking and choosing the laxest ruling from different *madhhab*s, potentially cobbling together a reprehensible lifestyle. In the Mamlūk period scholars quoted warnings such as that of Maᶜmar b. Rāshid (d. 770) that, if one were to take the early Medinan position allowing music and anal sex with women, the early Meccan ruling allowing temporary marriage, and the Kufan one permitting intoxicants, one would become 'the worst of all God's servants'.[18]

Three general approaches emerged to addressing the problem of 'fatwa shopping'. Some more atavistic or theoretical purists like the scholar ᶜIzz al-Dīn Ibn ᶜAbd al-Salām (d. 1262) approved of allowing lay folk to shop freely between muftis and their rulings. There was no ground to restrict them, he explained, since the exemplary generation of the Companions had freely chosen from among the legal opinions circulating among them. If Muslims in his own time sought out laxity and licences, Ibn ᶜAbd al-Salām concluded, they were only harming themselves. God judges actions by intentions.[19] Yet a prominent contemporary critic of Ibn ᶜAbd al-Salām pointed out the destabilising anachronism in his reasoning. The Companions had predated any systematic elaboration of law, and duplicating their example centuries later in the context of an elaborate menu of legal options would lead to rampant *rukhṣa* taking (and, indeed, Ibn ᶜAbd al-Salām did find himself forbidding such discretion to judges).[20]

A second, stricter approach to choosing between rulings or crossing *madhhab* boundaries is most associated historically with North African Mālikī scholars as well as Ḥanafīs in the Ottoman realm and modern South Asia. It required Muslims to choose and follow one authority only for all issues and strongly discouraged muftis from deviating from the standard ruling of their *madhhab*.[21] For centuries, many Mālikī muftis of North Africa could not even countenance deviating from the primary ruling of their own *madhhab* on an issue, let alone drawing on another school.[22] In underscoring the traditional legitimacy of the Ottoman's circa 1870 *Mecelle* law code, whose compilation he had overseen, Cevdet Paşa (d. 1895) noted how, even on the thorniest topics, he had remained within the Ottoman's revered Ḥanafī school.[23] For this stricter approach, the issue of controversy was whether a mufti could cite the non-primary ruling of the *madhhab* (it was allowed in cases of necessity); actually departing from the *madhhab* was not entertained.[24]

A third, intermediate position emerged in the works of two contemporaries in Mamlūk Cairo, Shihāb al-Dīn al-Qarāfī (d. 1285) and Ibn Daqīq al-ᶜĪd (d. 1302), both inventive Mālikī legal theorists.[25] Ibn Daqīq was considered a master of the Shāfiᶜī school as well, and this approach was further developed by his Shāfiᶜī successor in Damascus, Taqī al-Dīn al-Subkī (d. 1356).[26] It soon became a consensus in the Shāfiᶜī school. Their approach trod a middle ground by setting specific restrictions on choosing selectively between opinions within a *madhhab* or between *madhhab*s, either on the part of the scholar issuing a fatwa or that of the layperson weighing fatwas to choose from. Crossing *madhhab* boundaries or taking a secondary ruling within one school were permissible in two circumstances: when one believed that the alternate position enjoyed stronger evidence, or in the face of some legitimate need (*ḥāja*) or necessity (*ḍarūra*).[27] Even in such situations, crossing or mixing was only allowed provided that it did not result in transgressive combination (*talfīq*), meaning that the resulting act or transaction (like purification and then prayer) would be impermissible in both the person's original school and the alternate.[28] These restrictions precluded habitually taking licences (*tatabbuᶜ al-rukhaṣ*) and seeking out lax rulings based merely on illegitimate desires (*ahwāʾ*).[29]

This intermediate approach became progressively laxer as time went on. The Egyptian ᶜAbd al-Wahhāb al-Shaᶜrānī's (d. 1565) innovative and popular legal manual, the *Mīzān al-Kubrā*, envisioned the four Sunni schools of law as a common pool of valid rulings, ranging on every point of law from the strict (*ᶜazīma*) to the latitudinarian (*rukhṣa*). The rulings that an individual chose would differ for each person depending on his level of piety and religious practice. As A. F. Ibrahim has put it, al-Shaᶜrānī treated laypeople as being in 'a constant state of weakness' and thus 'in perpetual need of *rukhṣa*'.[30] Some later, admittedly briefer, discussions of this issue omitted the requirement of need and specified only that the resulting ruling not be something rejected by all schools of law. Scholars advocating this intermediate approach specified that one could only choose amongst the established *madhhabs*, and by the 1600s these were specified as only the four Sunni schools.[31]

The Dangers of Reaching Too Far Back

In 1234 CE the final stone was laid in Baghdad's great Mustanṣiriyya Madrasa, which would dominate the city's scholarly landscape from the Tigris shore even after the Mongol conquests. Unlike earlier madrasas, the Mustanṣiriyya made clear the range and limits of Sunni thought. It included four galleries, one for each of the four *madhhabs*.[32]

The eleventh century had already seen drastic advances in delimiting the circle of orthodoxy in order to rescue the umma from the unwieldy heritage of its own early diversity. Imām al-Ḥaramayn al-Juwaynī (d. 1085) reported a consensus amongst leading scholars (*muḥaqqiqūn*) that the masses should not follow the legal opinions of Islam's earliest generations, righteous and superior in knowledge though they were. Rather, they should only follow the *madhhabs* of those imams who had 'examined and investigated, organized legal issues topically, and noted their contexts (*awḍā*ᶜ).'[33]

By the thirteenth century, this need to enforce institutional limitations seems to have been felt even more keenly. It even attracted the attention of the Ayyūbid sultan, who in the mid 1200s rebuked the revered Ibn ᶜAbd al-Salām for the (false) charge of trying to start a new *madhhab*.[34] It was a palpable concern for scholars writing manuals for muftis in that era, such as the Damascene heirs to Baghdad's scholarly legacy, Ibn al-Ṣalāḥ (d. 1245) and al-Nawawī (d. 1277). In his *Kitāb al-Futyā*, Ibn al-Ṣalāḥ states that the only *madhhabs* that could be followed by the laity or used as bases for giving fatwas were those that had been 'set down and recorded (*yudawwanu*)' by the students of the founding figures and the subsequent generations of scholars following in their paths. This excluded drawing on the legal opinions of the Companions, since their legal methodologies were never described or compiled comprehensively. We might know ᶜUmar's or ᶜAlī's rulings on such and such an issue, but we do not know their *madhhab*, neither in its principles (*uṣūl*) nor in its substantive rulings (*furū*ᶜ), explained Ibn al-Ṣalāḥ.[35] This restriction also excluded turning to the opinions of Successors like the Seven Jurists (*al-fuqahā*ʾ *al-sab*ᶜ*a*) of Medina as well as the following generation, which preceded the earliest of the eponymous founders of the great *madhhabs*. These early scholars cannot be followed and taken as the basis for *taqlīd* (imitation) by later generations because one cannot know 'the true nature of their legal methodology (*ḥaqīqat madhhabi-him*).'[36]

Through the thirteenth century, however, scholars tended to discuss the notion of established *madhhabs* without specifying them, since a clear consensus on their number had not yet emerged. Certainly, the Sunni scholarly universe was beginning to settle around the four schools in the eleventh century. When the theologically engaged caliph al-Qādir (d. 1031) commissioned a set of epitomes produced for the major schools of law, he only specified the Shāfiᶜī, Mālikī, Ḥanbalī and Ḥanafī ones. But when the Shāfiᶜī scholar he chose, al-Māwardī (d. 1058), wrote how the 'cementing (*istiqrār*) of the *madhhabs*' had occurred by his time, he did not enumerate or identify them.[37] Other established schools, such as the Jarīrī school of al-Ṭabarī (d. 923), still flourished. Biographical dictionaries of jurists produced by eleventh-century contemporaries, al-ᶜAbbādī (d. 1065) and Abū Isḥāq al-Shīrāzī (d. 1083) (both Shāfiᶜīs), listed five *madhhabs* as having become 'widespread in the lands'. They included the Ẓāhirī school along with the four well-known Sunni ones.[38] Roughly two centuries later Ibn al-Ṣalāḥ also mentions five *madhhabs* but includes Sufyān al-Thawrī (d. 778) alongside the other four '*madhhab* founders'.[39]

In the twelfth century, however, evidence suggests that the notion of four agreed upon *madhhabs* had come to predominate. As one Baghdad scholar wrote in a poem, the four eponymous founders of the great schools 'Are our proof signs, and whoever is guided by other than them will go astray.'[40] A writer fascinating for his mastery of jurisprudence and his experience as a high administrator for the ᶜAbbāsid caliphs in Baghdad, the Ḥanbalī vizier Ibn Hubayra (d. 1165), remarked how the umma had come to consensus on the four schools. All agreed, he stated, that each and any of the four schools could be acted upon and followed by judges because all agreed that they were authentically grounded in the Prophet's Sunna.[41]

For Ibn Rajab (d. 1392), there was no debate. There were only four legitimate schools. In his *Rebuttal Against Those Who Follow Other than the Four* Madhhab*s*, the Damascene Ḥanbalī jurist explained that restricting scholars and the laity to the four schools prevented them from straying from the body of Muslim scholarly consensus.[42] His treatise adds colour to Ibn al-Ṣalāḥ's concerns, explaining the particular danger of reaching back before the formation of the schools of law to the opinions of the early Muslim generations. Ibn Rajab offered his treatise as a rebuttal to those offended by criticisms he had previously levelled at an earlier Ḥanbalī scholar, by whom it is safe to assume he meant Ibn Taymiyya (d. 1328). Although a scholar steeped in the Ḥanbalī school, Ibn Taymiyya had broken with it on numerous issues and with all four *madhhabs* in his ruling that triple divorce (*ṭalāq*) statements made at the same time by a husband only counted as one, revocable statement. Ibn Taymiyya based his ruling on a *ṣaḥīḥ* hadith explaining that this was how divorce was practised during the Prophet's life as well as the opinions of Ibn ᶜAbbās, ᶜIkrima (d. 723) and Muḥammad Ibn Isḥāq (d. 767).[43] Ibn Rajab noted that opinions attributed to Companions were sometimes *shādhdh* (aberrant), especially those of Ibn ᶜAbbās, who had permitted both *mutᶜa* marriage and – seemingly – transactions of money with interest.[44] When the Meccan scholar Ibn Jurayj (d. 767) had visited Basra, Ibn Rajab recounted, the horrified scholars there 'raised their hands in prayer' when they heard the *shādhdh* opinions he had preserved from Ibn ᶜAbbās.[45] Whether due to the geographical segregation of hadiths (Ibn ᶜAbbās was apparently unaware of hadiths prohibiting the interest-yielding transactions he allowed)[46] or because the legal opinions of the early Muslim generations had not been comprehensively studied and understood within their circumstances and methodological contexts, such opinions could not be turned to in order to justify positions outside the four schools.

Anxiety over the Modern West and Reform

Describing his decades of Islamic scholarly activism, combatting the threats of Communism and Western liberal hegemony, Muḥammad al-Ghazālī (d. 1996) wrote with exasperation about those who insisted he follow only one source of authority. 'Our religion is being attacked on numerous fronts,' the prolific Egyptian scholar wrote in 1991, 'and I need to move between the opinions of all the imams … standing in the fortress of Abū Ḥanīfa in the system of Zakat, or in the fortress of Ibn Taymiyya when I am speaking about the system of divorce …'[47]

Al-Ghazālī's sense of the crisis brought on by the modern West had been keenly felt by *ᶜulamāʾ* from Egypt to India for over a century. How could the *ᶜulamāʾ* guide their flocks through the new perils of the modern era? A major reformist strain that emerged to respond to the challenge of European modernity proposed looking to the entire heritage (*turāth*) of Islamic thought for solutions, reaching into its trove and seeking to shape from its myriad parts an Islam both authentic and sturdily set between the pure fount of prophecy and the demands of a new world order. Al-Ghazālī's mentor, the former Shaykh al-Azhar Maḥmūd Shaltūt (d. 1964), had prefaced his controversial book of reformist fatwas by stipulating that he had not followed any one *madhhab* or scholarly authority in writing it. Rather, he had acted as a 'perspicacious jurist following the precepts of the Qurʾan, the authentic Sunna (*sunna ṣaḥīḥa*), and the eternal, general principles of Islam (*qawāᶜid al-islām al-ᶜāmma al-khālida*).'[48]

One remarkable controversy seemed to epitomise the tension over the legitimate use of the Islamic heritage against the fraught setting of foreign influence and Islamic reform. It was the notorious Transvaal fatwa issued by the progenitor of Islamic legal reform in Egypt, the Grand Mufti Muḥammad ᶜAbduh (d. 1905). In this 1903 fatwa, ᶜAbduh responded to Muslims from British South Africa who had asked about the permissibility of eating meat slaughtered by Christians even if it were slaughtered by stunning it with a blow to the head. ᶜAbduh allowed it, basing his ruling on an empowered reading of the Qurᵓanic verse that 'the food of those people granted revelation before is permitted for you' (Q. 5:5) and his citation of precedent, namely the twelfth-century Mālikī jurist Abū Bakr Ibn al-ᶜArabī (d. 1145), who had also ostensibly allowed it.[49] In the wake of the fatwa, ᶜAbduh was pilloried by *ᶜulamāᵓ* and in the popular press alike, accused of misusing evidence and picking selectively from various schools of law to achieve his desired result. The Qurᵓan explicitly forbade eating animals killed by stunning (Q. 5:3), it was argued, and Ibn al-ᶜArabī's fatwa on the issue was aberrant and broke with scholarly consensus.[50]

Drawing on the utility – perhaps with legitimate reason – of the Shariᶜa's diverse heritage was not new. But the temptation to do so and the intensity of crisis that it engendered in the modern era were unprecedented. So was the conservative anxiety over the fatal dangers that this threat presented. Responding to reformists like Shaltūt and al-Ghazālī in duelling Egyptian journals, the Ottoman exile Muḥammad Zāhid al-Kawtharī (d. 1952) underscored the tremendous danger of cherry picking between *madhhab*s in so fraught an era. Those *ᶜulamāᵓ* and Egyptian statesmen trying to modernise Islamic law by doing so were no more than 'ersatz Muslim imposters (*muta-muslim mundass*)' working on behalf of the colonial powers, al-Kawtharī blasted.[51] Founded in 1866 as a bastion against British cultural domination of Muslim thought in India, the Dār al-ᶜUlūm madrasa at Deoband urged India's Muslims to adhere strictly to the Ḥanafī school of law. This focus and discipline, they believed, was essential to protect the Muslim laity from the cultural confusion and temptations around them. In tending to the needs of their followers, however, the leading scholars of Deoband reserved the right to select positions from other *madhhab*s when giving fatwas on topics of critical salience.[52]

Whether in the former Ottoman lands or South Asia, few topics have proven as controversial in contact between the Islamic tradition and the modern West as marriage (read, sexuality) and the conventions of finance. Oddly, in two pivotal questions in both areas it would be the person of Ibn Shubruma around whom debate would turn over the use and abuse of the Shariᶜa's obscure past.

Ibn Shubruma and Limits on Marriage Age

Abū al-Ṭufayl ᶜAbd Allāh Ibn Shubruma (d. 761) was a leading scholar of Kufa in the mid eighth century. Unlike his contemporaries Abū Ḥanīfa, al-Awzāᶜī (d. 774) and Sufyān al-Thawrī, Ibn Shubruma's corps of students and intellectual output never morphed into the critical mass necessary for a *madhhab* to form. But both during his lifetime and as recorded in later legal compendia, his opinions were noted regularly along with those of other titans of Kufan legal discourse in his time, such as Ibn Abī Laylā (d. 765) and the Basran ᶜUthmān al-Battī (d. 760).

Ibn Shubruma was a scholar who worked closely with the Muslim rulers, first under the Umayyads as a court favourite and a judge in Yemen, Basra, Sijistān and finally as a judge of the *maẓālim* court in Kufa. Under the ᶜAbbāsids, Ibn Shubruma cultivated equally close relations with the new caliphs in Baghdad and was assigned as a judge in the environs of Kufa.[53] It is therefore not surprising that many of the rulings reported from him involve court procedure. As the Sunni movement coalesced in the ninth century, Ibn Shubruma was appreciated as a transmitter in the canonical Sunni hadith collections but was not used very frequently.[54] His legacy featured much more prominently in the legal compendia that catalogued the various opinions of jurists (*ikhtilāf*), like the *Ikhtilāf al-fuqahā*ʾ of al-Ṭabarī, the *Ishrāf* of Ibn al-Mundhīr (d. 930) and later the *Bidāyat al-mujtahid* of Ibn Rushd (d. 1198), the *Mughnī* of Ibn Qudāma (d. 1223) and the *Majmū*ᶜ of al-Nawawī. Posterity breathed new life into Ibn Shubruma's legacy in the 1920s, when his legal opinion became a crucial point in debates over reforms of marriage laws in Egypt.

The late nineteenth and twentieth centuries saw debates in the Ottoman world swirl around a variety of issues related to marriage and Islamic law, from calls to restrict polygamy to limiting men's unilateral right to divorce. One of the most heated debates concerned prohibiting or severely restricting the marriage of young girls. In the 1830s, Edward William Lane had remarked that Egyptian women married as young as ten (only a few remained single by sixteen), noting that they 'tend to arrive at puberty much earlier than the natives of colder climates.'[55] The economic reforms carried out under the dynasty of Mehmet Ali and then under the British 'veiled protectorate' after 1882, however, brought about sudden and significant change. In the first decades of the twentieth century Egypt's population burgeoned, and family structures in rural areas fragmented as peasants flocked to the cities. With educational reforms, literacy rates improved dramatically. By the 1920s, exposure to Western norms and modernisation efforts had changed how marriage and appropriate marriage ages were viewed among sections of Egyptian society, particularly the newly created urban middle class. When censuses were carried out in 1907 and 1917, they showed that less than ten percent of Egyptian women were marrying before the age of twenty.[56]

Even before the British occupation in 1882, the health and welfare concerns of child marriage had already risen to the surface in Egypt. Health reforms under Mehmet Ali's successors in the mid nineteenth century had created a cadre of midwives called *Ḥakīmas*, who had begun raising alarm about the health risks of pubescent girls giving birth. Ironically, cuts in funding under the British occupation brought this new service to an end.[57] Passing legislation to restrict and possibly terminate the marriage of girls under sixteen became one of the causes to which Hudā Shaᶜrāwī (d. 1947) and the newly formed Egyptian Feminist Union devoted themselves. In 1923 the organisation's lobbying efforts helped convince Egypt's Parliament to pass a law setting the minimum marriage age for women at sixteen and men at eighteen.[58] The law accomplished this by prohibiting notaries from registering marriages if the bride was under sixteen and prohibiting courts from hearing disputes for any marriage that had been contracted with a girl under that age.

This proved highly controversial amongst Egypt's *ᶜulamāᵓ*, who disagreed vehemently amongst each other on the Shariᶜa legitimacy of such a law. According to the Shariᶜa tradition, the two legal moments relevant to marriage age for women were the contracting of the marriage (*ᶜaqd/nikāḥ*) and the consummation of the marriage (*dakhl*). These could be and often were separated by lengthy periods of time. Concerning the marriage contract, the majority of legal schools held that a girl who had reached the age of maturity (*bulūgh*, i.e. either menstruating or, if menstruation had still not occurred, the age of eighteen at the maximum) could not be married off by her guardian without her consent. In the case of a daughter who was underage (i.e. premenstrual), however, all four Sunni schools of law permitted a father to contract a marriage for her *without* the daughter's consent. As a minor, her consent was meaningless (though the Ḥanafī school allowed such a bride to annul this marriage contract upon reaching maturity).

The consummation was a wholly different matter. It was based on the discretion of the families and the physical maturity of the bride. It could occur shortly after the marriage contract or years later. Such was the case with the Prophet's marriage to ᶜĀᵓisha. Al-Ṭabarī reports that, when the marriage contract occurred, ᶜĀᵓisha was only six and 'too young for intercourse'. The couple thus waited several years, until ᶜĀᵓisha was nine according to an accepted hadith, for the consummation.[59] Pre-modern *ᶜulamāᵓ* did not devote a great deal of attention to the age *terminus ante quem* for permitting sex, primarily because the point at which any one girl was fit for intercourse could vary too much to be legislated firmly. The predominant theme in Shariᶜa discourse on this issue was that the matter was most appropriately left to the bride, the groom and the bride's guardian to determine. The norm on which the *ᶜulamāᵓ* did come to consensus was only a general guideline: they prohibited sexual intercourse for girls 'not able to undergo it', since otherwise sex could cause physical harm. As phrased in the late Ḥanbalī tradition, sex was allowed when the bride was 'at the age at which others like her have intercourse', with ᶜĀᵓisha's age of nine setting a general *terminus ante quem.*[60] In the Ḥanafī school, if the groom and his wife or her guardian disagreed about her capacity for sex, a Shariᶜa court judge would decide, perhaps after a female expert witness had examined her.[61]

Because the Prophet had married ᶜĀᵓisha when she was so young, and because the Islamic legal tradition had not set bright line rules for marriage age, introducing Shariᶜa complaint marriage age restrictions was highly problematic. Whatever the Prophet did is by definition permissible unless clearly specified as an exception, and blocking Muslims from following his precedent is highly suspect. The Qurᵓan even corrects the Prophet himself for restricting those sexual relations that God has allowed (Q. 66:1). In the strongly reformist climate of early twentieth-century Egypt, however, and assisted by the compelling power of the state, a number of prominent Egyptian *ᶜulamāᵓ* approved of the 1923 law. One of them was the Shaykh al-Azhar at the time, Muḥammad Abū al-Faḍl al-Gīzāwī (d. 1927), who penned a defence of the bill in the legal journal *al-Muḥāmāt.*

Al-Gīzāwī's argument in favour of the bill was based on three main points. First, he invoked the notion of executive authority in the application of the Shariᶜa. Specifically, the Shaykh al-Azhar cited the ruler's (*walī al-amr*) right to set administrative restrictions for judges (*takhṣīṣ al-qaḍāᵓ*). Even if a marriage contract agreed on by a groom and his bride/her guardian was valid before God, this did not mean that Shariᶜa courts or notaries had to register these marriages or admit them for dispute. It was well recognised that a ruler could issue directions for judges in his domain concerning administrative procedures.[62]

The second pillar in al-Gīzāwī's argument was to conflate the age of maturity in marriage with the age of maturity for competence in other contracts (a theme prominent in American reforms on marriage age laws). A minor cannot engage in a valid contract, since that requires sound reason (*ᶜāqil*), which, by definition, a minor lacks. Al-Gīzāwī built this argument by explaining that the Qurᵓan orders Muslims to 'test out the orphans until they reach the age of marriage (*balaghū al-nikāḥ*)' (Q. 4:6) before giving them any inheritance that had been held in trust for them. This command implied two things necessarily. First, maturity (*bulūgh*) and the capacity to marry were contemporaneous. Second, maturity was essential for taking up the responsibility of managing one's finances. Since marriage was theoretically a lifetime commitment and thus even weightier than finances, *a fortiori* no one underage could marry. Moreover, marriage only becomes necessary when a person reaches the point of having the physical desires that come with maturity (in Islamic law, puberty).[63] Al-Gīzāwī then invoked the furthest limits of when puberty could occur, along with the position of some jurists that sixteen to eighteen years old is the appropriate age for seniority regarding financial capacity (*sinn al-rushd al-mālī*), to make sixteen the earliest age at which girls could marry. This was justifiable, he claimed, because marriage is more consequential than managing money, and because it was clearly in the common good (*maṣlaḥa*) not to allow women to marry earlier.[64]

The third pillar of al-Gīzāwī's argument was precedent. Like the earlier two points, he had not developed this argument on his own. Neither had the group of senior *ᶜulamāᵓ* who endorsed with their signatures a 1923 *Al-Ahram* article supporting the marriage age restriction, including the respected author, scholar and dean at the School of Shariah Judges (*Madrasat al-Qaḍāᵓ al-Sharᶜiyya*), Muḥammad al-ᶜAfīfī al-Khuḍarī (d. 1927). These Egyptian *ᶜulamāᵓ* had been inspired by the Ottoman Family Law of 1917 (*Osmanlı Hukuk-ı Aile Kararnamesi*), articles 4, 5 and 6 of which prohibited marriage to girls under seventeen and boys under eighteen, unless the groom and bride were adolescents (*murāhiq*) approved of by the judge, and the bride had her guardian's permission. Article 7 took an even firmer stance, prohibiting marriage completely for a boy under eleven and a girl under nine years of age.[65] The Ottoman *ᶜulamāᵓ* tasked with justifying these laws as expressions of the Shariᶜa found the challenge almost insuperable, since none of the four Sunni *madhhab*s allowed restricting a father's right to contract a marriage for his underage daughter. Ottoman jurists thus reached outside the schools to the two classical scholars who supposedly did allow it. One was early Muᶜtazilite scholar Abū Bakr al-Aṣamm (d. 816), and the second was the much more respected Ibn Shubruma.[66] It was Ibn Shubruma and al-Aṣamm who seemed to have first developed the Qurᵓanic argument against underage marriage that lay at the core of the Ottoman and Egyptian laws.[67] Because Ibn Shubruma was a respected earlier figure in both the Kufan and Sunni traditions, while al-Aṣamm was a heretical Muᶜtazilite, the former served as a more stable anchor for the prohibition.

Opponents of the 1923 marriage age law attacked it and its supporters vociferously. One such opponent was the former Grand Mufti of Egypt, Muḥammad Bakhīt al-Muṭīᶜī (d. 1935).[68] Addressing the argument that the Muslim ruler had the right to shape law through administrative restrictions, al-Muṭīᶜī replied that *takhṣīṣ al-qaḍāᵓ* involved the procedures and details of adjudication and was only valid if it aimed at some common good (*maṣlaḥa*). Quite the contrary, the marriage restriction law would result in public harm, since it meant refusing to notarise or adjudicate a whole field of legal agreements. Since even advocates of the law acknowledged that marriage contracts conducted between underage partners were still valid in God's eyes, refusing to admit them in court would leave many validly married Egyptians with no legal recourse for marriage disputes. This would be tantamount to making what was *ḥalāl* in God's eyes *ḥarām* with no basis.[69]

Al-Muṭīʿī drew much of his substantive rebuttal of the Qurʾanic argument attributed to Ibn Shubruma from earlier Ḥanafī responses to it, such as that of al-Sarakhsī (d. circa 1096) and Kamāl al-Dīn Ibn al-Humām (d. 1457). Mainly, al-Muṭīʿī argued that Ibn Shubruma's argument contradicted the Qurʾan, the Sunna of the Prophet, and the early Muslims as well as the consensus of Muslim scholars. The Qurʾanic verses ordaining a waiting period of three menstrual cycles before a divorced woman could remarry add that those who are either menopausal or who 'have not menstruated (*allāʾī lam yaḥiḍna*)' should wait three months instead of the three courses before remarrying (Q. 65:4). That the Qurʾan detailed the proper post-divorce procedure for women who had not menstruated yet indicates indirectly that women too young to menstruate can still engage in marriage contracts. Furthermore, the Prophet's marriage contract with the six-year-old ʿĀʾisha was known by unimpeachable, parallel reports (*tawātur*), claimed al-Muṭīʿī, and many of the Companions and Successors had also conducted marriage contracts with young brides. Zubayr b. al-ʿAwwām (d. 656), in fact, had married his daughter to Qudāma b. Maẓʿūn (d. 656) on the day she was born. So whoever held or advocated restricting marriage contracts for underage girls, concluded al-Muṭīʿī, was advocating a 'false and rejected stance that contradicted the explicit meaning of the Book of God, the Sunna, and consensus. So it cannot be acted on.'[70]

Our chief concern here, however, is al-Muṭīʿī's response to the justification via classical precedent that the Ottoman and Egyptian *ʿulamāʾ* had attempted by citing Ibn Shubruma. This was not a valid tactic, explained al-Muṭīʿī, since the legal opinions of Ibn Shubruma and al-Aṣamm had neither been set down (*mudawwan*) nor attracted the attention needed of later followers (*aṣḥāb*) to properly understand and explain their legal methodology. In fact, al-Muṭīʿī ventured, the ambiguous language that those classical scholars who reported Ibn Shubruma's and al-Aṣamm's anomalous views, such as 'it is reported from them' or 'it is attributed to them', suggests that the attributions themselves were not reliable. Since the report about Ibn Shubruma comes down to us only as a disconnected artefact, we cannot even be sure that he had ever held this position or what he had meant by it if he had. This was compounded by the fact that another Ḥanafī *fiqh* manual, the *Badāʾiʿ al-ṣanāʾiʿ*, attributed the position to Ibn Shubruma and ʿUthmān al-Battī, not al-Aṣamm.[71]

Ibn Shubruma and Islamic Finance

In an influential 1976 book, the Egyptian Azhari Sāmī Ḥasan Ḥammūd offered a comprehensive treatment of the challenges that the modern financial landscape posed for those committed to compliance with the Shariʿa.

In what had become an established feature of modern financial life, credit had increasingly allowed people to acquire goods and services before they had accumulated all the funds necessary to pay for them. They were thus able to meet their needs more conveniently. This was made possible because merchants felt comfortable selling on credit due to a stable system for holding buyers and borrowers accountable. If Islamic banks and a Shariᶜa-conscious public wanted to compete in this new market, they had to offer such credit without veering into the sin of *al-ribā*. Ḥammūd suggested that this would be possible via the type of transaction known as *al-murābaḥa li-l-āmir bi-l-shirā*ᵓ, or a sale with an agreed upon profit carried out by an assigned agent (henceforth MAS), which the Shāfiᶜī school of law explicitly approved of.[72]

In this species of transaction, a Buyer engages an Agent to buy X item on his behalf from a Seller with the understanding that the Buyer will pay the Agent some premium for his services. Superimposed onto a financed purchase of a car or home, the Buyer engages the Agent (here, a Bank) to purchase the car/home from the Seller. After the Agent/Bank has bought the car/home, the Buyer then takes possession of it and pays the Agent/Bank the cost of the car/home according to some agreed upon schedule of instalments, with a premium added in as a counterpart to interest in a conventional loan.

This MAS transaction avoids transgressing the Shariᶜa's red lines. There is no interest paid, only the premium that the Prophet's Sunna had affirmed that the Buyer should pay for goods purchased on credit (if this premium tracks the conventional interest rates, that is no matter). Furthermore, the Agent/Bank is not guilty of selling what it does not have (a violation of the Prophet's command 'do not sell what you do not have') since it does not actually receive any payment from the Buyer or hand him the good until the Agent/Bank has received it from the Seller.[73] Finally, it is not 'profit with no liability (*ribḥ mā lam yuḍman*)', which the Prophet also prohibited, since the Agent/Bank bears the risk of damage befalling the goods until the Buyer takes possession.[74]

There was one snag in the MAS transaction, however. The Shariᶜa placed appreciable restrictions on the type of conditions or stipulations that could be attached to a sales contract. At the very least, any condition that contradicted the contract's entailment was prohibited, such as the sale of a horse on the condition that the buyer not ride it. So were any conditions that would result in the prohibited phenomena of interest (*al-ribā*) or excessive risk and uncertainty (*gharar*).[75] This latter concept included the prohibition on 'two transactions in one transaction (*bayᶜatān fī bayᶜa*)', in which case two parties agreed on one sale on the condition that they would then add another, separate sale (for example, Party A offers to buy X from Party B on the condition that Party B agrees to buy Y from Party A).[76] This involved elements of buying/selling what one does not own as well as transaction without liability.

In the case of the MAS, this prohibition meant that the Buyer and the Agent could not contractually agree that, if the Agent bought the item from the Seller, the Buyer would then buy it from the Agent. There could be no guarantee. The Buyer could arrange to buy a home through an Agent/Bank, but there was no way for the Agent/Bank to guarantee that the Buyer would actually uphold that commitment once the Agent/Bank had bought the house from the Seller. The Agent/Bank could be left holding an asset it had never wanted. Addressing this objection to the MAS serving as an Islamic counterpart to conventional loans, Ḥammūd replied that the percentage of buyers who would renege on their desire to buy an item through the Agent was tiny. Thus it was not worth dismissing the MAS as a financial solution. 'If the train derails once,' Ḥammūd offered, 'is the solution for the Ministry of Transport to stop all trains running so that this will not happen again?'[77] Of course, anyone who has experienced the modern mortgage market knows that this risk would be totally unacceptable in the conventional lending environment. No bank would purchase an asset for a potential borrower without a guarantee that the borrower would buy it in turn. Scholars of Islamic finance had to find some means to make the second stage of the MAS binding.

Again, Ibn Shubruma provided the key. In the late ninth century, al-Ṭabarī had already described a recognisable version of the MAS and had noted the challenge of the invalidity of the conditions required to make it binding. Though his *Ikhtilāf al-fuqahā'* contains only a handful of references to Ibn Shubruma, al-Ṭabarī refers to the Kufan scholar's ruling that, in the case of a sale with conditions, both the sale and the condition are valid. One could therefore conceivably undertake the MAS on the valid condition that the buyer guarantee that he would purchase the item from the agent.[78]

Al-Ṭabarī did not come across this information because Ibn Shubruma had offered an opinion on the MAS transaction. Rather, a report circulating amongst jurists in the ninth century described one ᶜAbd al-Wārith b. Saᶜīd going to Mecca and encountering Abū Ḥanīfa, Ibn Abī Laylā and Ibn Shubruma, all leading scholars of Kufa. He asked each his ruling on someone who 'made a transaction with a condition (*bāᶜa bayᶜan wa-sharaṭa sharṭan*)'. Abū Ḥanīfa replied that both the sale and the condition were void and invalid (*bāṭil*), citing a hadith in which the Prophet forbade sales with conditions. Ibn Abī Laylā responded that the sale was permissible and valid but the condition was void and invalid. He cited as his evidence a hadith in which a party sold a slave girl to ᶜĀ'isha, who intended to free her on the condition that the slave girl's *walā'* (patronage and the owner's share of the slave's estate) would remain with the party. Upon learning this, the Prophet affirmed the sale but nullified the condition, explaining that the *walāʾ* belonged to the manumitter of the slave. Ibn Shubruma, in turn, replied that both the sale and the condition were valid, since the Companion Jābir had sold a camel he was riding to the Prophet on the condition that Jābir be allowed to ride it back to his home before handing the animal over.[79]

As a result of this report, jurists like al-Ṭabarī, Ibn Rushd and others all assumed that Ibn Shubruma considered sales with conditions to be categorically valid.[80] Ibn Shubruma's ruling thus provided the ideal Shariʿa justification for the MAS with a binding agreement, bringing the financial device fully in line with modern lending. This was realised in 1979 at the First Conference of Islamic Finance (*Muʾtamar al-Maṣraf al-Islāmī al-Awwal*) in Dubai. The approval of the MAS depended on Ibn Shubruma's fatwa at its centre.[81]

As in the case of marriage age restrictions, the acceptance of the binding MAS attracted withering criticism. The most comprehensive came from the Palestinian *ʿālim* Muḥammad Sulaymān al-Ashqar (d. 2009), a longtime resident of Riyadh and Kuwait before settling in Jordan. In a comprehensive study on the binding MAS presented to the Dubai conference's 1983 follow-up in Kuwait, al-Ashqar undermined every argument for the practice. In short, he contended that conditions cannot be binding in such sales, since they would constitute unacceptable risk (*gharar*). As a result, any claim to a binding MAS would be prohibited. Furthermore, the various classical opinions that advocates of this species of transaction had marshalled as evidence were misplaced. Any rulings that extended some approval to binding promises or conditions could not conceivably have been intended to whitewash what was clearly meant to facilitate an interest-bearing transaction.[82]

As in the case of marriage age, al-Ashqar identified the longstanding problem with turning to the artefacts of defunct schools of thought as proof. The evidence for Ibn Shubruma having judged conditions on sales to be categorically valid and binding, namely the hadith in which Jābir sold the Prophet his camel, was not germane to the MAS issue. The binding MAS involved more than a simple condition in a transaction; it involved a promise to accomplish a whole other transaction. Unlike a condition, which becomes operative the moment one party in the contract fulfils its obligations (or at least begins to), the MAS involved a promise without consideration. It was a commitment made by one party to the other without either party giving up anything of detriment to the other.[83] Jurists from al-Ṭabarī to Ibn Ḥazm (d. 1064) and Ibn Rushd had assumed not only that Ibn Shubruma considered all conditions to be valid and binding, but also that all promises were 'binding, with the one making the promise subject to legal action and compulsion (*lāzim wa-yuqḍā bi-hi ʿalā al-wāʿid wa-yujbar*).' All this rested on reading a tremendous amount into how Ibn Shubruma interpreted one hadith.[84]

Ibn Shubruma's actual position, by contrast, along with his reasoning and interpretation of scriptural evidence were not clear at all. His argument was 'neither well recorded (*muḥarrar*) nor clarified (*mubayyan*)', observed al-Ashqar. Ibn Shubruma 'had no followers to record and edit (*yuḥarrirūn*) his legal methodology (*madhhaba-hu*), so that his categorical statements might be restricted and his general statements specified in light of what he intended in other utterances.' How could modern scholars be sure that Ibn Shubruma did not intend that conditions were valid provided they did not allow something *ḥarām*, like interest or *gharar*? That would seem much more likely, concluded al-Ashqar, and it would also be in line with an opinion that Ibn Ḥazm attributed to the Mālikī school in his day, namely that a promise or condition was binding if it fell within local custom and convention (*al-waʿd bi-l-maʿrūf*).[85]

Conclusion: The Political, Self Interest or Interpretive Hierarchy

Contemporary Sunni scholars outraged by calls for *mutʿa* marriage and other controversies, such as public campaigns promoting women leading Friday prayers, have been quick and confident in their dismissal of the rare, anomalous precedents that supporters of these practices draw upon from the classical heritage of Islamic law. Ibn ʿAbbās had allowed *mutʿa* marriage. Ninth-century Sunni luminaries like Abū Thawr (d. 854) and al-Ṭabarī had indeed allowed women to lead communal prayers. Ali Gomaa, then the Grand Mufti of Egypt, acknowledged all this in a 2005 fatwa on women-led prayers. But the anomalous opinions of Abū Thawr and others had no evidentiary weight when compared to the massive agreement of the *ʿulamāʾ* prohibiting women leading communal prayer, he responded. In fact, he added, 'advocating this aberrant (*shādhdh*) opinion is to impugn the umma in its early and latter days.'[86]

Yet the very scholarly establishments and claims of *ʿulamāʾ* consensus that so firmly rejected reaching back into the odd corners of the past on *mutʿa* and leading prayer embraced this same tactic on the equally controversial issues of restricting marriage age and Islamic financial transactions. The beloved Shaykh al-Azhar ʿAbd al-Ḥalīm Maḥmūd (d. 1978), though a passionate advocate of moving Egyptian law closer to the Shariʿa, approved of restricting marriage to girls over sixteen.[87] So did the Syrian shaykh and Shariʿa family court judge ʿAlī al-Ṭanṭāwī (d. 1999) when Syria adopted the same law, also on the basis of Ibn Shubruma's position.[88] During Gomaa's tenure as Grand Mufti of Egypt in the 2000s, in fact, the country's marriage restriction was further raised to eighteen for both men and women.[89] The

1979 Islamic finance conference in Dubai, in which Ibn Shubruma's opinion proved so crucial for accepting the binding MAS, is described by Mahmood El-Gamal as having 'ushered the birth of contemporary Islamic banking'. The permissibility of the binding MAS was reaffirmed at the second conference of Islamic banks in Kuwait in 1983 and again by the Jedda-based Islamic Legal Academy (*Majma*ᶜ *al-Fiqh al-Islāmī*) in 1988.[90] Both the Academy and the prolific Syrian scholar Wahba al-Zuḥaylī (d. 2015) noted that the binding MAS fast became the mainstay of lending in Islamic finance.[91]

From at least the thirteenth century to the present day, there has been consistent and strong concern over reaching beyond the primary rulings of a *madhhab* or crossing between schools. Concern has been even greater on the question of reaching outside the established *madhhab*s for precedents for legal rulings, let alone reaching back before the formation of the *madhhab*s altogether, either to authorities like the Companions or to early scholars whose *oeuvres* failed to generate lasting schools of law. From Ibn al-Ṣalāḥ and Ibn Rajab to scholars in Mauritania training muftis today, one finds the resounding conclusion that the scattered fatwas of the Companions and Successors or the sundry, uncontextualised rulings of scholars like Ibn Shubruma could not be understood well enough to serve as the basis for imitation in latter ages.[92]

In the case of Ibn Shubruma's supposed categorical allowance for conditions on sales, this wariness seems apt. In addition to tenuous evidence that he ever held this opinion to begin with, we find evidence that Ibn Shubruma's stance was less pronounced than claimed. A report in Wakīᶜ's (d. 918–19) *Akhbār al-quḍāt* describes Ibn Shubruma ruling in the case of one man urging another to arrange to have the latter man's slave purchase his own freedom over instalments (*mukātaba*). Concerning a promise offered by the first man to the second man (the slave's owner), that, if the soon-to-be manumitted slave were to fail in any of his duties, the first man would bear the financial responsibility, Ibn Shubruma ruled that the promissory condition was void.[93] It seems likely that the Kufan scholar ruled as such because the man's offer of guarantee bore too many traces of excessive risk and uncertainty (*gharar*), which would lend support to al-Ashqar's view that Ibn Shubruma had not approved of conditions for transactions categorically. Rather, he would never have approved of conditions that resulted in prohibited phenomena like *gharar* and *riban* (*al-ribā*). In the case of marriage age restriction, however, the eleventh-century sources that preserve what was ostensibly Ibn Shubruma's position provide ample explanation. In fact, drawing directly on the Qurᵓan and the expectations of marriage, Ibn Shubruma's argument is quite compelling.

Yet what of contemporary *ᶜulamāᵓ* like Ali Gomaa who seem to condemn reaching back before the *madhhab*s but also support the very legal reforms made possible by Ibn Shubruma?[94] From one perspective, this could be understood as the inconsistency that inevitably rears its head in the ineluctable presence of the political. Debates over marriage age restriction began and continue today from Egypt to Indonesia in the context of looming disapproval from colonial powers, Western observers and multilateral development organisations, as well as local segments of society convinced of these objections. A brief sampling of news media and the blogosphere illustrate the persistent disapproval of underage marriage amongst Western publics and those elements of Muslim populations that share their outlook. The pressures of the global financial system are even more intense. Sāmī Ḥammūd's observation that the Shariᶜa-minded could not compete in the financial marketplace without a competitive counterpart to the conventional mortgage was exact – the binding MAS has become the *sine qua non* of Islamic finance. Critics of Islamic finance, like al-Ashqar, find themselves in much the same position as *ᶜulamāᵓ* critics of Ottoman cash endowments almost 500 years ago: standing alone against the irresistible forces of economic reality and its concomitant apparatus of Shariᶜa legitimation.

Furthermore, both marriage age restrictions and the development of Islamic finance have been supported by state governments from Egypt to Malaysia. Deference to the political and legislative will of the state has been a prominent theme in Shariᶜa discourse in the Ottoman and post-Ottoman world. A state mufti like Ali Gomaa has no qualms about acknowledging this, explaining that, if there are two valid rulings on an issue, and the government favours one over the other, it is better to please the state.[95] One can only wonder, if the public mood in a country like Egypt or the will of the state were to shift dramatically on the issue of *mutᶜa* marriage, would Ibn ᶜAbbās' and Zufar's seemingly misguided support for the practice be embraced as prescient beads of wisdom plucked from the heritage of the past to justify reforms in the present?

From another, less cynical perspective, however, the tension over reaching back into the obscure past to legitimate present legal reform may be less an inconsistency than a question of who has the right to do so. In other words, it may not be a matter of whether one can access the distant past but rather who is qualified to access it. We find hints of this as far back as the fourteenth century. Despite the widespread agreement that the opinions of Companions could not be taken as the basis for rulings, al-Zarkashī (d. 1392) noted that some scholars maintained that senior jurists (*mujtahid*) could do so. He added that, in his own opinion, a mufti can base a fatwa on the opinion of an early, pre-*madhhab* scholar (*salaf*) provided that he is familiar with the reasoning behind the opinion.[96] Three centuries later, another prominent Egyptian jurist, al-Munāwī (d. 1622), also conceded that a *mujtahid* (for him, any scholar senior enough to dispense with *taqlīd*), could follow an early exemplar outside the four *madhhab*s as long as he did not lapse into habitual licence-taking (*tatabbuᶜ al-rukhaṣ*).[97]

We also find allusions to this framework of limited authoritative access to the past in the writings of al-Kawtharī, who was supremely critical of mid-twentieth-century efforts to reform personal status law in Egypt. He lambasted pseudo-*ᶜulamāʾ* assigned to state projects drawing from all the Sunni (and Shiᶜite) *madhhab*s in order to find laws 'appropriate for this day and age (*munāsib li-hādhā al-zamān*)'.[98] He called out the transparent strategy of finding some anomalous Companion or Successor ruling that fortuitously agreed with a point of contentious legal reform. Such theatre might provide reformers with 'an excuse before the people', he warned, 'but not before God'.[99] Indeed, as a staunch Ḥanafī and the last academic dean (*shaykh dars*) of the Ottoman Empire, al-Kawtharī adhered to the most conservative views on crossing *madhhab* lines.[100] But he was careful to affirm that it was the duty of the *ᶜulamāʾ* to bring Islam's heritage to bear on the challenges of the present day, so that they could offer Muslims those rulings that were 'most conducive to the umma'. To do so, they could even reach back to scholars outside the four *madhhab*s, al-Kawtharī added, even citing Ibn Shubruma as an example. But this was a responsibility only to be undertaken by truly qualified scholars, who alone had the right to access the obscurities of the past.[101]

The relationship between scholars undertaking this task and the Islamic legal heritage thus depends greatly on how those scholars are viewed, or at least on how they view their own authority. Even by the more conservative gradations of *ijtihād*, those who are deemed to have reached the highest qualifications of the position of *mujtahid* are, in fact, not required to remain within the boundaries of any one *madhhab*, though they would, in reality, remain rooted primarily in one.[102] In analysing a particular legal question or responding to a request for a fatwa, they can choose not only between the various opinions within one *madhhab* but also amongst the various *madhhab*s and even from the opinions of scholars like Ibn Shubruma who existed before and outside the *madhhab* framework. One scholar responsible for training foreign muftis in Egypt's Fatwa Ministry (*Dār al-Iftāʾ*) outlined the broad resources available to a qualified mufti as (1) the Qurʾan and Sunna, (2) the Islamic legal heritage (*turāth*), and (3) the aims of the Shariᶜa (*maqāṣid*). For such a mufti, the objectives of the Shariᶜa guide him or her to choose the appropriate ruling from the legal heritage, and the Qurʾan and the Sunna provide the best and most 'intimate' means of communicating it to the person seeking the fatwa.[103]

Scholars like Ali Gomaa consider themselves to be the living vessels of the Shariᶜa tradition brought to bear on the questions raised in the present day.¹⁰⁴ It is their confident mastery of the Shariʿa's interpretive tradition that provides them with their rulings and fatwas, not any one body of law or legal reference. Yet, because the Islamic scholarly tradition is a precedential one, in which statements must be rooted in the past to earn credibility, referring directly to the Qurʾan, the Prophet's words or the rulings of classical scholars embodies the scholar's own opinion in the currency of tradition. A recent survey on what makes a fatwa compelling to members of the public illustrates the suitability of this mode of presenting a Shariʿa argument. While an overwhelming percentage of those surveyed (94 per cent) replied that, in order to be confident in the validity of a fatwa, it should come from a reputable mufti or fatwa institute, 86 per cent of respondents wanted the fatwa to provide textual evidence from the Qurʾan and Sunna, and 67 per cent noted the importance of referencing earlier works of law.¹⁰⁵

There is thus an ironic convergence between the cynical and the sincere in the modern recourse to the obscure reaches of Islam's legal heritage. A modern scholar may well be using the opinion of Ibn Shubruma as a fig leaf to mask his own opinion, and he may call for other scholars to be prohibited from doing the same. But, if he is truly a senior scholar, he may also consider it his right and responsibility to act as the channel for the Shariʿa tradition, invoking some obscure reach of its heritage not as the substance of his argument but only to maintain that link between the present and the past that gives any tradition its strength.

Notes

1. Al-Khaṭīb al-Baghdādī, *Tārīkh Baghdād*, ed. Muṣṭafā ʿAbd al-Qādir ʿAṭā (Beirut: Dār al-Kutub al-ʿIlmiyya, 1417/1997), 14: 202–3; Ibn Khallikān, *Wafayāt al-aʿyān*, ed. Iḥsān ʿAbbās (Beirut: Dār Ṣādir, 1397/1977), 6: 150.
2. This took place in 1575–6. The nine-wife ruling was based on a cumulative reading of Qurʾan 4:3 instead of the standard, disjunctive one. For the main hadith evidence against this cumulative reading, see *Jāmiʿ al-Tirmidhī*: *kitāb al-nikāḥ, bāb mā jāʾa fī al-rajul yuslimu wa-ʿinda-hu ʿashar niswa*. The *mutʿa* decision took place in the presence of several leading Sunni scholars and chief judges of the Mughal realm, such as Qāḍī Yaʿqūb (d. 1589–90) and Ḥājj Ibrāhīm al-Sirhindī (d. 1585–6). Qāḍī Yaʿqūb disapproved of the ruling and thus fell from imperial favour: ʿAbd al-Qādir al-Badāunī, *Muntakhabu-t-Tawārīkh*, ed. and trans. W. H. Lowe *et al.* (Delhi: Renaissance Publishing, 1986), 2: 211–13; Ruby Lal, *Domesticity and Power in the Early Mughal World* (Cambridge: Cambridge University Press, 2005), 172–3; ʿAbd al-Ḥayy al-Ḥasanī, *Nuzhat al-khawāṭir fī bahjat al-masāmiʿ wa-l-nawāẓir*, 3rd edn (Hyderabad: Dāʾirat al-Maʿārif al-ʿUthmāniyya, 1989), 4: 193–4.
3. Ṣāliḥ al-Wardānī, *Zawāj al-mutʿa ḥalāl fī al-kitāb wa-l-sunna* (Cairo: Kunūz, 2008), 107.

4. Muḥammad Ḥāmid, *Nikāḥ al-mutᶜa ḥarām fī al-Islām* (Cairo: Dār al-Salām, 2008), 8, 93.
5. Jon Mandaville, 'Usurious piety: the cash waqf controversy in the Ottoman Empire', *International Journal of Middle East Studies* 10 (1979), 297, 302.
6. For the most recent and comprehensive discussion of *tatabbuᶜ al-rukhaṣ*, Islamic theories of legal pluralism and boundary crossing, see Ahmed Fekry Ibrahim, 'Al-Sharᶜānī's response to legal purism: a theory of legal pluralism', *Islamic Law and Society* 21:1–2 (2013), 110–40. Other useful, data-filled studies include Muḥammad Rifᶜat Saᶜīd, *al-Rukhṣa fī al-sharīᶜa al-islāmiyya wa-taṭbīqu-hā al-muᶜāṣira* (Mansoura: Dār al-Wafāᵓ, 1423/2002) and Usāma Muḥammad al-Ṣallābī, *al-Rukhaṣ al-sharᶜiyya aḥkāmu-hā wa-ḍawābiṭu-hā* (Alexandria: Dār al-Īmān, 2002).
7. For rabbis and Eastern Christian metropolitans being impressed by Shariᶜa court procedures in ninth- and tenth-century Baghdad, see Uriel Simonsohn, *A Common Justice: The Legal Allegiances of Christians and Jews under Early Islam* (Philadelphia: University of Pennsylvania Press, 2011), 107, 186–7.
8. This is reminiscent of Ibn al-Muqaffaᶜ's (d. 759) prescient suggestion that the caliph solicit the *fiqh* opinions from amongst the regional schools of thought (*amṣār*), examine their evidence from the Qurᵓan and Sunna, and then select one ruling to be part of a binding book of law: ᶜAbd Allāh Ibn al-Muqaffaᶜ, 'Risāla fī al-ṣaḥāba', in *Āthār Ibn al-Muqaffaᶜ* (Beirut: Dār al-Kutub al-ᶜIlmiyya, 1409/1989), 317.
9. Shaykh Niẓām *et al.*, *al-Fatāwā al-Hindiyya*, ed. ᶜAbd al-Laṭīf Ḥasan ᶜAbd al-Raḥmān (Beirut: Dār al-Kutub al-ᶜIlmiyya, 2001), 1: 4. One example is the fatwa in which the Deoband scholars take Mālikī positions to facilitate divorce for women in India: Fareeha Khan, 'Tafwīḍ al-Ṭalāq: transferring the right of divorce to the wife', *Muslim World* 99:3 (2009), 503.
10. Rudolph Peters, 'What does it mean to be an official madhhab?: Hanafism and the Ottoman Empire', in Peri Bearman *et al.* (eds), *The Islamic School of Law* (Cambridge, MA: Harvard University Press, 2005), 153.
11. Abū al-Ḥasan al-Māwardī, *Adab al-qāḍī*, ed. Muḥyī al-Hilāl Sarḥān (Baghdad: Maṭbaᶜat al-Irshād, 1971), 1: 165–85.
12. David Powers, 'Four cases relating to women and divorce in Al-Andalus and the Maghrib, 1100–1500', in Muhammad Khalid Masud, Rudolph Peters and David Powers (eds), *Dispensing Justice in Islam* (Leiden: Brill, 2006), 383–409; Leo Africanus, *The History and Description of Africa*, trans. John Pory, ed. Robert Brown (London: Hakluyt Society, 1896), 2: 444–5 (where the author describes an appeals court in Fez). In one instance in Cairo in 1524 CE, a Mālikī judge in the Ottoman Empire fell into conflict with the chief judge (Ḥanafī) overseeing him because the chief judge insisted that his junior rule by the *mashhūr* of his school while the latter insisted on his right as a senior scholar to choose among the Mālikī school's rulings on an issue: Reem Meshal, 'Antagonistic *Sharīᶜa*s and the construction of orthodoxy in sixteenth-century Cairo', *Journal of Islamic Studies* 21:2 (2010), 182–212 (200).

13. Abū ᶜĪsā Sīdī al-Mahdī b. Muḥammad al-Wazzānī (also al-Wāzzānī) (d. 1923–4), *al-Nawāzil al-jadīda al-kubrā fī-mā li-ahl Fās wa-ghayrihim min al-badū wa-l-qurā/al-Miᶜyār al-jadīd al-jāmiᶜ al-muᶜrib ᶜan fatāwā al-mutaᵓakhkhirīn min ᶜulamāᵓ al-maghrib*, ed. ᶜUmar ᶜImād (Casablanca: Maṭbaᶜat al-Faḍāla, 1418/1997), 4: 16. This approach must have been well-known in Fez since at least the fifteenth century, as Shaykh Sīdī Ibrāhīm Ibn Hilāl of Sijilmas (d. 1497–8) objected fiercely to it, affirming that 'it is not permissible to give fatwas except by the *mashhūr* ruling, and there is no acting except by the *mashhūr*.' He added that the opinion attributed to ᶜAlī b. Abī Ṭālib, which was seen as the anchor for local Fezi practice, was inauthentic: ibid. 81; ᶜAbd al-Ḥayy al-Kattānī, *Fahris al-fahāris*, ed. Iḥsān ᶜAbbās (Beirut: Dār al-Gharb al-Islāmī, 1406/1986), 2: 1107. For more on al-Wazzānī, see Etty Terem, *Old Texts, New Practices: Islamic Reform in Modern Morocco* (Stanford: Stanford University Press, 2014), 19–50.
14. Mohammed Fadel, 'The social logic of *Taqlīd* and the rise of the *Mukhtaṣar*', *Islamic Law and Society* 3:2 (1996), 219–32; Yossef Rapoport, 'Legal diversity in the age of *taqlīd*: the four chief *qāḍī*s under the Mamluks', *Islamic Law and Society* 10:2 (2003), 216, 226–8.
15. For a statement of this position in both Ḥanafī and Shāfiᶜī texts, see Muḥyī al-Dīn al-Nawawī, *Rawḍat al-ṭālibīn* (Beirut: al-Maktab al-Islāmī, 1405/1985), 11: 101; idem, *Adab al-muftī wa-l-mustaftī*, ed. Bassām ᶜAbd al-Wahhāb al-Jābī (Damascus: Dār al-Fikr, 1988), 77; Ibn Qayyim al-Jawziyya, *Iᶜlām al-muwaqqiᶜīn ᶜan rabb al-ᶜālamīn*, ed. Muḥammad ᶜIzz al-Dīn al-Khaṭīb, 4 vols (Beirut: Dār Iḥyāᵓ al-Turāth al-ᶜArabī, 1422/2001), 4: 220–1; Badr al-Dīn Muḥammad b. Bahādur al-Zarkashī, *al-Baḥr al-muḥīṭ fī uṣūl al-fiqh*, ed. Muḥammad Muḥammad Tāmir, 4 vols (Beirut: Dār al-Kutub al-ᶜIlmiyya, 2007), 4: 597; Aḥmad Zarrūq, *Qawāᶜid al-taṣawwuf*, ed. ᶜUthmān al-Ḥuwaydī (Tunis: al-Maṭābiᶜ al-Muwaḥḥada, 1987), 30; Abū al-Ikhlāṣ Ḥasan al-Shurunbulālī, 'al-ᶜIqd al-farīd fī bayān al-rājiḥ min al-khilāf fī jawāz al-taqlīd', in Khālid b. Muḥammad al-ᶜArūsī (ed.), *Majallat Jāmiᶜat Umm al-Qurā* 17:32 (1425/2005), 701; Muḥammad Amīn Ibn ᶜĀbidīn, *Ḥāshiyat Radd al-muḥtār*, 8 vols (Beirut: Dār al-Fikr, 2000), 2: 411 (reprint of the 1966 Cairo Muṣṭafā al-Bābī al-Ḥalabī edn); Sayyid ᶜAlawī b. Aḥmad al-Saqqāf, 'Mukhtaṣar al-fawāᵓid al-makkiyya', in *Majmūᶜat sabᶜa kutub mufīda* (Cairo: Muṣṭafā al-Bābī al-Ḥalabī, n.d.), 91.
16. *Rukhṣa* in this context, and as discussed in this chapter overall, should be distinguished from *rukhṣa* in the sense of scripturally granted dispensations, like the permission for those sick or travelling not to fast during Ramadan (Q. 2:184–5) and hadiths like 'Indeed God loves His *rukhṣa*s to be taken as He hates disobedience to Him to be done (*inna Allāh yuḥibbu an tuᵓtā rukhaṣu-hu ka-mā yakrahu an tuᵓtā maᶜṣiyatu-hu*)'; *Musnad Ibn Ḥanbal*: 2:108 (Maymaniyya print). Ibn Ḥajar al-ᶜAsqalānī noted that taking these dispensations, even when not strictly necessary (like shortening one's prayers during travel even when the travel is not burdensome), is a form of extra obedience to

God and thus better (*afḍal*) than carrying out the ordinary duty: ʿAbd al-Raʾūf al-Munāwī, *Fayḍ al-qadīr sharḥ al-Jāmiʿ al-ṣaghīr*, ed. Ḥamdī al-Damardāsh Muḥammad, 13 vols (Mecca: Maktabat Nizār Muṣṭafā al-Bāz, 1998), 4: 1686.

17. Abū Ḥafṣ ʿUmar al-Suhrawardī, *ʿAwārif al-maʿārif*, ed. ʿAbd al-Ḥalīm Maḥmūd and Maḥmūd al-Sharaf (Cairo: al-Īmān, 1426/2005), 149.
18. Ibn Ḥajar al-ʿAsqalānī, *Talkhīṣ al-ḥabīr*, ed. ʿAbd Allāh Hāshim al-Yamānī (Cairo: Sharikat al-Ṭibāʿa al-Fanniyya, 1384/1964), 3: 187. For a similar, much earlier attested statement attributed to Ibn Ḥanbal, see ʿAbd Allāh b. Aḥmad b. Ḥanbal, *Masāʾil al-imām Aḥmad b. Ḥanbal riwāyat ibni-hi ʿAbd Allāh b. Aḥmad*, ed. Zuhayr al-Shāwīsh (Beirut: al-Maktab al-Islāmī, 1401/1981), 449.
19. ʿIzz al-Dīn Ibn ʿAbd al-Salām, *Kitāb al-Fatāwā*, ed. ʿAbd al-Raḥmān ʿAbd al-Fattāḥ (Beirut: Dār al-Maʿrifa, n.d.), 153.
20. Al-Nawawī, *Adab al-muftī*, 77. Ibn ʿAbd al-Salām warned that judges in his day who ruled by their discretion and not by the main opinion of their *madhhab* tended merely to rule according to 'corrupt aims (*aghrāḍ fāsida*)'; Ibn ʿAbd al-Salām, *Fatāwā*, 90.
21. Muḥammad Zāhid al-Kawtharī, *Maqālāt al-Kawtharī* (Cairo: Dār al-Salām, 2007), 109–10; Muḥammad ʿUbaydallāh al-Asʿadī al-Qāsimī, *Dār al-ʿulūm dayūband* (Deoband, India: Akādīmiyyat Shaykh al-Hind, 1420/2000), 795; Ibn ʿĀbidīn, *Sharḥ ʿUqūd rasm al-fatwā*, 2nd edn (Hyderabad: Markaz Tawʿiyat al-Fiqh al-Islāmī, 2000), 1: 7–8; Rudolph Peters, 'Muḥammad al-ʿAbbāsī and Mahdī (d. 1987), Grand Muftī of Egypt, and his Fatāwā al-Mahdiyya', *Islamic Law and Society* 1:1 (1994), 66–82.
22. Al-Wazzānī, *al-Nawāzil al-jadīda*, 4: 81.
23. ʿAlī Ḥaydar, *Durar al-ḥukkām sharḥ Majallat al-aḥkām*, trans. Fahmī al-Ḥusaynī (Riyadh: Dār ʿĀlam al-Kutub, 1424/2003), 1: 11–12, re: section 1.4 in the *Mecelle*.
24. Ibn ʿĀbidīn (d. 1836) states that one can leave the primary ruling of the Ḥanafī school (*rājiḥ*, *ẓāhir*) in cases of necessity (*ḍarūra*) or if changing convention (*ʿurf*) has led to the adoption of a non-primary ruling for fatwas in that time/place. Mālikīs like Ibn Abī Ḥamza (d. 1202) and ʿAbd al-Qādir al-Fāsī (d. 1680–1) also allow *rukhṣa*s on occasion due to necessity. The Mālikī al-Qarāfī (d. 1285) notes that, though the mainstay position in the Mālikī school prohibited moving between schools on particular issues, according to him, even those who hold this position would allow switching schools in cases of necessity (*ḍarūra*). This seems to be the case for Aḥmad Zarrūq (d. 1493), who only allows taking permission from another *madhhab* in cases of necessity (*ḍarūra*); Ibn ʿĀbidīn, *Sharḥ Rasm al-fatwā*, 20, 21, 40, 44; al-Wazzānī, *al-Nawāzil al-jadīda*, 4: 9–10, 40–1; Shihāb al-Dīn Aḥmad b. Idrīs al-Qarāfī, *al-Iḥkām fī tamyīz al-fatāwā ʿan al-aḥkām wa-taṣarrufāt al-qāḍī wa-l-imām*, ed. ʿAbd al-Fattāḥ Abū Ghudda (Aleppo: Maktab al-Maṭbūʿāt al-Islāmiyya, 1387/1967), 213, 230; Zarrūq, *Qawāʿid*, 30–1.
25. Al-Qarāfī explains that crossing between schools must not result in *talfīq* (he gives the example of the prayer of someone who had taken the Shāfiʿī ruling

of wiping only part of one's head with water in ablutions and then taking the Mālikī position of not reciting the *basmala* out loud. The prayer would thus be invalid for Shāfiᶜīs, since the *basmala* was not said aloud, and for Mālikīs, since the whole head had not been wiped). Furthermore, a mufti should not draw on another *madhhab* for a fatwa or give a fatwa to a person asking about the ruling of their own *madhhab* (i.e. not the mufti's) if the mufti feels that the other school's opinion (1) contradicts consensus (*ijmāᶜ*), (2) contradicts basic maxims of law (*qawāᶜid*), (3) contradicts an explicit scriptural text (*naṣṣ*), or (4) contradicts *a fortiori* reasoning (*qiyās jalī*). Al-Qarāfī admits, however, that only item (1) would be agreed upon by all scholars. Interestingly, he gives the same items as conditions in which a judge's ruling would become void: al-Qarāfī, *al-Iḥkām*, 88, 210–11, 233.

26. Taqī al-Dīn al-Subkī recalls meeting Ibn Daqīq in Cairo as a boy but never studied with him at length: Tāj al-Dīn al-Subkī, *Ṭabaqāt al-shāfiᶜiyya al-kubrā*, eds ᶜAbd al-Fattāḥ Muḥammad al-Ḥulw and Maḥmūd Muḥammad al-Ṭanāḥī, 2nd edn (Cairo: Hujr, 1413/1992), 10: 145.
27. For a useful discussion of how necessity (*ḍarūra*) should be distinguished from need (*ḥāja*) or hardship (*ḥaraj*, *mashaqqa*), see ᶜAbd Allāh Bin Bayyah, *al-Farq bayn al-ḍarūra wa-l-ḥāja taṭbīqan ᶜalā baᶜḍ aḥwāl al-aqalliyyāt al-muslima*, available at http://www.binbayyah.net/portal/sites/default/files/the%20diffrent%20bettween%20aldarorah%20and%20alhajah.pdf (last accessed 31 December 2014). A. F. Ibrahim observes how, in a revealing instance, al-Zarkashī and al-Subkī use the term *ḍarūra* not as a life-threatening necessity but rather as intense need or 'taxing necessity': Ibrahim, 'Al-Sharᶜānī's response', 134. Al-Suyūṭī (d. 1505) offers a taxonomy of need: *ḍarūra* means a situation in which a person will perish, or come close to perishing, if a solution is not found, and it makes the *ḥarām* permissible. *Ḥāja* causes great hardship (*ḥaraj*, *mashaqqa*) and allows a person to take dispensations like breaking their fast due to fierce hunger: Jalāl al-Dīn al-Suyūṭī, *al-Ashbāh wa-l-naẓāʾir*, ed. Muḥammad al-Muᶜtaṣim al-Baghdādī (Beirut: Dār al-Kitāb al-ᶜArabī, 1414/1993), 176.
28. Such a case could include praying after touching a dog (pure according to the Mālikīs but impure to other schools) but not wiping one's whole head during ablutions (not required by other schools but required by Mālikīs).
29. Taqī al-Dīn al-Subkī gave this fatwa in 1345: Taqī al-Dīn al-Subkī, *Fatāwā*, 2 vols (Beirut: Dār al-Maᶜrifa, n.d.), 1: 147–8; Tāj al-Dīn al-Subkī *et al.*, *Ḥāshiyat al-ᶜallāma al-bannānī ᶜalā sharḥ al-Jalāl Shams al-Dīn al-Maḥallī ᶜalā matn jamᶜ al-jawāmiᶜ*, 2 vols (Beirut: Dār al-Fikr, 1402/1982), 2: 400–1; al-Zarkashī, *al-Baḥr al-muḥīṭ*, 4: 599; al-Suyūṭī, *al-Ḥāwī li-l-fatāwī* (Beirut: Dār al-Kitāb al-ᶜArabī, n.d.), 2: 5; Shihāb al-Dīn Aḥmad Ibn Ḥajar al-Haytamī, *al-Fatāwā al-ḥadīthiyya*, ed. Muḥammad ᶜAbd al-Raḥmān al-Marᶜashlī (Beirut: Dār Iḥyāʾ al-Turāth al-ᶜArabī, 1419/1998), 155–6; idem, *al-Fatāwā al-kubrā al-fiqhiyya* (Cairo: ᶜAbd al-Ḥamīd Aḥmad al-Ḥanafī, n.d.), 4: 304–5, esp. 307; Zarrūq, *Qawāᶜid*, 31; Shihāb al-Dīn

al-Ramlī, *Ghāyat al-maʾmūl fī sharḥ waraqāt al-uṣūl* (Cairo: Muʾassasat Qurṭuba, 2005), 396.

30. Ibrahim, 'Al-Sharʿānī's response', 133.
31. See Ibn Ḥajar al-Haytamī, *al-Fatāwā al-kubrā*, 4: 325–6 (here the author specifies that only the four *madhhabs* can be used in courts and for fatwas, though a person can follow another *madhhab* in his private life); Burhān al-Dīn Ibrāhīm al-Bayjūrī, *Ḥāshiyat al-imām al-Bayjūrī ʿalā jawharat al-tawḥīd*, ed. ʿAlī Jumʿa, 3rd edn (Cairo: Dār al-Salām, 1427/2006), 250–1; al-Saqqāf, 'Mukhtaṣar al-fawāʾid al-makkiyya', 89, 91 (citing Abū Bakr b. al-Qāsim al-Ahdal); Ṣāliḥ al-Fullānī, *Īqāẓ himam ūlī al-abṣār li-l-iqtidāʾ bi-sayyid al-muhājirīn wa-l-anṣār* (Beirut: Dār al-Maʿrifa, 1978), 54.
32. Ibn Abī al-Wafāʾ al-Qurashī, *al-Jawāhir al-muḍiyya fī ṭabaqāt al-ḥanafiyya*, ed. 'Abd al-Fattāḥ Muḥammad al-Ḥulw, 5 vols (Giza: Muʾassasat al-Risāla, 1978–88), 2: 663. This was followed in the madrasas endowed by the Ayyūbids in the 1240s: Ibrahim, 'Al-Sharʿānī's response', 116. Al-Dhahabī attests to the Mustanṣiriyya Library's preeminence through the 1320s: Shams al-Dīn al-Dhahabī, *Tadhkirat al-ḥuffāẓ*, ed. Zakariyyā ʿUmayrāt, 4 vols in 2 (Beirut: Dār al-Kutub al-ʿIlmiyya, 1419/1998), 4: 190.
33. ʿAbd al-Malik al-Juwaynī, *al-Burhān fī uṣūl al-fiqh*, ed. ʿAbd al-ʿAẓīm al-Dīb, 2 vols (Cairo: Dār al-Anṣār, 1400/1980), 2: 744.
34. Al-Subkī, *Ṭabaqāt*, 8: 231.
35. It is important to note that Ibn al-Ṣalāḥ and others discussing this issue mean the fatwas or rulings of the Companions that had not already been integrated into the *madhhabs* – in other words, anomalous ones. All the Sunni schools of law drew substantially on the rulings of Companions like ʿUmar and ʿAlī.
36. Al-Nawawī, *Adab al-muftī*, 77; al-Zarkashī, *al-Baḥr al-muḥīṭ*, 4: 571.
37. Yāqūt al-Ḥamawī, *Muʿjam al-udabāʾ*, ed. Iḥsān ʿAbbās (Beirut: Dār al-Gharb al-Islāmī, 1993), 5: 1955; al-Māwardī, *al-Aḥkām al-sulṭāniyya* (Cairo: Muṣṭafā al-Bābī al-Ḥalabī, 1966), 66; idem, *Adab al-qāḍī*, 1: 165–85.
38. Abū Isḥāq al-Shīrāzī, *Ṭabaqāt al-fuqahāʾ*, ed. Iḥsān ʿAbbās (Beirut: Dār al-Rāʾid al-ʿArabī, [1970]), 97ff.
39. Ibn al-Ṣalāḥ, *Muqaddima fī ʿulūm al-ḥadīth*, ed. Nūr al-Dīn ʿItr (Beirut: Dār al-Fikr, 1397/1977), 335. Interestingly, al-Thawrī's name is missing in ʿĀʾisha ʿAbd al-Raḥmān's edition of the *Muqaddima*: see *Muqaddimat Ibn al-Ṣalāḥ* (Cairo: Dār al-Maʿārif, 1989), 579.
40. Ibn al-Jawzī, *al-Muntaẓam fī tārīkh al-mulūk wa-l-umam*, ed. Muḥammad ʿAbd al-Qādir ʿAṭā and Muṣṭafā ʿAbd al-Qādir ʿAṭā (Beirut: Dār al-Kutub al-ʿIlmiyya, 1992), 18: 32.
41. Yaḥyā b. Muḥammad Ibn Hubayra, *Ikhtilāf al-a'imma al-aʿlām*, ed. al-Sayyid Yūsuf Aḥmad (Beirut: Dār al-Kutub al-ʿIlmiyya, 2002), 2: 395.
42. That only the four *madhhabs* have been sufficiently well documented and repeatedly refined was an opinion shared by Aḥmad Zarrūq and ʿAbd al-Ghanī al-Nābulusī (d. 1731), though for Zarrūq this was merely a function of them being the only surviving *madhhabs*. Al-Suyūṭī stated that at one

time or another there had been 'around ten *madhhabs* whose scholars were imitated (*muqallada*) and books set down.' Other book titles contemporaneous to Ibn Rajab convey the same understanding of the four *madhhab* limit, such as the *Kitāb al-Arkān fī al-madhāhib al-arbaʿa* by ʿAbd al-ʿAzīz al-Dayrī al-Shādhilī of Egypt (Shāfiʿī, d. 1297–8), the *Zubdat al-aḥkām fī ikhtilāf madhāhib al-aʾimma al-arbaʿa al-aʿlām*, by Sirāj al-Dīn Abū Ḥafṣ ʿUmar b. Isḥāq al-Hindī al-Ghaznawī (Ḥanafī, d. 1373) and *ʿUyūn al-madhāhib al-arbaʿa*, by Qiwām al-Dīn Muḥammad al-Kākī (d. 1349); Zarrūq, *Qawāʿid*, 30; ʿAbd al-Ghanī al-Nābulusī, *al-Ḥadīqa al-nadiyya sharḥ al-Ṭarīqa al-muḥammadiyya*, 2 vols (Istanbul: Āstāna, n.d.; reprint of the Maṭbaʿa-i ʿĀmira, 1290/[1873]), 2: 696; al-Suyūṭī, *al-Ḥāwī*, 2: 340 (treatise entitled *Kitāb al-Aʿlām bi-ḥukm ʿĪsā ʿalay-hi al-salām*); Ḥājjī Khalīfa Muṣṭafā Kātib Chelebī, *Kashf al-ẓunūn ʿan asāmī al-kutub wa-l-funūn*, ed. Muḥammad ʿAbd al-Qādir ʿAṭā (Beirut: Dār al-Kutub al-ʿIlmiyya, 1429/2008), 2: 250, 441; 3: 19.

43. Ibn Rajab al-Ḥanbalī, 'al-Radd ʿalā man ittabaʿa ghayr al-madhāhib al-arbaʿa', in Ṭalʿat Fuʾād al-Ḥulwānī (ed.), *Majmūʿ rasāʾil al-ḥāfiẓ Ibn Rajab al-Ḥanbalī* 2 vols (Cairo: al-Fārūq al-Ḥadītha, 1423/2002), 2: 626. In this hadith, Ibn ʿAbbās explains that ʿUmar had changed the ruling and counted three declarations in one setting as the three necessary for a terminal divorce: *Ṣaḥīḥ Muslim*: *kitāb al-ṭalāq, bāb ṭalāq al-thalāth*; Ibn Taymiyya, *Majmūʿat fatāwā*, eds Sayyid Ḥusayn al-ʿAffānī and Khayrī Saʿīd, 35 vols (Cairo: al-Maktaba al-Tawfīqiyya, n.d.), 32: 205–6, 212.
44. In *ṣarf*, the exchange must occur in the same sitting whether the coin (gold or silver) is of the same species or not and, in addition, be of the exact same quantities/weight if the same species: Ibn Ḥajar al-ʿAsqalānī, *Fatḥ al-Bārī sharḥ Ṣaḥīḥ al-Bukhārī*, eds ʿAbd al-ʿAzīz b. ʿAbdallāh b. Bāz and Muḥammad Fuʾād ʿAbd al-Bāqī, 16 vols (Beirut: Dār al-Kutub al-ʿIlmiyya, 1997), 4: 480–1.
45. Ibn Rajab, 'al-Radd', 623.
46. Al-Ḥākim (d. 1014) includes a report of Ibn ʿAbbās changing his position when he was told about the hadith in which the Prophet prohibited exchanging the same species of good at different amounts: al-Ḥākim al-Naysābūrī, *al-Mustadrak ʿalā al-Ṣaḥīḥayn* (Hyderabad: Dāʾirat al-Maʿārif al-ʿUthmāniyya, 1917–25), 2: 20, 43, 49.
47. Muḥammad al-Ghazālī, *Turāthu-nā al-fikrī* (Cairo: Dār al-Shurūq, 1991), 153.
48. Maḥmūd Shaltūt, *Fatāwā* (Cairo: Dār al-Shurūq, 1983), 15.
49. Muḥammad ʿAbduh, *al-Aʿmāl al-kāmila li-l-imām al-shaykh Muḥammad ʿAbduh*, ed. Muḥammad ʿAmāra (Cairo: Dār al-Shurūq, 1414/1993), 2: 509. For ʿAbduh's source, see Aḥmad b. Yaḥyā al-Wansharīsī, *al-Miʿyār al-muʿrib*, eds Muḥammad Ḥajjī *et al.* (Beirut: Dār al-Gharb al-Islāmī, 1981–3), 2: 9–10. ʿAbduh's argument hinged on whether the permission to eat the meat of the People of the Book superseded clear Qurʾanic prohibitions on types of slaugh-

ter. ʿAbduh draws on al-Wansharīsī's fatwa, which states that one can eat whatever Christians deem fit to eat, even though their methods of slaughter differ from Muslims', as long as it is not something clearly forbidden like pork. The question, then, is whether the Qurʾanic prohibition against eating animals killed by stunning (*mawqūdha*) constitutes such a firm rule, and on this al-Wansharīsī is silent. The source he relied on, Abū Bakr Ibn al-ʿArabī, however, specifically remarks that animals killed in ways prohibited by the Qurʾan are prohibited (*ḥarām bi-l-naṣṣ*) just like pork: Abū Bakr Ibn al-ʿArabī, *Aḥkām al-Qurʾān*, ed. Muḥammad Bakr Ismāʿīl (Cairo: Dār al-Manār, 2002), 2: 37. Supporters of ʿAbduh pointed out that Christians might only stun the animal with a blow but kill it with a knife. A young Muḥammad al-Ṭāhir Ibn ʿĀshūr (d. 1973) (anonymously) wrote a lengthy and ingenious tract supporting the fatwa: Rashīd Riḍā (ed.), *al-Manār* 6:21 (19 Jan 1904), 821–8. For more about this response, see Muḥammad Bilqāsim al-Ghālī, *al-Shaykh al-Jāmiʿ al-Aʿẓam Muḥammad al-Ṭāhir Ibn ʿĀshūr ḥayātu-hu wa-āthāru-hu* (Beirut: Dār Ibn Ḥazm, 1417/1996), 134–5.

50. Indira Falk Gesink, *Islamic Reform and Conservatism* (London: I. B. Tauris, 2010), 182, 188ff.; ʿAbd Allāh b. al-Ṣiddīq al-Ghumārī, *al-Khawāṭir al-dīniyya*, 2 vols in 1 (Cairo: Maktabat al-Qāhira, 2004), 1: 103; Muḥammad Jaʿfar al-Kattānī, *al-Riḥla al-sāmiya ilā al-Iskandariyya wa-Miṣr wa-l-Ḥijāz wa-l-bilād al-Shāmiyya*, eds Muḥammad Ḥamza al-Kattānī and Muḥammad ʿAzzūz (Beirut: Dār Ibn Ḥazm, 1426/2005), 136. I thank my friend Garrett Davidson for this last citation.
51. Al-Kawtharī, *Maqālāt*, 108.
52. Rashīd Aḥmad Gangūhī (d. 1906) stated that, though a committed Ḥanafī, he would draw on other *madhhabs* in cases of necessity (*ḍarūra*) and matters that had created widespread hardship (*ʿumūm al-balwā*): Rashīd Aḥmad Gangūhī, *Fatāwā Rashīdī* (Karachi: Dār al-Ishāʿāt, 2003), 4; al-Qāsimī, *Dār al-ʿUlūm Dayūband*, 793.
53. The most detailed information on Ibn Shubruma's biography is in Wakīʿ Muḥammad b. Khalaf (d. 918–19), *Akhbār al-quḍāt*, ed. Saʿīd Muḥammad al-Laḥḥām (Riyadh: ʿĀlam al-Kutub, n.d.), 512–27, 557–73. Ibn Shubruma also lived for three years in Mecca. See ibid. 561, 568–70. See also the impressive biography by Nāṣir Guzashti, s.v. 'Ibn Shubruma', *Dāʾirat al-Maʿārif-i Buzurg-i Islāmī* (Tehran: Markaz Dāʾirat al-Maʿārif al-Islāmiyya, 1991–), 4: 64–5. A very useful study of Ibn Shubruma's legal opinions is Muḥammad Riḍā al-ʿĀnī, *Fiqh al-imām Ibn Shubruma al-Kūfī* (Beirut: Dār al-Kutub al-ʿIlmiyya, 2008).
54. Ibn Shubruma seems to have been a crucial link for the legal opinions of al-Ḥasan al-Baṣrī (d. 728) and his fellow Kufan al-Shaʿbī al-Ḥimyarī (d. 721). In terms of hadith, he was a major source for Prophetic reports prohibiting all types of intoxicants in Kufa, which no doubt were controversial in legal discourse there: Wakīʿ, *Akhbār al-quḍāt*, 516–18, 521–2, 527ff. Al-Bukhārī includes only a handful of hadiths via Ibn Shubruma and on two occasions

cites him for his opinion on legal or *tafsīr* matters (see *Ṣaḥīḥ al-Bukhārī: kitāb faḍā'il al-Qur'ān, bāb fī kam yuqra'u al-Qur'ān; kitāb al-aḥkām, al-qaḍā' fī kathīr al-māl wa-qalīli-hi*). Muslim uses him for only three narrations and Abū Dāwūd for one, all supplementary ones. Ibn Mājah uses him for only one report. Al-Nasā'ī uses him most, including eight narrations from Ibn Shubruma in two subchapters. Along with Aḥmad Ibn Ḥanbal in his *Musnad*, al-Nasā'ī uses Ibn Shubruma as a source for reports from the Successor Abu Zur'a al-Bajalī < Abū Hurayra.

55. Edward Lane, *Manners and Customs of the Modern Egyptians* (New York: Cosimo, 2005), 160.
56. Beth Baron, 'Making and breaking marital bonds in modern Egypt,' in Nikkie Keddie and Beth Baron (eds), *Women in Middle Eastern History* (New Haven: Yale University Press, 1991), 282.
57. Leila Ahmed, *Women and Gender in Islam* (New Haven: Yale University Press, 1992), 152–3; Liat Kozma, *Policing Egyptian Women* (Syracuse: Syracuse University Press, 2011), 31–8.
58. 1923 Update to Article 101 of Law 31, 1910; Muḥammad Abū al-Faḍl al-Gīzāwī, 'Qānūn Taḥdīd sinn al-zawāj', *al-Muḥāmāt* 4:4 (1924), 398.
59. Muḥammad b. Jarīr al-Ṭabarī, *Tārīkh al-Ṭabarī*, 6 vols (Beirut: Dār al-Kutub al-ᶜIlmiyya, 2003), 2: 211; *Ṣaḥīḥ al-Bukhārī: kitāb al-nikāḥ, bāb inkāḥ al-rajul walada-hu al-ṣighār; Sunan al-Nasā'ī: kitāb al-nikāḥ, bāb inkāḥ al-rajul ibnata-hu al-ṣaghīra.*
60. Al-Nawawī, *Sharḥ Ṣaḥīḥ Muslim*, 15 vols (Beirut: Dār al-Qalam, 1987), 9/10: 218; Manṣūr b. Yūnus al-Buhūtī, *al-Rawḍ al-murbiᶜ*, ed. Bashīr Muḥammad ᶜUyūn (Damascus: Maktabat Dār al-Bayān, 1999), 383; Ibrāhīm Bin Ḍuwayyān, *Manār al-sabīl fī sharḥ al-dalīl*, ed. Zuhayr al-Shāwīsh, 2 vols, 7th edn (Damascus: al-Maktab al-Islāmī, 1989), 2: 216; Mahmoud Yazbak, 'Minor marriages and *khiyar al-bulugh* in Ottoman Palestine: a note on women's strategies in a patriarchal society', *Islamic Law and Society* 9:3 (2002), 395.
61. Shaykh Niẓām *et al.*, *al-Fatāwā al-Hindiyya*, 1: 316.
62. Al-Gīzāwī, 'Qānūn taḥdīd', 398.
63. Al-Sarakhsī, *al-Mabsūṭ* (Beirut: Dār al-Maᶜrifa, [1978]), 4: 212.
64. Al-Gīzāwī, 'Qānūn taḥdīd', 397.
65. For more on the Ottoman Family Law of 1917, see Judith Tucker, 'Revisiting reform: women and the Ottoman Law of Family Rights, 1917', *Arab Studies Journal* 4:2 (1996), 4–17.
66. From the text of the Ottoman Family Law and the Münâkehât ve Müfârakât Kararnâmesi Esbâb-ı Mucıbe Lâyihası, included as an appendix in Ibrahim Alhalalsheh, 'Ürdün Ahvâl-i Şahsiyye Kanununun Osmanlı Hukuk-ı Âile Kararnamesi İle Mukayesesi', PhD thesis, Marmara University (2009), 246–7, 273.
67. Al-Sarakhsī, *al-Mabsūṭ*, 4: 212.
68. For more on this fascinating figure, see Syed Junaid Ahmed Quadri,

'Transformations of tradition: modernity in the thought of Muḥammad Bakhīt al-Muṭīʿī', PhD dissertation, McGill University, 2013.

69. Muḥammad Bakhīt al-Muṭīʿī, 'Taḥdīd sinn al-zawāj', *al-Muḥāmāt* 4:4 (1924), 409–11.
70. Al-Muṭīʿī, 'Taḥdīd sinn al-zawāj', 404–5. Here al-Muṭīʿī cites the fourteenth-century Alexandrian Ḥanafī scholar Ibn al-Humām that the hadith of ʿĀʾisha consummating her marriage at nine years old was 'close to (*qarīb min*) *mutawātir*': Kamāl al-Dīn Muḥammad b. ʿAbd al-Wāḥid Ibn Humām, *Sharḥ Fatḥ al-Qadīr* (Beirut: Dār al-Fikr, n.d.), 3: 274.
71. Al-Muṭīʿī, 'Taḥdīd sinn al-zawāj', 401; al-Sarakhsī, *al-Mabsūṭ*, 4: 212; ʿAlā' al-Dīn al-Kāsānī, *Badāʾiʿ al-ṣanāʾiʿ*, 7 vols (Beirut: Dār al-Kitāb al-ʿArabī, 1982), 2: 240.
72. Sāmī Ḥasan Ḥammūd, *Taṭwīr al-aʿmāl al-maṣrafiyya bi-mā yattafiqu wa-l-sharīʿa al-islāmiyya* (Cairo: Dār al-Ittiḥād al-ʿArabī, 1397/1976), 476, 478–80. This book was originally the author's 1976 dissertation at al-Azhar University.
73. *Sunan* of Abū Dāwūd: *kitāb al-ijāra, bāb al-rajul yabīʿu mā laysa ʿinda-hu.*
74. Ḥammūd, *Taṭwīr al-aʿmāl*, 479; *Sunan* of Abū Dāwūd, *kitāb al-ijāra, bāb al-rajul yabīʿu mā laysa ʿinda-hu.*
75. Frank Vogel and Samuel T. Hayes III, *Islamic Law and Finance* (The Hague: Kluwer Law International, 1998), 100–02.
76. *Sunan* of Abū Dāwūd: *kitāb al-ijāra, bāb fīman bāʿa bayʿatayn fī bayʿa.* Al-Tirmidhī includes al-Shāfiʿī's description of this type of transaction: *Jāmiʿ al-Tirmidhī*: *kitāb al-buyūʿ, bāb mā jāʾa fī al-nahy ʿan bayʿatayn fī bayʿa.*
77. Ḥammūd, *Taṭwīr al-aʿmāl*, 480.
78. Al-Ṭabarī, *Ikhtilāf al-fuqahāʾ* (Beirut: Dār al-Kutub al-ʿIlmiyya, n.d.), 286. Interestingly, according to his son, the Shāfiʿī scholar Taqī al-Dīn al-Subkī also held that upholding a promise was required (*wājib*), though it is not clear if this means a promise could be enforced in court: al-Subkī, *Ṭabaqāt*, 10: 232.
79. Wakīʿ, *Akhbār al-quḍāt*, 518; Abū Sulaymān Ḥamd al-Khaṭṭābī, *Maʿālim al-sunan*, 4 vols, 3rd edn (Beirut: al-Maktaba al-ʿIlmiyya, 1981), 3: 145–6. See *Ṣaḥīḥ al-Bukhārī*: *kitāb kaffārāt al-aymān, bāb idhā aʿtaqa fī al-kaffāra li-man yakūnu walāʾuhu*; ibid., *kitāb al-shurūṭ, bāb idhā ishtaraṭa al-bāʾiʿ ẓahr al-dābba ilā makān musammā jāza.*
80. Ibn Ḥazm, *al-Muḥallā*, ed. Muḥammad Munīr al-Dimashqī, 11 vols (Cairo: Maṭbaʿat al-Munīriyya, n.d.), 8: 28; Ibn Rushd, *Distinguished Jurist's Primer*, trans. Imran Khan Nyazee, 2 vols (Reading: Garnet, 1996), 2: 193. For a useful summary of juridical opinions on keeping promises, see al-Nawawī, *al-Adhkār* (Cairo: Dār al-Manār, 1420/1999), 245–6 (chapter *bāb al-amr bi-l-wafā' bi-l-ʿahd wa-l-waʿd*).
81. Mahmoud El-Gamal, *Islamic Finance* (Cambridge: Cambridge University Press, 2006), 66; Wahba al-Zuḥaylī, *Islamic Jurisprudence and its Proofs: Financial Transactions in Islamic Jurisprudence*, trans. Mahmoud El-Gamal, 2 vols (Beirut: Dār al-Fikr, 2009), 1: 361; al-Zuḥaylī, *Mawsūʿat al-fiqh al-Islāmī wa-l-qaḍāyā al-muʿāṣira* (Damascus: Dār al-Fikr, 2010), 4: 500–02. I have

not been able to find the original proceedings of the 1979 Dubai conference, but they seem to appear in a non-paginated online resource at http://shamela.ws/browse.php/book-1611/page-1286. The text of Fatwa #8 actually makes no mention of Ibn Shubruma, describing the MAS as hinging on 'a promise that is legally binding (*mulzim … qaḍāʾan*) on both parties on the basis of the Mālikī school and religiously binding (*mulzim … diyānatan*) on both parties on the basis of other schools.' Scholars like al-Zuḥaylī, who were familiar with the conference discussions and reports, however, note the role played by Ibn Shubruma, as do scholars who published criticisms of the conference's conclusions.

82. Muḥammad Sulaymān al-Ashqar, 'Bayᶜ al-Murābaḥa kamā tujrīhi al-bunūk al-islāmiyya', in M. Sulaymān al-Ashqar, Muḥammad ᶜUthmān Shabīr, Mājid Muḥammad Abū Rakhkhiyya and ᶜUmar Sulaymān al-Ashqar (eds), *Buḥūth fiqhiyya fī qaḍāyā iqtiṣādiyya muᶜāsira* (Amman: Dār al-Nafāʾis, 1418/1998), 1: 69–133.
83. Vogel and Hayes, *Islamic Law and Finance*, 125.
84. Ibn Ḥazm, *al-Muḥallā*, 8: 28.
85. Al-Ashqar, 'Bayᶜ al-Murābaḥa', 1: 78, 91–3. This was, in fact, how Cevdet Paşa had negotiated the Ḥanafī school's notoriously rigid stance on accepting conditions in sales. Since the vast majority of conditions put upon contemporary sales in various professions are commonplace for the parties involved and serve to provide benefit, Cevdet observed, and since 'custom and convention are determinative (*al-ᶜurf wa-l-ᶜāda qāṭiᶜān*)', these conditions are valid. There was thus no need, he wrote, to reach outside of the Ḥanafī school and take the opinion of Ibn Shubruma. Although he was a great scholar (*imām*), Cevdet notes, his following had become extinct: ᶜAlī Ḥaydar, *Durar al-ḥukkām*, 1: 11–12; cf. *Mecelle* Book 1 section 4, #188: 'In the case of a sale concluded subject to a condition sanctioned by custom established and recognised in a particular locality, both sale and condition are valid'; available at http://www.iium.edu.my/deed/lawbase/al_majalle/al_majalleb01.html (last accessed 25 June 2014).
86. ᶜAlī Jumᶜa, *al-Bayān fī mā yashghalu al-adhhān* (Cairo: al-Muqaṭṭam, 1425/2005), 61.
87. ᶜAbd al-Ḥalīm Maḥmūd, *Fatāwā*, 2 vols (Cairo: Dār al-Maᶜārif, 2002), 2: 132.
88. J. N. D. Anderson, 'The Syrian Law of Personal Status', *Bulletin of the School of Oriental and African Studies* 17:1 (1955), 36–7; Alī al-Ṭanṭāwī, *Dhikrayāt*, 6 vols (Jeddah: Dār al-Manāra, 1985–6), 4: 290–2, 296; idem, *Fatāwā*, ed. Mujāhid Dayrāniyya (Jeddah: Dār al-Manāra, 1985), 122–3.
89. Law #1 in 2000 reiterated that no legal claims can be accepted/adjudicated on the basis of Shariᶜa marriage contracts if the bride was under sixteen and the groom under eighteen. A 2008 addition says that no marriage contract (*ᶜaqd*) can be legally documented if both the bride and groom are not eighteen or older (in solar years).

90. El-Gamal, *Islamic Finance*, 66; al-Zuḥaylī, *Islamic Jurisprudence and its Proofs*, 1: 361.
91. Al-Zuḥaylī, *Mawsūᶜat al-fiqh al-Islāmī*, 4: 500–2. For the text of the decision by the Majmaᶜ al-Fiqh al-Islāmī (*qarār* #2–3 of its fifth conference, round 5, held in Kuwait in 1988), see ibid. 9: 533–4. The opinion makes no mention of the evidence, but it adds nuance to the decision by noting that the promise of the buyer and agent is 'binding upon the promiser in terms of religious devotion except in the case of some excuse (*mulzim li-l-wāᶜid diyānatan illā li-ᶜudhr*)' and becomes 'binding by force of law (*mulzim qaḍāʾan*)' if it is premised on an action and then that action is taken and cost is incurred by the promised party as a result of the promise.
92. This opinion was stated by Dr Muḥammad Mukhtār Wald Ambāla, President of the Council of Fatwa and Maẓālim, Mauritania, during his speech at the *Muʾtamar li-Taᶜzīz al-Silm fī al-Mujtamaᶜāt al-Muslima* in Abu Dhabi, 9–10 March 2014; Shams al-Dīn ᶜAbd al-Raʾūf al-Munāwī, *Fayḍ al-qadīr sharḥ al-jāmiᶜ al-ṣaghīr*, ed. Ḥamdī al-Damardāsh Muḥammad, 13 vols (Riyadh: Maktabat Muṣṭafā al-Bāz, 1418/1998), 1: 401. See also, Tarek Elgawhary, 'Restructuring Islamic Law: the opinions of the ᶜUlama towards codification of Personal Status Law in Egypt', PhD dissertation, Princeton University (2014), 56.
93. Wakīᶜ, *Akhbār al-quḍāt*, 565.
94. For example, see El-Gamal, *Islamic Finance*, 138–51.
95. Ali Gomaa, personal communication.
96. Al-Zarkashī, *al-Baḥr al-muḥīṭ*, 4: 568, 595. Ibn Qayyim al-Jawziyya mentions that it is only the lowest level of mufti who cannot consider the fatwas of the Companions. Independent *mujtahids* and accomplished scholars seem to be above this restriction: Ibn Qayyim al-Jawziyya, *Iᶜlām al-muwaqqiᶜīn*, 4: 181.
97. Al-Munāwī's phrasing for such a scholar is noteworthy: '*ghayr ᶜāmmī min al-fuqahāʾ al-muqallidīn*'; al-Munāwī, *Fayḍ al-qadīr*, 1: 402. Ibn Ḥajar al-Haytamī shares this opinion in an illuminating discussion: al-Haytamī, *al-Fatawā al-kubrā*, 4: 307.
98. It is worth noting that the Ḥanafī jurist Muḥammad b. ᶜAbd al-Raḥmān al-Sinjārī (d. 1321) of Mardin wrote a book he claimed was unprecedented, *ᶜUmdat al-ṭālib fī maᶜrifat al-madhāhib*, which included the major positions within the Ḥanafī school, as well as primary positions of the Shāfiᶜī, Ḥanbalī, Mālikī and Ẓāhirī schools as well as the 'Shīᶜa': Kātib Chelebī, *Kashf al-ẓunūn*, 2: 425–6.
99. Al-Kawtharī, *Maqālāt*, 114.
100. If someone asked for a fatwa, al-Kawtharī states bluntly, then the mufti must give the *muftā bi-hi* opinion of his school without even mentioning differences of opinion within the school or between schools. The person asking for the fatwa is seeking clarity, al-Kawtharī explains, not more confusion; al-Kawtharī, *Maqālāt*, 114–15.
101. Al-Kawtharī, *Maqālāt*, 91–2, 192.

102. Most discussions among the *ᶜulamāᵓ* concerning levels of *mujtahid*/muftis are based on Ibn al-Ṣalāḥ's five-tier distinction. In summary, it consists of (1) independent/absolute *mujtahids*, who derive rules directly from the primary sources and follow no imam; (2) *mujtahids* who are qualified to derive rules independently but identify mostly with a prior imam/*madhhab*; (3) the early scholars of a *madhhab* who extend its rulings on the basis of its methodology; (4) those leading scholars after the 900s who refine the *madhhab* and select between its rulings; (5) scholars only qualified to cite the main ruling of their *madhhab* to those who ask. One major difference in discourse on this topic is whether the independent/absolute *mujtahid* exists after the time of the *madhhab* founders. Ibn al-Ṣalāḥ held that there had been none for 'a long time', while Ibn al-Qayyim, ᶜAbd al-Ḥayy al-Laknawī (d. 1887), and contemporary scholars like ᶜAbd Allāh al-Ghumārī (d. 1993) maintained that there are always absolute (*muṭlaq*) *mujtahids* qualified to act outside the four *madhhabs*, though they cannot be independent (*mustaqill*) because this would imply developing new sources and methods for deriving law (*uṣūl*), and the early imams had exhausted these. Al-Suyūṭī took a middle ground, affirming that absolute (*muṭlaq*) *mujtahids* exist in every age but adding that they identify with and operate under the aegis of one particular *madhhab*. His longtime student, the Ḥanafī Muḥyī al-Dīn Muḥammad b. Sulaymān al-Kāfiyājī (d. 1474), seconded his teacher in his *Wajīz al-niẓām fī iẓhār mawārid al-aḥkām*, which cites an opinion attributed to Ibn Ḥanbal that *mujtahids* will exist until Judgement Day: al-Nawawī, *Adab al-muftī*, 22–31; Ibn Qayyim, *Iᶜlām al-muwaqqiᶜīn*, 4: 179–81; al-Suyūṭī, *al-Radd ᶜalā man akhlada ilā al-arḍ wa-jahila anna al-ijtihād fī kull ᶜaṣr farḍ*, ed. Khalīl al-Mays (Beirut: Dār al-Kutub al-ᶜIlmiyya, 1403/1983), 113–23; Ibn Ḥajar al-Haytamī, *al-Fatāwā al-fiqhiyya al-kubrā*, 4: 302–3; ᶜAbd al-Ḥayy al-Farangī Maḥallī al-Laknawī, 'al-Nāfiᶜ al-kabīr li-man yuṭāliᶜu al-Jāmiᶜ al-ṣaghīr', in Nuᶜaym Ashraf Aḥmad (ed.), *Majmūᶜat rasāᵓil ᶜAbd al-Ḥayy al-Laknawī* (Karachi: Idārat al-Qurᵓān wa-l-ᶜulūm al-Islāmiyya, [1998]), 3: 17–21; ᶜAbd Allāh al-Ghumārī, *al-Khawāṭir al-dīniyya*, 1: 101–2; Kātib Chelebī, *Kashf al-ẓunūn*, 3: 523. See also Muḥammad Tawfīq al-Būṭī, 'Uṣūl al-fatwā wa-khaṣāᵓiṣihā', presented at *al-Muᵓtamar al-ᶜĀlamī: Manhajiyyat al-iftāᵓ fī ᶜālam maftūḥ*, Kuwait, 2007.

103. The scholar termed these three as the components of *ᶜilm ijtimāᶜ al-fatwā*; Shaykh ᶜAmr al-Wardānī, personal communication at the Dār al-Iftā', Cairo, August 2008.

104. For Gomaa, truly qualified muftis use the aims of the Shariᶜa and procedural and substantive maxims (*qawāᶜid uṣūliyya wa-fiqhiyya*) to draw on the entirety of the Islamic legal heritage. Following on a controversial fatwa that drew on a Ḥanafī ruling allowing Muslims to engage in transactions that would otherwise be prohibited when outside the Muslim world, Gomaa explains that every *madhhab* allows for crossing *madhhab* lines in cases of necessity (*ḍarūra*) and widespread need (*ᶜumūm al-balwā*). Both in his writing and in his class lectures, Gomaa traces his thinking to an articulation of the necessity/

need principle made by the Shaykh al-Azhar al-Bayjūrī (d. 1860), and earlier by al-Shirwānī (al-Dāghistānī) in the context of discussing the prohibition on using silver or gold vessels for eating and drinking. They note that the minority position in the Ḥanafī school allows such vessels for drinking coffee, adding, 'And whoever is afflicted by such as this, as often occurs, [let him] follow what preceded so that he may be free from the prohibition (*man ubtuliya bi-shayʾ min dhālik kamā yaqaᶜu kathīran taqlīd mā taqaddama li-yatakhallaṣa min al-ḥurma*).' Only al-Shirwānī's original text in the 1938 edition has the correct reading: Jumᶜa/Gomaa, *al-Bayān*, 103–4; ᶜAbd al-Ḥamīd al-Shirwānī (al-Dāghistānī) *et al.*, *Ḥawāshī tuḥfat al-muḥtāj bi-sharḥ al-minhāj* (Cairo: Maṭbaᶜat Muṣṭafā Muḥammad, 1938), 1: 118–9; al-Bayjūrī, *Ḥāshiyat al-Shaykh Ibrāhīm al-Bayjūrī ᶜalā sharḥ Ibn al-Qāsim al-Ghazzī ᶜalā matn Ibn Abī Shujāᶜ*, ed. Muḥammad ᶜAbd al-Salām Shāhīn, 4 vols (Beirut: Dār al-Kutub al-ᶜIlmiyya, 1420/1999), 1: 75.

105. Musa Furber, 'Elements of a fatwa and their contribution to confidence in its validity', Tabah Analytic Brief, no. 14 (2013), 3–4, available at http://www.tabahfoundation.org/research/pdfs/Musa-Furber-Fatwa-Confidence-Elements-Tabah-En.pdf (last accessed 3 July 2014).

5

Reading Sūrat al-Anᶜām with Muḥammad Rashīd Riḍā and Sayyid Quṭb[1]

Nicolai Sinai

Introduction

One of the central themes pervading modern Qurᵓanic exegesis (*tafsīr*) is a marked emphasis on the literary and thematic coherence of Qurᵓanic suras or even of the entire Qurᵓanic corpus. As Mustansir Mir has pointed out, exegetes from different regions of the Islamic world such as Ḥamīd al-Dīn al-Farāḥī (d. 1930) and Amīn Aḥsan Iṣlāḥī (d. 1997) in the Indian subcontinent, the Iranian scholar Muḥammad Ḥusayn al-Ṭabāṭabāᵓī (d. 1981) or the Egyptian Sayyid Quṭb (executed in 1966) all concur that Qurᵓanic suras are structured around thematic 'pivots' (sg. *miḥwār*), 'hubs' (sg. *ᶜamūd*) or 'aims' (sg. *gharaḍ*), and at least to some extent these exegetes interpret the Qurᵓan accordingly.[2] Holistic leanings are also discernible in what is widely considered to be the inaugural work of modern Qurᵓanic exegesis in Arabic, the *Tafsīr al-Manār*, published by Muḥammad Rashīd Riḍā (d. 1935) on the basis of lectures by Muḥammad ᶜAbduh (d. 1905).[3]

At first sight, such tendencies form a noticeable contrast with pre-modern *tafsīr* works, which often limit their attention to single verses or brief verse groups. Nevertheless, some consideration of aspects of textual coherence is by no means absent from the earlier exegetical tradition.[4] For instance, already the Qurᵓanic commentary of Fakhr al-Dīn al-Rāzī (d. 1210) explores the linear connections or interrelationships (sg. *munāsaba*) between adjoining verses,[5] and some 250 years later the Mamluk exegete al-Biqāᶜī (d. 1480) programmatically declared that understanding such interrelationships required the discovery of the 'aim (*gharaḍ*) at which a particular sura is directed' and to which all of its components are subordinate.[6] To some degree, then, the uptake of such holistic and coherentist precedents by modern exegetes resembles the career of concepts like *ijtihād* or *maṣlaḥah*, which are likewise traditional notions that are accorded new prominence and are significantly re-cast from the late nineteenth century onwards.[7]

It has been pointed out that the 'progression from an atomistic to an organic approach runs parallel in literature and in *tafsīr*, with a slightly delayed reaction in the latter'.[8] In part, the increased attention of twentieth-century exegetes to the Qurᵓan's coherence is therefore due to literary and aesthetic factors. Sayyid Quṭb, for one, had been a secular writer and literary critic before reinventing himself as an Islamic ideologue,[9] and his understanding of the unique literary qualities of the Qurᵓan, as first expressed in his 1944 study of *Artistic Depiction in the Qurᵓan* (*al-Taṣwīr al-fannī fī al-Qurᵓān*), is informed by his close association with the Egyptian writer and poet ᶜAbbās Maḥmūd al-ᶜAqqād (d. 1964), who demanded that poetry exhibit organic unity.[10] In tandem with such aesthetic trends, though, there is also a distinctly religious dimension to the prominence of holistic or coherentist approaches in twentieth-century exegesis. Mir plausibly describes them as geared towards endowing scripture with a higher degree of hermeneutical self-sufficiency or, as he puts it, as aiming to replace 'extra-quranic hermeneutical constraints' by hermeneutical constraints arising from the Qurᵓan itself.[11] To see his point, it is useful to remind ourselves that in pre-modern commentaries on the Qurᵓan the meaning attributed to a given verse or verse group will often be governed by non-Qurᵓanic traditions – for example, by reports about the circumstances or 'occasions of revelation' (*asbāb al-nuzūl*) that allegedly triggered the proclamation of the passage at hand, or by lexical explanations and narrative amplifications that are traced back to early exegetical authorities or even to the Prophet himself. Exegetical holism constitutes a potent way of prying apart this interpretive symbiosis between scripture and extra-scriptural paratexts. For example, Iṣlāḥī rejects the widespread tradition that the initial five verses of Sura 96 were the first Qurᵓanic passage to be revealed to Muḥammad and that they originally constituted a free-standing revelatory utterance. Instead, Iṣlāḥī finds the passage to be inextricably connected to the sura's remaining verses, whose content indicates a later date of revelation.[12]

Why might the disentangling of scripture and extra-scriptural tradition that is facilitated by exegetical holism have appeared, and continue to appear, appealing to many modern Islamic thinkers? At least in part, the answer would seem to be that it supports the modernist strategy of jettisoning secondary layers of the Islamic textual heritage in order to fortify the position of more basic layers (in particular, of the Qurᵓan itself) in the face of an unprecedented need to keep Islam relevant under rapidly changing social, economic, political and intellectual conditions. In this respect, one may discern a structural analogy between the proposition that Qurᵓanic suras are structured around thematic 'hubs' or 'aims', and the view that the rulings of

Islamic law give expression to underlying 'principles', the so-called *maqāṣid al-sharīʿa*, a position that has likewise acquired considerable popularity in the twentieth century.[13] Both notions can be used to impart a quasi-axiomatic quality to exegetical and legal discourse: novel claims can be justified, and entrenched views dismissed, by summarily invoking a limited number of axiom-like principles that supposedly underlie the textual surface of scripture or of the relevant legal proof texts. Rather than having to engage the accumulated tradition at close range and with limited room for manoeuvre, as pre-modern scholars tend to do, the tradition can be judged from a much more detached vantage point that is nevertheless perceived to be authentically Islamic. In this sense, exegetical holism ties in not only with developments in the literary realm, but can also play a crucial function in the project of re-articulating Islamic belief and practice under the conditions of an imposed modernity.

Due to its important precedents in the earlier *tafsīr* tradition, the phenomenon of exegetical holism is evidently relevant to the present volume's interest in gauging how and to what extent modern Islamic writers are in conversation with and transform the pre-modern Islamic heritage. The topic itself certainly merits additional study: despite the pioneering work of Mustansir Mir and also of Kate Zebiri, much scholarship on modern *tafsīr* tends to be interested in other questions,[14] and the manner in which coherentist notions affect the actual interpretive work done by modern Qurʾanic exegetes remains yet to be fully described. A promising point of departure for further study of the topic would appear to be the introductory remarks that in various modern commentaries precede the detailed treatment of individual suras (for Suras 4–11, the *Tafsīr al-Manār* also includes concluding epitomes).[15] Ideally, one would undertake a comprehensive study of the content of such prefaces across a significant number of suras and in different Qurʾanic commentaries, and then compare and contrast them with the ensuing verse-by-verse commentary. Being acutely conscious of the limited space of a book chapter, I shall confine myself to an examination of the prefaces preceding Sura 6, traditionally called Sūrat al-Anʿām (after the reference to livestock, *anʿām*, in vv. 136 and 138) in the *Tafsīr al-Manār* and in Sayyid Quṭb's *Fī ẓilāl al-Qurʾān* (*In the Shade of the Qurʾan*), composed several decades apart in Egypt.[16]

Although I do not aim at making any interpretive claims about Sūrat al-Anʿām itself, it will be helpful to briefly acquaint ourselves with the general contents of the sura. Islamic exegetes generally consider it to be 'Meccan', that is, to have been revealed before the *hijra*, although, as we shall see, various reports maintain that in its present shape it contains a number of 'Medinan' verses, namely, verses that were allegedly revealed after the *hijra*.

Following Angelika Neuwirth, the text can be subdivided into three main parts.[17] The first part, vv. 1–73, consists of an introductory hymn (vv. 1–3) and extended polemics against a group of opponents who refuse to acknowledge the Qurᵓanic messenger's claim to prophecy and who are accused of 'associating' (*shirk*) other beings with God (cf. vv. 14, 19, 22–3). The middle part, vv. 74–153, provides a historical *exemplum* for this confrontation by narrating how Abraham, portrayed as the ideal believer, came to espouse monotheism and to renounce *shirk* (vv. 74–90). This is followed by further polemics, touching again on the Qurᵓan's revelatory nature (cf. vv. 91–3, 109–14) and the sin of *shirk* (cf. vv. 94, 100–8) as well as on God's creative activity in nature (vv. 95–9). This part also insists on the need to invoke God's name over slaughtered animals (vv. 118–21), berates those guilty of *shirk* for assigning a portion of their harvest and livestock to beings other than God (vv. 136–9), and criticises Jewish dietary restrictions (vv. 146–7). The sura's concluding part, vv. 154–65, again defends the Qurᵓan's revelatory nature and closes with a sequence of statements about God's omnipotence and unicity (vv. 161–4). In sum, while the sura evidently encompasses a wide range of topics whose interrelationship is not always readily evident, we may still make the preliminary observation that the defence of monotheism against *shirk* occupies a prominent, perhaps dominant, position in the text.

In order to get a sense of the potential resonance of pre-modern exegesis in Riḍā's and Quṭb's treatment of Sūrat al-Anᶜām, we must attempt to pick up some of the issues that are traditionally associated with the sura as a whole. I shall therefore begin by browsing through a number of earlier commentaries.

Some Pre-modern Prefaces to Sūrat al-Anᶜām

Summary introductions to entire suras are not an indispensable component of classical commentaries; the well-known commentary of al-Ṭabarī (d. 923), for example, launches straight into a discussion of the first verse of the sura at hand. Where a pre-modern commentary does include preface-like material, this will often state whether a given sura, or its component parts, were revealed before or after Muḥammad's emigration from Mecca to Medina. A case in point is the introduction to Sūrat al-Anᶜām in the commentary of Fakhr al-Dīn al-Rāzī,[18] which, as we shall see below, is quoted in the *Tafsīr al-Manār*. Al-Rāzī's introduction opens with a tradition ascribed to the early exegete Ibn ᶜAbbās (d. 687).[19] It assigns Sūrat al-Anᶜām to Muḥammad's Meccan period and states, inter alia, that it was revealed 'in one whole' (*jumlatan wāḥidatan*) and in the company of 70,000 angels. I shall baptise this tradition, which exists in numerous variants and echoes a term conspicuously used in Q. 25:32,[20] the '*jumlatan wāḥidatan* tradition'.[21] In the version cited by al-Rāzī, it explicitly excludes six verses allegedly stemming from Muḥammad's Medinan period, but other versions of it do not enumerate any such additions.[22] (Incidentally, Islamic scholarship also preserves reports that assign Sūrat al-Anᶜām to the Meccan period and list a number of allegedly Medinan verses without maintaining that the sura was revealed 'in one whole'.)[23] Al-Rāzī follows the report cited on the authority of Ibn ᶜAbbās with a second one, ascribed to the Prophet via his companion Anas b. Mālik, which begins by highlighting that the feature of having been revealed as a unitary piece is unique to Sūrat al-Anᶜām: 'The only sura of the Qurᵓan that was sent down to me as a whole (*jumlatan*) is Sūrat al-Anᶜām.'

Al-Rāzī goes on to suggest that Sūrat al-Anᶜām's unique feature of virtually integral revelation is due to its peculiar content. He reports that according to 'the *uṣūliyyūn*' – which here presumably designates the practitioners of *uṣūl al-dīn*, 'theology'[24] – the reason for the sura's having been revealed 'in one stroke' (*dufᶜatan wāḥidatan*) and in the company of 70,000 angels consists in the fact that it 'encompasses proofs for the unity of God, for [divine] justice, for prophecy, and for the Resurrection' and refutes the views of 'the deniers and heretics'.[25] Al-Rāzī adds, apparently still from the perspective of the *uṣūliyyūn*, that unlike revelations indicating legal judgements (*mā yadullu ᶜalā al-aḥkām*) and for which it may be advantageous (*qad takūnu al-maṣlaḥa an*) to be revealed 'in accordance with the need for them', the knowledge of the 'fundamentals of the faith' (*ᶜilm al-uṣūl*) must be revealed at once (*ᶜalā al-fawr*). The fact that almost the whole of Sūrat al-Anᶜām was revealed in one stroke, then, is due to the fact that it is devoted to an exposition of the fundamentals of the faith. Sura 6 thus emerges as a summa of Qurᵓanic theology.

A similar understanding of the subject matter of Sūrat al-Anᶜām informs the brief preface to al-Biqāᶜī's commentary on the text,[26] which identifies the sura's 'intended aim' (*maqṣūd*) with 'demonstrating the truth of the unity of God to which Scripture has summoned in the previous sura [namely, in Sura 5]'.[27] Al-Biqāᶜī also alludes to the *jumlatan wāḥidatan* tradition, and he appears to recycle part of al-Rāzī's report of the view of the *uṣūliyyūn* when he states that

> the fact that it [the sura] was sent down in the fashion described above points to the fact that the fundamentals of the faith (*uṣūl al-dīn*) occupy a most exalted position and that it [the science of the *uṣūl al-dīn*?] must be learned all at one (*ᶜalā al-fawr*), due to the fact that it [the sura] was sent down as a whole – as opposed to legal judgements, for these are dispersed (*tafarraqa*) in accordance with what is advantageous (*bi-ḥasab al-maṣāliḥ*).

I shall leap into the early nineteenth century now, to the commentary of the Iraqi scholar al-Ālūsī (d. 1854),[28] who, like al-Rāzī, is explicitly cited in the *Tafsīr al-Manār* and therefore deserves close attention. Al-Ālūsī is sceptical of the reports that Sūrat al-Anᶜām was revealed on one occasion and finds fault with their weak transmitter chains (sg. *isnād*), an assessment that he supports by invoking a statement by the famous hadith critic Ibn al-Ṣalāḥ (d. 1245).[29] He then proceeds to a discussion of inter-sura complementarity, or *munāsaba*, much of which is cited from Jalāl al-Dīn al-Suyūṭī (d. 1505).[30] The quoted passage begins by tying the beginning of Sura 6 to the end of Sura 5. The first link proposed constitutes a sort of exegetical rail shot leading through a third passage: Sura 6 opens with praise of God, while Sura 5 closes with God's eschatological judgement (*qaḍāʾ*) – two themes that are concomitant in Q. 39:75: 'They are judged according to the truth, and it is said: "Praise belongs to God, Lord of all beings."' Al-Suyūṭī also identifies a direct link, however, by maintaining that the beginning of Sura 6 constitutes an 'explanation' (*sharḥ*) and 'elaboration' (*tafṣīl*) of Sura 5's concluding statement that God possesses 'the sovereignty of the heavens and the earth and what is in them' (5:120).[31] The passage quoted from al-Suyūṭī then widens its focus and characterises Sūrat al-Anᶜām as an 'explanation' and 'elaboration' not merely of the ending of Sura 5, but of miscellaneous brief and general references (*ᶜalā sabīl al-ījāz, ᶜalā sabīl al-ijmāl*) from all of the five preceding suras. For instance, Sūrat al-Anᶜām is said to unpack and elucidate the call not to 'forbid the good things that God has made lawful for you' at Q. 5:87, the brief censure of various ways of consecrating animals at Q. 5:103, and the reference to 'livestock and tilled land' (*al-anᶜām wa-l-ḥarth*) at Q. 3:14.[32]

In general, al-Ālūsī appears markedly less interested in Sūrat al-Anᶜām's internal thematic unity than in its thematic complementarity with other parts of the Qurʾanic corpus: at the centre of his attention is not sura coherence but corpus coherence. It is true that he, too, reiterates the idea that Sūrat al-Anᶜām is a theological sura: 'it might be said', he observes, 'that the axis (*quṭb*) of this sura revolves around establishing the Creator and proofs for monotheism.'[33] However, this immediately leads into another quotation, attributed to Abū Isḥāq al-Isfarāʾīnī (or al-Isfarāyīnī; d. 1027),[34] which returns to the topic of inter-sura complementarity – this time between Sūrat al-Anᶜām and Q. 1, 18, 34 and 35, all of which commence with the invocation 'Praise be to …' (*al-ḥamdu li-*).

The *Tafsīr al-Manār* on Sūrat al-Anᶜām

As we have seen, pre-modern commentators do make some effort to characterise the overarching theme of Sūrat al-Anᶜām and to explore how it complements other Qurʾanic suras; they also discuss whether the sura was revealed on one occasion and thus is marked not only by thematic but also genetic unity. Nevertheless, such introductory discussions in the pre-modern tradition are generally short. By contrast, in the *Tafsīr al-Manār* and in Sayyid Quṭb's *Fī ẓilāl al-Qur'ān*, comments on the sura as a whole become much more expansive: while Al-Ālūsī's preface to Sūrat al-Anᶜām only runs to about two pages, the *Manār* commentary devotes eight pages to an introductory discussion of the *jumlatan wāḥidatan* tradition and to issues of *munāsaba*, in addition to a twenty-four-page concluding epitome (*khulāṣa*), and Quṭb's preface encompasses approximately twenty-six pages.

Let us start with Riḍā.[35] The first three and a half pages of his introduction are clearly responding to al-Ālūsī, who is explicitly named towards the end of this section.[36] The latter, it will be recalled, was sceptical of the authenticity of the *jumlatan wāḥidatan* tradition, whereas Riḍā ultimately insists that the tradition's multiple attestation 'does not leave any room for personal opinion (*ra'y*)'.[37] Still, Riḍā exhibits considerable patience in working towards this conclusion: discussion of the *jumlatan wāḥidatan* tradition itself is delayed until after Riḍā has managed to cast significant doubt on reports alleging that Sūrat al-Anᶜām, despite being substantially Meccan, contains a number of Medinan insertions. Already while presenting the relevant material, Riḍā appears unconvinced and points out that one such alleged addition, the two verses 6:151–2, treat a typically 'Meccan' topic and are solidly linked to what follows (*muttaṣilatān bi-mā baᶜdi-hā*).[38] He then reproduces a passage from al-Suyūṭī's famous manual of Qur'anic sciences, *al-Itqān fī ᶜulūm al-Qur'ān*, which lists various reports about Medinan additions to Sūrat al-Anᶜām.[39] Moving on to give his own opinion, Riḍā is disinclined to set much store by traditions alleging that a particular verse 'was revealed with respect to' (*nazalat fī*) some person whom Muḥammad encountered during his Medinan period: it is possible, he writes, that when a Companion of Muḥammad said that a particular verse 'was revealed with respect to' something, he merely meant to say that the verse in question was applicable to this event, not that it 'was sent down when this thing happened'.[40] Riḍā therefore insists that traditions about Medinan verses in Meccan verses or Meccan verses in Medinan suras are to be treated with caution and that they should only be accepted if equipped with an incontrovertibly sound transmitter chain and are perfectly unequivocal.[41] At most, Riḍā is willing to take seriously a tradition, deemed to be authentic (*ṣaḥīḥ*) by al-Suyūṭī, according to which 6:151–3 are later additions to Sūrat al-Anᶜām – but even these, he doubtfully remarks, appear perfectly Meccan in content (*hunna min mawḍūᶜ al-suwar al-makkiyya*).

Riḍā's style of writing is continuous with traditional Islamic scholarship, and he is clearly at pains to engage the exegetical tradition in considerable detail, an impression that is highlighted by his use of extensive quotations.

Nevertheless, what Riḍā has said so far would appear to imply a default reluctance to concede the presence of Medinan insertions in suras otherwise assigned to the Meccan period (and, vice versa, of Meccan verses in suras otherwise considered to be Medinan). This position, although justified by invoking traditional-sounding scholarly scruples about the potential ambiguity of the expression *nazalat fī* and the strength of transmitter chains, is in fact far from traditional and is plausibly viewed as rooted in a distinctly modern preference for treating Qurᵓanic suras as unitary literary wholes. In this sense, Riḍā appears to presuppose a much stronger nexus between thematic and genetic unity than, for example, al-Rāzī, who despite his characterisation of Sūrat al-Anᶜām as a systematic exposition of basic theological tenets did not dispute that the text contained Medinan additions.

After these somewhat preliminary skirmishes, Riḍā introduces the obvious trump card supporting a holistic approach to Sūrat al-Anᶜām, namely, the *jumlatan wāḥidatan* tradition. As soon as it is broached, Riḍā's caution vis-à-vis potentially unreliable transmitter chains decreases markedly. To be sure, he is careful to cite Ibn al-Ṣalāḥ's complaint about the tradition's weak *isnād* in an even fuller version than al-Ālūsī,[42] but he ultimately maintains that the *jumlatan wāḥidatan* tradition's multiple attestation makes it 'inevitable that there is an authentic root to it'.[43] In line with his studied use of traditional patterns of argument, Riḍā further justifies his espousal of the *jumlatan wāḥidatan* tradition by citing the principle that 'an affirmative report takes precedence over a negative report' (*al-muthbit muqaddam ᶜalā al-nāfī*).[44] Still, Riḍā is unwilling to categorically dismiss the claim that at least 6:151–3 could be a Medinan addition, given that a report to this effect attributed to Ibn ᶜAbbās was deemed to be authentic (*ṣaḥḥaḥa*) by no less an authority than al-Suyūṭī.[45] Nonetheless, Riḍā continues to discredit this tradition's probative force by remarking that Ibn ᶜAbbās had not committed Qurᵓanic texts to memory prior to the *hijra* and that his exception of the three verses at hand might simply be a case of personal judgement (*raᵓy*). In any case, Riḍā writes, even if the three verses in question are Medinan, it would still be the case that virtually all of Sūrat al-Anᶜām was revealed on one occasion, which disproves the view that this was not the case for any of the long and medium-sized suras. Finally, Riḍā proceeds to an explicit rebuttal of al-Ālūsī's doubts about the authenticity of the *jumlatan wāḥidatan* tradition.[46]

Having shown that Sūrat al-Anᶜām is likely to be a genetic unity, Riḍā next reproduces the passage from al-Rāzī suggesting that the sura's integral revelation was due to its theological content. Sūrat al-Anᶜām, Riḍā agrees, is essentially devoted to an exposition of the 'doctrines of religion' (*ᶜaqāᵓid al-dīn*),[47] and in his concluding epitome he calls it 'the sura of the doctrines of Islam, or the sura of monotheism' (*sūrat ᶜaqāᵓid al-Islām aw sūrat al-tawḥīd*).[48] These doctrines of religion, he adds in the preface, must be taught 'according to the Qur'anic method (*ʿalā ṭarīqat al-Qurʾān*), not according to the method of the theologians (*al-mutakallimūn*) and the Greek philosophers'.[49] This concise demand is substantially expanded in Riḍā's concluding epitome: the most eloquent (*ablagh*) mode of treating 'doctrinal questions' is the style of the Qurʾan (*asālīb al-Qurʾān*), which proceeds by means of 'disputation and debate' (*bi-uslūb al-munāẓara wa-l-jidāl*) and by presenting the truth 'in response to questions' (*jawāban baʿda suʾāl*), thereby combining persuasion of people's intellects (*iqnāʿ al-ʿuqūl*) with an impact on their hearts (*al-taʾthīr fī al-qulūb*) and leading to a synthesis of certainty (*al-yaqīn*) and faith (*al-īmān*).[50] Regrettably, though, 'the Greek philosophers caused the scholars of theology (*ʿulamāʾ al-kalām*) to stray from this [Qurʾanic] style (*min hādhihi al-asālīb*)'.[51] While the notion that the Qurʾan is distinguished by a particular mode of discourse that is superior to that of philosophy and theology does not figure in Fakhr al-Dīn al-Rāzī's preface to Sūrat al-Anʿām, it appears elsewhere in his *oeuvre*.[52] According to al-Rāzī, the superiority of the Qurʾanic method is due to what Ayman Shihadeh has described as the Qurʾan's 'spiritually transformative features',[53] which constitutes a neat parallel to Riḍā's emphasis on the Qurʾan's ability to exert an impact on people's hearts. As we shall see below, these ideas will have a strong resonance in Sayyid Quṭb.

In spite of his disagreement with al-Ālūsī over the soundness of the *jumlatan wāḥidatan* tradition, Riḍā follows the basic structure of the latter's preface by next addressing the topic of inter-sura complementarity or *munāsaba*. As a matter of fact, so close is Riḍā's relationship to his Iraqi predecessor that he concludes this section of the preface by reproducing the entire *munāsaba* passage from al-Ālūsī's commentary, the main part of which, as we saw above, consists in turn of a quotation from al-Suyūṭī, followed by a shorter quotation from Abū Isḥāq al-Isfarāʾīnī.[54] Prior to citing al-Ālūsī, though, Riḍā gives his own analysis of the matter. He frames the rationale behind the *munāsaba* approach in terms of its contribution to explaining the order of suras in the Qurʾanic corpus: while these are generally ordered by decreasing length, throughout the corpus one encounters instances where shorter suras precede longer ones. This, he explains, is due to relationships of fit between the meanings of suras (*al-tanāsub fī maʿānī al-suwar*).[55] Riḍā then outlines the various ways in which the long suras at the beginning of the Qurʾanic corpus complement one another. In doing so, he frequently uses the verbs *atamma* and *faṣṣala*, as well as the latter's inverse *ajmala*. For example, Suras 3 to 7 are said to provide an 'elaboration' (*tafṣīl*) of 'the theological, prophetological, and eschatological doctrines (*ʿaqāʾid*) that were presented in a general fashion (*ujmila*) in sura 2'; it is thus 'fitting (*nāsaba*) that afterwards [namely, in Suras 8 and 9] there should be mention of what completes its [namely, Sura 2's] general presentation of legal rulings (*mā ujmila fī-hā min al-aḥkām*), especially rulings concerning war and the hypocrites.'[56] As we have seen, the passage that al-Ālūsī quotes from al-Suyūṭī – reproduced at the end of Riḍā's preface – also conceives of the relationship between the first six suras of the Qurᵓan as one of *ijmāl* versus *tafṣīl*. Riḍā thus deploys traditional tools in order to present the Qurᵓan as a work that exhibits a systematic order and proceeds from the general to the specific: Sura 2 broaches various issues in a general way (*ajmala*) and subsequent suras then go into further detail (*faṣṣala*). It seems plausible that this presentation is not free from modern assumptions about ideal expositional structures.

Riḍā's general introduction to the *Tafsīr al-Manār* dwells on the dangers of an overly technical type of exegetical scholarship that distracts (*shaghala, ṣarafa, alfata*) the reader from the essence of the Qurᵓan, which is to provide moral 'guidance' (*hidāya*).[57] Nonetheless, Riḍā's preface to Sūrat al-Anᶜām is a pastiche of dense scholarly arguments and extended quotations from earlier scholars that presents him as an author who is in intimate engagement with a centuries-long exegetical tradition. The contrast with the introduction that results from this is noteworthy, and different explanations may be suggested. It would not be unfair to suspect Riḍā of occasionally giving in to a desire to prove his scholarly credentials. Moreover, however unsatisfied he may have been with the existing kind of Qurᵓanic exegesis, an entrenched literary genre such as *tafsīr* is difficult to remake at will, even if the need to do so is programmatically asserted. It is therefore only to be expected that a traditionally trained *ᶜālim* like Riḍā will exhibit a certain tendency to relapse into ingrained patterns of writing, at least when dealing with a topic also discussed by earlier interpreters – which is certainly the case for the issues treated in Riḍā's introduction to Sūrat al-Anᶜām. In addition to these two factors, though, I find it difficult not to see Riḍā as trying to utilise thoroughly traditional resources in order to work towards an overall understanding of the Qurᵓan that is distinctly novel – namely, an understanding of the Qurᵓan as a work that answers to modern expectations of unity and coherence, expectations that would no doubt have been fuelled by new methods of education and written communication introduced during the nineteenth century. Sūrat al-Anᶜām, as suggested by Riḍā's adroit recycling of multifarious traditional material, is a catechetic text employing a specifically Qurᵓanic mode of theological instruction that is geared to having a genuine impact on people's 'hearts', a text whose thematic coherence is underscored by the fact that it was revealed in one piece – and, finally, a text that is embedded in a scripture exhibiting an optimal expositional organisation, moving from the general to the specific.

Sayyid Quṭb on Sūrat al-Anᶜām

That the *Manār* commentary is in conversation with the exegetical tradition preceding it is hardly a surprise. For Quṭb's commentary, an analogous conclusion would be much more unexpected. His very style of writing marks an obvious break with the conventions of scholarly Arabic that still govern the *Manār* commentary: his clauses and paragraphs are brief, he makes ample use of exclamation and question marks and points of ellipsis, and his general discursive stance is mostly paraenetic rather than scholarly.[58] The dynamism of Quṭb's prose almost immediately gives away his background in literature and journalism: this is not the work of an *ᶜālim*. Nevertheless, I shall try to show that at least some of the topics and concepts that feature in Quṭb's preface to Sūrat al-Anᶜām can be plausibly linked to the works encountered above. Unlike Riḍā, however, Quṭb does not extensively and ostentatiously reproduce earlier material, which makes his participation in the tradition much less conspicuous.

Quṭb's treatment of the sura begins with a general introduction to the Meccan Qurᵓan (*al-Qurᵓān al-makkī*),[59] occasioned by the fact that Sūrat al-Anᶜām is the first Meccan sura to occur in the corpus and, as he later writes, constitutes a 'perfect exemplar' of the Meccan Qurᵓan.[60] According to Quṭb, the latter is devoted to one overarching topic, 'the issue of the doctrine (*qaḍiyyat al-ᶜaqīda*)'.[61] Quṭb considers the pithiest expression of this Qurᵓanic doctrine to be the traditional Islamic formula of *tawḥīd*, 'there is no God but God' (*lā ilāha illa al-llāh*), but gives an extremely far-reaching interpretation to it: recognition of God's oneness and His exclusive claim to human worship also implies recognition of His sole right to 'rulership' (*ḥākimiyya*), thereby demanding a 'revolution' (*thawra*) against all merely human systems of social organisation and political rule.[62] Although Quṭb writes about the 'doctrine' of the Meccan Qurᵓan in general, the fact that the topic is developed in the preface to Sūrat al-Anᶜām recognisably echoes the topos, going back at least as far as Fakhr al-Dīn al-Rāzī, that Sūrat al-Anᶜām is, as Riḍā puts it, 'the sura of the doctrines of Islam' (*sūrat ᶜaqāᵓid al-Islām*).[63]

Yet the topos is given an idiosyncratic inflection. The Meccan Qurᵓan, Quṭb says, confined itself to reiterating and explaining the doctrine of *tawḥīd* and did not 'go beyond it and in no way addressed details of the system [of life] that was to rest on it (*tafṣīlāt al-niẓām alladhī yaqūmu ᶜalay-hā*) or the laws that were to govern the Islamic society that embraced it'.[64] Only after God's exclusive right to worship and rulership 'became firmly established' in the hearts of a 'chosen band (*al-ᶜuṣba al-mukhtāra*) of humans', could the latter go about creating a social order reflecting its religious re-orientation and commence the implementation of a properly Islamic social and political order.[65] Quṭb understands this two-stage model not just to correspond to the Meccan and the Medinan stage of Muḥammad's career, but also to constitute a paradigm for how an Islamic revolution is to be achieved in the present age, and he consequently insists that details of how the future Islamic society is to function can only be worked out after such a society has been brought into existence.[66] In his introduction to Sūrat al-Anᶜām, Quṭb explains that it was due to the necessity of following such a two-stage procedure that Muḥammad, during his Meccan period, consciously abstained from taking on the role of a social and ethical reformer or even of an anti-colonial liberator of the Arabs from Byzantine and Persian oppression; to work towards an incremental 'reform' (*iṣlāḥ*) of the existing order would have been the diametrical opposite of the way in which God wanted to establish Islam at the time of Muḥammad: namely, on the basis of a thorough internalisation of the Islamic *ᶜaqīda*.[67] Quṭb thus reconfigures the notion of *ᶜaqīda*, whose connection to Sūrat al-Anᶜām he inherits from earlier commentaries, to denote an existential and revolutionary doctrinal commitment to monotheism that must precede all moral, social and political change. This reconstructed notion of *ᶜaqīda* is then used to give check to the concept of 'reform' – which is of course a favourite term of Riḍā and his teacher ᶜAbduh.[68] Muḥammad did not come with a 'call to reform' (*daᶜwa iṣlāḥiyya*),[69] and neither should contemporary Muslims:

> the souls must first become faithfully devoted to God and announce their servitude to him by accepting, as a matter of principle, His law and refusing anyone else's law, before they can be given any details (*tafṣīl*) pertaining to this law that would awaken their desire for it.[70]

Further echoes of the exegetical tradition are audible when we turn to Quṭb's view of how the Meccan Qurᵓan treats 'the issue of the doctrine':

> It does not treat it in a 'theoretical' form! It does not treat it in the form of 'divinity' (*lāhūt*), nor does it treat it in the form of theological disputations (*jadal kalāmī*), as was subsequently practised by what is called 'the science of divine unity' (*ᶜilm al-tawḥīd*) or 'the science of theology' (*ᶜilm al-kalām*)![71]

The statement echoes al-Rāzī's and Riḍā's notion of a specifically Qurᵓanic 'method' of teaching theology, distinct from that of *kalām* and *falsafa*. Theoretical disputations and theology would not have been the 'appropriate' manner of instilling the Islamic *ᶜaqīda* in the Qurᵓan's audience.[72] In effect, the Qurᵓan aimed not merely at changing people's doctrine but their very 'way of thinking'[73] – 'to give us, the adherents of Islam's call (*al-daᶜwa al-Islāmiyya*), a special way of thinking by means of which we become free from the sediments of the pagan ways of thinking (*rawāsib manāhij al-tafkīr al-jāhiliyya*) that hold sway on earth'.[74] Hence, it would not be inaccurate to say that for Quṭb, just as for al-Rāzī, the Qurʾan is characterised by 'spiritually transformative features'.[75] Yet arguably, Quṭb significantly increases this dimension of the Qurʾan by conceiving the latter as designed to trigger a fundamental remaking of the human person; for Quṭb, true believers must perform the daunting task of completely extricating themselves from the reality in which they have so far grown up and lived, and the only lever that could bring about such an extrication is the Qurʾan. Encountering the Qurʾan thus takes on a positively soteriological significance.

The way in which the Qurʾan is able to perform this function, Quṭb maintains, is by addressing its audience aesthetically, with pre-rational immediacy, rather than theoretically. When describing the effect of Sūrat al-Anʿām, Quṭb characteristically resorts to visual and aural metaphors and to subjective interjections:

> Yes! It is true! A truth that I find in my soul and senses while following the flow of the sura (*siyāq al-sūra*) and its scenes (*mashāhid*) and rhythms ... And I do not think that any human endowed with a heart (*qalb*) would fail to find in it the tinge (*lawn*) that I find in it.[76]

The Qurʾanic manner of addressing its audience is to speak to the human heart, then, not – or not primarily – to human reason. One is reminded of Riḍā's insistence that the Qurʾanic 'method' of teaching theology does not confine itself to convincing people's intellects but also exerts an 'impact on their hearts' (*al-taʾthīr fī al-qulūb*).[77] The term *qalb*, which recurs at several junctures,[78] is of course a word with long-standing Sufi connotations,[79] thus reinforcing Quṭb's insistence that the Qurʾan does not merely aim at rational persuasion but at a fundamental reshaping of its addressees.

What Quṭb's commentary is trying to achieve is first and foremost to assist its readers in opening up their 'innate receiving devices' (*ajhizat al-istiqbāl al-fiṭriyya*)[80] to this transformative aesthetic impact of the Islamic scripture. As Quṭb says, he strives to erect a bridge (*qanṭara*) between the Qurʾan and those 'who are isolated from this Qurʾan – because of their distance from life in the atmosphere of the Qurʾan'.[81] When this bridge is crossed, one will 'arrive in a different region (*minṭaqa ukhrā*)', where one can 'live in the atmosphere of the Qurʾan'.[82] The purpose of Quṭb's commentary is thus not properly exegetical: his aim is not to elucidate the Qurʾanic text for its own sake, nor even to unlock the Qurʾan's ethical 'guidance', as the *Manār* commentary strives to do.[83] Rather, Quṭb's objective is to amplify the Qurʾan's inherent aesthetic appeal in such a way that it can overcome the 'sediments of the pagan ways of thinking'[84] within the psyche of his readers.

It is against this background that Quṭb proceeds to discuss the *jumlatan wāḥidatan* tradition,[85] for which he has at least as much sympathy as Riḍā. To Quṭb, an essential aspect of scripture's aesthetic impact consists in its coherence, which he also describes in terms of a sura's possession of a unique 'personality',[86] thereby assimilating one's reception of a Qurᵓanic sura to encountering a human other. As for Riḍā, the tradition that Sūrat al-Anᶜām was revealed on a single occasion is apt to underscore its unity of theme and content.[87] It is therefore ultimately in the service of his transformative aesthetics that Quṭb successively takes on the sura's allegedly inserted verses by deploying a string of highly respectable philological arguments. His general strategy is to assess putative insertions against their literary context and against whether they contain any obviously 'Medinan' references. In following this approach, which he designates as 'thematic analysis' (*taḥlīl mawḍūᶜī*),[88] Quṭb may conceivably be taking a cue from Riḍā's assessment that 6:151–2, alleged to be Medinan insertions, treat a perfectly Meccan topic and are seamlessly connected to the following verses.[89]

Let us take a closer look at Quṭb's examination of a tradition according to which vv. 91 and 141 are later insertions. That 6:91 could be an addition is deemed possible, as the verse would fit a Medinan context: it mentions the Mosaic scripture and confronts the Jews, who are addressed in the second person.[90] Yet Quṭb goes on to point out an alternative reading of the verse that transposes the direct address into the third person and thus does not imply that Jews were actually present when the verse was revealed.[91] This reading would also be supported by the fact that the context of the verse deals with the Meccan polytheists. Uncharacteristically, Quṭb even adds an argument from traditional authority, remarking that al-Ṭabarī likewise appears to prefer the third-person variant.[92] All things considered, then, Quṭb appears to prefer the alternative reading and to view v. 91 as an original constituent of the sura. He is less circumspect in the case of v. 141: it cannot be a Medinan insertion, he holds, because excising it from the sura would interrupt the context, as the verse constitutes an indispensable transition between the one preceding it and the one following it.[93] After having thus examined the allegedly inserted verses in considerable detail, Quṭb inclines towards giving credence to those traditions stating that Sūrat al-Anᶜām was revealed on one occasion without enumerating any exceptions.[94] He concludes his exercise in source criticism by reiterating the aesthetic vision that ultimately fuels it:

> the flow (*siyāq*) of the sura, in terms of its cohesion (*tamāsuk*), its drive forward (*tadāfuᶜ*), and its gushing forth (*tadaffuq*), impresses upon the heart (*qalb*) that this sura is a river gushing forth (*nahr yatadaffaqu*), or a stream

> rushing forward (*sayl yatadaffaᶜu*), without impediment or interruption, and that its very structure (*bināʾ*) completely verifies these traditions [about the sura having been revealed in one whole], or at least endows them with a strong probability.[95]

After having philologically vindicated the genetic unity of Sūrat al-Anᶜām, Quṭb goes into further details about the 'basic topic of the sura and its general personality', which I shall briefly recap.[96] Similar to the passage quoted at the end of the previous paragraph, Quṭb re-employs water imagery in order to emphasise the sura's indivisible unity. 'The main theme that it [the sura] treats is continuous; hence it is impossible to divide the sura into sections (*maqāṭiᶜ*) treating particular aspects of the topic … rather, it consists in waves … every wave agrees with the one preceding it and complements it.'[97] This is followed by a summary and partial quotation of the text's first thirty-six verses, subdivided into five 'waves' and interspersed with Quṭb's own remarks and exclamations.[98] He then turns to the particular manner in which the sura treats its 'basic topic' (namely, 'establishing the true nature of divinity, acquainting people with their true lord, and making them serve Him alone').[99] The text does so, Quṭb holds, in a way that generates a mood of 'dazzling awe' (*rawᶜa bāhira*),[100] a description that recurs several times throughout his preface.[101] This proposition again leads into extensive quotations. Finally, Quṭb highlights Sūrat al-Anᶜām's 'coherent way of presenting scenes and situations' (*tanāsuq fī manhaj al-ᶜarḍ li-l-mashāhid wa-l-mawāqif*).[102] Three features are listed: (1) the sura's great vividness, which 'seizes the hearer and puts him before the scene' at hand;[103] (2) the fact that the sura, at various junctures, contains 'scenes invoking witnesses' (*mawāqif al-ishhād*);[104] and (3) the recurrence of certain words and phrases, described as the text's 'terminological coherence' (*al-tanāsuq al-taᶜbīrī*), which according to Quṭb serves to emphasise that one and the same truth is being discussed in different forms.[105] Unlike all the other sura prefaces reviewed in this study, Quṭb thus maintains that the sura's thematic unity entails a stylistic and terminological unity as well.[106] The extent to which other parts of his commentary view a sura's unity of content as intertwined with the possession of a unitary literary and terminological form would deserve a separate study.

Some Concluding Remarks on the Study of Modern Qurʾanic Exegesis

I shall not belabour the fact, amply demonstrated above, that both Riḍā and Quṭb intimately participate in a centuries-long exegetical conversation. Without situating them against this backdrop, a scholar risks significantly impoverishing the range of interpretive frequencies that he or she will be able to pick up. For instance, the fact that Quṭb responds to and appropriates two topoi going back at least as far as Fakhr al-Dīn al-Rāzī – namely, Sūrat al-Anᶜām's constituting a summa of Qurᵓanic theology and the Qurᵓan's being distinguished by a unique 'method' of presenting theology – would simply not be audible without prior study of the pre-modern exegetical tradition. At least to some degree, even the interpretive moves made by someone as ostentatiously modern in style as Quṭb are therefore moves made on a chessboard many of whose squares were marked off centuries ago (which is not to preclude that the structure of the board evolved over time).

Riḍā's participation in the tradition is much more readily apparent, of course, as he extensively quotes and engages with earlier interpreters. In his case, the danger resides more in perceiving this traditional dimension as a redundant and tedious topping that must somehow be cleared away to allow us to get at the real content of his exegetical work. Scholarship on modern *tafsīr* ought to resist the temptation of being interested in its object primarily or even exclusively insofar as exegesis can serve as a forum for debating the fraught relationship between Islam and modernity. That is to say, it would be insufficient to pursue the study of modern Qurᵓanic exegesis mainly as a study of how modern exegetes grapple with two classes of verses: verses that are likely to invite explicit or implicit references to modern Western concepts, and verses that do not seem easily reconcilable with modern values or modern science. The present contribution shows, I would contend, that nineteenth- and twentieth-century *tafsīr* is more than just a source to comb for tell-tale manifestations of modernity or the rejection thereof. Such an approach would be unlikely to do full justice to hermeneutic developments that go beyond the conspicuous projection of ready-made Western ideas onto the Islamic scripture or setting the latter up as a bulwark against them (the modern emphasis on the Qurᵓan's thematic and literary coherence being a case in point).

The study of modern Qurᵓanic exegesis can contribute to, but must not be identified with, doxography (what did a particular interpreter happen to think about democracy, or science, or the status of non-Muslims?). Rather, it ought to be an exercise in reconstructive reading: what are the implicit assumptions and the patterns of observation, inference and presentation by means of which an interpreter makes sense of the Qurᵓanic text in the context of debates that may have a pre-history of more than a millennium? From my reading of Riḍā's and Quṭb's introductions to Sūrat al-Anᶜām, I come away with the impression that a due appreciation of the multifarious ways in which modern Islamic exegesis can be in conversation with the antecedent tradition – by re-evaluating ancient reports, by scrutinising and critiquing the views of earlier authorities, by reconfiguring existing topoi – is indispensable to gauging its full sophistication.

Notes

1. English citations of Qurʾanic verses are based on the translation by Alan Jones (Gibb Memorial Trust, 2007) with occasional modifications.
2. Mustansir Mir, 'The Sūra as a unity: a twentieth century development in Qurʾān exegesis', in G. R. Hawting and Abdul-Kader A. Shareef (eds), *Approaches to the Qurʾān* (London and New York: Routledge, 1993), 211–24; M. Mir, *Coherence in the Qurʾān: A Study of Iṣlāḥī's Concept of* Naẓm *in* Tadabbur-i Qurʾān (Indianapolis: American Trust Publications, 1986). This development seems to have occurred independently in the Indian subcontinent and in the Arab world (in particular, Egypt) during the first decades of the twentieth century (Mir, 'Unity', 217).
3. Charles C. Adams, *Islam and Modernism in Egypt: A Study of the Modern Reform Movement Inaugurated by Muḥammad ʿAbduh* (New York: Russell & Russell, [1933] 1968), 201–2; Kate Zebiri, *Maḥmūd Shaltūt and Islamic Modernism* (Oxford: Clarendon Press, 1993), 143. The standard narrative of the *Tafsīr al-Manār*'s genesis locates its ultimate origin in exegetical lectures delivered by Muḥammad ʿAbduh that Muḥammad Rashīd Riḍā subsequently revised for publication in his journal *al-Manār*. Later, Riḍā expanded the material into a free-standing commentary, entitled *Tafsīr al-Manār*, which also covered suras not previously treated by ʿAbduh and which by the time of Riḍā's death in 1935 had reached Sura 12. On the *Tafsīr al-Manār* in general and the issue of authorship in particular, see Adams, *Islam and Modernism*, 198–202; Johannes J. G. Jansen, *The Interpretation of the Koran in Modern Egypt* (Leiden: Brill, 1974), 18–34; Zebiri, *Shaltūt*, 132–7; Kosugi Yasushi, '*Al-Manār* revisited: the "Lighthouse" of the Islamic Revival', in Stéphane A. Dudoignon *et al.* (eds), *Intellectuals in the Modern Islamic World: Transmission, Transformation, Communication* (London and New York: Routledge, 2006), 3–39 (17–19). The complex genesis of the *Tafsīr al-Manār* and Riḍā's editorial strategies are patently in need of an in-depth study, which would have to undertake systematic textual comparisons between (1) the exegetical material in the *Manār* journal, (2) the independent exegetical publications that have appeared under the name of Muḥammad ʿAbduh, and (3) the first and second editions of the *Tafsīr al-Manār* itself. In this article, I shall adhere to the customary practice of using the second edition of the commentary.
4. See Mir, *Coherence*, 10–19; Mir, 'Unity', 211–12.
5. Mir, 'Unity', 211–12; Mir, *Coherence*, 17–18. For a general introduction to Fakhr al-Dīn al-Rāzī and his commentary, see Roger Arnaldez, *Fakhr al-Dîn al-Râzî: Commentateur du Coran et philosophe* (Paris: Librairie Philosophique J. Vrin, 2002). On the concept of *munāsaba*, see Jalāl al-Dīn al-Suyūṭī, *Al-Itqān fī ʿulūm al-Qurʾān*, 2 vols (Beirut: Dār al-Kutub al-ʿIlmiyyah, n. d.), 2: 234–47 (*nawʿ* 62).
6. See the quotation in Walid A. Saleh, *In Defense of the Bible: A Critical Edition and an Introduction to al-Biqāʿī's Bible Treatise* (Leiden: Brill, 2008), 15

(Arabic text given in n. 40, English translation modified). For an introduction to al-Biqāᶜī and his commentary see Saleh, *Defense*, 7–35.

7. I refrain from attempting an enumeration of recent scholarship, but see the remarks in Albert Hourani, *Arabic Thought in the Liberal Age 1798–1939* (Cambridge: Cambridge University Press, 1983), 144, 151–2, 233–4, 344.
8. Zebiri, *Shaltūt*, 174.
9. Two recent intellectual biographies of Sayyid Quṭb are John Calvert, *Sayyid Qutb and the Origins of Radical Islamism* (New York: Columbia University Press, 2010) and James Toth, *Sayyid Qutb: The Life and Legacy of a Radical Islamic Intellectual* (Oxford: Oxford University Press, 2013).
10. See Calvert, *Sayyid Qutb*, 65 and 67 (on al-ᶜAqqād's and Quṭb's demand for organic unity) and 112 (on *al-Taṣwīr al-fannī*).
11. Mir, 'Unity', 218.
12. Ibid. 219.
13. On Riḍā's use of the concept see Yasir S. Ibrahim, 'Rashīd Riḍā and *Maqāṣid al-Sharīᶜa*', *Studia Islamica* 102/103 (2006), 157–98.
14. For example, Wielandt's otherwise comprehensive encyclopaedia entry on modern Qurᵓanic exegesis does not count holism as one of the five 'main trends' distinguished by her (Rotraud Wielandt, 'Exegesis of the Qurᵓān: early modern and contemporary', in Jane Dammen McAuliffe (ed.), *Encyclopaedia of the Qurᵓān* (Leiden: Brill, 2001–6), 2: 124–42). As a matter of fact, holistic tendencies cut across her classification, which assigns the *Tafsīr al-Manār* and Quṭb's commentary to different categories.
15. On sura introductions and epitomes in the *Manār* commentary see Zebiri, *Shaltūt*, 143, and Yasushi, '*Al-Manār*', 19–20.
16. Note that the *Tafsīr al-Manār*'s extensive concluding epitome on Sura 6 (8: 270–94) will only be referred to very selectively. For literature on the *Tafsīr al-Manār*, see note 3 above. On Quṭb's commentary, see Olivier Carré, 'La Lecture du Coran par Sayyid Quṭb', *Arabica* 32 (1985), 261–88; Ronald Nettler, 'A modern Islamic confession of faith and conception of religion: Sayyid Quṭb's Introduction to the *Tafsīr, fī Ẓilāl al-Qurᵓān* [sic]', *British Journal of Middle Eastern Studies* 21 (1994), 102–14; R. Nettler, 'Guidelines for the Islamic community: Sayyid Qutb's political interpretation of the Qurᵓān', *Journal of Political Ideologies* 1 (1996), 183–96. The process of its publication and subsequent revision is summarily sketched in Calvert, *Sayyid Qutb*, 205.
17. See Angelika Neuwirth, *Studien zur Komposition der mekkanischen Suren*, 2nd edn (Berlin: de Gruyter, 2007), 290–1.
18. Fakhr al-Dīn al-Rāzī, *Tafsīr Fakhr al-Dīn al-Rāzī al-mushtahir bi-l-Tafsīr al-kabīr wa-mafātīḥ al-ghayb*, 32 vols (Beirut: Dār al-Fikr, 1981), 12: 149.
19. On Ibn ᶜAbbās, see Claude Gilliot, 'Portrait "mythique" d'Ibn ᶜAbbās', *Arabica* 32 (1985), 127–84.
20. 'Those who disbelieve say, "Why has the recitation/the Qurᵓan (*al-qurᵓān*) not been sent down to him in one whole (*jumlatan wāḥidatan*)?" [We have sent it

down] thus so that We may strengthen your [singular] heart by it, and We have sent it down distinctly.'

21. For a compilation of numerous variants of this tradition, see Jalāl al-Dīn al-Suyūṭī, *Al-Durr al-manthūr fī l-tafsīr bi-l-maʾthūr*, ed. ᶜAbdallāh b. ᶜAbd al-Muṣin al-Turkī, 17 vols (Cairo: Markaz Hajar li-l-Baḥth wa-l-Dirāsāt al-Islāmiyyah, 2003), 6: 5–9 (with further references); cf. also al-Suyūṭī, *Itqān*, 1: 82 (*nawᶜ* 13).
22. The verses that were inserted according to the version cited by al-Rāzī would seem to be vv. 151–3, v. 91, and vv. 93–4. As customary for Islamic exegetes, al-Rāzī does not give verse numbers and adduces only the opening of v. 93, which overlaps with that of v. 21; it appears that v. 94 must be understood to be included in order to bring the number up to six.
23. A selection is cited in *Manār*, 7: 283, l. 4 from bottom – 284, l. 7; see below. *Manār* = Muḥammad ᶜAbduh and Muḥammad Rashīd Riḍā, *Tafsīr al-Qurʾān al-ḥakīm al-mushtahir bi-sm Tafsīr al-manār*, 12 vols (Cairo: Dār al-Manār, 1947–61). Note: page and line numbers for this reprint may exhibit minor divergences from the original printing of the second edition.
24. This is also how the term is construed in *Manār*, 7: 287, ll. 7–8.
25. The nineteenth-century scholar al-Ālūsī, whose introduction to Sura 6 is briefly discussed below, cites the Ashᶜarite theologian Abū Isḥāq al-Isfarāʾīnī (d. 1027) as having maintained that Sura 6 contains 'all the foundations of monotheism' (*kull qawāᶜid al-tawḥīd*) (Shihāb al-Dīn Maḥmūd al-Ālūsī, *Rūḥ al-maᶜānī fī tafsīr al-Qurʾān al-ᶜaẓīm wa-l-sabᶜ al-mathānī*, 30 vols (Beirut: Dār Iḥyāʾ al-Turāth al-ᶜArabī, n.d.), 7: 77, l. 13). While this suggests that al-Rāzī might have derived the notion that Sūrat al-Anᶜām is essentially a theological text from the Ashᶜarite tradition in which he was himself trained, the fact that his *uṣūliyyūn* highlight divine justice (*ᶜadl*) has a distinctively Muᶜtazilite ring to it. The ultimate origin of the idea clearly requires further study.
26. Burhān al-Dīn Ibrāhīm b. ᶜUmar Al-Biqāᶜī, *Naẓm al-durar fī tanāsub al-āyāt wa-l-suwar*, 22 vols (Cairo: Dār al-Kitāb al-Islāmī, n.d.), 7: 6–7.
27. According to al-Biqāᶜī, this aim features especially prominently in the passage criticising the pagan customs relating to livestock (*Naẓm al-durar*, 6: 136–9).
28. On the author and his commentary, see Basheer M. Nafi, 'Abu al-Thanaʾ al-Alusi: an Alim, Ottoman mufti, and exegete of the Qurʾan', *International Journal of Middle East Studies* 34 (2002), 465–94; on al-Ālūsī's exegesis, see the brief characterisation in Mir, *Coherence*, 18–19. The preface to Sura 6 is found in al-Ālūsī, *Rūḥ*, 7: 75–7.
29. Al-Ālūsī, *Rūḥ*, 7: 76, ll. 18–19, the wording of which is slightly closer to the version cited in al-Suyūṭī, *Itqān*, 1: 82 (*nawᶜ* 13) than to the original (Ibn al-Ṣalāḥ, *Fatāwā wa-masāʾil Ibn al-Ṣalāḥ fī l-tafsīr wa-l-ḥadīth wa-l-uṣūl wa-l-fiqh*, ed. ᶜAbd al-Muᶜṭī Amīn Qalᶜajī, 2 vols (Beirut: Dār al-Maᶜrifah, 1986), 1: 249).
30. See Jalāl al-Dīn al-Suyūṭī, *Asrār tartīb al-Qurʾān*, ed. ᶜAbd al-Qādir Aḥmad ᶜAṭā (Cairo: Dār al-Iᶜtiṣām, 1978), 97–100 (l. 2) = Jalāl al-Dīn al-Suyūṭī,

Tanāsuq al-durar fī tanāsub al-suwar, ed. ʿAbdallāh Muḥammad al-Darwīsh (Damascus: Dār al-Kitāb al-ʿArabī, 1983), 49–52. Al-Suyūṭī is explicitly named as a source in al-Ālūsī, *Rūḥ*, 7: 76, l. 23 and the ultimate line, but already the immediately preceding lines (ll. 20–2) are lifted from his *Asrār*.

31. The first half of this statement, it is suggested, corresponds to the assertion that God has 'created the heavens and the earth' (6:1), while the second part can be mapped onto the affirmation that God has 'made darkness and light' and 'created you [plural] from clay and then fixed a term' (6:1–2).
32. The relevant passages in Sura 6 would seem to be 6:118–21 (for 5:87), 6:136–9 (for 3:14 and 5:103), and 6:146–7 (for 5:87).
33. Al-Ālūsī, *Rūḥ*, 7: 77, ll. 12–13.
34. On him, see *Encyclopaedia of Islam*, 2nd edn (*EI2*) (Leiden: Brill, 1960ff) [accessed online at http://referenceworks.brillonline.com/entries/encyclopaedia-of-islam-2 (July 2014)] 'al-Isfarāyīnī' (Wilferd Madelung), and *EI3*, (Leiden: Brill, 2007ff) [accessed online at http://referenceworks.brillonline.com/entries/encyclopaedia-of-islam-3 (July 2014)], 'Abū Isḥāq al-Isfarāyīnī' (Angelika Brodersen), both of whom report that none of al-Isfarāʾīnī's works are extant.
35. *Manār*, 7: 283–91.
36. Ibid. 286, ll. 14ff.
37. Ibid. 285, l. 10.
38. Ibid. 284, ll. 3–4. Riḍā also opines, in ll. 2–3, that at least from the perspective of content, 'the preceding' – presumably, 6:146–147 – would be much more likely to be Medinan, given that these verses criticise the Jews, 'who were present in Medina'. Note the methodological parallel between these remarks and Iṣlāḥī's treatment of Q. 96:1–5, briefly presented in the introduction above.
39. Cf. *Manār*, 7: 284, ll. 8–13 with al-Suyūṭī, *Itqān*, 1: 27 (*nawʿ* 1, *faṣl fī taḥrīr al-suwar al-mukhtalaf fīhā*).
40. *Manār*, 7: 284, ll. 14ff. As Riḍā himself remarks, this train of thought is derived, via al-Suyūṭī (cf. *Itqān*, 1: 64–5 = *nawʿ* 9), from Ibn Taymiyya. See also Ibn Taymiyya, *Muqaddima* [= Musāʿid b. Sulaymān al-Ṭayyār, *Sharḥ al-Muqaddimah fī uṣūl at-tafsīr li-Ibn Taymiyyah* (Al-Dammām: Dār Ibn al-Jawzī, 1428 AH)], 67.
41. A similar view is expressed in introduction to the *Manār* commentary, according to which most exegetical traditions (*akthar al-tafsīr al-maʾthūr*) may be disregarded, as it 'goes back to transmitters (*ruwāt*) who were Jewish or Persian freethinkers (*zanādiqa*) or converted Jews and Christians' rather than to the Prophet, his Companions and 'the scholars among the Successors' (*Manār*, 1: 7–8).
42. *Manār*, 7: 285, ll. 5–8, quoted from al-Suyūṭī, *Itqān*, 1: 82 (*nawʿ* 13). This citation is followed by a passing reference to al-Suyūṭī, *Durr*, 6: 5–9 at *Manār*, 7: 285, ll. 8–10.
43. *Manār*, 7: 285, l. 11.

44. See Wael B. Hallaq, *A History of Islamic Legal Theories: An Introduction to Sunnī* Uṣūl al-Fiqh (Cambridge: Cambridge University Press, 1997), 68. Riḍā understands the *jumlatan wāḥidatan* tradition to be 'affirmative' and reports about Medinan insertions to be 'negative'.
45. Al-Suyūṭī, *Itqān*, 1: 27 (*nawᶜ* 1, *faṣl fī taḥrīr al-suwar al-mukhtalaf fī-hā*), referenced in *Manār*, 7: 285, ll. 18–19.
46. In doing so, Riḍā cites and refutes an argument that al-Ālūsī quotes from 'the *imām*' – namely, that the general consensus that Sūrat al-Anᶜām was revealed 'as a whole' is contradicted by the fact that 'about each of its verses it is said that the occasion of its revelation consisted in such and such' (al-Ālūsī, *Rūḥ*, 7: 76, ll. 14–15; for Riḍā's response see *Manār*, 7: 286, ll. 14–23). This enigmatic *imām* is exasperatingly difficult to identify. Like Riḍā, I first looked to Fakhr al-Dīn al-Rāzī as the obvious candidate, for 'when the title *imām* is used in works by exegetes, theologians, legal hermeneuticians and logicians subsequent to al-Rāzī, it refers to him' (*Manār*, 7: 287, ll. 9–10); yet, as Riḍā also points out, al-Rāzī's preface to the sura does not contain 'what al-Ālūsī has quoted from him' (*Manār*, 7, 287, l. 8; emend *ᶜan* to *ᶜan-hu*).
47. *Manār*, 7: 287, l. 7.
48. *Manār*, 8: 270, l. 16.
49. *Manār*, 7: 287, ll. 7–8.
50. *Manār*, 8: 271, ll. 9–17.
51. Ibid. antepenultimate and penultimate lines.
52. According to Ayman Shihadeh, *The Teleological Ethics of Fakhr al-Dīn al-Rāzī* (Leiden and Boston: Brill, 2006), 200–3, this view is frequently encountered in the later writings of Fakhr al-Dīn al-Rāzī (Shihadeh, *Ethics*, 200ff.). That Riḍā did indeed derive the notion from al-Rāzī is supported by the fact that the reference to the 'Qurᵓanic method' (*ṭarīqat al-Qurᵓān*) comes immediately in the wake of Riḍā's quotation of the end of al-Rāzī's preface to the sura. Thus, although al-Rāzī's preface to Sūrat al-Anᶜām does not explicitly refer to the 'Qurᵓanic method', Riḍā seems to have included the statement as a supplementary clarification of al-Rāzī's intent.
53. Shihadeh, *Ethics*, 201–2.
54. *Manār*, 7: 289, l. 16 – 291, l. 6 = al-Ālūsī, *Rūḥ*, 7: 76, l. 20 – 77, l. 19. For references to al-Suyūṭī, see note 30 above.
55. Ibid. 287, ll. 20–1.
56. Ibid. 289, ll. 2–4. The 'hypocrites' (*al-munāfiqūn*) are traditionally understood to be those inhabitants of Medina who were unwilling to fully embrace Islam and even actively plotted against the Prophet.
57. *Manār*, 1: 7.
58. The 'sermon-like' quality of Quṭb's commentary is noted in Jansen, *Interpretation*, 79.
59. Sayyid Quṭb, *Fī ẓilāl al-Qurᵓān*, 6 vols (with continuous pagination) (Cairo: Dār al-Shurūq, [1972] 2003), 1004–17.
60. Ibid. 1015, ll. 21–2.

61. See, for example, Quṭb, *Ẓilāl*, 1004, ll. 7–8; 1005, l. 9. The term *^caqīda* is part of Quṭb's vocabulary elsewhere, too; see Nettler, 'Modern Islamic confession', 106–7.
62. Cf. Quṭb, *Ẓilāl*, 1005, ll. 9–21. On Quṭb's understanding of *ḥākimiyya* and its counterpart, the concept of *jāhiliyya*, see William E. Shepard, 'Sayyid Qutb's doctrine of Jāhiliyya', *International Journal of Middle East Studies* 35 (2003), 521–45 and Yvonne Haddad, 'Sayyid Qutb: ideologue of Islamic revival', in John L. Esposito (ed.), *Voices of Resurgent Islam* (New York and Oxford: Oxford University Press, 1983), 67–98 (85–7 and 89–90).
63. *Manār*, 8, 270, l. 16.
64. Quṭb, *Ẓilāl*, 1005, ll. 6–8. On Quṭb's understanding of Islam as a system, see William E. Shepard, 'Islam as a "system" in the later writings of Sayyid Qutb', *Middle Eastern Studies* 25 (1989), 31–50.
65. Ibid. 1005, ll. 1–4. As pointed out in Jeffry R. Halverson, H. L. Goodall Jr and Steven R. Corman, *Master Narratives of Islamist Extremism* (New York: Palgrave Macmillan, 2011), 45, Quṭb's 'chosen band' clearly echoes Lenin's notion of the revolutionary vanguard.
66. Sayyid Quṭb, *Ma^cālim fī l-ṭarīq* (Cairo: Dār al-Shurūq, 1979), 33 (quoted in Shepard, 'Islam', 39; translation slightly modified): 'When this [Islamic] society actually exists it will have a practical life that will require organisation and legislation … Only then will this religion begin to establish systems and make laws for a people who are prepared to submit to such systems and laws in the first place.' Cf. similarly Quṭb, *Ẓilāl*, 1009–11 and 1014–15.
67. Quṭb, *Ẓilāl*, 1005–8.
68. See *EI2*, 'Iṣlāḥ'. On Quṭb's criticism of ^cAbduh and his 'school' see Carré, 'Lecture', 263–4.
69. Quṭb, *Ẓilāl*, 1007, l. 26.
70. Ibid. 1011, ll. 22–3.
71. Ibid. penultimate line – 1012, l. 1. Further references to *^cilm al-tawḥīd* and *al-lāhūt* occur in Quṭb, *Ẓilāl*, 1012, ll. 9–11.
72. Ibid. 1012, ll. 9–11.
73. Ibid. 1014, ll. 7–8.
74. Ibid. ll. 16–17. On Quṭb's use of the term *jāhiliyya*, which in pre-modern Islam designates the 'age of ignorance' prevailing in the Arabian Peninsula prior to the revelation of the Qur^oan, to describe the modern world see Shepard, 'Quṭb's doctrine'.
75. The expression is again borrowed from Shihadeh, *Ethics*, 201–2.
76. Quṭb, *Ẓilāl*, 1015, ultimate line – 1016, l. 1. Note that the points of ellipsis here and elsewhere are Quṭb's. The term *mashhad*, frequently employed by Quṭb, is also used by ^cĀ^oisha ^cAbd al-Raḥmān in *al-Tafsīr al-bayānī* (Cairo: Dār al-Ma^cārif, 1990, 1: 103, l. 3). The observation illustrates the need for a thorough study of the literary vocabulary of Quṭb in the context of twentieth-century Egyptian literature and literary criticism.
77. *Manār*, 8: 271, ll. 9–17.

78. In addition to the passage just quoted, see Quṭb, *Ẓilāl*, 1016, ll. 27–8; 1020, l. 11; 1022, l. 10.
79. Sufis use it to refer to the part of the human self that is receptive to divine inspirations (see Ahmet T. Karamustafa, *Sufism: The Formative Period* (Edinburgh: Edinburgh University Press, 2007), 15, 19, 41–2, 45, 107–8). When Quṭb speaks of man's 'innate receiving devices' (*ajhizat al-istiqbāl al-fiṭriyya*; Quṭb, *Ẓilāl*, 1012, l. 3), this appears to mean essentially the same as the term *qalb*.
80. Ibid. 1012, l. 3.
81. Ibid. 1016, ll. 4–5 from bottom.
82. Ibid. 1017, ll. 9–10. Cf. Quṭb, *Ẓilāl*, 1016, l. 3 from bottom – 1017, l. 1: 'Life in the atmosphere of the Qurʾan does not mean studying the Qurʾan, reciting it, becoming familiar with Qurʾanic scholarship … Rather, what we mean by living in the atmosphere of the Qurʾan is for man to live in an atmosphere, in circumstances, in a movement, and in suffering, and in a struggle, and in ambitions … like those within which this Qurʾan was revealed … [It means] for man to live in confrontation with this age of paganism (*jāhiliyya*) that encompasses the surface of the earth today.'
83. *Manār*, 1: 7.
84. See Quṭb, *Ẓilāl*, 1014, ll. 16–17
85. Ibid. 1020–2.
86. Ibid. 1022, l. 13.
87. Quṭb does not deny that other suras might be composite (see Quṭb, *Ẓilāl*, 1020, ll. 18–20). Note, however, that elsewhere, too, his commentary takes issue with the alleged presence of Medinan insertions; see, for example, his introduction to Sura 11 (Quṭb, *Ẓilāl*, 1839).
88. Quṭb, *Ẓilāl*, 1022, ll. 8–9.
89. *Manār*, 7: 284, ll. 3–4.
90. Quṭb, *Ẓilāl*, 1020–1. The verse runs as follows: 'They have not measured God's power properly when they said, "God has not sent down anything to any mortal." Say, "Who sent down the Scripture that Moses brought as a light and a guidance to the people? You [plural] put it [on] parchments, revealing them, but concealing much. And you were taught what you did not know – neither you nor your forefathers." Say, "God", then leave them playing in their idle talk.'
91. Instead of *tajʿalūna-hu* and *tubdūna-hā*, the reading variant has *yajʿalūna-hu* and *yubdūna-hā*. See Aḥmad Mukhtār ʿUmar and ʿAbd al-ʿĀl Sālim Makram, *Muʿjam al-qirāʾāt al-qurʾāniyyah*, 2nd edn, 8 vols (Kuwait: Dhāt al-Salāsil, 1988), 2: 292.
92. See Muḥammad b. Jarīr al-Ṭabarī, *Jāmiʿ al-bayān ʿan taʾwīl āy al-Qurʾān*, ed. ʿAbdallāh b. ʿAbd al-Muḥsin al-Turkī, 26 vols (Cairo: Dār Hajar, 2001), 9: 398 (on Q. 6:91).
93. Quṭb, *Ẓilāl*, 1021, ll. 9–10. Once again, note the methodological parallel to Iṣlāḥī's treatment of Q. 96:1–5, briefly presented in my introduction.
94. Ibid. 1021, penultimate line–1022, l. 9.

95. Ibid. 1022, ll. 10–12.
96. Ibid. 1022–9.
97. Ibid. 1022, ll. 23–4.
98. Ibid. 1022, l. 25–1025, l. 6.
99. Ibid. 1025, l. 12.
100. Ibid. l. 8.
101. Ibid. 1015, l. 3 from bottom; 1023, l. 5; 1027, l. 6.
102. Ibid.1027, ll. 6–7.
103. Ibid. l. 11.
104. Ibid. 1028, ll. 8–20. Quṭb points to various verses containing the phrase *law tarā* ('if you could see ...'), already quoted in support of the first of the three features (vv. 27, 30 and 93) and cites two verses employing derivatives of *sh-h-d* (vv. 19 and 150).
105. Ibid. l. 21 – 1029, l. 10. For instance, the phrase *bi-rabbi-him ya^c^dilūn* recurs in v. 1 and towards the end, in v. 150; and the word *al-ṣirāṭ* is repeated several times (Quṭb quotes vv. 126 and 153, but three more instances could be added: vv. 39, 87 and 161).
106. Once again, see Quṭb, *Ẓilāl*, 1028, l. 21: *al-tanāsuq al-ta^c^bīrī alladhī yaqtaḍī-hi al-taqrīr al-mawḍū^c^ī.*

6

Contemporary Iranian Interpretations of the Qur'an and Tradition on Women's Testimony[1]

Karen Bauer

Scholars of religion are well aware of the hermeneutical difficulty posed when a holy text says something that challenges widespread beliefs or values. In this paper I focus on modern Iranian methods of dealing with Q. 2:282. Qur'an 2:282 states that women's testimony in cases of debt is half that of men's, which poses a challenge to the notion of gender egalitarianism, and particularly to the notion that women's minds are equal to men's minds. I describe the conservative, the reformist and the neo-traditionalist methods of interpretation, categories which I have adopted from Ziba Mir-Hosseini, who uses the terms 'traditionalist', 'neo-traditionalist' and 'modernist'.[2] I have modified the terms she has used, because these terms imply that traditionalists are not modern and that reformists reject all aspects of tradition. Instead, all *ᶜulamā'* use some aspects of tradition, and all modify it in some ways to incorporate widespread values, and this is evident in their approaches to gender roles. I ultimately argue that gender egalitarianism is a widespread modern value (not just a 'Western' value) in part by showing how notions of egalitarianism influence the interpretations of all *ᶜulamā'*, including those who argue against egalitarian interpretations of the Qur'an.

Reformists and neo-traditionalists embrace elements of gender egalitarianism. Conservatives argue instead for 'complementarity', in which men and women have fixed, complementary roles. This is entirely in keeping with pre-modern interpretations, which, though varied in many respects, were unanimously gender hierarchical. However, unlike pre-modern interpreters, modern conservatives clarify that the roles of men and women are equally valuable. In other words, the notion of egalitarianism is evident in conservatives' justification for the ruling, rather than in its substance. Whereas pre-modern interpreters often justified their interpretations by pointing to women's defects, today such language has been jettisoned. Elements of equality between the sexes are emphasised, even in conservative interpretations where the ruling itself remains hierarchical or unequal. This is a prime example of the way that certain values can come to be a norm that is taken for granted, which in turn influences the interpretation of the Qurʾan. The differences between the *ʿulamāʾ* which form the parameters of the debate outlined below can tell us much about the local politics of interpretation. But the subtle elements of agreement between them are symptomatic of the way that the learned class of the *ʿulamāʾ* respond to wider currents of thought both in the Middle East and Iran, and beyond.

The Verse and its Interpretative Background

Qurʾan 2:282, the longest verse in the Qurʾan, speaks of the manner in which parties should contract a debt; one phrase addresses the status of women as witnesses to this transaction:

> Call to witness from among your men two witnesses; but if there are not two men, then one man and two women from among those who are pleasing witnesses, so that if one of the two women errs, one of the two may remind the other.

In the pre-modern period, the notion of women's word being worth half of men's word was acceptable. The rulings on women's testimony in pre-modern *fiqh* are varied and complex; but most jurists justified their rulings with reference to women's minds: women are deficient in rationality (*nāqiṣāt al-ʿaql*), or prone to forgetfulness, they do not have the judgement that men have, and for some jurists testimony carries a type of authority (*wilāya*) for which women are unsuited.[3] When jurists do not cite these rationales, they cite other factors: women's voices should not be heard in public, or women should not mix with men.[4] These justifications accord with the dominant idea at that time that women's and men's minds are unequal.[5] Furthermore, hadiths say that women are deficient in rationality and religion. There are several versions of the 'deficiency hadith', as I term it, in both Sunni and Shiʿi collections. These hadiths, however, have one thing in common: women are deemed to be deficient in rationality (*nāqisāt al-ʿaql*), because the 'testimony of two of them equals that of one man', as per this verse. Though the hadith is not cited in every work of *tafsīr* or *fiqh*, it is cited or referred to fairly often in order to explain this verse, or other verses that imply a gender hierarchy, such as Q. 4:34.

How do modern conservative, neo-traditionalist and reformist *ʿulamāʾ* deal with this history of interpretation? Conservatives seek to preserve pre-modern laws; yet they generally do not replicate the pre-modern justifications described above. Fariba ʿAlasvand upholds core aspects of pre-modern rulings on women's testimony, only granting women equal rights to testify in those areas that were allowed in pre-modern law, and denying women rights to testify in areas that were denied in pre-modern law, but she justifies her rulings with recourse to modern science. Unlike ᶜAlasvand, some modern *ᶜulamāʾ* advocate reform in the laws themselves. Grand Ayatollah Saanei, whom I classify as a neo-traditionalist,[6] promotes reform in the law and rejects hadiths that contravene the ideal of gender equality. He asserts that women's testimony equals men's in most areas, but is not willing to jettison all prior interpretations. The reformist Mehdi Mehrizi favours a wholesale reinterpretation of the verse, to allow women entirely equal rights to testify with men.

Tradition, with a Twist

All of the thinkers described above embrace some elements of tradition, but none more than the conservatives. Conservatives describe themselves as traditionalists; they actively seek to reproduce its most important elements, though it is well recognised that they modify and modernise that tradition.[7] And indeed, I would argue that the idea of gender egalitarianism influences their thought, even when they actively deny egalitarianism as a value. One example is found in the work of Fariba ᶜAlasvand, a prominent teacher and one of the foremost experts on women's issues in Qom.

During my interview with her, ᶜAlasvand immediately referred me to one of her books, which she proceeded to give me, entitled '*Critique of the Convention of Elimination of all forms of Discrimination Against Women* (*Naqd konvensiyūn rafᶜ kulliyya-i ashkāl tabᶜayiḍ ᶜalayhi zanān*)'.[8] The Convention of Elimination of all forms of Discrimination Against Women (CEDAW) is a treaty adopted in 1979 by the United Nations General Assembly. Ratifying states must agree to end legal discrimination against women and to treat men and women equally under the law. Iran is not a signatory. ᶜAlasvand's written critique of CEDAW explains why, in her view, the Convention contravenes Islamic law and human nature. The basic message of the book is that legal distinctions between men and women in Islamic law do not constitute a form of discrimination. She argues that these distinctions are beneficial to women, and to society in general. That is because, according to her, Islamic legal provisions reflect the natural differences between the sexes.

The *Critique* includes a few pages on women's testimony, in which she summarises the Imāmī Shiᶜi *fiqh* on women's testimony, according to the Marjaᶜ al-Ḥurr al-ᶜĀmilī (d. 1104/1693), who was a prominent Akhbārī jurist. In ᶜAlasvand's analysis, women's testimony can be divided into four different types of case: (1) cases in which women's testimony is accepted without men; (2) cases in which the testimony of one woman is valid against that of four men; (3) cases in which women's testimony, whether alone or with men's, is not accepted; (4) cases in which women's testimony is accepted along with men's.[9]

She gives a brief explanation of each type of case: the first has to do with areas in which women specialise, such as the birth of a live child. ᶜAlasvand points out that testifying to the birth of a live child may have important implications for inheritance. This case rates an entire paragraph; thus, she emphasises the importance of women's testimony alone, without men. The second case, that in which a woman's testimony may contravene that of four men, is in a case of fornication (*zinā*); this is when a woman can swear to her own innocence of the crime. The third case, in which women's testimony is not accepted at all, is in crimes requiring retaliation (*qiṣāṣ*), crimes against God (*ḥudūd*), and divorce. And the fourth case, when women's testimony is accepted along with men's, is in monetary matters.[10] Notably, her source for these rulings is a pre-modern jurist of the Akhbārī school; and though she does not go into detail, she reproduces these pre-modern rulings. I believe that her emphasis on the cases in which women's testimony is equal with men's is, however, her own subtle and adroit addition to her summary of these medieval rulings. She shifts the framing away from that presented in medieval texts, while maintaining the substance of the medieval rulings.

In her book, ᶜAlasvand does not clarify why women's testimony does not count equally to men's in all cases. In the interview with me, however, she explained that a woman's physiology is her defining feature. Women's hormonal cycles affect even basic decisions, such as buying shoes or sitting for exams. Thus, women need to look at themselves first as women, and organise their lives around this principle:

Fariba ᶜAlasvand: Being a woman is a reality, and we need to take everything into account from this framework. First it is necessary to see yourself as a woman, and from there take everything else into consideration. For instance the issue of menstruation is very important, and you must plan for it. Now it has been established that for three weeks out of the month, women are under the influence of pre-menstrual tension.

Karen Bauer: Three weeks!

FA: For three weeks you are involved with that and for only one week you are relaxed.

KB: Have you noticed that? I have never noticed that. Maybe for one week.

FA: No, only one week you can be completely relaxed. But three weeks out of every month a woman is involved with this [hormonal shift]. Scientists have counted two thousand signals to indicate this. This affects all of women's issues. You cannot, for instance, buy shoes when you are

> menstruating, because the size of your feet may change. Or you may feel uncomfortable because of having to take a test at the university. So it affects everything that has to do with women, everything in your life. You should consider the reality of the differences between women and men and then make a programme to deal with it. You should not think that women and men are equal and then not take our differences into consideration. We must look into the framework in which men and women differ, and then take these differences into consideration.[11]

For ᶜAlasvand, the physiological differences between the sexes show that equality is a myth; treating men and women the same is unfair to women. Only by being treated as women, with a different set of rules, can women feel truly relaxed and free. By paying attention to their own physiology, women can feel relaxed and free. Ignoring it leads women into a state of being oppressed. As she says, 'it is a mistake for women to say that they wish to have the equal right to testify with men. No. God has in this way disentangled us from a difficult responsibility, by not forcing us to do this.'[12] Her assertion that unequal testimony is an aspect of God's care and protection marks an important shift away from the medieval discourse, in which authors often attributed it to women's deficiencies. And, in another shift from the medieval discourse, hadiths are entirely absent from her discussions of women's testimony in both book and interview. She frames the medieval rulings within an entirely modern scientific discourse.

Indeed, science is at the heart of ᶜAlasvand's argument, which rests on her claims about women's hormonal balance and other measurable physiological signals. The reason that women cannot testify equally with men, she explains, is also established through science: 'we have scientific proof that women pay more attention to details, so they remember less. There is more likelihood that they will forget, because they pay attention only to details.'[13] Thus, as in medieval texts, women's minds are at the root of their inability to assume full weight in testimony. But unlike medieval interpreters, ᶜAlasvand does not say that women's minds are less able than men's minds, or that they are 'deficient'. She concurrently insists on their equal value and their intrinsic differences. In her words: 'This does not mean that one is flawed and the other is flawless; it means that women and men have different functions, and so this is actually perfection for each of them.'[14] For her, the unequal rulings on women's testimony are beneficial for women; the burden is lightened on them.

The emphasis on science is common among modern conservative interpreters. Zibaei Nejad, *Ḥujjat al-Islām wa-l-Muslimīn*,[15] director of the Center where ᶜAlasvand works, quotes the findings of Alan and Barbara

Pease, authors of the book *Why Men Don't Listen and Women Can't Read Maps*,[16] on the differences between men's and women's eyes in order to justify the ruling that women cannot testify to having seen the new moon, which signals the beginning and end of Ramaḍān. In doing so, he uses science to back up a pre-modern legal ruling in the Imāmī school:

> One reason that women cannot testify about the moon is that women's eyes are capable of receiving more visual signals than men's. So women can see in a wider range; and as for men, they have better tunnel vision and can focus on things that are small and far away, particularly in darkness. Therefore, their testimony in seeing the moon is acceptable. Allan and Barbara Pease who have written this book say that women are better drivers during the day, but men are better at night because of these differences in their eyesight. Testimony about seeing the moon is because men have better tunnel vision, whereas women have better peripheral vision.[17]

Allan and Barbara Pease, who are popular psychologists, probably never imagined that their arguments would be used by conservative clerics in Iran to justify women's testimony not being counted equally to men's in court. But for ᶜAlasvand and Zibaei Nejad, their work embodies the central idea of the conservative worldview on gender: men and women, while equal as humans, are essentially different in body and mind.

The work of Pease and Pease has the added appeal that it is written in the West. These authors are from a society where the sexes have equal rights, but they still insist on the intrinsic differences between the sexes. Their books are a part of a global trend in popular science: detailed scientific studies are appropriated to make assertions that often go well beyond the conclusions of their academic authors. The science of sexual differences is a major bestseller in the West, where it is billed as relationship self-help. It is hardly surprising that this literature has been picked up by religious conservatives to justify traditional roles for men and women. While authors of popular science have appropriated neuroscientific findings to make broad and general statements about the sexes that were probably never intended by the scientists who produced the studies, pop science is in turn appropriated in ways equally unintended by its authors, by groups who have an interest in promoting social or legal differences between the sexes. In Iran, works like this lend credence to the conservatives' view that the differences between the sexes in Islamic law reflect innate, unchanging characteristics. Because these characteristics are not bound to particular circumstances, the laws based on them are also timeless, and not subject to change or reinterpretation.

The argument that human nature itself prevents women from giving reliable testimony is one that is inherently challenged by legal systems in which women's testimony is accepted in all instances. When I went to Iran in 2011, I questioned some of the *ᶜulamāᵓ* about whether Muslim women in England could testify on an equal basis with men since the customs and laws in England permit women's testimony. This question was a way of accessing a cleric's openness to the ruling changing according to circumstance. Grand Ayatollah Makarim Shirazi, a highly respected conservative cleric and an author of a work of *tafsīr*, answered that a woman should follow her religious law rather than the secular law of the land. Thus a Muslim woman in Britain may only testify if giving testimony is a necessity and it would cause hardship for her to resist; if she could avoid it, she should follow her religious law and refrain in cases where her testimony was not acceptable religiously.[18]

By giving her testimony alone, according to Makarim Shirazi, a woman might err due to her emotionality; when he was asked for the source of the information that women are more emotional than men, he replied: 'This is apparent. It is an obvious reality and everyone can see its effects in the society.'[19] It is common to appeal to an idea of common sense against testable hypotheses. Zibaei Nejad, for instance, repudiated the notion that women and men have the same IQ:

> You may say that some IQ tests show that women and men have the same memory. My answer is that they do not have the same memory in the specific circumstances in which they are going to testify, because they are emotional and their sentiments may affect their memory.[20]

Western science here stands in for Western equality; for conservatives, it is not tenable because it would mean reinterpreting the medieval core laws. This is precisely why arguments about women's innate nature take precedence; arguments that rely on circumstantial evidence, such as the argument that women have less experience in certain matters, could admit the possibility of change. And though conservatives may admit change in 'non-essential' matters, such as men testifying to the birth of a live child, for a variety of reasons women's testimony is considered to be a part of the unchanging core, rather than the changing periphery.

Reformists: Re-evaluating Tradition

While conservatives seek to preserve pre-modern laws, reformist *ᶜulamāᵓ* are open to rethinking laws entirely. However, they still base their arguments in tradition, which requires them to read familiar texts in a new way, and to extract new rulings from the sources. In Qom, one of the most vocal proponents of the equal rights of men and women to testify in court is Mehdi Mehrizi, *Ḥujjat al-Islām wa-l-Muslimīn* (one rank below Ayatollah). While Fariba ᶜAlasvand had been introduced to me as the foremost authority on women's issues in Qom, Mehdi Mehrizi was introduced to me in the same way – but this introduction came from another prominent reformist. Just as ᶜAlasvand speaks for many conservatives, so too does Mehrizi speak for many reformists on the subject of women's issues.

I met Mehrizi at his office in the Library of Hadith, in Qom. He says that, read correctly, the Qur'an guarantees women equal rights to testify with men. He explains why he cannot rely on received *fiqh*:

> The fundamental problem and the main doubt is connected with the opinion of the jurists, not with the Book or the *sunna*, because what is mentioned by them is some of the general opinions, some of which are specific to one time and particular circumstances … and the proof that the results which the jurists reach on the basis of returning to the Book and the *sunna* are something different from the source of the Book and the *sunna*, is that the jurists present, on some issues, opinions and views that are completely opposed, to the extent that some of them make certain matters obligatory, while others forbid these matters.[21]

Mehrizi observes that the jurists frequently disagree on basic premises in the law. Therefore, he asserts, *fiqh* cannot actually be considered to represent the Qur'an and the Sunna: it is a product of the jurists' own opinions and of their time and place. 'There is no doubt', he says, 'that the social circumstances in which the jurists live affects their thought.'[22] He sees *fiqh* as a living construct that is continually evolving.

The title of his book, *The Woman Question: Studies in Renewal of Religious Thought on Women's Issues* (*Mas'alat al-mar'a: dirāsāt fī tajdīd al-fikr al-dīnī fī qaḍiyyat al-mar'a*), indicates that he believes in renewal and change, rather than finding new justifications for medieval interpretations. But he does not abandon the idea that sacred history, tradition and religious law are binding for believers. His method is to re-examine the sources of law, particularly hadiths that indicate women's place in society. Mehrizi bases his opinion of women's testimony on the content of Q. 2:282, on events in its historical milieu and on a grammatical discussion. Each of these in some way relates to the traditional sources of Qur'an, history and *fiqh*.

In his analysis of the content of the verse, he asserts that the subject of the verse is not women's testimony, per se. It is about the writing down of testimony in order to protect the rights of the parties concerned in a debt.[23] According to him, it is a mistake to use this verse to speak about women's testimony in all arenas.

He uses historical example, as portrayed in Shiᶜi hadiths, in order to argue against strict limitations on women's testimony. It is clear, he says, that women's testimony was accepted among the Shiᶜa in the earliest period, because

Fāṭima, the Prophet's daughter, testified that her father had bequeathed to her the oasis of Fadak, and her word was believed:

> In the *Kitāb al-Kāfī*, there is a hadith regarding the incident of Fadak. This was an incident that occurred in which there was a difference between Fāṭima and Abū Bakr. Fāṭima went to Abū Bakr and claimed that Fadak was hers. She went, not [her husband] ᶜAlī, and said that Fadak is ours, and Abū Bakr judged in favour of Fāṭima. This hadith exists in *al-Kāfī*. If Fāṭima did not believe, and Abū Bakr did not believe that the testimony of a woman was worth half that of a man, then how is it possible that the testimony of women is not counted equally?[24]

Mehrizi argues that because the hadith exists in the well-respected hadith collection *al-Kāfī*, it shows that these early authorities took women's testimony for granted. Although this hadith was not used in prior juridical discussions of women's testimony, he cites it as evidence of historical precedent for his view, and asks how it could it be possible to include the hadith in this collection if women's word were worth less than men's word.

Mehrizi's next type of explanation is grammatical. The grammatical explanation engages both the words of the verse and also ideas in the theory of law. He focuses on the problematic particle spelled *ᵓ-n*, which appears in the phrase of the verse that I have translated 'if (*ᵓ-n*) one of the two women errs, the one shall remind the other'. The majority reading of the particle is '*an*', which means 'that', yet the majority interpretation of the phrase is '*if* one of the two women errs'. (A minority reading is *in*, which is properly translated as 'if').

Mehrizi takes the literal interpretation of the particle ('*that* one of the two errs'), and says that *an* is giving a cause (*ᶜilla*) for the second woman's testimony. Here he refers to legal theory of the ruling and its causes. He asserts that the ruling (*ḥukm*) of two women for one man rests on the literal interpretation of the term 'that' (*an*). Therefore, only in a case *when* (not 'if') a woman will err in her testimony, a second woman can be brought. According to him, this is not inevitable, it is circumstantial: 'if we were to look at a group of Bedouin, we might find a woman who does not enter into financial matters, and we can examine the situation to see if she will make a mistake.'[25] When the cause (the forgetfulness of the particular Bedouin woman) is removed, so is the effect. For him, the verse speaks about the testimony of men and women as equals:

> But if the situation and the time changes, then the cause (*ᶜilla*) changes and the ruling (*ḥukm*) changes. *When one of them errs, the other will remind her*, but when one of them does not err – for instance, today many women work

> in banks, many women are directors of factories, and the woman of this day and age does not differ from the man with regards to financial matters. So the verse makes things easier in this matter.[26]

Mehrizi rests his argument on grammatical analysis, but he also takes into account the changing times and historical circumstances of the verse. His interpretation uses traditional elements and methods in order to grant women and men equal rights to testify in all cases.

History is at the heart of Mehrizi's defence of women's rights. Many of his historical examples are from Shiᶜi sources, and involve ᶜAlī b. Abī Ṭālib. In one such example, he describes a battle between the Persian forces commanded by the daughter of Chosroes (bint Kisrā) and the Islamic forces, commanded by Khalīd b. Kaᵓs. When the Muslim forces captured her, they brought her to ᶜAlī, who offered to marry her to his son Ḥasan. However, she refused, saying that she would not marry anyone but ᶜAlī himself. A relative of hers came to ask for her hand, but ᶜAlī said that she could choose for herself.[27]

For Mehrizi, the main sources of law are the Qurᵓan and Sunna, whereas for the conservatives a core source of today's law is found in the majority opinions of reliable pre-modern sources. But basing his reinterpretation on the Sunna poses some problems: he must deal with uncomfortable hadiths, such as the 'deficiency' hadith mentioned above. He argues that this hadith cannot be used to determine the law on women's testimony. He dismisses this hadith using five main arguments, which I paraphrase here: (1) the version mentioned in the *Nahj al-Balāgha* (a collection of speeches attributed to ᶜAlī b. Abī Ṭālib) was limited to a specific circumstance; (2) the narrations about women's deficient religion and rationality (*nāqiṣ al-ᶜaql wa-l-dīn*) contradict the Qurᵓan 'because the Qurᵓan clarifies that the reason for the lack of equality between men and women in testimony is due to [circumstantial] forgetfulness which women may fall into, not due to a deficiency in their minds';[28] (3) this narration goes against reason (*ᶜaql*); (4) the deficiency in rationality in the narrations does not indicate a substantial difference between men and women, but rather refers to the circumstances and milieu; (5) this narration was propagated by some of the enemies of Fāṭima, the daughter of Muḥammad.[29] Three of these points refer to historical circumstances, while two of them indicate that the use of reason is appropriate in order to critique hadiths.

Just as he relies on traditional sources such as the Qurᵓan and hadith, Mehrizi's methods are well grounded in tradition. In particular, his use of grammatical analysis is a common method in medieval works of Qurᵓanic interpretation (*tafsīr*) and *fiqh*. The use of hadiths to point to historical circumstances is another method common in medieval sources. Yet the results he reaches are astonishingly different from his medieval counterparts, and from modern conservatives, because of his project to use these methods to examine the traditional sources anew.

Neo-traditionalism

Mehdi Mehrizi's view that women and men can testify equally is unusual even among reformist *ᶜulamāᵓ*. Far more common is the neo-traditionalist view: many aspects of testimony can be reconsidered, but some elements of the traditional rulings must be preserved. Like the reformists, neo-traditionalists assume that the Qurᵓan and medieval majority rulings can be reinterpreted; but they still ultimately refer to medieval *fiqh* and use it as their starting point. This is the method of Grand Ayatollah Saanei, for whom the issue of women's testimony is of great importance.[30]

Yusuf Saanei was born into a clerical family in 1937 and had a traditional education. He moved to Qom in 1951 and became a star pupil in the Hawzeh system there. In 1955 he began studying with Ayatollah Khomeini (d. 1989), and continued to study with him until 1963. In the post-revolution government, Ayatollah Saanei became the State Prosecutor-General and was a member of the Council of Guardians and the Supreme Judicial Council.[31] He ended his time in government and returned to the Hawzeh in 1984.

Grand Ayatollah Saanei adheres to the principle of Dynamic *Fiqh* (*fiqh-i pūyā*), which was developed by his teacher, Ayatollah Khomeini. Dynamic *Fiqh* means that, when deriving the laws, one must take into account time (*zamān*) and place (*makān*). There is a difference between this approach and the approach that says that the laws themselves can change; instead of changing the law, in Dynamic *Fiqh* a new ruling is imposed in response to changing circumstances.[32] Many of the reformist clerics whom I interviewed in Iran referred obliquely or directly to the principle of Dynamic *Fiqh*.

Grand Ayatollah Saanei has a commanding presence; yet he has a good sense of humour, which was apparent in our interview. He was also one of the few Grand Ayatollahs to attempt to establish common ground with me, to show that he understood the perspective of sexual equality:

> The problem is this: two women have been put in the place of one man. In the instance when both women and men see and hear something, and men and women both see as well as each other, one man is enough. But if a woman sees and hears the same thing, then two of them are needed in place of one man. Their sight is like one [man]. Their hearing is like one [man]. Their perception is the same. This is a certainty. Their understanding is like that of a man, and so why are two women put in place in one man?

> Why does Islam do this to women, putting two of them in the place of one man? I am restating the problem to show that I understand it well. If one understands the problem, it is much easier to answer it.
>
> According to scientific method, the difference between male and female is not justifiable. And in the place where a man's testimony is enough, a woman's testimony is also enough, without any difference between them. What we can deduce (*al-mustafad*) from the verse is that there is no difference between the testimony of a woman or that of a man. In some issues, it is necessary to have one witness, whether woman or man. In some matters, it is necessary to have two witnesses, women or men. This is my reading and understanding of the verse.[33]

Grand Ayatollah Saanei draws on science, but unlike the conservatives, he refers to science to assert that women's and men's minds are the same. In many ways, his methods are often similar to those of the conservatives, but his results are entirely different.

However, the most common method used by reformists differs from that used by conservatives. While conservatives argue that gendered laws are based on unchanging human nature, reformists historicise its text in order to say that aspects of it are time-bound. According to Grand Ayatollah Saanei, the verse was revealed at a time when women did not study arithmetic and go out of the house regularly. Even recently, he asserts, women were not educated in mathematics: 'I have seen a woman from my neighbourhood, and when her father came with the bill, if the sum came to three hundred thousand, she was not able to add it up. She said, "three hundred tomans!" She did not know three hundred thousand. That time was different from this time.'[34] This justification subtly reinforces the fact that social circumstances in Iran have changed even within his own lifetime. But we did not discuss whether his own personal opinion had changed over time; he simply used this personal anecdote as an example of why circumstances could require new laws. He explained further:

> There is not a change in the text of the Qur'an, but there can be a change in the interpretation of the Qur'an. Our understanding of the Qur'an changes through time. Our derivation of laws changes through time. One example. Women were at the time of the revelation of the verse ignorant of mathematical matters. But nowadays, women know about mathematics. Therefore nowadays the testimony of one woman who is knowledgeable in maths can take the place of two men who know nothing about mathematics. In this case, one woman equals two illiterate men.[35]

Ayatollah Saanei asserts that, although the Qur'an is a constant, new laws need to be derived over time. For him, knowledge about something determines the reliability of a witness. If a witness is not knowledgeable, then they will not remember something, and hence the statement in the verse that 'if one of the two women errs, the other will remind her'. Although grammatically the verse is clearly in the feminine and speaks about women, now it is not limited to women. He proposes a radical solution: the verse refers to knowledgeable people, so one knowledgeable woman's testimony could equal the testimony of two illiterate men.

When I asked him about the hadiths that contradict this view, he rejected them. He asserted that God created men and women equal, so the idea that women could be deficient was absolutely false. But he does not reject all tradition. In order to back up his view, he cites pre-modern jurists who accept women's testimony in some matters. For instance, al-Shaykh al-Mufīd (Abū ᶜAbd Allāh Muḥammad b. Nuᶜmān, d. 1022) said that two women could testify to marriage. According to Ayatollah Saanei, that is because women are knowledgeable about marriage. He uses this ruling to support his view that it is knowledge, rather than gender, that determines the reliability of a witness, and it reinforces his argument that women's minds are equal to men's minds. But for pre-modern jurists, allowing women to testify in certain areas does *not* necessarily indicate that their minds equal men's minds. Instead, women's testimony is allowed in cases of necessity, when no men are present (such as testifying to the birth of a live child). Ayatollah Saanei has a deep awareness of the pre-modern tradition and builds on it. Yet like the conservatives, his justifications for his rulings may differ from the original justifications in the pre-modern works of *fiqh*.

In the interview, I was given a clear and straightforward view of the reasons for women's testimony now being accepted on a par with men's, or in certain circumstances above men's: women and men are equal, and to say otherwise is false. However, in his book, his view of women's testimony was more nuanced. He had mentioned 'exceptions' in passing in the interview. A brief examination of the issue of fornication (*zinā*) shows that sometimes he aligns himself with the near consensus of pre-modern schools, rather than accepting women's word on a par with men's absolutely.[36] In the interview, he used a common-sense, rational, argument in order to justify his position. He said, 'this is not because of any deficiency but because of concealing matters. This is why the testimony of two men is not acceptable, because the goal is to narrow the incidence, and not cover up lewdness (*lā yastur al-faḥshāᵓ*).'[37] He told me that the entire matter was discussed in the book, and he did not dwell on the point.

In the book, his method is to cite several views of the matter, to compare and analyse them. By looking at all of the views on women's testimony, he shows that the supposed pre-modern consensus on these matters was not absolute. He cites certain pre-modern *ᶜulamāʾ* who accepted the testimony of three men and two women, or two men and four women in the case of *zinā*. Like these sources, he accepts women's limited testimony in *zinā*: two men and four women, or three men and two women.

Grand Ayatollah Saanei rejects women's testimony entirely in cases where the incident in question refers to homosexuality. He begins with many hadiths, such as the following: 'On the authority of ᶜAlī, peace be upon him, women's testimony is not permitted in *ḥudūd*, nor in retaliation (*qawad*).'[38] He then explains:

> The law builds on lessening *ḥudūd*, and on not enforcing it in the case of the least doubt, so the Lawmaker does not make the paths of establishing *ḥudūd* easy, especially the *ḥudūd* of honour (*ᶜirḍiyya*) which … shatters the sanctity of the whole society …
>
> With the comparison of the two sides together, we find that the stronger doctrine is non-acceptance of the testimony of women in lesbianism and gayness, and that is due to the sound narratives, with complete chains, that attest to that.[39]

There are two points to make here. The first is that Grand Ayatollah Saanei relies on hadiths that reject women's testimony. Though he rejects some hadiths, he accepts others: in this case, he argues, there is no proof for going against the narratives. His adherence to Dynamic *Fiqh* does not mean a complete abandonment of medieval *fiqh*; on the contrary, it means that in certain cases his views are predicated on the correctness of the medieval sources. For instance, his entire discussion of women's testimony in cases involving homosexual acts presumes that homosexuality is a crime punishable by death. This assessment of his relationship to medieval *fiqh* accords with Mir-Hosseini's assessment of Grand Ayatollah Saanei as a 'neo-traditionalist', rather than a 'modernist'.[40] The second point is that although he frames himself as a reformist, he uses pre-modern principles of law in his explanation: the well-established notion in *fiqh* that testimony must not be accepted in case of doubt. This is the same reason cited by medieval jurists against women's testimony in *ḥudūd*.

While my interview with Grand Ayatollah Saanei included general, common-sense proofs, and downplayed the exceptions, the book was more specific and detailed. That is, in part, because these are distinct genres, with distinct audiences. A verbal interview or sermon will not necessarily include the same level of detail and source citation as a written scholarly text. When I submitted this text to his office, they clarified the reason for these differences: 'it is worth mentioning that we believe an interview is more of a persuasive function rather than a detailed comprehensive reasoning and argument which you can come across reading the book. Thus, should one need to learn about Grand Ayatollah Saanei's views on women's testimony, certainly the book is the recommended source.'[41]

Conclusion

As many scholars have pointed out, conservative interpretations of the Qurᵓan are hardly medieval. Conservatives, like reformists, borrow much from modern terminology and concepts. Though the reformists' historicising method is unique to them, the other methods of interpretation are shared between conservatives and reformists. On the whole, it is not hermeneutics that divide these scholars, but rather their views on specific issues. The views of the adherents to each group fall roughly into patterns, with conservatives broadly adhering to aspects of pre-modern rulings and reformists questioning the conclusions of the pre-modern jurists. However, the views of modern jurists must be seen along a continuum, in which a jurist can exercise his own individuality and choose which aspects of law or tradition to maintain, and how and why.

It is striking that all of these interpreters respond to, and to some extent incorporate, modern notions of egalitarianism in their writings. While equality is an obvious factor in the writings of the reformists discussed above, the conservative ᶜAlasvand clearly states that the idea of equality is a myth. For her, true justice is served not through equality but rather through each sex understanding their nature and role in life. Nevertheless, women's roles do not preclude their activities outside of the house, and in groups of men, particularly with regards to the production and interpretation of religious knowledge. She does not believe in equality; yet her conception of women's roles rests on modern notions of their nature which have been informed by debates on gender equality in both West and East. The language around women and their abilities has shifted in crucial ways, even when the rulings themselves remain relatively stable.

The modern notion of equality is not the only context for the writings of these Iranian *ᶜulamāᵓ*. In the question of hermeneutics, the *ᶜulamāᵓ* profiled here are all responding subtly to currents of Salafi and jihadi ideology that are prominent in today's Middle East. Though the views of the three *ᶜulamāᵓ* profiled here are varied, their hermeneutical responses to the Qurᵓan and history of interpretation show that they all seek to promote a moderate vision of women's roles. The reformists reject the sources of interpretation used by the Salafis: they reject hadiths and, to a greater or lesser degree, they reject past laws. Yet conservatives like ᶜAlasvand may also reject hadiths on the basis that they do not make sense. And ᶜAlasvand asserted that she would, for instance, teach men if the necessity arose. This pits her against the more radical tendencies of interpreters who believe that women should not participate in such sessions, or that women's voices should not be heard by non-related men. In short, it is not only reformists who argue against more radical Salafi and jihadi elements that have emerged as a force in recent times, but it is also conservatives who seek to promote a moderate conservatism. These wider trends form the backdrop for the more local politics in Qom, which may also be expressed through the interpretation of the Qur'an.

Notes

1. This article has been adapted, in part, from my book *Gender Hierarchy in the Qur'an: Medieval Interpretations, Modern Responses* (Cambridge: Cambridge University Press, 2015), and is used with permission from the publisher.
2. Ziba Mir-Hosseini, *Islam and Gender: The Religious Debate in Contemporary Iran* (Princeton: Princeton University Press, 1999).
3. Karen Bauer, 'Debates on Women's Status as Judges and Witnesses in Post-Formative Islamic Law', *Journal of the American Oriental Society* 130:1 (2010), 1–21.
4. Ibid. 15–17.
5. For more on these hadiths, see Bauer, *Gender Hierarchy in the Qur'an*, ch. 1.
6. Following Mir-Hosseini.
7. For instance, most prominently, by Muhammad Qasim Zaman, *The Ulama in Contemporary Islam: Custodians of Change* (Princeton: Princeton University Press, 2007).
8. Fariba ʿAlasvand, *Naqd konvansiyūn rafʿ kuliyya-i ashkāl tabaʿyiḍ ʿalayhi zanān* (Qom: Markaz-i Mudīrīyat Ḥawzah-yiʿIlmīya, 1382/2004).
9. ʿAlasvand, *Naqd*, 84–5.
10. Ibid. *Naqd*, 85.
11. Fariba ʿAlasvand, Personal Interview, Qom, Iran, 8 June 2011.
12. Ibid.
13. Ibid.
14. Ibid.
15. This is a ranking in the hierarchy that is just below Ayatollah.
16. Allan and Barbara Pease, *Why Men Don't Listen & Women Can't Read Maps* (London: Orion, 1999).
17. Mohammed Reza Zibaei Nejad, Personal Interview, Qom, Iran, 28 May 2011.
18. Makarim Shirazi, Personal Interview, Qom, Iran, 25 June 2011.
19. Ibid. 2011.
20. Zibaei Nejad, Personal Interview, 2011.
21. Mehdi Mehrizi, *Masʾalat al-marʾa: dirāsāt fī tajdīd al-fikr al-dīnī fī qaḍiyyat al-marʾa*, trans. (into Arabic from Persian) ʿAlī Mūsawī (Beirut: Markaz al-Ḥaḍāra li-Tanmiyat al-Fikr al-Islāmī, 2008), 265–6.
22. Ibid. *Masʾalat al-marʾa*, 267.
23. Mehdi Mehrizi, Personal Interview, Qom, Iran, 9 June 2011.

24. Ibid.
25. Ibid.
26. Ibid.
27. Mehrizi, *Masʾalat al-Marʾa*, 234.
28. Ibid. 240.
29. These points are paraphrased from Mehrizi, *Masʾalat al-Marʾa*, 240.
30. His son Fakhr al-Din Saanei has written a book about his views, *The Testimony of Women in Islam: a Legal Reading, an Exposition of the Theory of the Great Marjaʿ, Grand Ayatollah Yusuf al-Saanei*: Fakhr al-Din Saanei, *Shahādat al-marʾa fī al-Islām qirāʾa fiqhiyya, ʿarḍ li-naẓariyyāt al-marjaʿ al-kabīr samāḥat Āyat Allāh al-ʿUẓmā al-Shaykh Yūsuf al-Ṣāniʿī* (Qom: Manshūrāt Fiqh al-Thaqlayn, 2007).
31. Mir-Hosseini, *Islam and Gender*, 144.
32. Ibid. 113.
33. Yusuf Saanei, Personal Interview, Qom, Iran, 13 June 2011.
34. Ibid.
35. Ibid.
36. There are also exceptions for more normal cases. The normal cases are summarised thus: 'With the elimination of personal affairs and the re-examination of the instances, the testimony of one woman, in these three instances, is like the testimony of one man; except if, in the instance, a proof is presented contrary to that, in which case the testimony of two women is equal to that of one man' (Saanei, *Shahādat al-marʾa fī al-Islām*, 202).
37. Saanei, Personal Interview, 2011.
38. Saanei, *Shahādat al-marʾa*, 220.
39. Ibid. 220–1.
40. Ziba Mir-Hosseini defined Ayatollah Saanei as a Neo-Traditionalist: in other words, a cleric who uses tradition but is open to reinterpretation. For Mir-Hosseini, this group is differentiated from the Modernists, who represent a 'theoretical break from conventional wisdoms of Islamic feqh': Mir-Hosseini, *Islam and Gender*, 19.
41. Personal email communication from the office of Grand Ayatollah Saanei, 1 July 2014.

7

Ibn Taymiyya between Moderation and Radicalism[1]

Jon Hoover

Ibn Taymiyya (d. 1328) was one of the most incisive and controversial religious scholars in the middle period of the Islamic tradition, and his writings have been read and marshalled to diverse ends in the modern era.[2] The Tunisian thinker Abū Yaᶜrub al-Marzūqī (b. 1947) sees Ibn Taymiyya as a great philosopher heralding a modern philosophical nominalism,[3] and the Pakistani intellectual and University of Chicago professor Fazlur Rahman (d. 1988) took Ibn Taymiyya as a model for his reformist modernism.[4] The centrism (*wasaṭiyya*) of Qatarī-based scholar Yūsuf al-Qaraḍāwī (b. 1926) harks back to Ibn Taymiyya's advocacy of the golden mean (*wasaṭ*) in matters of doctrine,[5] and al-Qaraḍāwī invokes Ibn Taymiyya in support of positive political engagement in a plural society,[6] a pragmatic jurisprudence of balancing benefits and harms,[7] and a strictly defensive approach to jihad against unbelievers.[8] Moreover, Saudi Arabian Wahhābism;[9] religious reform movements in nineteenth- and early twentieth-century Iraq,[10] Syria,[11] Yemen,[12] India[13] and Egypt;[14] and the contemporary global Salafi phenomenon that originated in Saudi Arabia in the 1960s[15] have all looked to Ibn Taymiyya for inspiration and appealed to his authority for legitimacy. Beyond this, Ibn Taymiyya is the main medieval Muslim authority cited by contemporary Muslim extremists, and the most forceful use of his writings for radical purposes is found in *al-Farīḍa al-ghāʾiba* (*The Neglected Duty*) by the electrician ᶜAbd al-Salām Faraj (d. 1982). This treatise served to justify Islamic Jihad's assassination of Egyptian President Anwar Sadat in 1981. Faraj quotes Ibn Taymiyya's fatwas against the Mongols and his fatwa on the legal status of Mardin, a city today in southern Turkey, in the course of arguing that rulers who fail to uphold Islamic law are apostates and must be fought.[16]

Faraj's interpretation of Ibn Taymiyya's fatwas has not gone uncontested, both in Egypt and beyond, and one particularly sophisticated counter-interpretation is found in the writings of Yahya Michot (b. 1952), currently a professor at Hartford Seminary in the USA. Michot argues vigorously that Faraj and his ilk are unfaithful to Ibn Taymiyya's intention, and, similar to al-Qaraḍāwī, he understands Ibn Taymiyya instead to be a moderate and pragmatic scholar who offers vision for Muslims seeking to live constructive and engaged lives in society, even in minority situations. The title of Michot's 2012 book *Against Extremisms* well captures his understanding of Ibn Taymiyya. On Michot's reading, the fourteenth-century jurist sought to avoid extremes in personal piety and behaviour and encouraged prudence and good will in interaction with others; he cannot be used to justify today's Islamist extremism.[17]

Michot rejects three claims that he finds commonly asserted, whether in the thought of Islamist radicals or in scholarly analysis: (1) that Ibn Taymiyya provides justification for declaring rulers apostate and fighting them; (2) that he holds a dualistic black and white view of the world divided into a domain of peace and a domain of war; and (3) that he readily declares Muslims who do not agree with him unbelievers and apostates.[18] This study examines how Michot overcomes the first two claims as they relate most directly to violent jihadism. As for the third, it will suffice to say here that Michot, following his usual custom, translates a number of Ibn Taymiyya's texts to show that he was normally reticent to call fellow Muslims unbelievers and apostates, especially if there were extenuating circumstances.[19]

Before discussing Michot's responses to the first two questions, I will situate Ibn Taymiyya's anti-Mongol fatwas in historical context and sketch a spectrum of their modern interpretations. In the latter part of the study, I look at how Michot deploys his Taymiyyan political theology in response to the Arab Spring of 2011 and then reflect on the key theme of utilitarianism that emerges from the preceding investigation. What will become apparent is that Ibn Taymiyya's utilitarianism lends itself to diverse uses, with both jihadists and Michot equally engaged in a creative process of appropriating Taymiyyan texts to their respective visions of Muslim life in the world today.

Ibn Taymiyya's Anti-Mongol Fatwas

The historical context of Ibn Taymiyya's anti-Mongol fatwas is the Mongol menace to the Mamlūk sultanate of Syria and Egypt. The Mongol invaders from Central Asia struck deep into the traditional Muslim heartlands and conquered Baghdad in 1258, but in 1260 the Mamlūks thwarted their further advance westward into Syria. Nonetheless, the Mongols continued to threaten Syria periodically into the early 1300s. The winter of 1299–1300 saw the most successful campaign. The Īlkhānid Mongol ruler Ghāzān (r. 1295–1304), a convert to Sunni Islam, defeated a Mamlūk army and occupied Damascus for three months. The Mongols then abandoned the city upon hearing rumours that a new Mamlūk army was approaching from Egypt. Ibn Taymiyya did not resist the Mongol occupation but instead engaged the Mongols in diplomacy to free prisoners and avert further bloodshed. Ghāzān embarked on another invasion of Syria the following winter. Ibn Taymiyya preached jihad to rally the Mamlūks and called on the people of Damascus to resist. However, Ghāzān, for unknown reasons, aborted his mission before reaching the city. Two years later, in the spring of 1303, Ghāzān attempted a third invasion of Syria but was defeated by a Mamlūk army before he could threaten Damascus. Later on in 1312, Ghāzān's successor Uljaytū (d. 1317), a convert to Shiᶜism, tried to invade Syria again, but to no avail.[20]

The fact that the Mongols confessed to being Muslims sowed doubts in Syrian minds about the legitimacy of fighting them since, according to traditional Islamic law, Muslims should not fight Muslims. This is the primary problem that Ibn Taymiyya addresses in three anti-Mongol fatwas printed in succession in volume 28 of the large collection of his writings *Majmūᶜ fatāwā*.[21] The third fatwa may be the first chronologically and perhaps dates to the first Mongol invasion in 1299–1300.[22] The first fatwa probably dates a little later to the second and third Mongol invasions of 1300–1 and 1303.[23] These two fatwas argue that the Mongols (*al-Tatār*) must be fought even though they pronounce the Muslim confession of faith. The Mongols were not just Muslim rebels (*ahl al-baghy*) rising up against a particular Muslim leader as when Muᶜāwiya fought against the fourth caliph ᶜAlī at the battle of Ṣiffīn in 657. Rather, they had abandoned some of the laws of Islam after the fashion of the Khārijīs and those who forbade paying *zakāt* in the days of the first caliph Abū Bakr (d. 634). The Mongols, explains Ibn Taymiyya, failed to uphold the Shariᶜa in full and forbid pagan worship; they colluded with unbelievers such as Christians and idolaters; and they did not fight on behalf of Islam but only to gain hegemony. Thus, it was obligatory to wage jihad against them.

Muslim jurists had traditionally grouped the Kharījīs and those who withheld *zakāt* from Abū Bakr together with Muᶜāwiya who fought ᶜAlī at the Battle of Ṣiffīn into the one category of Muslim rebels (*bughāt*). The opposing combatants simply held different interpretations (*taʾwīl*) of the political circumstances due to differences in independent legal reasoning (*ijtihād*), and these differences did not endanger their status as Muslims. Ibn Taymiyya, however, divided combatants into those who adhered to the laws of Islam (*sharāʾiᶜ al-Islām*), such as ᶜAlī and Muᶜāwiya, and those who did not, such as the Khārijīs and those who withheld *zakāt* from Abū Bakr. Whereas Muᶜāwiya was merely a political rebel, the Khawārij and those who withheld *zakāt* were religious heretics. So far as it was practically possible, the latter had to be fought until they followed the established laws of religion in full.[24]

Ibn Taymiyya's second and longest anti-Mongol fatwa repeats the argument of the first and third fatwas that the Mongols had to be fought because they resembled the Khārijīs.[25] However, Ibn Taymiyya also now details what he believes to be the Mongols' corrupt vision of Islam, and he censures them for converting to Shiᶜism.[26] This, along with various historical allusions, dates the second fatwa to after the conversion of the Mongol Īlkhānid ruler Uljaytu to Twelver Shiᶜism in 1309 and most likely to Uljaytu's attempt to invade Syria in 1312.[27]

Despite the Mongols' confession of Islam, Ibn Taymiyya complains in the second fatwa about Mongol legal syncretism, religious laxity, and theological pluralism. Few among the Mongols fasted and practised the Muslim prayer while many among them were religious innovators such as Shiᶜis and monistic Sufis. Additionally, the Mongols applied laws from the *yāsa*,[28] the pagan legal system of Genghis Khan, and they raised Genghis Khan to the same level as the Prophet Muḥammad, even confessing him to be the Son of God after the fashion of Christian belief about Christ. Moreover, Ibn Taymiyya alleges, some Mongols regarded Islam, Judaism and Christianity to be equally valid paths to God much as Sunni Muslims recognised the equal legitimacy of their four law schools. The Mongol conversion to Shiᶜism was particularly scandalous to Ibn Taymiyya because Shiᶜis had aligned with Christians to facilitate the Mongol conquests of central Muslims lands. Ibn Taymiyya combines the Mongols' affiliation with the treacherous Shiᶜis together with their use of Genghis Khan's legal system, the *yāsa*, to conclude that they are apostates (*murtaddūn*) even worse than those who withheld *zakāt* from Abū Bakr.[29]

Modern Interpretations of Ibn Taymiyya's Anti-Mongol Fatwas

ᶜAbd al-Salām Faraj's *Farīḍa*, which provided the rationale for assassinating Egyptian President Anwar Sadat in 1981, quotes extensively from Ibn Taymiyya's second and third anti-Mongol fatwas, along with some commentary from Ibn Taymiyya's student Ibn Kathīr (d. 1373) on Q. 5:50, to make the case that contemporary Muslim rulers are apostates and must be fought and replaced in order to establish an Islamic state.[30] The *Farīḍa* assimilates modern Muslim rulers to the Mongols just as Ibn Taymiyya assimilates the Mongols to the Khārijīs and those who withheld *zakāt* from Abū Bakr. Both modern Muslim rulers and the Mongols confess Islam, but they are nonetheless both apostates because they rule according to non-Islamic laws. Modern Muslim rulers who follow codes of law imported from imperialist unbelievers are in fact worse than the Mongols who ruled according to their *yāsa*, and the

Mongols were worse than the Khārijīs and those who withheld *zakāt* from Abū Bakr. Thus, the *Farīḍa* reasons, it is obligatory to fight modern Muslim rulers just as it was obligatory to fight the Khārijīs and the Mongols.[31] This justification for Islamic revolution, taken on its own, is powerful and coherent, and it continues to inform contemporary jihadist thinking.[32]

Following Sadat's assassination, the Egyptian religious establishment quickly moved to situate Ibn Taymiyya's fatwas in historical context in order to show that the *Farīḍa* incorrectly assimilated modern rulers to the Mongols of Ibn Taymiyya's day. In a 1982 fatwa, the Egyptian Mufti Jād al-Ḥaqq ᶜAlī Jād al-Ḥaqq (d. 1996) argues that unbelief had not pervaded Egypt and that reasonably pious modern Muslim rulers were not comparable to the savage and irreligious Mongols that Ibn Taymiyya had observed. Jād al-Ḥaqq also prohibits calling Muslim rulers apostates, refutes the various Qurᵓanic and legal arguments made in the *Farīḍa* concerning jihad, and invokes his authority as a religious scholar against the uneducated Faraj.[33]

This sharp response to Faraj appears to have induced some jihadists to skirt the *Farīḍa* by widening their base of classical and medieval authorities beyond Ibn Taymiyya.[34] In 1988 the Egyptian ᶜAbd al-Qādir b. ᶜAbd al-ᶜAzīz, also known as Dr Faḍl (b. 1950), published *al-ᶜUmda*, a jihad manual widely used by al-Qāᵓida.[35] While Ibn Taymiyya is the most frequently cited medieval source in the book, many other prominent and respected authorities such as al-Māwardī (d. 1058), al-Nawawī (d. 1277) and Ibn Ḥajar al-ᶜAsqalānī (d. 1449) are also used. Dr Faḍl allows that contemporary Muslim rulers may be assimilated to the Mongols in order to be declared apostates. However, he explains that this point may be made without reference to Ibn Taymiyya, and he does not rely on the anti-Mongol fatwas in the fashion of Faraj to build his overall case. Dr Faḍl does quote the first anti-Mongol fatwa, which was not used by Faraj, where Ibn Taymiyya discusses weighing up the pros and cons of fighting. Even if the intentions of the fighters are impure, it is obligatory to fight to protect religion if the danger to religion from not fighting is greater than that from fighting.[36] Osama bin Laden (d. 2011), former leader of al-Qāᵓida, invokes Ibn Taymiyya and his utilitarian rationale to the same ends in his 1996 Declaration of War against the USA and its allies. According to Bin Laden, it is an Islamic principle to repel the greater of two dangers at the expense of the lesser, and it is better for the unrighteous to fight alongside the righteous against the enemies of religion than to forgo fighting altogether.[37]

Utilitarian reasoning of this kind can also run in the opposite direction. Yūsuf al-Qaraḍāwī, in his large 2009 book *Fiqh al-jihād*, briefly mentions Ibn Taymiyya's anti-Mongol writing and the book *al-Farīḍa al-ghāᵓiba* in the midst of a lengthy juristic treatment on rising up against ruling regimes.

Against the extremists, al-Qaraḍāwī notes that fighting those who violate religion is the prerogative of the ruler himself, not the populace, and this is to avert anarchy.[38] More broadly, al-Qaraḍāwī invokes the traditional juristic bias toward social and political stability.[39] He asserts that it is impermissible to remove a wrong or harm by force when that would lead to even greater wrong or harm, and he sets out four conditions that must be met before forcefully confronting wrong (*munkar*): Muslim scholars must have come to a consensus that the alleged wrong is in fact a wrong; the wrong must be manifest and open, not hidden; one must possess sufficient strength to correct the wrong; and correcting the wrong by force must not entail a greater wrong such as anarchy. Implied throughout is that the jihadist agenda fails to meet these conditions.[40] According to al-Qaraḍāwī, patience is commended in the face of oppressive rulers since history shows that armed rebellions never succeed but lead only to bloodshed and chaos.[41] Al-Qaraḍāwī limits the means of change to democracy and other peaceful approaches.[42] Yahya Michot's response to jihadist use of Ibn Taymiyya's anti-Mongol fatwas is more philological, historical and theological, and less juristic than al-Qaraḍāwī's, but the vision of prudence and pragmatism is much the same. It is to Michot that we now turn.

Michot on Ibn Taymiyya's Anti-Mongol Fatwas

Yahya Michot spent his early career through 1997 at the Catholic University of Louvain where he established his reputation as a leading authority on Ibn Sīnā. He was then based at the University of Oxford, Faculty of Theology and the Oxford Centre for Islamic Studies for ten years before taking up his present professorship at Hartford Seminary in the USA in 2008. Michot's earlier scholarship is in his native French, and he continues to write in that language, although by now a substantial portion of his work appears in English or English translation. Michot started translating and commenting on Ibn Taymiyya in 1990, and he has continued strong ever since, establishing himself as the closest reader of Ibn Taymiyya in Western academia. Michot brings a high degree of philological skill and historical learning to his scholarship. A substantial number of his publications are philological and historical in the first instance and do not bear a normative religious stamp. The rest of his work is equally well informed by philological and historical rigour but adds as well the explicitly moral and theological voice of a Muslim religious scholar. Much of this latter body of scholarship consists of translated Taymiyyan texts with full scholarly apparatuses accompanied by historical, linguistic, moral and theological commentary, usually in the footnotes and introductory sections. The core of Michot's strategy for interpreting Ibn Taymiyya is translating and contextualising selected texts in ways that highlight the tolerant and pragmatic aspects of his ethics and spirituality. In addition to more than twenty five books and academic articles on Ibn Taymiyya, Michot has published three series of short selections from Ibn Taymiyya's writings in French translation.[43] Sixteen of these texts and two of Michot's smaller translation volumes are rendered into English in his 2012 book *Against Extremisms*.[44]

The challenge posed by Ibn Taymiyya's anti-Mongol activism and its appropriation by the likes of ᶜAbd al-Salām Faraj appears to have been at the forefront of Michot's mind in 1990 when he initiated the first of his three translation series. In the opening paragraph of the first instalment of 'Textes spirituels' published in the Parisian magazine *Le Musulman*, Michot writes:

> The oeuvre of Ibn Taymiyya (661/1263 – 728/1328) is in some ways a victim of his gigantism and his militancy. Outside academic works, the readings that it has been given too often suffer from ignorance of the essential texts or degenerate into ideological reductions. Preserving a rare relevance in a time where Islam is confronted with a neo-*jāhiliyya* having perhaps more severe consequences, over the long term, than the Mongol tidal wave against which the great Ḥanbalī scholar fought, this oeuvre however should deserve a better fate. Not being able to undertake at this stage a systematic presentation of the spirituality that animates it, we propose instead to translate into French some particularly rich pages for *Le Musulman* to be able to nourish still the faith and reflection of today's believers.[45]

In Michot's assessment contemporary Muslims face the threat of a 'neo-*jāhiliyya*' – presumably the bane of extremism – worse than that of the Mongol hordes invading Syria, and Ibn Taymiyya, rather than being the source of today's problems, is in fact part of the solution. Thus, Michot seeks to nurture a reflective and sophisticated faith among francophone Muslims by translating Ibn Taymiyya's texts into French. Michot does not here specify the core content of Ibn Taymiyya's spirituality, but in the course of his translation work in 'Textes spirituels' and beyond, it becomes clear that it consists in sincere obedience, moderation and prudent pragmatism in following the way of the Prophet.

For the most part, the sixteen instalments of 'Textes spirituels' published between 1990 and 1998 examine basics of Ibn Taymiyya's vision of God's moral economy with humankind, including correct worship of God, rightly ordered love for God, and the relation between revelation and reason. However, Michot breaks with these themes in contributions XI–XIII published in 1994 and 1995 to examine Ibn Taymiyya's anti-Mongol activism. As far as I am aware, this is the first time that Michot took up the question of Ibn Taymiyya's anti-Mongol fatwas directly. The immediate backdrop is the violent conflict in Algeria that erupted after the military cancelled parliamentary elections in January 1992 to preclude a victory by the Islamist Islamic Salvation Front (FIS).[46] Michot has this in view as he translates 'particularly "hot"' portions of Ibn Taymiyya's second anti-Mongol fatwa, provides it with extensive annotation, and discusses its historical and contemporary significance in an introduction. He also translates a passage quoting Ibn Taymiyya from the Algerian Islamist Ali Belhadj, FIS second in command.[47]

Michot's introduction to these three instalments of 'Textes spirituels' briefly outlines the Mongol invasions of Syria in the early 1300s and seeks to limit the significance of Ibn Taymiyya's anti-Mongol activism to his own historical context of the Mamlūk sultanate by casting him as a mere propagandist. Just as Mongol propagandists attributed Mongol military successes to the will of God, Ibn Taymiyya was himself a propagandist for the Mamlūks, and his opposition to the Mongols was driven as much by pro-Mamlūk patriotism and Arab anti-Turkish and anti-Persian sentiment as by the Mongols' defective Islam. Michot adds that the course of events vindicated the Mongol apologists because the Mongols eventually converted to Sunni Islam after flirting with Shiᶜism, and their conquests contributed to deeper penetration of Islam into Central Asia and the Indian subcontinent.

Michot then asks his Muslim readers how they should respond to all of this. Michot notes that ᶜAbd al-Salām Faraj's *Farīḍa* cited the Taymiyyan texts translated in this instalment of 'Textes spirituels' to justify jihad against Egyptian President Anwar Sadat. Likewise, Michot explains, Ali Belhadj used these texts in 1992 to call for armed insurrection against the Algerian government. Michot continues that both Faraj and Belhadj 'Mongolize' the governments of their own countries. That is, they turn Ibn Taymiyya's call to resist a foreign invader into a call to overthrow their own governments. Michot observes further that the Taymiyyan texts in question have been subject to completely opposing interpretations. On the one hand, for the radicals, 'the Mongols today are no longer outside the Muslim city; they are in its very heart', and Ibn Taymiyya's fatwas justify fighting them. But on the other hand, for the Muslim religious establishment, the Taymiyyan texts provide no religious or historical foundation for such opposition whatsoever. Michot himself does not take a stand for one side or the other, indicating that he wishes to avert misunderstanding and leave open the possibility of bringing other considerations to bear on the matter. At this point, Michot refers his readers to the earlier translation articles in the 'Textes spirituels' series, works that deal with Ibn Taymiyya's views on worship and love of God. Presumably, Michot wishes to signal to his readers that the interpretations of both the radicals and the religious establishment are incomplete in their understanding of Ibn Taymiyya and lack sufficient spiritual depth.[48]

Apart from indicating that Ibn Taymiyya's opposition to the Mongols was not prudent in light of the good that they ultimately achieved for Islam, Michot's questioning of contemporary Mongolisers in instalments XI–XIII of 'Textes spirituels' is not particularly robust. This changes in Michot's 2004 book in French on the Mardin fatwa, which was translated into English and published in 2006 as *Muslims under non-Muslim Rule*.[49] Michot now argues clearly that 'to use the writings of Ibn Taymiyya to "Mongolize" the governments of certain present-day Muslim countries is indeed to betray his thought'.[50] This is because Ibn Taymiyya adopted a religiously-based quietist stance toward his own Mamlūk rulers. Michot explains that Ibn Taymiyya never called for armed insurrection against the Mamlūks. Instead, he enjoined patience in the face of oppression, and he commanded obedience to rulers wherever possible.

To clarify this position, Michot quotes three fundamentals that Ibn Taymiyya outlines on allegiance to the ruling authorities: 'to obey within obedience to God, even if the one giving the order is unjust; to abstain from disputing the authority of those who dispose it; to take up the cause of the Truth without fear of any creature'.[51] Taking up 'the cause of the Truth without fear of any creature' provides Ibn Taymiyya room for his stubborn adherence to his own religious convictions, some of which famously landed him in Mamlūk prisons.[52] For Michot, Ibn Taymiyya's 'critical obedience' and 'non-violent quietism' are rooted either in strict adherence to the way of the Prophet or in a pragmatic morality that always favours the lesser evil – insurrection being a cause of greater evil than good – or most likely in both.[53] In Michot's eyes, this quietism grounded in religious conviction precludes any analogical transfer of Ibn Taymiyya's rulings on the Mongols, an external enemy, to one's own government.[54] Later in *Muslims under non-Muslim Rule*, Michot drives home his disagreement with both modern radicals and Western scholars of Islam who follow them in imagining Ibn Taymiyya to legitimise Mongolising Muslim rulers. Moreover, Michot wonders whether Western scholars nefariously adhere to this reading of Ibn Taymiyya in order to confirm that Islam is incompatible with modern and Western values.[55]

The question of 'Mongolizing' Islam is fundamentally about Ibn Taymiyya's doctrine of *jus ad bellum*, that is, what justifies war and armed rebellion. ᶜAbd al-Salām Faraj and jihadists who follow his lead justify rebellion against their own rulers by assimilating them to the Mongols whom Ibn Taymiyya deemed apostates for failing to uphold Islamic law. Michot rejects the Mongolising reading out of hand as unfaithful to Ibn Taymiyya's intention because his anti-Mongol fatwas were nothing more than Mamlūk war propaganda against a foreign invader and his political theology precluded insurrection against his own ruler.

Michot on the Mardin Fatwa

We turn now to the second issue that Michot confronts: what makes for a domain of peace and a domain of war in Ibn Taymiyya's vision of the world? This is the issue at the core of Michot's 2006 book *Muslims under non-Muslim Rule*, and here Michot argues that modern Islamists are unfaithful to Ibn Taymiyya in attributing to him a political vision of Islam concerned with the apparatus of the modern state and the imposition of Islamic law therein. Rather, Michot argues, Ibn Taymiyya is most concerned with the religious and ethical integrity of Muslims as individual persons.

Michot's book is a study in the interpretation and contemporary use of Ibn Taymiyya's short Mardin fatwa. The date of the fatwa is not known, but the city of Mardin, today in southern Turkey, was under Mongol Īlkhān rule. Ibn Taymiyya's fatwa addresses the legal status of the city and its Muslim inhabitants: was Mardin a domain of war, and did Muslims have an obligation to emigrate from it to the lands of Islam? Ibn Taymiyya responds that emigration (*hijra*) is not obligatory if Muslims can still practise their religion and that Mardin is neither a domain of war (*dār al-ḥarb*) nor a domain of peace (*dār al-silm*); rather its status is a composite (*murakkab*) of the two. Ibn Taymiyya further defines a domain of war as a place 'whose inhabitants are unbelievers' and a domain of peace as a domain 'in which the institutions (*aḥkām*) of Islam are implemented because its army (*jund*) is [composed] of Muslims'.[56]

As Michot explains in *Muslims under non-Muslim Rule*, ᶜAbd al-Salām Faraj and other modern militant Islamists such as the Palestinian jihadist ᶜAbd Allāh ᶜAzzām (d. 1989) equate the Mardin fatwa's 'institutions (*aḥkām*) of Islam' found in Ibn Taymiyya's 'domain of peace' with Islamic government and the legislation and institutions of the modern state. On this reading, a 'domain of peace' is a place where Islamic law, understood as a legal system enforced by the state, is applied. Conversely, a 'domain of war' is a place where a legal system informed by unbelief is in force even though, for Faraj at least, it is occupied by a majority of Muslims. This interpretation allows Faraj to consider the Egypt of his time a domain of war. As Michot correctly points out, Faraj misunderstands Ibn Taymiyya to say that Mardin is a domain of war despite being inhabited by Muslims. For Ibn Taymiyya, a domain of war is in fact defined by the absence of Muslims.[57]

Michot rejects the Islamist reading of Ibn Taymiyya's Mardin fatwa as 'politicizing', but, before coming to that critique, he sets the foundation for an alternative interpretation. Following what he calls an 'intertextual' method, he first seeks to enrich the interpretation of the Mardin fatwa by translating three additional Taymiyyan texts dealing with emigration (*hijra*).

Here Michot finds that true emigration is most fundamentally about fleeing from sin, not just leaving a place. Moreover, Ibn Taymiyya speaks of two kinds of emigration: one fleeing from sin and bad company, and the other shunning evil-doers in order to inflict a penalty on them. In both cases, Michot explains, Ibn Taymiyya counsels a prudent pragmatism in emigration. Emigration should be undertaken only if the good in it outweighs the harm. One should not, for example, turn away from sinners to punish them with a severity that leads to greater harm than the sins that they commit. Similarly, fleeing from sinners to avoid their evil runs the risk of abandoning the good that one might gain from them. This is exemplified in one of the texts that Michot translates. Ibn Taymiyya explains that the famous hadith scholar Aḥmad b. Ḥanbal (d. 855) did not completely shun his theological opponents the Qadarīs because there was no one strong enough to fight them. Moreover, fighting them would have cut him off from the knowledge that they transmitted through hadith reports.[58]

Michot draws three conclusions from Ibn Taymiyya's texts on emigration. First, Ibn Taymiyya provides no set answers for Muslims living in Western countries today who wonder whether they should emigrate to places more supportive of their Muslim identities. Rather, individual Muslims must weigh up the advantages and disadvantages of their own circumstances. Second, Ibn Taymiyya's approach to emigration is ethical, not political; there is no mention of Islamic government. Third, Michot calls Ibn Taymiyya 'a theologian of moderation' for his 'profound utilitarianism' in moral and religious matters and his avoidance of excessive risk and intolerance.[59]

With this moderate, personalist and utilitarian doctrine of emigration in view, Michot moves on in *Muslims under non-Muslim Rule* to what Ibn Taymiyya means in the Mardin fatwa by the terms 'domain of peace' and 'domain of war'. For Ibn Taymiyya, Michot explains, the status of a place depends on the quality of the people residing in it. It is the presence of unbelievers that defines a domain of war, and it is the presence of Muslims freely practising their faith that defines a domain of peace. Michot emphasises that this approach to the domains of war and peace is 'both personalist and religious, or ethical', but not 'political in the narrow sense'.[60] Mardin was then, for Ibn Taymiyya, a 'composite' domain, inhabited as it was by both unbelievers and Muslims, and the Muslims could stay if they were able to practise their religion unimpeded. As noted above, Michot takes it to be a matter of personal and individual assessment as to whether a particular 'composite' domain provides sufficient freedom for religious practice.

We turn now to the Islamist understanding of Ibn Taymiyya's domain of peace, which poses the primary challenge for Michot's interpretation. For ᶜAbd al-Salām Faraj and like-minded Islamists, Ibn Taymiyya's mention of 'the institutions (*aḥkām*) of Islam' refers to Islamic government and a state legal system. The status of a place depends on the character of the laws that the territorial state enforces, not on the ethical and religious condition of its residents. Michot strongly resists this 'politicizing' of Ibn Taymiyya. Again using his intertextual method, he ascertains that by 'institutions of Islam', Ibn Taymiyya intends not Islamic governance but personal matters pertaining to marriage, inheritance, burial, security and protection of property, matters that are up to individual Muslims to implement. A domain where Muslims have the ability to practise these 'institutions' is not a domain of war even if ruled by non-Muslims. Ibn Taymiyya's primary concern is the well-being and flourishing of Muslim people, not Muslim territorial dominance and the territorial imposition of Islamic law.[61] Michot concludes, 'The thinking of Ibn Taymiyya is of an essentially juridical-religious nature, and personalist. To that is added a concern that is in truth far less political than it is security-oriented, even humanitarian.'[62]

Ibn Taymiyya's definition of a 'domain of peace' poses one further difficulty for Michot's personalist interpretation. A 'domain of peace' is not only where the 'institutions of Islam are implemented' but also where this is so 'because its army is composed of Muslims'. The added condition of a Muslim army could be construed as political, but Michot thinks not. On Michot's reading, Ibn Taymiyya's foregrounding of the military pushes out civil authorities, as well as politics and the state in the modern senses of the words. His definition of a domain of peace simply reflects the realities of his experience in the Mamlūk sultanate. If it were to legitimise anything modern, Michot suggests, it would be contemporary (pre-Arab Spring) military regimes in the Middle East, not the Islamic state envisioned by Islamists.[63]

At the very end of the Mardin fatwa, Ibn Taymiyya specifies what it means for Mardin to be a composite between a domain of peace 'in which the institutions of Islam are implemented because its army is [composed of] Muslims' and a domain of war 'whose inhabitants are unbelievers'. This third type of domain is, following the Arabic text in *Majmūᶜ fatāwā*, one 'in which the Muslim shall be treated (*yuᶜāmal*) as he merits, and in which the one who departs from the Way/Law of Islam (*sharīᶜat al-Islām*) shall be combated (*yuqātal*) as he merits'.[64] Michot takes this as further evidence for Ibn Taymiyya's personalist rather than systemic or political approach to the question of Mardin's status. The focus is no longer on the status of the city as a whole, but rather on the individuals therein, who are to be treated according to what they each deserve.[65] However, Michot does not reflect on what it might mean that someone who departs from the Way of Islam should be 'combated' or 'fought' (*yuqātal*). Thanks to a textual emendation arising out of a conference on the Mardin fatwa held in 2010, Michot no longer faces this question.

Michot on the 2010 Mardin Conference

In 2011 Michot published an article in *The Muslim World*, of which he is the editor, providing a thorough account of a conference held in Mardin on 27–8 March 2010 to discuss Ibn Taymiyya's fatwa.[66] The conference was initiated by organisations linked to the prominent Mauritanian shaykh ᶜAbd Allāh bin Bayya and British-based writer Aftab Malik, and it brought together a diverse array of scholars to undo alleged misuse of the Mardin fatwa. Michot himself was not invited. Michot observes that the conference declaration[67] echoes much that he says in *Muslims under non-Muslim Rule*. Nonetheless, he sharply criticises the New Mardin initiative for shoddy scholarship and promoting a sugar-coated 'Genetically Modified Islam' that only feeds the cancer of Islamist extremism.

Michot points to the first conclusion of the Mardin declaration as the prime example of misguided scholarship. This states that Ibn Taymiyya's Mardin fatwa may not be used to justify rebelling against rulers and declaring fellow Muslims unbelievers. The problem is that contemporary jihadists justify acts of violence not from the Mardin fatwa but from Ibn Taymiyya's anti-Mongol fatwas and other sources. Michot shows from this and various statements given to the press that conference representatives obviously confused the Mardin fatwa with Ibn Taymiyya's anti-Mongol fatwas such that the full weight of responsibility for modern Muslim terrorism was loaded erroneously onto the Mardin fatwa.[68]

Michot also reproaches Bin Bayya and his American student Hamza Yusuf Hanson for making exorbitant claims about the import of a correction to the printed Arabic of the Mardin fatwa. In an interview on Aljazeera television, Bin Bayya notes that some Muslim youth in Europe carried out an attack on the basis of Michot's translation of *yuqātal* in the last line of the Mardin fatwa as 'combated'. Bin Bayya does not censure Michot himself: Michot was only translating the text he had at hand. Michot expresses appreciation for Bin Bayya's charity, but challenges Bin Bayya to produce evidence of a link between his translation and Islamist terrorism in Europe, especially as the whole tenor of *Muslims under non-Muslim Rule* opposes such a reading.[69] Bin Bayya continues that the general sense of the Mardin fatwa requires replacing *yuqātal* (combated) in the last line with *yuᶜāmal* (treated), and he refers to early sources to support his emendation. Michot accepts this emendation to the modern printing of the Mardin fatwa found in *Majmūᶜ al-fatāwā*, and he finds further support for it in a manuscript dating back to 1372 CE. The last line of the fatwa thus defines the third type of domain as one 'in which the

Muslim shall be treated (*yuᶜāmal*) as he merits, and in which the one who departs from the Way/Law of Islam shall be treated (*yuᶜāmal*) as he merits'. Michot readily accepts Bin Bayya's emendation of the text, but he does not think that it drastically changes the meaning. However, Bin Bayya and later Hamza Yusuf claim that contemporary Islamist extremism, including the terrorism of al-Qāᵓida, is all based on this fatwa misprint and that its correction has now pulled the rug out from under extremist ideology. Michot rejects this as preposterous grandstanding, especially as he has been unable to locate any mention of the Mardin fatwa in the writings of Osama bin Laden.[70]

Michot concludes that the pronouncements coming out of the Mardin conference deliberations were of such inferior academic quality that few would be persuaded by them, and he dismisses the Mardin declaration as little more than a publicity stunt that made a mockery of those involved and totally undermined their objective of opposing Islamist extremism. Michot further links the Mardin conference to the post 9/11 'industry' of refurbishing the tarnished image of Islam and promoting what he calls a soft and irenic Sufism and 'Genetically Modified Islam' designed to fight the spiritual cancer of Islamist terrorism. To Michot's mind this Genetically Modified Islam promotes a kind of 'spiritual diabetes' that does not cure the 'spiritual cancer' of Islamist extremism but instead exacerbates it. Michot then examines the responses of the American jihadists Anwar al-Awlaki (d. 2011) and Adam Gadahn to the 2010 Mardin conference to show that its extreme impotence in fact emboldened their Islamist extremism. Michot concludes colourfully, 'Among American Muslims as in the Middle East, hyperglycemia is carcinogenic'.[71]

Michot on the Arab Spring and Islamic Revolution

The Arab Spring afforded Michot opportunity to explore the import of Taymiyyan political theology further, especially in two essays published online in February and March 2011. The first interprets the Egyptian uprising as an 'Islamic Revolution', and the second probes the legitimacy of Yūsuf al-Qaraḍāwī's call to kill the Libyan leader Muammar Gaddafi (d. 2011).[72]

In the first essay, and in a similar and in parts identical discussion found in his 2012 book *Against Extremisms,* Michot outlines his religious argument against 'Mongolizing' Islam even more fully than before.[73] These discussions not only elaborate Michot's critique of how contemporary jihadists and Western academics read Ibn Taymiyya. They also go on to explain how the 2011 Egyptian uprising, as a nonviolent protest movement, was a specifically Islamic revolution. After reviewing how Ibn Taymiyya's rationale for fighting the Mongol invaders has been appropriated by modern Islamic radicals and Western observers, Michot condemns this appropriation in no uncertain terms:

> To legitimize armed struggle and the assassination of Muslim rulers by identifying them with the invaders attacked in the anti-Mongol fatwas of Ibn Taymiyya is indeed, quite simply, a hijacking of the text that transforms his writings calling to resist an incoming foreign invader into pamphlets challenging a power in situ. It is shocking that such a 'Mongolization' of Sadat and other Muslim rulers could be conceived as faithful to the thought of the Damascene Shaykh al-Islam [Ibn Taymiyya]. He himself indeed remained always loyal vis-à-vis his own sultan, the Mamluk al-Nasir Muhammad – even though the latter was, in respect of the Shari^c^a, not much stricter than a Mongol of that time or a modern Arab-Muslim ruler ... The writings of the Damascene shaykh are, moreover, explicit: for him, as for the great majority of classical Sunni authors, such a loyalty is the very foundation of the political theology of Islam.[74]

On Michot's reading, Ibn Taymiyya was religiously committed to loyalty to his own rulers in accord with classical Sunni political theory, and this trumped the rationale that he devised to justify fighting the Mongols. Ibn Taymiyya's quietism is not grounded in a judgement about the piety of the Mamlūks, nor the degree of their adherence to Islamic laws after the fashion of his ruling against the Mongols. Instead, it is rooted in the traditional Sunni conviction that armed insurrection against one's own ruler always entails more corruption than it prevents, as encapsulated in the maxim that Ibn Taymiyya occasionally cites, 'Sixty years of an unjust ruler are better than a single night without a ruler'.[75] Additionally, Michot explains, patience is the virtue that Ibn Taymiyya prescribes in the face of mistreatment and injustice at the hands of ruling authorities, and this can, in fact, be a means by which God tests his people.[76]

Turning to the Egyptian uprising, Michot clarifies that submission to rulers does not require total passivity in the face of injustice. Rather, 'there is room in Islam ... for conscientious objection, non-violent protest, and civil disobedience enlightened by faith'; these are in fact at times 'obligations of the religion, in the same way as are moderation and weighing the pros and cons in all things'.[77] In Islam and in Ibn Taymiyya's thinking, there is a place for 'speaking truth to power' and patiently enduring the consequences, or for what Michot calls 'the Muslim tradition of critical patience and of the *jihad* of the word'.[78] It is within this tradition that Michot locates the Egyptian Tahrir Square demonstrators of early 2011 and calls their non-violent stand for truth and justice 'a truly *Islamic* revolution'.[79]

Michot does not explain how the critical but loyal patience of Ibn Taymiyya provides a precedent for calling on a ruler such as former Egyptian President Hosni Mubarak to leave office entirely, not merely to change his ways. Yet, Michot finds in the Egyptian uprising a modern expression of Islamic activism that he believes to be far more faithful to the Taymiyyan spirit than 'the violent Ibn Taymiyya of the assassins of Sadat', who 'was nothing but a vicious fairy-tale, a Mongolizing bad dream'.[80] Put differently, for Michot, the example of Ibn Taymiyya adds greater legitimacy to non-violent revolution than to violent insurrection, and there apparently does come a point in a Taymiyyan political theology when a ruler may be called upon to leave office if preponderant benefit is in view.

Michot's second essay, dated 15 March 2011, seeks to make sense of Yūsuf al-Qaraḍāwī's calls on 21 and 25 February 2011 to kill Libyan ruler Muammar Gaddafi, an act that would appear out of step with Taymiyyan critical loyalty to rulers, not to mention al-Qaraḍāwī's own juristic principles. While there were medieval jurists who permitted rebellion in self-defence and rebellion that had a reasonable chance of success without causing preponderant harm,[81] neither Michot nor al-Qaraḍāwī invokes these precedents. Al-Qaraḍāwī does, however, justify his fatwa on the grounds that Gaddafi was a great danger to the Libyan people. He had already massacred many of his own people, and he needed to be prevented from wreaking the further havoc that he threatened. Thus, based on a 'jurisprudence of balancing (*muwâzanât*)', Gaddafi should be sacrificed for the greater good of all.[82]

Analysing this, Michot underlines al-Qaraḍāwī's role as a charismatic religious authority independent of state institutions and without coercive power to depose Gaddafi himself. Al-Qaraḍāwī speaks for Islam only insofar as ordinary Muslims give him their ear. Thus, Michot writes, 'By calling for the killing of Gaddafi, Shaykh al-Qaradâwî didn't in fact do anything other than fill his obligations as a renowned mufti and meet the expectations of a great number of believers.'[83] Additionally, Michot seeks to forestall a comparison of al-Qaradāwī's ruling with the *Farīḍa* of ᶜAbd al-Salām Faraj and the assassination of Egyptian President Sadat by noting two points. The first concerns scholarly authority. The respected al-Qaraḍāwī has better scholarly credentials than did the electrician Faraj, who had a poor understanding of the texts that he used. The learned al-Qaraḍāwī's legal reasoning is based on a careful weighing of benefits and harms in accord with traditional jurisprudence. Michot's second point is that Gaddafi was the aggressor and not the people. With Gaddafi, it was a matter of the ruler losing his legitimacy by turning on his people to massacre them, not the people rising up in arms against the ruler. Or, as Michot puts it, it is not an 'armed coming out against the sultan' (*khurūj ᶜalā al-sulṭān*) but an 'armed coming out of the power against its own people' (*khurūj al-sulṭān ᶜalā al-shaᶜb*). In such cases it is the responsibility of religious scholars to call for the death of the perpetrator, and, as al-Qaraḍāwī argued, it is appropriate to sacrifice one person for the sake of the people. Michot acknowledges that al-Qaraḍāwī's ruling entails a certain danger in that it could be misapplied to other circumstances. The antidote in his view is to recall that fatwas apply only to the particular situations for which they were given; they cannot be generalised into universal rules of religion.[84]

Michot does not mention explicitly that al-Qaraḍāwī also does not justify killing Gaddafi by denigrating his religious status. There is no charge here of apostasy. Al-Qaraḍāwī's reasoning is based solely on the pragmatic consideration of inflicting harm – killing Gaddafi – in order to achieve the greater good of saving the Libyan people from slaughter. This calculation would appear to counter al-Qaraḍāwī's view that rebellions always cause greater harm than good, as well as Michot's Taymiyyan vision of critical patience and loyalty. Michot's strategy of turning Gaddafi into the rebel instead of the populace might evade the issue momentarily, but it raises the question at what point does an oppressive ruler turn into an outright rebel. Clearly for both al-Qaraḍāwī and Michot there is a limit to how much oppression and injustice a people must endure before it becomes religiously imperative to respond with lethal force if possible. For Michot, the authority to demarcate that limit lies in the hands of learned religious scholars like al-Qaraḍāwī who are in tune with the widespread sensibilities of the Muslim community. It does not lie in the hands of uneducated extremists who cobble together some texts to justify a revolutionary view.[85]

Ibn Taymiyya's Utilitarianism and its Modern Appropriation

Summing up thus far, Michot privileges Ibn Taymiyya's quietism and ethical personalism over his anti-Mongol argument that those who abandon some aspect of Islamic law must be fought. The Prophet's command and the traditional juristic calculus that insurrections always cause more harm than benefit constrain Ibn Taymiyya to a stance of critical loyalty and patience before his own Mamlūk rulers, and it is obvious enough that he never judged his situation to be so severe – on the order of a modern Gaddafi – to warrant calling for his rulers' demise. Thus, Michot reasons, today's extremists cannot legitimately use Ibn Taymiyya to justify armed insurrection against their own rulers. Ibn Taymiyya's anti-Mongol fatwas were a matter of Mamlūk war propaganda limited in use to the circumstances for which they were written.

Yet, the contrast between the severity of Ibn Taymiyya's anti-Mongol fatwas on the one hand and the judicious and pragmatic moderation of his Mardin fatwa on the other raises a further question that Michot addresses in a long footnote in *Muslims under non-Muslim Rule*: 'Must we conclude that Ibn Taymiyya modulates and (in the negative sense) makes a tool of the religion, fitting it to whatever objectives he is pursuing, sometimes mobilizing people, sometimes calming them down?'[86] Michot does not deny this possibility, and he translates a text in which Ibn Taymiyya outlines his utilitarianism explicitly as the path of the Prophet. The jurist explains that religious judgments should take account of the circumstances and consider the preponderant good. If, for example, a king converts to Islam but still drinks wine, he should not be prohibited from drinking wine if that would lead to him apostatising. Ibn Taymiyya concludes that the judgments of the Prophet himself varied according to the circumstances and 'were of diverse kinds, whether it was a question for him of enjoining or prohibiting, or waging jihad or pardoning, [or when] implementing penalties, of being strict or merciful'.[87]

It is not, then, a matter of Ibn Taymiyya turning religion into a tool for pursuing his objectives. It is rather that, for Ibn Taymiyya, weighing up the benefits and harms of all actions is essential to the religion, and prudent utilitarianism is the path of the Prophet. The telos or overall preponderant good toward which this utilitarianism aims is exclusive worship of God,[88] and violence here comes into play as one tool for attaining this objective. In his well-known treatise on Islamic polity *Al-Siyāsa al-sharᶜiyya*, Ibn Taymiyya envisions the goal of humanity as worshipping God alone and the role of rulers as using their power to reform society to that end, through both religious guidance and the sword: 'The establishment of the religion is by the Book and the sword.'[89] He further explains that violent punishments are of two kinds: (1) those imposed on deviants living under Muslim rule, and (2) fighting against those not under Muslim control such as unbelievers living outside Muslim realms and heretics openly defying the Islamic religion.[90] Ibn Taymiyya in no way condones violence that is vengeful, senselessly destructive, or fuelled by greed. The ruler must consider the overall benefits and harms of actions and choose the preponderant good.[91] As Michot himself explains, coercive power is essential to Islam in Ibn Taymiyya's thinking but its exercise must be channelled solely toward the advancement of religion:

> A religion without the power (*sulṭān*) to assert itself, unable or unwilling to wage jihad, and devoid of resources (*māl*) would be threatened in its existence and remains imperfect, hence the usefulness of the Mamluks. On the other hand, the pursuit of power, wealth, and war for any purpose other than establishing the religion (*iqāmat al-dīn*) is obviously to be condemned – hence the necessity of the ᶜulamaᵓ to educate not only the people but also their rulers.[92]

Given that Ibn Taymiyya legitimises violence for no purpose other than establishing religion, Michot's characterisation of his anti-Mongol fatwas as merely patriotic Mamlūk war propaganda is not entirely persuasive. It is more plausible that the fatwas ensued from Ibn Taymiyya's calculation that fighting the Mongols would further the cause of Islam. This is a calculation that Michot, as we saw earlier, discounts as shortsighted because the Mongol invasions in fact led to the Islamisation of Central Asia and the Indian subcontinent. Such a judgement is, of course, retrospective. Ibn Taymiyya could not have known the full consequences of fighting the Mongols, and, more generally, judging the costs and benefits of waging war accurately is usually a precarious and highly subjective undertaking.

Permeating Michot's interpretation of Ibn Taymiyya as a beacon of prudent Islamic moderation for today's world is the assumption that utilitarian reasoning is inherently tolerant, sensible and accommodating. This makes Ibn Taymiyya's anti-Mongol fatwas look like an anomaly in a career otherwise marked by critical but prudent and loyal interaction with political power. The anti-Mongol fatwas make more sense, however, if we envision Ibn Taymiyya as a scholar and activist seeking ways to advance religion as he understood it by all means calculated to succeed. Alongside teaching, writing and moral activism, this meant critical obedience to his Mamlūk rulers – there was no practicable possibility of displacing them, and they could be useful for religious ends. But against alleged heretics whose defeat appeared possible and advantageous, Ibn Taymiyya was prepared to write and agitate.

Utilitarian reasoning depends on a large number of subjective human factors, and its outcomes depend to a great extent on the vision of the good to which it aspires. Thus, as with utilitarianisms more generally, Ibn Taymiyya's utilitarianism readily lends itself to different appropriations, and a wide spectrum of modern Muslims find within it the resources and flexibility to support their diverse visions of the religious good. As noted earlier, Bin Laden supported his 1996 call to war with the logic of Ibn Taymiyya's first anti-Mongol fatwa that fighting to protect religion is obligatory when the danger from not fighting is greater, even if the intentions of the jihad fighters are impure. Similarly utilitarian is al-Qaraḍāwī's centrist vision of political engagement, which draws on Ibn Taymiyya to support a jurisprudence of weighing up benefits and harms. As for Michot, he works hard to preclude use of Ibn Taymiyya for radical ends by underlining his critical but patient loyalty to the Mamlūk sultan and the prudence of his pragmatism. Yet, it is not certain that Ibn Taymiyya's loyalty to his ruler was absolutely unconditional. Ibn Taymiyya's loyalty might have reached a limit if the ruler had become unbearably corrupt and there had been reasonable possibility of replacing him with someone better. It could be argued that modern radicals believe at least implicitly that they have indeed reached such a limit and judged that taking up arms to dislodge allegedly apostate rulers will lead to the greater good of the religion in due course. Once such utilitarian calculations are complete, there begins the process of seeking authoritative precedents to support the chosen course of action. Ibn Taymiyya, due to the fecundity of his thought and the courageousness and diversity of his activism, all of which establish his prestige as an authority, provides precedents that may be taken in either direction: moderation or radicalism. Just as Ibn Taymiyya himself justifies fighting the invading Mongols who confessed Islam through creative interpretation of precedents from early Islamic history, so also ᶜAbd al-Salām Faraj and his followers appropriate Ibn Taymiyya's anti-Mongol fatwas to justify violent insurrection against their own rulers. And no less creatively, Michot draws on Ibn Taymiyya to inform his vision of non-violent Islamic revolution and prudent Muslim engagement in society. Both Ibn Taymiyya and his diverse heirs are equally engaged in the hermeneutical appropriation of the past to meet the needs of the present. It is Michot's contention that he is appropriating Ibn Taymiyya faithfully and to the greater interest of Muslims while Islamist radicals completely betray his vision. The radicals would certainly argue that Michot has got the utilitarian calculus of Muslim interests wrong. Michot would reply that the radicals not only lack the scholarly depth to render such judgements; they also lack the ear of the wider community of Muslim believers. Yet, all parties are in fact striving to gain a hearing within the Muslim community, and, like Ibn Taymiyya, they are no doubt seeking ways to support the Islamic religion by all means calculated to succeed. It remains a matter of difference whether and when violence is one of those means.

Notes

1. I would like to thank David Warren for his helpful comments on an earlier draft of this chapter.
2. There is as yet no comprehensive study and assessment of Ibn Taymiyya's reception in the modern world.
3. Georges Tamer, 'The curse of philosophy: Ibn Taymiyya as a philosopher in contemporary Islamic thought', in Birgit Krawietz and Georges Tamer (eds), *Islamic Theology, Philosophy and Law: Debating Ibn Taymiyya and Ibn Qayyim Al-Jawziyya* (Berlin: de Gruyter, 2013), 329–74 (361–9).
4. See especially Fazlur Rahman, *Revival and Reform in Islam: A Study of Islamic Fundamentalism*, ed. Ebrahim Moosa (Oxford: Oneworld, 1999). Rahman writes, 'We shall argue that for a genuine reconstruction of Islam to occur, the threads have to be traced back to Ibn Taymiyya with a reconsideration of certain factors' (p. 132). Martin Riexinger, 'Ibn Taymiyya's worldview and the challenge of modernity: a conflict among the Ahl-i Ḥadīth in British India', in Krawietz and Tamer, *Debating Ibn Taymiyya*, 493–517, critiques Muslim modernist appropriation of Ibn Taymiyya as inconsistent with his hadith-based vision.
5. Bettina Gräf, 'The concept of *wasaṭiyya* in the work of Yūsuf al-Qaraḍāwī', in

Jakob Skovgaard-Petersen and Bettina Gräf (eds), *Global Mufti: The Phenomenon of Yusuf al-Qaradawi* (London: Hurst, 2009), 213–38.

6. Mona Hassan, 'Modern interpretations and misinterpretations of a medieval scholar: apprehending the political thought of Ibn Taymiyya', in Yossef Rapoport and Shahab Ahmed (eds), *Ibn Taymiyya and His Times* (Oxford: Oxford University Press, 2010), 338–66 (351–5).
7. Andrew March, *Islam and Liberal Citizenship: The Search for an Overlapping Consensus* (Oxford: Oxford University Press), 253, 264.
8. Muhammad Qasim Zaman, *Modern Islamic Thought in a Radical Age: Religious Thought and Internal Criticism* (Cambridge: Cambridge University Press, 2012), 265–6, 304–5.
9. Key works on Wahhābism and Saudi Arabia include Guido Steinberg, *Religion Und Staat in Saudi-Arabien: Die Wahhabitischen Gelehrten 1902–1953* (Würzburg: Ergon, 2002); David Commins, *The Wahhabi Mission and Saudi Arabia* (London: I. B. Tauris, 2006); ᶜAbd Allāh Ṣāliḥ al-ᶜUthaymīn, *Muḥammad ibn ᶜAbd al-Wahhāb: The Man and his Works* (London: I. B. Tauris, 2009); Madawi Al-Rasheed, *A History of Saudi Arabia*, 2nd edn (Cambridge: Cambridge University Press, 2010); Thomas Hegghammer, *Jihad in Saudi Arabia: Violence and Pan-Islamism since 1979* (Cambridge: Cambridge University Press, 2010); Stéphane Lacroix, *Awakening Islam: The Politics of Religious Dissent in Contemporary Saudi Arabia* (Cambridge, MA: Harvard University Press, 2011); Nabil Mouline, *The Clerics of Islam: Religious Authority and Political Power in Saudi Arabia*, trans. Ethan S. Rundell (New Haven: Yale University Press, 2014).
10. Itzchak Weismann, 'Genealogies of fundamentalism: Salafi discourse in nineteenth-century Baghdad', *British Journal of Middle Eastern Studies* 36:2 (2009), 267–80; Basheer M. Nafi, 'Salafism revived: Nuᶜmān Al-Alūsī and the trial of two Aḥmads', *Die Welt des Islams* 49 (2009), 49–97.
11. David Dean Commins, *Islamic Reform: Politics and Social Change in Late Ottoman Syria* (New York: Oxford University Press, 1990); Itzchak Weismann, *Taste of Modernity: Sufism, Salafiyya, and Arabism in Late Ottoman Damascus* (Leiden: Brill, 2001).
12. Bernard Haykel, *Revival and Reform in Islam: The Legacy of Muhammad Al-Shawkānī* (Cambridge: Cambridge University Press, 2003).
13. Claudia Preckel, 'Screening Ṣiddīq Ḥasan Khān's library: the use of Ḥanbalī literature in 19th-century Bhopal', in Krawietz and Tamer, *Debating Ibn Taymiyya*, 162–219.
14. Especially with Rashīd Riḍā (d. 1935), on whom see Charles Adams, *Islam and Modernism in Egypt; a Study of the Modern Reform Movement Inaugurated by Muḥammad ᶜAbduh* (New York: Russell & Russell, 1933), 202–4.
15. Key contributions to the study of contemporary Salafism include Quintan Wiktorowicz, 'Anatomy of the Salafi movement', *Studies in Conflict & Terrorism* 29 (2006), 207–39; Roel Meijer (ed.), *Global Salafism: Islam's New Religious Movement* (London: Hurst, 2009); Laurent Bonnefoy, *Salafism in Yemen:*

Transnationalism and Religious Identity (London: Hurst, 2011); Terje Østebø, *Localising Salafism: Religious Change among Oromo Muslims in Bale, Ethiopia* (Leiden: Brill, 2012); Richard Gauvain, *Salafi Ritual Purity: In the Presence of God* (London: Routledge, 2013); Chanfi Ahmed, *West African ᶜUlamāᵓ and Salafism in Mecca and Medina: Jawāb Al-Ifrīqī – The Response of the African* (Leiden: Brill, 2015); Lloyd Ridgeon (ed.), *Sufis and Salafis in the Contemporary Age* (London: Bloomsbury, 2015). On the genealogy of the appellation 'Salafism', see Henri Lauzière, 'The construction of *Salafiyya*: reconsidering Salafism from the perspective of conceptual history', *International Journal of Middle East Studies* 42 (2010), 369–89.

16. Johannes J. G. Jansen, *The Neglected Duty: The Creed of Sadat's Assassins* (New York: Macmillan, 1986; reprint, New York: RVP Press, 2013), which includes a full translation of Faraj's *al-Farīḍa al-ghāᵓiba* (151–229). Page references are to the reprint edition, the pagination of which differs slightly from that of the original edition. The reprint also includes a photocopy of the Arabic text (1–55, Arabic). Gilles Kepel, *Muslim Extremism in Egypt: The Prophet and the Pharaoh* (Berkley: University of California Press, 2003), 191–222, also provides an account of Islamic Jihad and the assassination of Sadat.
17. Yahya Michot, *Ibn Taymiyya: Against Extremisms* (Beirut: Dar Albouraq, 1433/2012). The book consists of English renderings of Michot's earlier translations of Taymiyyan texts into French.
18. Michot, *Against Extremisms*, xxi; Yahya M. Michot, 'Ibn Taymiyya', in *The Princeton Encyclopedia of Islamic Political Thought*, ed. Gerhard Bowering (Princeton: Princeton University Press, 2013), 238–41 (239).
19. On the third question, see especially Michot, *Against Extremisms*, 34–82, which is a full translation of Yahya Michot, *Ibn Taymiyya: Mécréance et pardon* (Beirut: Dar Al-Bouraq, 1426/2005).
20. Denise Aigle, 'The Mongol Invasions of Bilād Al-Shām by Ghāzān Khān and Ibn Taymīyah's Three "Anti-Mongol" Fatwas', *Mamlūk Studies Review* 11:2 (2007), 89–120, available at http://mamluk.uchicago.edu/MSR_XI-2_2007-Aigle.pdf (last accessed 14 July 2014). For a detailed chronology of the three Mongol invasions in the period 1299 to 1303, see Jean R. Michot, *Ibn Taymiyya: Lettre à Un Roi Croisé (Al-Risâlat al-Qubruṣiyya)* (Louvain-la-Neuve: Bruylant-Academia, 1995), 35–62. See also Reuven Amitai, 'The Mongol occupation of Damascus in 1300: a study of Mamluk loyalties', in Michael Winter and Amalia Levanoni (eds), *The Mamluks in Egyptian and Syrian Politics and Society* (Leiden: Brill, 2004), 21–39.
21. Ibn Taymiyya, *Majmūᶜ fatāwā Shaykh al-Islām Aḥmad Ibn Taymiyya* [MF], eds ᶜAbd al-Raḥmān b. Muḥammad b. Qāsim and Muḥammad b. ᶜAbd al-Raḥmān b. Muḥammad, 37 vols (Riyadh: Maṭābiᶜ al-Riyāḍ, 1961–7), 28: 501–8 (first fatwa), 28: 509–43 (second fatwa), and 28: 544–53 (third fatwa); the reprint of MF (Medina: Mujammāᶜ al-Malik Fahd, 2004) is typeset differently but retains the pagination of the original and is available at https://archive.org/details/mfsiaitmmfsiaitm (last accessed 14 July 2014). Faraj, *al-Farīḍa al-ghāᵓiba*,

accessed the second and third fatwas from an older collection of Ibn Taymiyya's works: *Kitāb majmū*ᶜ*at fatāwā Shaykh al-Islām Taqī al-Dīn Ibn Taymiyya* [KMF], 5 vols (Cairo: Matbaᶜat Kurdistān al-ᶜIlmiyya, 1326–9/1908–11), 4: 280–98 (second fatwa) and 4: 298–302 (third fatwa); this collection is known in jihadist circles as *al-Fatāwā al-kubrā* or simply *Fatāwā*.

22. Aigle, 'Mongol Invasions', 117.
23. Aigle, 'Mongol Invasions', 117, suggests that this fatwa dates to the Mongol occupation of Damascus in 1300 when Ibn Taymiyya was mediating between the Mongols and the local population. However, the fatwa inquiry (MF 28: 501) speaks of the Mongol invasion 1299–1300 as already come and gone.
24. Aigle, 'Mongol Invasions', 101–2. For further exposition of Ibn Taymiyya's distinction between political rebels such as Muᶜāwiya and religious heretics such as the Khārijīs from different texts, see Khaled Abou El Fadl, *Rebellion and Violence in Islamic Law* (Cambridge: Cambridge University Press, 2001), 271–9.
25. Ibn Taymiyya, MF 28: 509–43.
26. Ibid. 527.
27. Aigle, 'Mongol Invasions', 117–20; Yahya Michot, 'Textes spirituels d'Ibn Taymiyya. XII: Mongols et Mamlûks: l'état du monde musulman vers 709/1310 (suite)', *Le Musulman* (Paris) 25 (January 1995), 25–30 (30, n. 36); J. Y. Michot, 'Un important témoin de l'histoire et de la société mamlûkes à l'époque des Īlkhāns et de la fin des Croisades: Ibn Taymiyya (ob. 728/1328)', in U. Vermeulen and D. DeSmet (eds), *Egypt and Syria in the Fatimid, Ayyubid and Mamluk Eras: Proceedings of the 1st, 2nd and 3rd International Colloquium Organized at the Katholieke Universiteit Leuven in May 1992, 1993 and 1994* (Leuven: Peeters, 1995), 335–53 (344, n. 30).
28. Recent studies on the *yāsa* and its relation to Islamic law include Denise Aigle, *The Mongol Empire between Myth and Reality: Studies in Anthropological History* (Leiden: Brill, 2015), 134–56; David Morgan, 'The "Great Yasa of Chinggis Khan" Revisited', in Reuven Amitai and Michal Biran (eds), *Mongols, Turks, and Others: Eurasian Nomads and the Sedentary World* (Leiden: Brill, 2005), 291–308.
29. Ibn Taymiyya, MF 28: 520–31. For further exposition of the second fatwa, see Aigle, 'Mongol Invasions', 101–3, 111–20; Michot, *Lettre*, 62–70; and Michot, 'Un important témoin', 345–53. The text of MF 28: 530 referring to the *yāsa* of Genghis Khan is corrupt; for correction and discussion, see Yahya Michot, 'Textes spirituels d'Ibn Taymiyya. XIII: Mongols et Mamlûks: l'état du monde musulman vers 709/1310 (fin)', *Le Musulman* (Paris) 25 (September 1995), 25–30 (25–6, n. 7); and Michot, 'Un important témoin', 345–6.
30. Ibn Kathīr's commentary on 'Do you desire the judgment of the Jāhiliyya' (Q. 5:50) condemns the Mongols for preferring the *yāsiq* (i.e. *yāsa*) legal system of Genghis Khan over the Qurᵓan and the Sunna of the Prophet and explains that anyone who does that is an unbeliever (*kāfir*) who must be fought. For a translation of Ibn Kathīr's comments, see Michot, 'Un important témoin', 347, n. 38.

31. In Jansen, *The Neglected Duty*, 160–8, 171–3 (§21–35, 40–2). For further analysis, see Rachel Scott, 'An "official" Islamic response to the Egyptian al-jihād movement', *Journal of Political Ideologies* 8:1 (2003), 39–61 (46–50); Emmanuel Sivan, 'Ibn Taymiyya: Father of the Islamic Revolution: Medieval Theology & Modern Politics', *Encounter* 60:5 (1983), 41–50.
32. See, for example, Joas Wagemakers, *A Quietist Jihad: The Ideology and Influence of Abu Muhammad al-Maqdisi* (Cambridge: Cambridge University Press, 2012), 59–74, which discusses Abū Muḥammad al-Maqdisī's relegation of the modern legal systems in Muslim countries to the domain of unbelief.
33. Jād al-Ḥaqq ᶜAlī Jād al-Ḥaqq, 'Kutayb *al-Farīḍa al-ghāᵓiba* wa-l-radd ᶜalay-hi' (3 January 1982), in *Al-Fatāwā al-Islāmiyya min dār al-iftāᵓ al-Miṣriyya*, 2nd printing (Cairo: Wizārat al-Awqāf, 1997), 3724–59 (vol. 10, no. 1326) (followed by the full text of *al-Farīḍa al-ghāᵓiba*, pp. 3761–91), available at https://ia600500.us.archive.org/23/items/waq61121/61121.pdf (last accessed 15 July 2014); Jansen, *The Neglected Duty*, 3–5, 55–62; Scott, 'An "official" Islamic response', 50–5; Hassan, 'Modern interpretations', 359.
34. Such is the argument of Simon Wolfgang Fuchs, 'Do excellent surgeons make miserable exegetes? Negotiating the Sunni tradition in the *ǧihādī* camps', *Die Welt des Islams* 53:2 (2013), 192–237, which is derived from the author's book, *Proper Signposts for the Camp: The Reception of Classical Authorities in the Ǧihādī Manual* al-ᶜUmda fī Iᶜdād al-ᶜUdda (Würzburg: Ergon, 2011). References will be to the 2013 article.
35. ᶜAbd al-Qādir b. ᶜAbd al-ᶜAzīz (a.k.a. Dr Faḍl), *Al-ᶜUmda fī iᶜdād al-ᶜudda li-l-jihād fī sabīl Allāh* (Word document), available at www.tawhed.ws/dl?i=f8ro5d45 (last accessed 10 July 2014), (pagination may vary on different computers). For biographical information on Dr Faḍl, see Nelly Lahoud, 'Jihadi recantations and their significance: the case of Dr Fadl', in Assaf Moghadam and Brian Fishman (eds), *Fault Lines in Global Jihad: Organizational, Strategic, and Ideological Fissures* (London: Routledge, 2011), 138–57 (139–40). Writing from an Egyptian prison in 2007 and following, Dr Faḍl polemicised against the jihad activities of al-Qāᵓida, but Lahoud doubts the sincerity of these writings. For a thorough account of the history of al-Qāᵓida, especially in relation to Saudi Arabia, see Hegghammer, *Jihad in Saudi Arabia*.
36. Fuchs, 'Excellent surgeons', 203–4, 217–9, 233, 237; Dr Faḍl, *Al-ᶜUmda*, 70–1, 381–2, twice quotes the last three pages of Ibn Taymiyya's first anti-Mongol fatwa, MF 28: 506–8.
37. See the English translation, 'Bin Laden's Fatwa', available at http://www.pbs.org/newshour/updates/military-july-dec96-fatwa_1996/ (last accessed 14 July 2014); the passage begins, 'The ultimate aim of pleasing Allah …' I was unable to locate an Arabic version of the text. For analysis of the fatwa, see Rosalind W. Gwynne, 'Usama Bin Ladin, the Qurᵓan and Jihad', *Religion* 36 (2006), 61–90.
38. Yūsuf al-Qaraḍāwī, *Fiqh al-jihād: Dirāsa muqārana li-aḥkāmi-hi wa-falsafati-hi fī ḍawᵓ al-Qurᵓan wa-l-Sunna*, 2 vols (Cairo: Maṭbaᶜat al-Madanī, n.d.; also, Cairo: Maktabat Wahba, 2009), 2: 1032.

39. Ibid. 1033.
40. Ibid. 1040–51.
41. Ibid. 1054–5.
42. Ibid. 1067.
43. 'Textes spirituels d'Ibn Taymiyya', *Le Musulman* (Paris, 1990–8); 'Pages spirituelles d'Ibn Taymiyya', *Action* (Mauritius, 1999–2002); and 'Textes spirituels d'Ibn Taymiyya. Nouvelle série' (2009–present), available at http://www.muslimphilosophy.com/it/ (last accessed 15 July 2014); the first two series are available on the same website.
44. Michot's curriculum vita with publications through 2008 is available at http://www.hartsem.edu/sites/default/files/Michot_CV.pdf (last accessed 15 July 2014), and further works are listed in his *Against Extremisms*, 279–83.
45. Yahya Michot, 'Textes spirituels d'Ibn Taymiyya. I. L'extinction (fanâ°)', *Le Musulman* (Paris), 11 (June–September 1990), 6–9, 29 (6).
46. For a recent account of the Algerian conflict, see James D. Le Sueur, *Between Terror and Democracy: Algeria since 1989* (London: Zed Books, 2010).
47. Yahya M. Michot, 'Textes spirituels d'Ibn Taymiyya. XI. Mongols et Mamlûks: l'état du monde mususlman vers 709/1310', *Le Musulman* (Paris), 24 (October 1994), 26–31 (28); idem, 'Textes spirituels ... XII', 25–30; idem, 'Textes spirituels ... XIII', 25–30.
48. Ibid. 27–8.
49. Yahya Michot, *Ibn Taymiyya: Mardin: Hégire, fuite du péche et 'demeure de l'Islam'* (Beirut: Dar Al-Bouraq, 1425/2004); idem, *Ibn Taymiyya: Muslims Under Non-Muslim Rule* (Oxford: Interface Publications, 1427/2006); all references are to the English volume.
50. Michot, *Muslims*, 49.
51. Ibn Taymiyya, MF 3: 250; trans. Michot, *Muslims*, 54.
52. Hasan Qasim Murad, 'Ibn Taymiya on trial: a narrative account of his Miḥan', *Islamic Studies* 18 (1979), 1–32.
53. Yahya M. Michot, 'Textes spirituels d'Ibn Taymiyya. Nouvelle série. IV. L'obéissance aux autorités', (December 2009), available at http://www.muslimphilosophy.com/it/works/ITA-TexSpi-NS04.pdf (last accessed 30 January 2014), gives Ibn Taymiyya's political quietism a firmer evidential base than that found in *Muslims under non-Muslim Rule* by translating relevant passages from his *Minhāj al-sunna al-nabawiyya*, a refutation of Shi^cism written sometime toward 1317. Here Ibn Taymiyya explains that, contrary to the views of the Khārijīs, Zaydīs and Mu^ctazilīs, armed insurrection against an unjust ruler always entails excessive corruption to the community and is also prohibited by the Prophet. Rulers should also be obeyed in whatever agrees with God's command, even if they are themselves sinners. The texts are also translated into English in Michot, *Against Extremisms*, 220–30. Later in *Against Extremisms*, 259, n. 2, Michot calls Ibn Taymiyya's stance 'critical loyalism'.
54. Michot, *Muslims*, 49–56.
55. Ibid. 123–9.

56. Ibn Taymiyya, MF 28: 240–1; idem, KMF 4: 279–80; English trans. Michot, *Muslims*, 63–5 (quoting Michot's translation, 65).
57. Michot, *Muslims*, 38–45 (discussion), 101–22 (translated texts), 103–4, n. 2 (Faraj's misunderstanding). See also Jansen, *The Neglected Duty*, 158–9, 169–70 (§20, 37).
58. Ibid. 11–17 (discussion), 66–100 (translated texts).
59. Ibid. 17–20 (20).
60. Ibid. 20–3 (23).
61. Ibid. 19–20, n. 2, 23, 25.
62. Ibid. 26.
63. Ibid. 23, 59–61.
64. Translation adapted from Michot, *Muslims*, 65, with reference to the Arabic of the Mardin fatwa in MF 28: 240–1.
65. Michot, *Muslims*, 26–7.
66. Yahya Michot, 'Ibn Taymiyya's "New Mardin Fatwa". Is Genetically Modified Islam (GMI) Carcinogenic?' *The Muslim World* 101:2 (2011), 130–81.
67. 'The New Mardin Declaration', 28 March 2010, available at http://www.mardin-fatwa.com/attach/Mardin_Declaration_English.pdf (last accessed 25 September 2013).
68. Michot, 'New Mardin', 137–8, 139–41, 143–4, 148–9.
69. Ibid. 138–9.
70. Ibid. 138–9, 144–51. For Hamza Yusuf's account, see the video, 'The Mardin Fatwa & Al Qaeda', available at http://www.youtube.com/watch?v=77QODDURVMg (last accessed 15 July 2014). Curiously, Faraj transcribes the relevant text from the Mardin fatwa in *al-Farīḍa al-ghāʾiba* in one place *yuʿāmal* and in a second place *yuqātal*. See the text in Jansen, *The Neglected Duty*, 7 (Arabic §20 *yuʿāmal*) and 14 (Arabic §36 *yuqātal*). Even more curiously, Jansen translates both occurrences as 'treated' (pp. 159 and 169). I am grateful to Jabir Sani Maihula for drawing the second occurrence to my attention.
71. Michot, 'New Mardin', 155–63 (163).
72. Yahya Michot, 'An Islamic Revolution', 18 February 2011, available at www.scribd.com/doc/65025050/An-Islamic-Revolution (last accessed 23 September 2013); and idem, 'The fatwa of Shaykh Yûsuf al-Qaradâwî against Gaddafi', 15 March 2011, available at http://www.scribd.com/doc/51219918/The-fatwa-of-Shaykh-Yusuf-al-Qaradawi-against-Gaddafi (last accessed 6 July 2014).
73. Michot, *Against Extremisms*, xxv–xxix.
74. Michot, 'An Islamic Revolution', 2; almost exactly the same text is found in Michot, *Against Extremisms*, xxvi.
75. See for example Ibn Taymiyya, MF 20: 54, translated with slight differences in Michot, *Against Extremisms*, 258–9. Other occurrences of the maxim include Ibn Taymiyya, MF 14: 268 and 30: 136.
76. Michot, 'An Islamic Revolution', 2.
77. Ibid. 3; nearly identical wordings of the quotations in this and the following two references are found in Michot, *Against Extremisms*, xxvii–xxviii.

78. Michot, 'An Islamic Revolution', 4.
79. Ibid.
80. Michot, *Against Extremisms*, xxix.
81. Abou El Fadl, *Rebellion and Violence*, 194, 283–7.
82. Michot, 'The fatwa of Shaykh Yûsuf al-Qaradâwî', 2–3. David H. Warren, 'The ᶜUlamāᵓ and the Arab Uprisings 2011–13: considering Yusuf Al-Qaradawi, the "Global Mufti," between the Muslim Brotherhood, the Islamic Legal Tradition, and Qatari Foreign Policy', *New Middle Eastern Studies* 4 (2014), available at http://www.brismes.ac.uk/nmes/archives/1305 (last accessed 16 July 2014), includes discussion of al-Qaraḍāwī's fatwa against Gaddafi and provides an assessment of the bases of his religious authority.
83. Michot, 'The fatwa of Shaykh Yûsuf al-Qaradâwî', 3.
84. Ibid. 3–4.
85. Yahya M. Michot, 'L'autorité, l'individu et al communauté face à la *sharīᶜa*: quelques pensées d'Ibn Taymiyya', *Mélanges de l'Université Saint-Joseph* 54 (2012), 261–86, provides further investigation of Ibn Taymiyya's approach to religious authority in the direction of individual conscience.
86. Michot, *Muslims*, 50–3, n. 3 (question on p. 51).
87. Ibn Taymiyya, MF 35: 32, as translated in Michot, *Muslims*, 53.
88. On the centrality of exclusive worship of God in Ibn Taymiyya's theology and ethics, see Jon Hoover, *Ibn Taymiyya's Theodicy of Perpetual Optimism* (Leiden: Brill, 2007), 26–9.
89. Ibn Taymiyya, *al-Siyāsa al-sharᶜiyya*, MF 28: 244–397 (264); trans., Omar A. Farrukh, *Ibn Taymiyya on Public and Private Law in Islam* (Beirut: Khayat, 1966); trans., Henri Laoust, *Le traité de droit public d'Ibn Taymiyya* (Damascus: Institut fraçais de Damas, 1948).
90. Ibn Taymiyya, *Siyāsa*, MF 28: 349.
91. Ibid. 284. For additional discussion of Ibn Taymiyya's utilitarian or consequentialist legitimisation of violence, see Jon Hoover, 'Squaring Ibn Taymiyya's legitimization of violence with his vision of universal salvation', forthcoming in the proceedings of the 'Legitimate and Illegitimate Violence in Islamic Thought' conferences, University of Exeter, 2010–12.
92. Michot, 'Ibn Taymiyya', 240.

8

The Impact of a Sixteenth-Century Jihad Treatise on Colonial and Modern India

Carole Hillenbrand

Introduction

This chapter analyses the views on Islam of a little-known early Orientalist scholar working in Madras, Michael John Rowlandson (1804–94), and of two modern Muslim scholars in India, Muhammad Husayn Nainar and Ahamad Ilyaas Vilayatullah. The discussion here will focus on a most interesting Arabic jihad treatise called *Tuḥfat al-mujāhidīn fī ba*ᶜ*ḍ aḥwāl al-Burtugāliyyīn*.[1] Written by a Keralan scholar, Sheikh Zainuddin Makhdum (d. 1583), this work deals with events from his own time, the period of Portuguese domination of the Indian Ocean, and their violent attacks on Malabar.

This treatise urges the Muslims in Bijapur to wage jihad against these ferocious invaders. Zainuddin makes telling comparisons between the famous jihad waged by the Levantine Muslims in the twelfth and thirteenth centuries against the Franks and the much less well-known jihad fought by the Indian Muslims in Bijapur against the Portuguese in his own time, three centuries later. Thus the relevance of medieval concepts of jihad, developed and refined in the Levant in the context of the Crusades, remained firmly in place in early modern India.

Zainuddin calls the Portuguese invaders the Franks (*al-Afranj*) and he records their history from the time of their arrival in Calicut in 1498 under Vasco da Gama. In his author's preface, Zainuddin expressly states that he has composed his narrative to arouse the faithful to engage in jihad against 'the worshippers of crosses' (ᶜ*abada al-ṣulbān*).[2] Zainuddin stresses the great reward that awaits those who engage in fighting jihad against the Portuguese. He is not, however, hostile to the Hindus with whom he and his fellow-Muslims have long lived harmoniously. The jihad he advocates is a *defensive* one against the foreign European Christian invaders of Malabar. Zainuddin frequently uses the same kind of anti-Frankish tropes and formulaic curses regularly found in the twelfth- and thirteen-century Arabic chronicles of the Levant that recount the history of the Crusades. For example, when he mentions the attacks of the group he calls 'the Portuguese Franks', Zainuddin writes 'May God forsake them' (*khadhala-hum Allāh*),[3] a curse frequently used in Muslim chronicles of the Crusading period in the Levant.[4]

This chapter hopes to demonstrate how, just as Arabic chroniclers at the time of the Crusades provided a model of jihad which Zainuddin could use to inspire his fellow-Malabari Muslims to resist the terrible onslaughts of the Portuguese 'Franks', so too his own work, translated into English, could be used for different purposes in the context of nineteenth-century British colonial India and also in Kerala today.

The *Tohfut-Ul-Mujahideen* was translated for the first time from Arabic into English in 1833 in Madras by Michael John Rowlandson, a serving British army officer (see Figure 8.1).[5] This chapter will focus on aspects of his translation, the context in which he undertook it, his possible motives for doing so, and his explanations of Islamic doctrines, including jihad. Of course this work has its own interest in the context of sixteenth-century Indian history, and, beyond that, of the Portuguese enterprise of exploration. But it also has its place in the very different context of the present volume. For it shows how a work written for a specific and urgent purpose, namely to encourage South Indian Muslims to take up jihad against the hated foreign invaders, could spring to life and acquire an unexpected relevance in nineteenth-century India, when the region was under the control of quite another set of foreign invaders. As this chapter will show, it served an apparently innocuous purpose as a teaching tool for both Europeans and Indians interested in the study of the Arabic language. It also fitted into the wider nineteenth-century pattern of increasing – and increasingly meticulous – non-Muslim European scholarly engagement with the literature of the Islamic world. However, it was also manipulated (and that is not too strong a word) to serve the missionary purposes of its devoutly evangelical translator. There is a rich irony in the use of a jihad text as a call to accepting the Christian gospel. But that so to speak undercover purpose itself fitted into the wider project, so dear to many a Victorian heart, of converting Indians to Christianity.

Who was Michael John Rowlandson?

It was a phenomenon of British India in the nineteenth century that a number of Orientalist scholars came from the ranks of the army and the civilian government.[6] Michael John Rowlandson, the translator of the *Tohfut-Ul-Mujahideen*, was no exception to this. He is very little known. He fails to figure in any list of the galaxy of British Orientalist scholars who served in India in the nineteenth century.[7] Copies of his *Tohfut* translation are found in only a few libraries outside India.[8]

Rowlandson was born on 23 November 1804, in Hungerford, Berkshire; his father was Vicar of Warminster.[9] He joined the Indian army as a cadet in 1820, becoming a lieutenant in 1821 and a major in 1824. Before going to India, in accordance with the rules of the Indian Colonial Service (ICS), Rowlandson must have attended Haileybury College, as did all serving administrative and military officers, where he would have learned Latin and Greek, as well as one or more of the languages that were important for governing India – Persian, Arabic and Urdu. These studies were probably followed up with further informal language sessions with local *munshīs* once he had graduated from Haileybury and had arrived in Madras. He was awarded a brevet commission in 1836.[10]

Details about Rowlandson's activities in Madras are scarce. One snippet of information, suggesting that he enjoyed a respected status in Madras government circles, is to be found in the records of divorce proceedings in the Supreme Court of Judicature in 1837, where his name appears as one of the signatories to a new divorce bill.[11] Rowlandson is also mentioned in the *Journal of the Royal Asiatic Society* in 1899 as having been a Corresponding Fellow and as Persian Interpreter to the Headquarters of the Army, Fort St George.[12] Rowlandson retired from the Indian army in 1852 and he died in 1894 in England.[13] It is not clear when he returned home and there is little known in official records about how or where he spent the rest of his life.

Rowlandson did, however, write at least three other books in addition to his translation of *Tohfut*, and these provide further biographical evidence about him. They shed valuable light on his academic credentials and religious convictions. One of these books was published as early as 1828 in Madras and it demonstrates clearly his commitment to the teaching of Arabic and Persian. It is entitled *An Analysis of Arabic Quotations which Occur in the Gulistan of Muslih-ud-Deen Sheikh Sadi.* The text beneath this title on the frontispiece reads:

> the book is intended for the use of the College of Fort St George by Lieut. M. J. Rowlandson, Acting Secretary to the Board of the College, and for public instruction.

This work of 220 pages is a textbook. The first part (pages 1–142) explains aspects of Arabic grammar at considerable length; the second part gives a selection of Arabic quotations in the Persian work of Saᶜdī, the *Gulistān*, and an explanation of them. This latter part, Rowlandson writes, 'is designed more particularly for the use of the native students in the College of Fort St

George'. Such a statement makes it clear that local Indian students as well as serving British army officers and administrators were attending his classes in the College. It is probable that Rowlandson taught them. On matters concerned with Arabic he says that he has consulted the opinion of the 'Arabic Head master [*sic*] of the College of St George'. He also writes that it is hard to know whether the Arabic language is so little studied because of a belief that it is difficult or because it is not useful. He has no such problem with appreciating the importance of Persian 'as long as the process of the courts is in Persian'.[14]

Whatever the intended readership for this book might be, Rowlandson is uncompromisingly scholarly in his copious footnotes, often quoting verbatim from Latin sources, as well as those in Arabic, Persian and French. The work is dedicated to the Governor of Fort St George, the Right Honourable Stephen Rumbold Lushington, to whom Rowlandson explains his intention of facilitating a better reading of a work 'with the beauties of which you are familiar'.[15] This work makes it clear that Rowlandson was equipped with a sound knowledge of Arabic grammar by this time and thus he would have felt ready to embark on the translation of the *Tohfut*, which was published five years later.

Two of Rowlandson's other published works reveal him to be an 'evangelical Orientalist', as Avril Powell said of Rowlandson's much more illustrious compatriot, Sir William Muir.[16] Like Muir, Rowlandson wrote proselytising Christian tracts, with long, grandiose titles. One such work by Rowlandson is called *A Basket of Fragments and Crumbs for the Children of God*, and another is entitled *Specimens of 'Much Fine Gold' or The Unsearchable Riches of Divine Grace*.[17] The *Specimens of Gold* makes its Christian missionary intention clear, explaining that its title refers to the Gospel message which is 'to be preached amongst and offered to the Gentile nations of the earth'.[18] The tone is that of British nineteenth-century militant Christianity and perceived European superiority:

> To people of all colours and countries and climes; to the civilized European, and the debased African; to the Mohamedan sensualist and the Hindoo idolater; to Scythian, barbarian, bound or free, the Son of God cries, 'Come!'[19]

Hinting perhaps at his own feelings of 'otherness' during his time in Madras, as well as his openly declared Christian faith, Rowlandson describes the resurrected Jesus as: 'walking through the world, no longer as a native inhabitant, but (as Europeans dwell in India) as a foreigner and stranger, having his affections in another and better country'.[20]

The preceding discussion of the sparse extant biographical and personal material available about Rowlandson's life and attitudes prompts a number of reflections. He never enjoyed posthumous fame, such as that accorded to certain other British Orientalists serving in India, such as William Muir and Thomas Arnold. Indeed, were it not for his translation of the *Tohfut* of Sheikh Zainuddin Makhdum, an Islamic Arabic text hardly known in Europe outside Portugal, it is almost certain that Rowlandson's name would have sunk into almost total obscurity.[21]

It is, however, valuable to examine the views of a forgotten British colonial Orientalist scholar on Islam and especially on jihad. Indeed, it will be argued in what follows here that Rowlandson, who began writing in the 1830s, fills a gap between the well-known British Orientalist figures from earlier generations, such as Sir William Jones, and famous British scholars of the second half of the nineteenth century, such as Sir William Muir.

An Analysis of Rowlandson's Preface and Footnotes to his *Tohfut* Translation

Preface to the translation

Rowlandson introduces his translation of the *Tohfut* with a ten-page explanatory preface, outlining the historical context in which Zainuddin (d. 1583) wrote his treatise.[22] Rowlandson's tone in his preface is calm, un-polemical, and at times even laudatory of the Malabari Muslims. Rowlandson explains that Zainuddin lived in the reign of Sultan ᶜĀdil Shāh, the fifth ruler of the ᶜĀdil Shāhī dynasty in Bijapur. Zainuddin dedicates his book to ᶜĀdil Shāh and praises him for his 'unwearied zeal and activity' in fighting the infidels and in particular for his vigorous resistance against the 'Christian heretics' who had invaded Malabar.[23] Rowlandson singles out the term '*Al-Afrunj*' [*sic*] (Franks) used by Zainuddin to refer to the Portuguese.[24]

Rowlandson then describes the structure of the *Tohfut*. The first chapter discusses how the Prophet Muḥammad explained to his followers 'the meritorious nature and ultimate reward' of fighting non-believers. Thus, says Rowlandson, Zainuddin aims to arouse his fellow Muslim brethren to wage 'a holy war against the infidel intruders – the cursed "Franks"'.[25] After two more background chapters about the origins of the indigenous peoples of Malabar, Rowlandson turns to the fourth chapter of the *Tohfut*, in which Zainuddin tells how the Portuguese arrived in Malabar in 1498.[26] Here Rowlandson praises Zainuddin for the 'fidelity of his narrative' and its 'very minute and extraordinary agreement with the Portuguese sources'. He adds that when Zainuddin mentions the 'furious and persecuting spirit which the Portuguese invariably displayed throughout their Indian rule' he was not guilty of exaggeration.[27]

Thus Rowlandson's preface shows clear approval of the historical accuracy of Zainuddin's account and an admiration for the spirited resistance shown by the Malabari Muslims against the Portuguese colonial invaders from the arrival of Vasco da Gama onwards. Any hostility in the main body of Rowlandson's preface is directed at the Portuguese Catholics. No evidence of anti-Muslim sentiment or proselytising Christian zeal is expressed in his preface. It should, moreover, be emphasised that Rowlandson's translation is couched in grand, resonant English prose.

Rowlandson's footnotes

It is unfortunate that Rowlandson does not number his footnotes. Instead, on each page he uses a series of symbols. His footnotes providing geographical or historical information about Malabar, its Muslim rulers and the Portuguese invasions are generally sound. He draws on earlier sources in Latin, French, Persian and Arabic. He includes lengthy Latin quotations (which he does not translate) from the work of the seventeenth-century Jesuit scholar, Joannes Petrus Maffeius (Giovanni Pietro Maffei, 1533–1603), as well as providing references to revered early British Orientalists such as Pococke and Sale. For a number of his footnotes about Islam, Rowlandson cites Muslim sources such as the well-known works of Abū al-Fidāᵓ (d. 1331), al-Suyūṭī (d. 1505), al-Bayḍāwī (d. between 1282-91), al-Shāfiᶜī (d. 820), al-Bukhārī (d. 870) and others.

It is clear, however, from the very outset that Rowlandson's stance in his footnotes is often polemical. Zainuddin's treatise opens with a preface in praise of the Islamic revelation, exalted above all other creeds, and of the Prophet Muḥammad. But already in Rowlandson's third footnote,[28] there are clear signs of nineteenth-century Christian apologetic and anti-Muslim feeling. When speaking of chapter 3 of the Qurᵓan, *Sūrat ᶜImrān*, Rowlandson says that the Qurᵓan gives an account of Jesus' birth 'very similar to that recorded by the Evangelists' but he then strongly denies in very intemperate tones that Jesus brought to life a 'bird that he had made of clay',[29] a story that he attributes to the Prophet Muḥammad. He seems to be unaware that this narrative is found in one of the Apocryphal Christian Gospels, *The Infancy Gospel of Thomas*.[30]

Rowlandson's views on the concept of jihad, such as they are, are revealed in his footnotes to chapter 1 of the *Tohfut*,[31] which has the lengthy title 'Regarding certain divine commands, wherein war against infidels is enjoined. Treating, also, of the reward that shall await that act of religious duty, and being an exhortation of it.'[32] This chapter sets out the views of Zainuddin on the meaning of jihad and the reward for those who engage in it. Rowlandson provides copious footnotes with his own interpretation of the contents of the chapter. In his first footnote for this chapter Rowlandson expresses opinions about the Qurʾan, and in particular about the concept of jihad, which would certainly not be acceptable to pious Muslims.[33] He clearly disapproves of the promises of good things in the hereafter for those who fall in the pursuit of jihad. But in general he is much more interested in explaining the basic tenets of Islam than in the details of jihad. Rowlandson quotes from a work written in Latin, *De fatis linguarum orientalium*, some fifty years earlier. Its author, unnamed by Rowlandson, the Austrian scholar Bernard von Jenisch (d. 1807), praises in Latin the matchless style of the Qurʾan. Rowlandson then quotes some derogatory comments by Sir William Jones (d. 1796), the founder of the Asiatic Society of Bengal, significantly couched in Latin rather than English, about the authorship of the Qurʾan, and those of the Anglican divine Jeremy Taylor (d. 1667) about the Prophet Muḥammad. All this is frankly scurrilous and it sits ill with the otherwise neutral tone that dominates the footnotes. Rowlandson himself then ridicules the details of the paradise promised to Muslim believers. The first footnote on page 26 of Rowlandson's translation continues in this anti-Muslim polemical vein, strongly criticising the Qurʾanic denial of Jesus' crucifixion, and he refers to Islamic belief in Dajjāl (the Antichrist) as 'idiotic vagaries'.[34] Such material in his footnotes reveals Rowlandson's underlying Christian evangelical agenda. And he often lets himself down with snide sarcasms.[35]

Why did Rowlandson Translate the *Tohfut*?

It is worth considering why Rowlandson chose to translate a sixteenth-century Arabic text about the Malabari Muslims' jihad against the Portuguese in Madras in 1833. A partial answer to this question can be found in the preface and in his footnotes. In addition, the fact that he was living and working in Madras could no doubt have produced other reasons for his choosing to translate this particular treatise.

The neighbouring region of Malabar, the area from which the *Tohfut* originated, had a large number of Muslims. This would have been relevant to the British administrators, policy-makers and military men who were working in Madras. How Rowlandson came to gain access to the *Tuḥfat al-mujāhidīn* is not clear, but the copy of it shown here (Figure 8.2) indicates that Edward Law, Lord Ellenborough, the Governor-General of India 1842–4, had asked for it to be printed for him. The English translation of the *Tohfut* would certainly have highlighted for the British administrators in Madras the versatility of the classical Islamic theory of jihad, as it had been applied to certain specific historical episodes of great significance involving European invasions of Muslim territory, firstly the Levant in the Crusading period from 1099 to 1291, and then the colonial enterprise of the Portuguese, who seized much of the coastal lands of south-west India in the sixteenth century.[36] The relevance of these parallels to British officers and administrators ruling Indian Muslims would have been obvious to all. It is likely that, as the local interpreter and teacher of Persian and Arabic at Fort St George, Rowlandson would have been seen as a suitable person to translate the manuscript copy of the *Tohfut* in the possession of Lord Ellenborough.

The tone and content of Rowlandson's footnotes suggest several possible motives, or a combination of these, that would help to explain why he translated this text. It is reasonable to assume that selected folios from the Arabic text of Zainuddin, together with copies of Rowlandson's translation and footnotes, would have been a convenient teaching tool. They would have been useful for his pupils from the Indian Civil Service, both military and administrative, at Fort St George for studying classical Arabic and also for learning about the Qurʾan, and in particular jihad.

Moreover, Zainuddin's scathing attacks on the Catholic Portuguese colonising invaders in the sixteenth century would have had familiar anti-Catholic resonances in the Protestant evangelical context of the Indian Colonial Service and the British rivalry with the Portuguese in the nineteenth century. Sir William Muir was to be openly critical of the 'harmful' presence of Catholicism in Goa,[37] but Rowlandson hints at animosity towards Catholics back in England in his tract entitled *Specimens of Gold*. In that work he is hostile to Roman Catholicism and the Anglo-Catholic Oxford movement, condemning both the Pope and Edward Pusey who 'cause Christian believers to have doubts about their own salvation'.[38]

As already mentioned, Rowlandson's translator's preface reveals that he is sympathetic to the plight of the Muslims of sixteenth-century Bijapur. Indeed, he writes that Zainuddin, when describing the cruelties perpetrated by the Portuguese, has been 'guilty of no exaggeration'. Rowlandson, as a British soldier but also an Orientalist scholar from a European Christian background, who is working in the colonial period of British rule in India, argues strongly that the Muslims of Bijapur were fighting a just war (jihad) in defence of themselves and their families, their lands, and their possessions.

However, Rowlandson's analysis of the Islamic paradise and its promised delights to the faithful believers contains unequivocally hostile remarks about Muḥammad that regurgitate medieval Western European stereotypes and slurs found in the work of Dante and others.[39] So Rowlandson has obviously inherited an anti-Islamic stance which can be traced back to medieval European polemic and which, despite more tolerant attitudes to Islam during the Enlightenment, as expressed by thinkers such as Edward Gibbon and Thomas Carlyle, persisted in Christian evangelical circles throughout the nineteenth century.

Rowlandson's views on jihad accord well with those of his famous contemporary Sir William Muir (d. 1905).[40] Like Rowlandson, Muir learned Arabic at Haileybury College, but unlike Rowlandson he rose very high in the Indian Civil Service, reaching the level of Lt Governor of the North-West Province.[41] Muir is also recorded as speaking Urdu.[42] Clinton Bennett points out that Muir gave a full account of the life of Muḥammad but that he 'wanted to convince Muslims that Muḥammad was not worth their allegiance'. Muir's aims were thus at the same time scholarly and evangelical.[43] By the time of the Indian Mutiny in 1857, Muir was able in his *Life of Mahomet* to pronounce a criticism of jihad as scathing as that of Rowlandson in his footnotes more than twenty years earlier: 'The sword of Mahomet and the Coran are the most fatal enemies of Civilization, Liberty and Truth which the world has yet known.'[44] In his book *The Caliphate. Its Rise, Decline and Fall from original sources*, first published in 1883, and reprinted in 1915, Muir writes, with eerily misplaced assurance:

> If Christian nations have too often drawn the sword in propagation of their faith, it was in direct contravention of their Master's word ... Far different is the Muslim's case. Tribes and peoples for ages rushed into the battlefield, fulfilling what they believed their Maker's law, 'to fight in the ways of the Lord'; and as its immediate effect, the world was drenched in blood from the Mediterranean to the Caspian Sea.[45]

Avril Powell also speaks of Muir's 'unsympathetic understanding of Islam in scholarly publications which criticised the military propensities of both the Prophet's early Islamic state and the subsequent caliphates.'[46]

It has been convincingly argued by many historians and thinkers that, in the Indian context, British officials used their knowledge of the indigenous languages and culture for 'purposes of control'.[47] As prominent figures such as Lord Cromer pointed out, Christianity was a great ally in Britain's efforts to civilise India.[48] Moreover, in a recent publication Eric Germain writes that in British society of the late Victorian period, jihad was the issue most highlighted by those wishing to 'advocate the barbarian and backwards [*sic*] nature of Islam, anti-modern by essence, whose ultimate fate was to be overruled by Christianity'.[49] Germain further points to an essentialist vision of Islam on the part of Christian missionary, political and military circles, a vision which emphasises, on the basis of the Qurʾan and the career of Muḥammad, alleged Muslim military aggression and forced conversion.[50]

The Reception of Rowlandson's Translation and a Discussion of Two Recent Translations of the *Tohfut-Ul-Mujahideen*

Rowlandson's translation is criticised in a review by Donald Ferguson written in 1899 about a Portuguese translation of the *Tuḥfat* by David Lopes, published in Lisbon in 1898.[51] After heaping praise upon Lopes for his excellent scholarship, Ferguson writes: 'Our only regret is, that, being in Portuguese, Mr Lopes's work will be read by so few English scholars.' Ferguson also remarks that Rowlandson's work has often been quoted, although he does not cite any examples of its use, and he then launches into an attack on the inaccuracy of Rowlandson's translation 'in many places' and his often erroneous citing of proper names.[52] Ferguson also points out that, unlike Rowlandson who says that he has used only one manuscript of the *Tohfut*, Lopes drew on the evidence of four manuscripts.[53] In their famous book *Hobson-Jobson*, Henry Yule and A. C. Burnell also criticise Rowlandson's translation, writing that 'the want of editing in this last book is deplorable'.[54] This bad press apart, Rowlandson's translation of the *Tohfut* remained neglected for a long time.

Two English translations of the *Tohfut* have appeared in recent years.[55] The relationship between these two books is very close. The first translation was published by Muhammad Husayn Nainar in Madras in 1942 and revised and republished in Kuala Lumpur in 2006. The second translation, by Ahamad Ilyaas Vilayatullah, appeared in 2012. These recent publications provide footnotes with solid, uncontroversial historical and geographical information and explanations of Islamic terms. Both the Nainar and Vilayatullah books claim that there have been many translations of the *Tohfut* but at no point are any references given to such works. To quote Vilayatullah: 'Portuguese, Latin, French, German, Spanish, English etc. are a few of the foreign languages in which it appeared at various stages and in different shapes.'[56] He also states that the *Tohfut* has been translated into English previously on several occasions by many people and for various purposes. He says that these works are either out of print or not available for modern readers or inadequate for other reasons: 'Some translations are available only in fragments and some others are not sufficiently annotated.'[57] These remarks remain totally unsubstantiated and unreferenced and one may question their accuracy. According to the foreword of Nainar's book written in July 2005 by K. K. N. Kurup, Director of the Malabar Institute for Research and Development in Vatakara, the *Tohfut* has been translated into many languages, including Latin, French, Spanish, Czech, Malayalam and Tamil.[58] Once again no details of these alleged translations are mentioned. However, a recent discussion by David Thomas provides more concrete information;

he notes, giving titles and full details, that the *Tohfut* has been translated into Persian, Malayalam, Portuguese and English.[59]

Vilayatullah remarks that the most important section of the *Tohfut* is the fourth, consisting of fourteen chapters, that truthfully describes the Malabar people's heroic resistance to the Portuguese invasion. Describing this resistance as a glorious episode in the history of the global Muslim community, Vilayatullah sees the Malabaris' struggles against the Portuguese, 'the foremost imperialistic power of the time', as inspirational, as in the past against the British and Portuguese, and now for the present generation in resisting the imperialistic ambitions 'of the US and its allies'.[60] So the notion of jihad once again proves highly adaptable to changing times and situations.

It is regrettable that the powerful analogy made by Zainuddin between the Crusaders in the twelfth and thirteenth centuries and the Portuguese in the sixteenth century is lost in the translations of both Nainar and Vilayatullah by the use of the word 'Portuguese' instead 'Franks' when translating the term 'Al-Afranj' in the Arabic text. Thus the impact of the reused trope of the 'Franks' is lost in these modern English translations produced in India. It is, of course, well known now that modern Islamic anti-Western propaganda, such as that used by Osama bin Laden (d. 2011), involves Crusading imagery to denote the USA and the Western powers more generally.

Concluding Remarks

This discussion has shown how a sixteenth-century Arabic text, the *Tohfut-Ul-Mujahideen*, written by Zainuddin Makhdum, a Malayalam-speaking Muslim scholar from South India, drew on concepts of jihad which had inspired Muslims in the Middle East in their struggles again the Crusaders (the Franks) in the twelfth and thirteenth centuries. In the nineteenth century, Rowlandson, a serving British army officer and Persian interpreter, found time to produce an English translation of the *Tohfut*; this is an isolated early example of Orientalist interest in jihad in an Indian Muslim context. In the twenty-first century this text has reappeared in two English translations prepared by two Keralan scholars, Nainar and Vilayatullah, who, as will shortly appear, have their own reasons for drawing attention once again to the *Tohfut*.

It is clear from the preface to Rowlandson's translation of the *Tohfut* that as a military man he admires the courageous armed struggle of the Malabari Muslims in the sixteenth century against violent Portuguese invaders and that he is very interested in this episode of South Indian history. Rowlandson is careful to praise the historical accuracy of Zainuddin's account, having consulted for himself the relevant European sources to include in his copious footnotes. Given his firmly held evangelical Protestant Christian beliefs, he was no doubt pleased to translate a text which portrays the Catholic Portuguese in a most unfavourable light. They were, after all, in his own time Britain's main rivals for the control of South India.

However, when Rowlandson, as a member of the British colonial class serving in India, launches into the religious aspects of Zainuddin's text and begins to write explanatory footnotes to explain Islamic doctrines to his students and other readers, he attacks and ridicules certain Islamic doctrines, including the rewards of jihad, with full evangelical fervour. Drawing on deep-rooted prejudices and stereotypical views, he perpetuates the Western European medieval Christian image of jihad. He says nothing about the precise rules of jihad laid down in the books of the Shari^{c}a nor about Sufism and the greater jihad. Rowlandson feels it imperative to underline the superiority of Christianity over Islam. Indeed, just like Muir, Rowlandson would no doubt have believed that 'If Christianity is anything, it must be everything'.[61]

In short, then, Rowlandson's book reveals several distinct facets of this enigmatic man. At one level he is a competent professional 'Orientalist', using that word in its familiar pre-Saidian sense. He was obviously a gifted linguist, using Latin, French, Arabic and Persian with facility. He cites his references in the approved manner of his time. So far so good. Next, he is a military man with a particular pedagogical brief to help both Indian and British employees of the East India Company acquire the linguistic skills required for their work. The translation of the *Tohfut* admirably dovetailed with these two aspects of Rowlandson's life. The fact that his book dealt with the history of the principal Muslim state close to Madras was a further and obvious bonus, and ensured a lively local interest in his project. But this context, detailed as it is, is by no means the full story.

Rowlandson also cherished an anti-Catholic and anti-Muslim agenda, and it is hard to deny that these were factors in his choice of text. This double bias does not, it seems, affect the translation itself, but its presence in the footnotes is unmistakable. Rowlandson's evangelical, missionary zeal frequently breaks through the tone of academic impartiality that characterises most of the footnotes. The change of tone triggered by references to Jesus (for example, on the issue of his crucifixion)[62] and to Muḥammad (for example in the context of the Battle of Badr)[63] and paradise[64] is nothing short of disturbing to a modern reader. The chords touched here seem to take us to the very heart of this complex man and to what made him tick. The discussion above has sought to contextualise him against the wider background of the nineteenth-century civilising and Christianising mission pursued by many of the British ruling elite in India. But one has only to read Gibbon and Carlyle on Islam to recognise that more temperate British assessments of that faith were possible immediately before and after Rowlandson's work. By that standard,

Rowlandson's comments on the Prophet Muḥammad take on the colouring of a rant: crude and tasteless vilification that belongs firmly to the Middle Ages, more worthy of Dante than Diderot. There are of course parallels for such intemperate language on the Muslim side too, for example the descriptions in Muslim sources of how Saladin cleansed the holy places of Jerusalem from the filth of Christian occupation; but such sentiments seem thoroughly out of place in a nineteenth-century English gentleman wearing a frock coat and breeches. Rowlandson, then, partakes of both Jekyll and Hyde.

Nainar and Vilayatullah have a different agenda in their treatment of Zainuddin's text. As well as a justified pride in their Keralan ancestors who stood up against the Portuguese, they are concerned to point out to the global Muslim community how this sixteenth-century jihad struggle can serve as a role model for combating current Western military interference across the Muslim world today. Thus the capacity of the classical jihad concept to speak to Muslims and non-Muslims (Rowlandson) of very varied backgrounds and traditions is as strong today as it was in the twelfth or sixteenth centuries.

The main purpose of this chapter has been to exhume a long-buried work of British scholarship on the South Asian Muslim world. But that task has inevitably led into a series of cognate enquiries. For while the text's purpose in its own time was, it seems, straightforward – namely to inspire beleaguered Deccani Muslims to fight for their faith against the rapacious Portuguese – its revival in the nineteenth and twenty-first centuries was nothing of the kind. In both those periods it demonstrated how certain concepts like jihad are evergreen, and how easily they can adapt to new situations and acquire sometimes startling new resonances. There is no telling what Rowlandson's South Indian Muslim students really thought of the text which Rowlandson was interpreting for them, and whether a connection that is obvious to a modern eye, namely the similarity between the Portuguese imperialists and the British ones, was equally plain to them. Similarly, whether they picked up on a Christian misappropriation of a Muslim text for missionary aims pursued under the cover of academic study and research remains unclear. What is certain is that modern South Indian Muslims working on this same text are in no doubt about the modern implications of this sixteenth-century text. In some quarters, at least, the concept of jihad is every bit as alive and well in Kerala today as it is in Syria, Iraq or Afghanistan. It merely takes a different form.

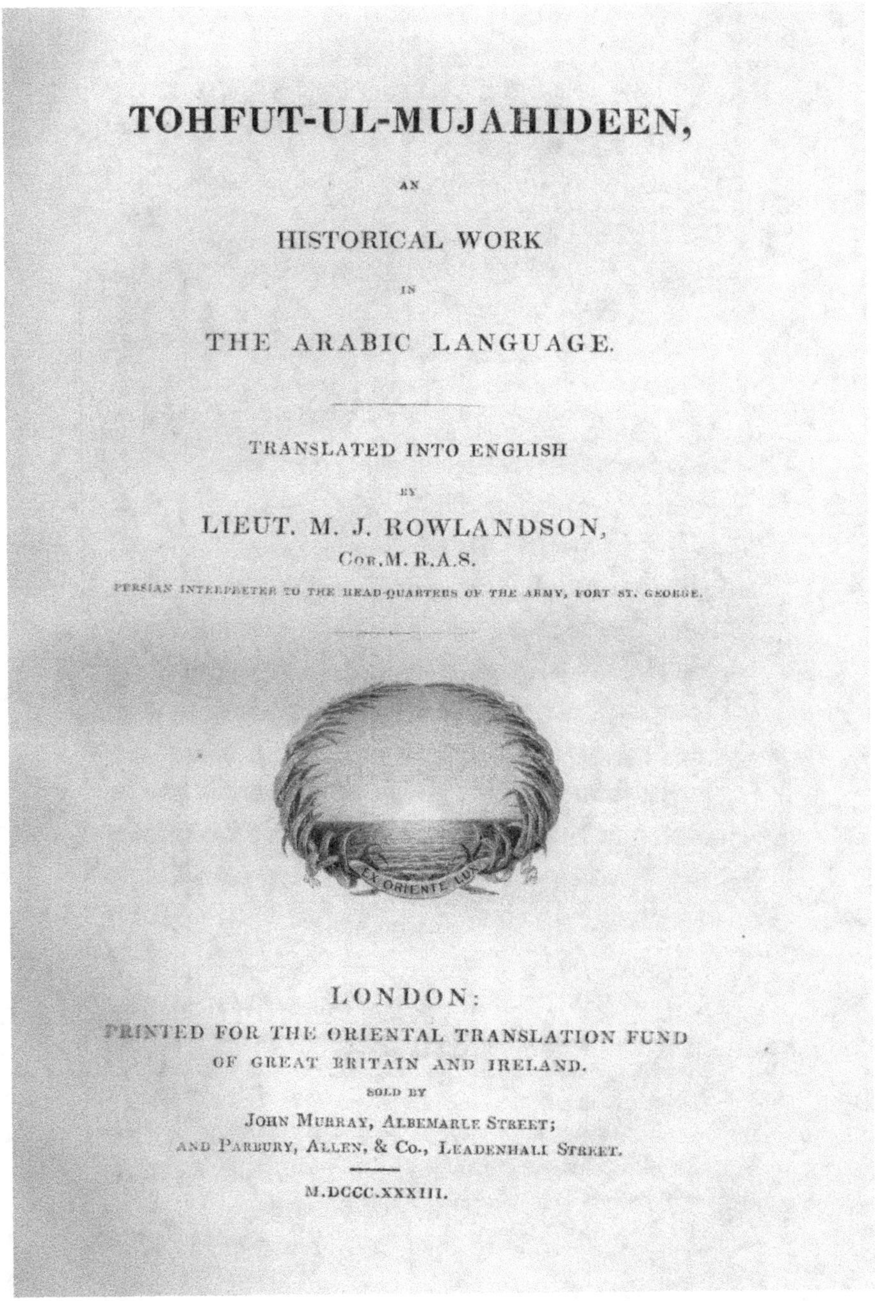

TOHFUT-UL-MUJAHIDEEN,

AN

HISTORICAL WORK

IN

THE ARABIC LANGUAGE.

TRANSLATED INTO ENGLISH

BY

LIEUT. M. J. ROWLANDSON,

COR.M. R.A.S.

PERSIAN INTERPRETER TO THE HEAD-QUARTERS OF THE ARMY, FORT ST. GEORGE.

LONDON:

PRINTED FOR THE ORIENTAL TRANSLATION FUND

OF GREAT BRITAIN AND IRELAND.

SOLD BY

JOHN MURRAY, ALBEMARLE STREET;

AND PARBURY, ALLEN, & CO., LEADENHALL STREET.

M.DCCC.XXXIII.

Figure 8.1 The opening title page of the *Tohfut-Ul-Mujahideen*, published in London in 1833.

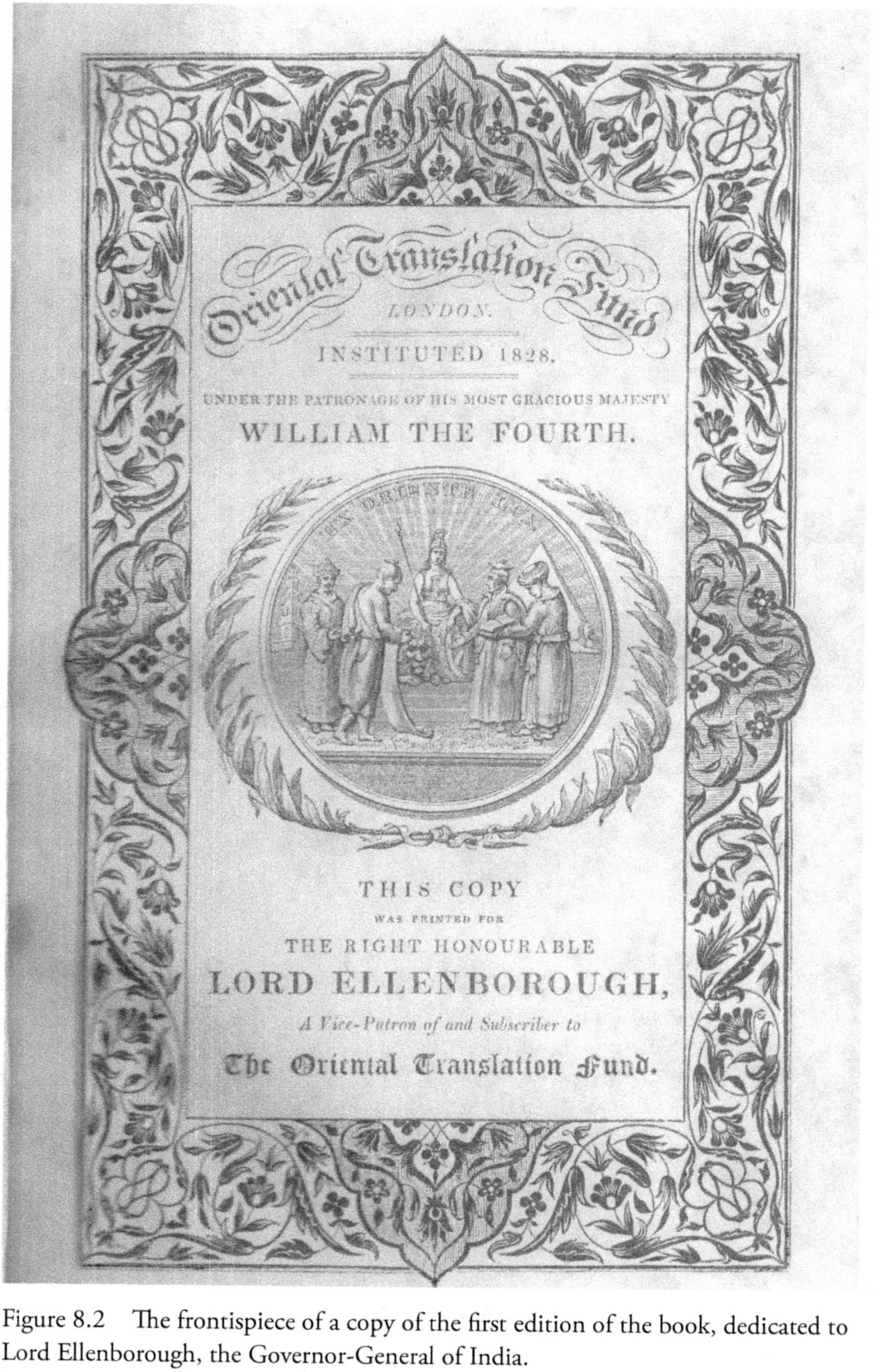

Figure 8.2 The frontispiece of a copy of the first edition of the book, dedicated to Lord Ellenborough, the Governor-General of India.

Notes

1. Zainuddin Makhdum, *Tuḥfat al-Mujāhidīn. History of the early Muhammadans in Malabar and their Struggles with the Portuguese*, Journal of the Royal Asiatic Society, Arabic ms. 28. Copied in Madras in 1830. For the sake of consistency, the transliteration of the name of the work under discussion here will follow throughout that of M. J. Rowlandson, *Tohfut-Ul-Mujahideen*, although such transliteration is unacceptable today in academic circles.
2. JRAS Arabic ms. 28, folio 0046.
3. Ibid.
4. Niall Christie, '"Curses, foiled again!" Further research on early use of the "Khadhala-hum Allāh" invocation during the Crusading period', *Arabica* 58 (2011), 561–70.
5. *Tohfut-Ul-Mujahideen: An Historical Work in The Arabic Language (1833)*, translated into English by Lieut. M. J. Rowlandson (London: Murray, 1833).
6. Clinton Bennett, *Victorian Images of Islam* (London: Grey Seal, 1992), 104.
7. Rowlandson does not, for example, appear in A. J. Arberry, *British Orientalists* (London: W. Collins, 1943).
8. I was fortunate to find by chance a rare copy of Rowlandson's translation of the *Tohfut* in the library of the Islamic Art Museum in Qatar in its collection of rare nineteenth-century European books on the Crusades.
9. *England and Wales, National Probate Calendar (Index of Wills and Administrations), 1858–1966* (search.ancestry.com/search/db.aspx?dbid=1904); *India Office Family History Search* (indiafamily.bl.uk/ui/home.aspx).
10. *Alphabetical list of the officers of the Indian Army; with the dates of their respective promotion, retirement, resignation, or death, whether in India or in Europe, from the year 1760 to the year 1834 inclusive, corrected to September 30, 1837*, see http://familysearch.org/search/catalog/817808.
11. *Collection of Nineteenth Century British Divorce Proceedings*, 4 vols (London, 1824–57), 2 (1829): 45, 56–7. e-book, see http://babel.hathitrust.org/cgi/pt?id=uc1.31158008184128;view=1up;seq=27.
12. Donald Ferguson, 'Review of *Historia dos Portugueses no Malabar, por Zinadim, Manscripto Arabe de Seculo XVI, publicado e traduzido por David Lopes,* Lisboa, 1898', *Journal of the Royal Asiatic Society*, July 1899, 677–8.
13. *India Office Family History Search* (indiafamily.bl.uk/ui/home.aspx).
14. Michael John Rowlandson, *An Analysis of Arabic Quotations which Occur in the Gulistan of Muslih-ud-Deen Sheikh Sadi* (Madras: College Press, 1828).
15. Rowlandson, *Gulistan*, 1.
16. Avril A. Powell, *Scottish Orientalists and India. The Muir Brothers, Religion, Education and Empire* (Woodbridge: Boydell Press, 2010), 94.
17. The date and place of publication of the first of these two titles is unknown. The second is still in print: Michael John Rowlandson, *Specimens of 'Much Fine Gold': or, The Unsearchable Riches of Divine Grace. By the author of 'A basket of fragments and crumbs for the children of God'* (London: Wertheim and Macintosh, 1852).

Hugh Goddard quotes a passage from Muir's *The Mohammadan Controversy* which speaks of the 'light and teaching of the Gospel' and which uses the same imagery as that of Rowlandson in *Specimens*: 'England now pours forth her gold in the merciful and blessed work of enlightening the people'. See Hugh Goddard, *A History of Christian–Muslim Relations* (Edinburgh: Edinburgh University Press, 2000), 133.

18. Rowlandson, *Specimens*, 2.
19. Ibid. 9.
20. Ibid. 44. The phrase 'as Europeans dwell in India' is written in brackets in Rowlandson's text.
21. For a rare reference to Rowlandson's *Tohfut*, see Margaret Anderson, *Arabic Materials in English Translation. A Bibliography of Works from the pre-Islamic period to 1977* (Boston: G. K. Hall, 1980), 126.
22. Rowlandson, *Tohfut*, vii–xvi.
23. *Tohfut*, vii–viii.
24. Ibid. ix.
25. Ibid. xi.
26. Ibid. xiv–xv.
27. Rowlandson concludes by thanking two British officials in Madras: the Hon. W. Oliver, a Council member at Fort St George, who gave him the manuscript, and Mr J. Lushington, the Secretary of the Madras Auxiliary Branch of the Royal Asiatic Society, who provided him with valuable information about the Arabic original. The copy of the Arabic manuscript of *Tohfut* used in this paper has Rowlandson's name on folio 0038; written in a sloping hand which is hard to decipher are the words: 'Copy of the Tohfat al-Mujahedeen to accompany Capt. Rowlandson's Translation when sent to the Oriental Translation Committee'. The date of completion of the translation was probably 1830.
28. Rowlandson, *Tohfut*, 2–3.
29. Qur᾿an 3:49.
30. *The Infancy Gospel of Thomas*, see www.gnosis.org., II, I.
31. JRAS, Arabic ms. 28, ff. 0040–0059; Rowlandson, *Tohfut*, 15–16.
32. Rowlandson, *Tohfut*, 15.
33. Ibid. 15–16.
34. Ibid. 41.
35. Ibid. 34, 36, 40.
36. A rare reference to Rowlandson's translation of the *Tohfut* is given by Serjeant. He writes that 'The cruel, ruthless, and insulting attitude of the Portuguese towards the Muslims has been described by Zain al-Dīn Ma'barī'; Robert B. Serjeant, *The Portuguese off the South Arabian Coast, Hadrami Chronicles*, (Oxford: Clarendon Press, 1963), 30. Note 4 cites Rowlandson, 103–10.
37. Powell, *The Muir Brothers*, 94.
38. Rowlandson, *Specimens*, 38.
39. Rowlandson, *Tohfut*, 16.
40. Avril Powell speaks of the Muir brothers' 'decisions, early in their Indian service,

to lend their linguistic training and historical interests to support missionary agendas'; Powell, *The Muir Brothers*, 14.

41. Bennett, *Victorian Images*, 103.
42. Powell, *The Muir Brothers*, 214.
43. Bennett, *Victorian Images*, 113.
44. Quoted in ibid. 109.
45. William Muir, *The Caliphate: Its Rise, Decline, and Fall, from Original Sources* (London: Forgotten Books, 2013), p. 608.
46. Powell, *The Muir Brothers*, 179.
47. Bernard S. Cohn, *Colonialism and its Forms of Knowledge: The British in India* (Princeton: Princeton University Press, 1996), 1–5; Goddard, *A History*, 124–5.
48. Dayne E. Nix, 'Muhammad Iqbal: restoring Muslim dignity through poetry, philosophy and religious political action', in H. Chad Hillier and Basit Bilal Koshul (eds), *Muhammad Iqbal. Essays on the Reconstruction of Modern Muslim Thought* (Edinburgh: Edinburgh University Press, 2015), 203; Muhammad Qasim Zaman, *The Ulama in Contemporary Islam: Custodians of Change* (Princeton and Oxford: Princeton University Press, 2002), 63.
49. Eric Germain, '"Jihadists of the Pen" in Victorian England', in Elisabeth Kendall and Ewan Stein (eds), *Twenty-First Century Jihad. Law, Society and Military Action* (London and New York: I. B. Tauris, 2015), 297.
50. Ibid. 297.
51. Ferguson, 'Review of *Historia dos Portugueses*', 677–8. In his book Lopes provides a long introduction which covers the history of Malabar from ancient times until the seventeenth century. His sections include Indian trade, a history of the St Thomas Christians, the Malabar Church and the arrival of Vasco da Gama; see David Lopes, *Historia dos Portugueses no Malabar, por Zinadim, Manscripto Arabe de Seculo XVI,* Introducção (Lisbon, 1898), ix–lxxxi.
52. Ibid. 678.
53. One in the British Museum Library, one in the Royal Asiatic Society, and two in the India Office Library: Ferguson, 'Review', 678.
54. Henry Yule and A. C. Burnell, *Hobson-Jobson* (originally published 1903; republished New Delhi, 2000), 159. See also their comment 'Very badly edited', xlv.
55. Zainuddin Makhdum, *Tuḥfat al-Mujāhidīn,* English translation by S. Muhammad Husayn Nainar Shaykh Zainuddin Makhdum: *Tuḥfat al-Mujāhidīn: A Historical Epic of the Sixteenth Century* (Kuala Lumpur and Calicut: Islamic Book Trust, 2006). Zainuddin Makhdum, *Tuḥfat al-Mujāhidīn,* English translation by Ahamad Ilyaas Vilayatullah as *Sheikh Zainuddin Makhdum's Tuhfatul Mujahideen. A Twenty First Century Translation* (Saarbrücken: Lambert Academic Publishing, 2012).
56. Vilayatullah, '*Tuhfatul Mujahideen*', 9.
57. Ibid. 5.
58. Nainar, '*Tuḥfat al-Mujāhidīn*', xiv–xv.
59. David Thomas, 'Al-Maᶜbarī', in David Thomas and John A. Chesworth (eds),

Christian-Muslim Relations. A Bibliographical Survey (Leiden: Brill, 2015), 7: 887.

60. Vilayatullah, '*Tuhfatul Mujahideen*', 10.
61. Powell, *The Muir Brothers*, 261 and n. 59.
62. Rowlandson, *Tohfut*, 27.
63. Ibid. 18–19.
64. Ibid. 33.

9

Jihadist Propaganda and its Exploitation of the Arab Poetic Tradition

Elisabeth Kendall

Introduction

A leading scholar of Islamist militancy recently posed a blunt question: 'Why is it that hunted terrorists spend time on poetry when they could be training?'[1] This is a powerfully pertinent question. The answer goes to the heart of the social dynamics, motivation and recruitment techniques of jihadist groups.[2] I have written previously on the significance and functions of poetry in winning hearts and minds for the militant jihadist cause.[3] This chapter departs from my previous research in that it focuses specifically on how and why contemporary jihadists use the Arab classical poetic tradition as a propaganda tool.

First, it is important to understand that poetry holds a revered position in Arab culture and that it enjoys widespread appeal in both popular and elite circles. Generally considered to be the oldest art form in the Arab world, poetry permeates all sectors of the social hierarchy and deals with a vast range of life's activities, from politics to pleasure, and from war to wisdom. Over the centuries it has been used widely not only to record history but also actively to shape it. In other words, more than simply reflecting the world we see, Arabic poetry has the capacity to influence *how* we view the world. Small wonder then that jihadist movements, both under the umbrella of what we now know as al-Qāᶜida and of the so-called Islamic State, make liberal use of this vast and venerable resource. It is reasonably well known that leading jihadists penned their own poetry, including both the former and current global leaders of al-Qāᶜida, Osama bin Laden (d. 2013) and Ayman al-Ẓawāhirī, as well as Abū Muṣᶜab al-Zarqāwī (d. 2006), leader of al-Qāᶜida in Iraq, the group that metamorphosed into Islamic State. What is less well explored is the way in which jihadists have drawn on the classical poetic heritage, even in poetry that has been deemed to be their own creation. This therefore is the focus of this chapter.

The incorporation of canonical texts from the classical poetic tradition into today's jihadist narratives mirrors the use of canonical religious texts. Both categories of text are 'claimed' and reinterpreted within contexts that buttress the ideals of modern militant jihad. The classical poetic tradition is embedded in today's jihadist narratives in two ways: first, by the appropriation of whole works or select verses directly from the classical heritage, and second, by the adoption of classical poetic structures, themes, tropes and idioms in the composition of new poetry. In understanding the motivation and appeal of jihadist groups, their choice of poetry is as revealing as the functions that they might expect the poetry to perform. This is particularly instructive in their surprising and seemingly contradictory choice of *jāhilī* poetry (poetry from the 'age of ignorance' before Islam) to back a radical Islamist agenda. This raises awkward questions about the extent to which jihadists are aware of their sources or, equally incongruous, whether tribal values and identifications dating back to pre-Islamic times in reality resonate as strongly as Islamic religious ones.

Jihadist use of poetry has received little attention from scholars, analysts and translators. This may in part be because the poetry has been considered peripheral in comparison with pronouncements on religious doctrine or military tactics. It may also be because the classical style of the poetry makes it difficult to translate and analyse. Whereas the target audience for such poetry need not understand every word in order for their hearts to be stirred and their minds to grasp the over-arching message, any translator or analyst adhering to even the loosest methodology cannot similarly pick and choose phrases here and there to translate in their briefs – either the poetry is included or it is not. Most of the time it is not, and this can blinker our understanding of jihadist thinking in significant ways. For example, Flagg Miller's analysis of the audio cassette featuring Osama bin Laden's 1996 speech that came to be known, inaccurately, as the 'Declaration of War Against the United States' reveals that the original contained no fewer than fifteen poetry excerpts – of which more than two thirds can be traced to the classical poetic heritage. Most of these poems were omitted from translated versions, yet they cast the speech in a different light. Significantly, they reveal Bin Laden's anger to have been directed primarily against the Saudi monarchy, perceived as Westernised, secular and corrupt, rather than overwhelmingly focused on America and the West itself. As Miller puts it, 'Bin Laden's primary audience would have understood the full measure of his political radicalism through his poetry.'[4] In other words, by failing to take account of key ways in which the poetry refines and targets messages, Western media and intelligence agencies are approaching jihadist ideology through a skewed prism that is out of synch with that of its primary Arab audience.

This chapter seeks to address this gap in understanding by investigating how and why the Arab poetic tradition is being appropriated, reconfigured, redeployed and even reinvented by contemporary jihadists. More specifically, it also asks which elements of the poetic heritage have been resurrected and what this can tell us. To establish firm evidence for the kind of poetry that jihadists favour in their propaganda, a basic content analysis is undertaken of the main Arabic magazine of al-Qāᶜida in the Arabian Peninsula, which is generally considered to be the most active, entrenched and aggressive branch of al-Qāᶜida today. The chapter then looks at how the poetic tradition is selectively reconstructed by jihadists and explores issues of both plagiarism and modern simulation. It ends with further discussion of the possible motivations behind and effects of this reclamation of the poetic tradition, particularly in terms of bolstering jihadist legitimacy and providing alternative claims to authority.

Appropriating the Poetic Tradition

The classical poetic tradition, in its capacity as a repository of history and not simply as a canon of aesthetic works, presents an important tool for appropriating the past and reconfiguring it to support a contemporary militant jihadist agenda. But first, what do we mean here by the classical poetic tradition? For the purposes of this chapter, the classical poetic tradition encompasses two poetic spheres. The first sphere is the vast canon of the classical *qaṣīda* (ode), which can be viewed as the dominant poetic form stretching from the pre-Islamic era arguably as far as the twentieth century, after which major shifts in poetic sensibility began to emerge. The second sphere comprises poetry from the twentieth century onwards in which we see the persistence of many of the fundamental elements of the classical *qaṣīda*, alongside or intertwined with new poetic forms and techniques. At its most basic, the classical *qaṣīda* model might be defined as verses comprised of two hemistiches (or half lines), structured using a variety of set metres and with each line or verse (*bayt*) ending in the same mono-rhyme. As Stetkevych has shown, the *qaṣīda* form has been inextricably bound up with social and political functions over the centuries, rather than being produced simply as art for art's sake,[5] and this may have much to do with its staying power. Contrary to some popular accounts,[6] Islam does not consider poetry to be sinful or frivolous. Indeed, the Prophet Muḥammad himself used poetry as a propaganda tool to spread the new religion of Islam.[7] There is also extensive historical precedent for the use of poetry to connect with, sustain, encourage and document the exploits of Muslim soldiers in holy war.[8] Contemporary jihadists, like their warrior ancestors, favour those genres of the traditional *qaṣīda* that best suit their needs and aspirations, namely *madīḥ* (eulogy), *rithāʾ* (lament), *hijāʾ* (lampoon or derogation), *fakhr* (boasting) and *ḥamāsa* (warmongering).

The poetry is used as part of a battle for cultural identity, which is essential for garnering support, whether this be for a resistance movement (al-Qāʿida's current focus) or a state-building project (Islamic State's current focus). Just as English literature helped to construct a British imperialist identity that constructed Africans as ignorant savages that needed to be saved and taught, so jihadist literature, especially poetry, helps to construct a pure Islamic identity against enemy 'others'. In a reversal of orientalist strategies famously exposed by Edward Said, in which stereotypes of Arabs and 'easterners' become embedded in the psyche through constant repetition in 'institutions' such as the literary canon, militant jihadist literature constantly repeats the idea of a corrupt Western(ised) enemy defined in opposition to a pure warrior of Allah. This overarching theme of virtue battling corruption is replayed time and again in various guises throughout the poetry. As a consequence of this insidious polarisation of good and evil, the jihadist position starts to appear clear and justified without the need for complex doctrinal argument.

Cultural legitimacy is further claimed through implanting the notion of continuity, both historical and geographic. Here, two factors are important: the linguistic medium of the poetry and its cultural genealogy. With regard to the first, al-Qāʿida in the Arabian Peninsula (AQAP), like other jihadist groups, overwhelmingly favours poetry in classical Arabic as opposed to fielding Nabaṭī poetry, which features the vernaculars of the tribes of the Arabian Peninsula and the Syrian desert, or Ḥumaynī poetry featuring Yemeni vernaculars. Of the 173 poems and poetry extracts featured in *Ṣadā al-Malāḥim* (2008–11), the AQAP Arabic magazine, only one is fully in local dialect. At a local level, audiences are engaged through the very use of poetry as the medium of communication owing to its popular appeal and deep cultural resonance even in the absence of instantly accessible dialect. Simultaneously, at a global level, the jihadist project is served through harnessing the kind of pure linguistic register that is sanctified by the Qurʾan and is thus recognisable across the entire Arab and Islamic worlds. The connection between language and power has been well explored in scholarship. Just as Benedict Anderson has shown how language played an important role in the constructing concepts of nationalism,[9] so too is language a key part of constructing the jihadist ideal of a caliphate that bonds together a global community of Muslims whose fundamental texts are in classical Arabic. The jihadist adoption of and composition of poetry in classical Arabic is therefore a conscious strategy, one function of which is to jump modern man-made borders. These borders are likewise erased by the oral transmission of poetry, which enables ideas to travel quickly, imperceptibly, cheaply and, once absorbed into the collective memory, permanently.

With regard to the second factor in establishing continuity – cultural genealogy – mining the classical heritage for poetic support is a powerful foil in the battle for Arab hearts and minds because it enables jihadist groups to operate on the inside of inherited cultural traditions and hence actively to manipulate the collective memory. The selective redeployment of the classical poetic heritage creates two important impressions among its primary Arab audience. First, it creates the impression that modern interpretations of militant jihad were always part of the cultural fabric of Arab society. Second, it re-casts Arab shared cultural history and collective memory such that it appears to have always been pointing towards a future that is today finally being realised. This has the effect of making the contemporary jihadist battle for a utopian Islamic society seem natural and fatalistically inevitable.

In this respect, jihadists are constructing what philosopher and literary theorist Jean-François Lyotard might term a 'grand narrative' or 'metanarrative'. A metanarrative is a totalising story whose function is to legitimise authority by making connections between disparate episodes with reference to a universal explanatory schema. Lyotard perceives metanarratives to be in decline with the advance of what he calls 'the postmodern condition', which refers to a progressive outlook that acknowledges diverse experiences and localised contexts as opposed to a single grand universalising narrative. He writes, 'The narrative function is losing its functors, its great hero, its great dangers, its great voyages, its great goal.'[10] Jihadist propaganda marks a reversal of this (perceived) progressive trend with its return to a grand narrative formed by dipping selectively into the classical poetic heritage. Although the poetry is often deployed with reference to highly localised grievances and experiences, it frames these as part of a grand narrative. The grand narrative performs the function of totalising all experience into an overarching and apocalyptic battle between good and evil involving great heroes facing great dangers and making great sacrifices.

What Poetry do Jihadists Like?

In order to appreciate the extent to which poetry, and in particular the poetry of the classical tradition, contributes to the construction of jihadist narratives, deeper investigation of a 'data set' was undertaken. This data set consisted of the main Arabic magazine of al-Qāᶜida in the Arabian Peninsula, *Ṣadā al-Malāḥim*. Basic content analysis of all issues of the magazine reveals that, on average, a fifth of the pages (19 per cent) feature poetry, usually only a few verses but sometimes whole poems. Of the 173 separate instances of

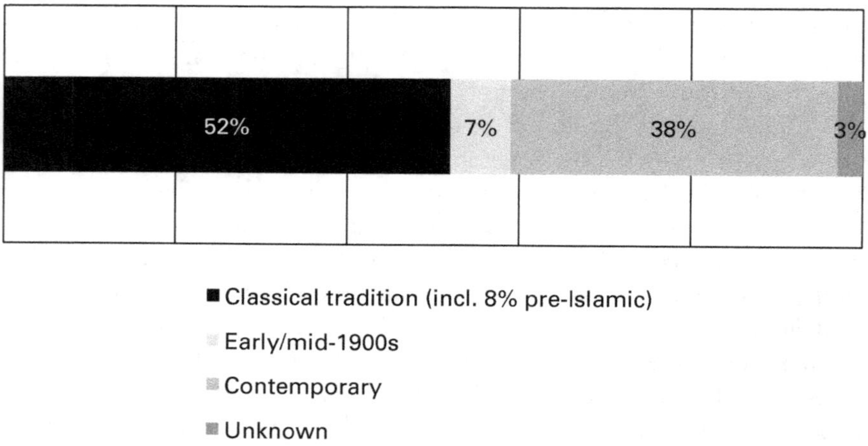

Figure 9.1 The provenance of the poetry featured in the AQAP magazine *Ṣadā al-Malāḥim.*

poetry, 89 per cent are composed in the classical *qaṣīda* form consisting of two hemistiches and a mono-rhyme and, as mentioned above, 99 per cent are composed in the classical Arabic language. This unequivocally demonstrates the significance of, at the very least, the external trappings of the classical poetic tradition. In other words, looking and sounding authentic is extremely important. But to what extent is the poetry new work dressed up in old robes? This is difficult to attest since less than one quarter of the poetry is attributed to any specific poet – not even to a pseudonym, which sometimes occurs with the modern composition. So, in a long and painstaking process, the provenance of each poetic verse was traced. The results indicate that the internal content of the classical poetic tradition, not just its superficial features, thrives within the contemporary jihadist context (see Figure 9.1).

Over half of the poetry featured over the life cycle of *Ṣadā al-Malāḥim* was traced back to bygone poets of the classical poetic heritage and, within this, the vast majority (89 per cent) was produced before the end of the Abbasid era in 1258. The most frequently quoted poet is Abū Ṭayyib al-Mutanabbī (d. 965), which fits well with his reputation as a warrior poet inspired by contemporary Muslim battles against the Byzantine Christians. In tied second place with regard to frequency are Abū Tammām (d. 843) and Ibn al-Mubārak (d. 797). Both were enthusiastic poetic proponents of militant jihad, although both are perhaps better known for their compilations – in Ibn al-Mubārak's case for his prose compilation of *The Book of Jihad* – than for their own original poetry. On initial inspection, Osama bin Laden also appears to be in tied second place, except that on closer investigation several of his verses can be traced back to the classical poetic tradition, rather than being original to him.

Pre-Islamic material

Several interesting observations arise from the analysis of the poetic material included in al-Qāᶜida's magazine. Perhaps the most intriguing discovery from tracing the provenance of the jihadists' poetic material is that some of it (approximately 16 per cent of the poetry taken from the classical tradition; or 8 per cent of the poetry overall) predates Islam, coming from the so-called 'age of ignorance' (*jāhiliyya*). In only one instance is the pre-Islamic origin acknowledged – this equates to a rate of source acknowledgement that is three times lower than the magazine's average for poetry.

There are several possible reasons for this discrepancy, all of them revealing about jihadist motivation. First, this lack of source acknowledgement might logically be considered intentional, since it would be counter-intuitive for jihadists to admit that their source of inspiration and/or argumentation springs from the 'age of ignorance' before Islam. However, given that the lack of acknowledgement of pre-Islamic sources is not universal – Bin Laden himself sometimes acknowledged such sources in his speeches – this is unlikely to be the main explanation. A second possible explanation is that, because the material was produced in the distant past and transmitted orally over generations, its true origins are not known by the jihadists, being lost on the wings of time. A third more likely explanation is that precise provenance, pre-Islamic or otherwise, is simply not an issue for jihadists so long as the poetry has an authentic ring. The point is that the tribal values of honour, chivalry and purity exemplified in this distant desert poetry continue to run deep, alongside their (by comparison relatively recent) religious values.

Another surprising discovery is that poetry, including pre-Islamic poetry, is comfortably placed alongside the Qurᵓan as an apparently parallel source of authority. An article ominously entitled 'When will you strike out?',[11] which appeared just as the so-called 'Arab spring' was breaking in Yemen, denounces the Ṣāliḥ regime for its rampant corruption and, by extension, also the Americans ('the perpetrators of the crimes in Guantanamo, the grandees of torture in Abū Ghrayb') for propping it up. 'Here in Yemen, everything is stolen and sold: land, air, sea.' Note how the fundamental drivers here are local concerns. The article confidently predicts, 'What happened in Tunisia will be repeated in Yemen' and incites readers/listeners to rise up. This directive is backed up by a verse from the Qurᵓan, as one might expect, but also by a pre-Islamic poetic verse placed after the Qurᵓanic verse as though it were an equally valid source. The source of this verse is not acknowledged but it can be traced to the famous pre-Islamic Ode of Zuhayr:

He who does not rise up to defend with his weapon
is defeated and he who does not fight oppression is oppressed

It is clearly ironic that hardened jihadists should be using poetry from the 'age of ignorance' before Islam alongside the Qurʾan in support of their plan to restore Islamic rule. Again, this non-Islamic choice evidences the strong tribal and cultural identities still at play in Yemen. This chimes with the findings of political scientist Laurent Bonnefoy that Yemen's jihad is motivated in the first instance by local Yemeni concerns and values.[12] Thus these pre-Islamic verses demonstrate how literary investigation can help to shed the light on the contemporary political landscape.

One particularly striking example of poetry evidencing the persistence of ancient tribal tradition can be found in an article entitled 'The propagandists of defeatism and confusion'.[13] This article heaps criticism on deviant Muslims who have forsaken the basic principles of the Qurʾan to collaborate with the regime and hence also the West. The point is not clinched with reference to the Qurʾan, however, but rather with reference to pre-Islamic poetry. Specifically, the Arabs of the *jāhiliyya* are praised for upholding values of honour, such as protecting the virtue of their womenfolk to avoid shame, even going so far as to bury them alive. The verses quoted can be traced to the pre-Islamic vagabond (*ṣuʿlūk*) poet, al-Shanfarāʾ:

[How much] she pleased me when she walked abroad
Not letting her veil fall nor being spoken of in disapproval

As she makes her way, it is as though [her eyes] search for something she has dropped on the ground;
and when she talks to you, she does not say much[14]

These verses have clearly been selected to highlight suitable feminine behaviour: cover up, keep your gaze lowered and don't talk too much. These directives have much in common with those issued by today's Islamic State,[15] but on the Arabian Peninsula at least, their catchy encapsulation in classical poetry invoking age-old customs is likely to carry more appeal. It is worth pointing out that other verses from the same poem, such as the poet's yearning for the woman or his descriptions of her body, are conspicuously absent. This illustrates the selective reconstruction of the poetic heritage to suit the jihadist agenda.

Poetic outliers and what they tell us

While jihadist poetry makes several references to women, generally either as models of submissive modesty in this world or as seductive temptresses waiting for martyrs to join them in the next, poetry by women is not favoured.

Only one woman poet is ever featured in the al-Qāᶜida magazine and she hails back to the time of the Prophet.[16] On the one hand this seems at odds with the strategic inclusion of female voices by other recent jihadist groups, such as Islamic State. Islamic State has championed female voices, such as the young Syrian poet Aḥlām al-Naṣr, who composed a series of propaganda poems for the new Islamic State upon her arrival in Raqqa in 2014.[17] Islamic State also makes efficient use of its women on social media to win over other women for the jihadist cause. On the other hand, however, even Islamic State has not (yet) attempted to galvanise women's voices, including their poetry, on the Arabian Peninsula.

In the AQAP magazine, we find rudimentary attempts to appeal to women in the regular women's section 'The Grand-daughters of Umm ᶜAmmāra' but the emphasis is very much on men furnishing female role models from the Islamic past for women to emulate rather than empowering new female voices. Nevertheless, interestingly, the models offered are of active fighting women like the eponymous heroine of the women's section,[18] not of passive wives and mothers. The featured verse by Khawla bint Thaᶜlaba is addressed to 'he who flees from God-fearing women' and it encapsulates well the message of the article in which it is embedded: women should encourage their men to stand firm for the jihad. Otherwise, readers are reminded of how women had to resort to stoning the male deserters and killing the Byzantines themselves at the Battle of Yarmūk in 636. The verse thus offers a potent blend of passive and active roles for women, not to mention a veiled threat to the masculinity of stay-at-home Muslim men.[19] This implies that attracting recruits has been a challenge and that strategies for getting women in the family/tribe on side with the jihad therefore merit attention.

The importance of tribal politics is also revealed by the poetry's greatest outlier, in terms of historical period at least. The only poetry extract featured in the al-Qāᶜida magazine to be produced between the mid-fifteenth and twentieth centuries is an interpolation from local Yemeni tradition. This unattributed verse can be traced to a *qaṣīda* by a prominent Yemeni religious scholar, Muḥammad bin al-Amīr al-Ṣanᶜānī (d. 1769), although it is clearly modelled on a near identical verse by the pre-Islamic poet al-Mutalammis. Al-Ṣanᶜānī advocated a literal interpretation of the Qurᵓan and Sunna and his teachings helped to form the republican model of Salafism that eventually rose to power in Yemen in the 1970s.[20] Moreover, a tract that he wrote on militant jihad was appended in full to Yūsuf al-Qaraḍāwī's infamous 2009 tome, *Fiqh al-Jihād* (The jurisprudence of Jihad),[21] while the verse quoted by AQAP suggests that his poetry too remains in circulation. Some of al-Ṣanᶜānī's verses, including this one, were quoted by Ayman al-Ẓawāhirī in his 2008 book *al-Tabriᵓa* (Exoneration), which seeks to justify militant jihad:[22]

No one would dwell in enforced shame,
Except the two most contemptible things: the tribe's tent pole and tent peg.[23]

It is worth dwelling on this verse briefly as it exemplifies some of the insights into al-Qāᶜida's dynamics that the poetry makes possible. These insights are not presented as hard facts, but rather as reasoned conclusions suggested by the analysis. First, the poetry demonstrates the subtle way in which tribal grievances are grafted onto a jihadist agenda. The verse suggests that the jihadists are finding it difficult to embed within tribes. The reference to the tent pole and peg (symbols of structure and power) as contemptible is a metaphor for the contempt felt towards tribal sheikhs deemed to be in league with the regime of former President ᶜAlī ᶜAbd Allāh Ṣāliḥ. The shelter metaphor also hints that these tribal sheikhs are refusing to offer traditional hospitality to the jihadists. The broader article in which this classical verse is embedded goes on to make these points explicitly and addresses popular anger at corruption, asking 'How many people today have been wronged by tribal sheikhs?' The article then attaches an aura of historicity and legitimacy to this general complaint, complementing that created by the use of the classical poetic verse, by drawing a much-loved parallel between the hardships of today's jihadists and the hostility faced by the Prophet Muḥammad and his early followers. Second, the verse demonstrates that jihadist publications do have reach and are passed on. Al-Ẓawāhirī's book was almost certainly the inspiration behind this use of the poetry verse, since the AQAP verse blends elements from both of the two different renditions of the same verse quoted by al-Ẓawāhirī (although it is closer to al-Ṣanᶜānī than to the pre-Islamic al-Mutalammis). Third, it shows that the poetry embedded in jihadist publications does resonate and does spread the message of jihad orally. Had the AQAP author been copying from al-Ẓawāhirī's *written* publication, he would have cited one verse or the other, rather than remembering a mix of the two (to no artistic effect).

Selectively Reconstructing the Poetic Tradition

From the pre-Islamic examples mentioned above, it is reasonable to conclude that the content of the poetry takes precedence over notions of authorship and context. Al-Qāᶜida naturally chooses from the poetic heritage those verses that resonate with its own agenda; in other words, it is selectively reconstructing the poetic tradition by reproducing some verses of a poem whilst ignoring the others. For example, the unacknowledged verse from the Ode of Zuhayr cited above, which is deployed by the jihadists as a passionate call to war, is actually from a poem that carries an overwhelmingly anti-war message. The original poem refers to death as 'the blundering of a blind camel' and rails against the pointless ravages of war, referring to it in the same poem as 'a grindstone', 'a doubly-fertile begetter of evil progeny', 'an accursed thing', 'a blood-polluted water source' and a 'plague infested pasture'.

There is plenty of further evidence in the poetry at large to attest to the fact that the credibility of the source and context is less important than the nature of the message being pinpointed. For example, verses cited in praise of masculine virtues[24] were originally composed by the poet Ḥamza b. Bīḍ (d. 734), famous for blackmail, alcohol consumption and libertinism. Other poetic verses deployed to seal the idea of jihadists as *ghurabāʾ* (strangers or outsiders) – a semi-romantic notion that places their circumstances on a par with those of the earliest Muslims – can be traced to Abū Nuwās (d. 814), a poet famous for his love of wine, women and song.[25] A further example of the incongruous poetic choices made by jihadists is a verse again introduced to capture the image of the jihadists as courageous outsiders forced to renounce worldly pleasures.[26] The verse can be traced to Qaṭarī b. al-Fujāʾa (d. 698), a brutal leader of the uncompromisingly militant Kharijite sect that rebelled against the Umayyad caliphate in the mid-seventh century and declared all those who disagreed with their views to be apostates worthy of death. Although this might seem like an appropriate role model, in fact today's jihadists consider themselves mainstream and so vehemently reject the glaring parallels drawn between them and Kharijites. Unlike Osama bin Laden who cited the same verse in a 1993 speech and acknowledged Qaṭarī b. al-Fujāʾa as the poet,[27] the more recent jihadist usage does not acknowledge the source. Whether or not this omission is intentional, today's jihadists are at pains to renounce the label 'Kharijite' which is considered synonymous with 'terrorist'.[28] Thus the deployment of poetry by an infamous Kharijite leader to back up their cause is at odds with the image they seek to portray of themselves as the true Muslims rather than the deviants.

This strategy of selective reconstruction also happens with the more modern poetic heritage. For example, the classical style *qaṣīda* read on video by AQAP ideologue Khālid Bāṭarfī to lament the loss of their leader Nāṣir al-Wuḥayshī, killed by drone in 2015, was not attributed to any previous poet. Yet it is recognisable as *Aḥzān wa-Iṣrār* (Sorrows and persistence) by the famous Yemeni poet ʿAbd Allāh al-Baradūnī (1929–99), but from which AQAP has expurgated about half the verses. While al-Baradūnī and al-Qāʿida shared a vehement dislike of the Yemeni government, the poet was also an outspoken champion of democracy and women's rights, both anathema to al-Qāʿida. It might therefore seem counter-intuitive to find al-Baradūnī cited by those who ultimately seek caliphal rule and place strict limits on the behaviour, dress and movement of women.

It is therefore safe to conclude that the immediate cultural resonance of specific verses is far more important than their original authorship or context. For jihadists then, the meaning of a poetic work is not determined by the original author's intention but rather resides in the interpretation of the reader, listener and we might also add 'user' – referring to a jihadist author who recycles bygone poetic works. This provides an interesting practical illustration of the conclusions reached by cultural theorists over recent decades. Poststructuralist and postmodern approaches to the literary text have moved ever further away from the notion of a text/poem (written or spoken) containing a definitive meaning that the audience passively absorbs. These approaches demonstrate a more contingent understanding of the role of the audience in producing meaning as opposed to the author delivering meaning.[29] There is no one-directional transfer of knowledge and understanding from the poetic text/performance to the reader/listener. Our comprehension of the interactive process of interpretation is facilitated by thinking about it in terms of the concept of discourses (frameworks of knowledge).[30] It is in the creation of discourses that the power to guide interpretation lies. While the poetry itself can generate a discourse within it, the range of interpretations open to the audience shrinks drastically when that poetry is placed in the context of an overarching discourse. This is precisely what happens when jihadists lift poetry from the classical tradition and place it in a new context such as a speech, sermon or magazine article. The 'framing' discourse envelops the poetry and guides the interpretation of it, thereby reconstructing the classical poetic tradition to support the contemporary agenda of militant jihad.

Plagiarising the Poetic Tradition?

This brings us on to broader questions about authorship. Although the poetry lifted by jihadists is rarely attributed to its source poet, it would not be appropriate to condemn this as plagiarism in the sense that jihadists are trying to pass off the poetry as their own. There are three main reasons for this: cultural, practical and ideological. First, culturally, the notion of plagiarism versus originality from the perspective of the Arab poetic tradition is not as clear-cut as it tends to be in 'the West' today. Arab poets would take apprentice poets, who would learn their master's verses as well as composing their own. The objective was more to imitate and perfect rather than to break with tradition and create something totally original. Originality and novelty may be literary concepts that we in the West value, but these were not similarly conceptualised in the Arab classical poetic tradition. Genius was measured by the demonstration of dexterity in verbal acrobatics within the bounds of traditional frameworks and metres. Such creativity was held in higher esteem than straying from the revered *qaṣīda* structures themselves. In short, the idea was to improve the existing poetic recipe by juggling, improving and finessing the traditional ingredients rather than by concocting an entirely new dish.

Second, practically, oral transmission by its very nature blurs claims of authorship and can obscure original provenance. We have already seen how one verse went through several iterations that we even know about (from al-Mutalammis to al-Ṣanᶜānī to al-Ẓawāhirī to al-Hudaydī). Given that poetry continues to spread orally, particularly in desert environments such as al-Qāᶜida's strongholds in eastern Yemen, but also in urban environments and enhanced in recent decades through the circulation of audio cassettes, it is quite possible that original authorship would genuinely be forgotten or lost.

Third, ideologically, the idea that the poetry cited in support of a jihadist agenda is inherited from tradition rather than being solely a new invention provides a valuable supportive function. It constructs a powerful sense of historical continuity and inevitability. Hence, even where a poetic verse is not precisely sourced, it is frequently attributed to an 'assumed' ancestor by the use of vague phrases like 'as the poet said' or 'in the words of the poet'. Such phrases imply a general repository of cultural reference that the primary Arab audience shares with the writer/speaker, the precise details of which are less important than the simple fact of the existence of this mutual cultural history.

Yet there are instances when the classical tradition appears to be exploited in more manipulative ways. Existing verses can be subtly tweaked, such as when Bin Laden switched the phrase in one poem from the original 'striking their castles' to his own 'striking their towers', thus aligning the poem with contemporary events and suggesting a certain fatalism about the destruction of New York's Twin Towers in 2001.[31] Jihadists are also fond of grafting whole verses of their own onto older material in ways that they do not acknowledge transparently. The faint familiarity of the classical tradition will imbue the modern message with a certain legitimacy. An example of this is Bin Laden's 1996 speech in which he begins one poem with threats against the US Secretary of Defense William Perry, then follows up with verses highly reminiscent of the pre-Islamic tribal warrior poet ᶜAntara Ibn Shaddād, himself the subject of famous collections of heroic epic romance.[32]

This strategy of linking new with old is also practiced by al-Qāᶜida in the Arabian Peninsula. In an article entitled 'Seven years of crusades', AQAP's leader Nāṣir al-Wuḥayshī (d. 2015) positions the jihadist struggle as a new crusade being fought both militarily and in the media. One of the main points of the article, that 'the legitimate way to establish the caliphate, consolidate territory, topple the thrones of the tyrants and banish injustice is to fight', is sealed using two verses of poetry which sum up the would-be jihadist's choice:

> There are two strategies: either captivity and submission
> Or blood; and being killed a free man is worthier
>
> Will you answer to us or to them?
> Which of the two sides is following the right path?[33]

The verses are not attributed to any poet, but the first can be traced to the pre-Islamic poet Taᵓabbata Sharran.[34] The second verse appears to be a contemporary invention and can be traced to the Yemeni cleric ᶜAbd al-Majīd al-Raymī al-Hitārī (who it turns out was one of the clerics negotiating with the Yemeni government to halt US drone strikes against suspected al-Qāᶜida operatives 2013 – clearly he had influence with the group). This poetic grafting strategy has the effect of linking the classical heritage, and its encapsulation of the tribal honour code, to the modern dilemma of whether or not to give one's life to jihad. It is a culturally powerful way of justifying the act of joining al-Qāᶜida by equating it directly with the act of the traditional tribal warrior nobly resisting captivity.

In another article addressed to al-Shabaab jihadists in Somalia, AQAP leader Nāṣir al-Wuḥayshī praises al-Shabaab's refusal to negotiate and encourages acts of piracy: 'the sea is full of ships of the Zionist Crusader campaign'.[35] He upholds al-Shabaab as an inspirational model and paints a picture of Muslim youth everywhere rushing out to emulate them. This image climaxes in a short poem of which the first two verses appear to be original compositions by al-Wuḥayshī. They are cleverly sandwiched onto two further verses that can be traced to the Abbasid poet ᶜAlī b. Muḥammad, better known as Ṣāḥib al-Zanj, whose verses cement the image of a confident warrior, reliant only on his sword and answerable only to Allah. This is a significant choice in the Somali context, since Ṣāḥib al-Zanj is said to have been of African-Arab origin. He led the Zanj revolt, an African slave rebellion in ninth-century Iraq, setting up a state and refusing until death/martyrdom to compromise with the Abbasid caliph.[36] Whether conscious or not, this choice of poet and the narrative of oppression that it raises, hints at a postcolonial flavour to the struggle of Somali jihadists standing up to Zionist Crusader superpowers. This strategy of subtly coupling faintly familiar verses with new verses, producing what writer and critic Hélène Cixous might term a 'pirate reading' of the original (forgive the pun),[37] provides pseudo-authentic historical justification for contemporary acts.

Simulating the Poetic Tradition

Even modern poetry genuinely authored by contemporary jihadists is heavily styled on the classical poetic heritage.[38] This is most obvious in the poetic form and language – the use of the traditional *qaṣīda* with its two hemistiches and mono-rhyme, composed in the classical Arabic language. However, the content too of modern compositions draws on elements of the poetic tradition. The powerful natural imagery that has peppered desert poetry since pre-Islamic times is still a favourite with today's jihadists on the Arabian Peninsula. Other classical images in current use may appear anachronistic but are entirely in keeping with the construction of today's jihadist identity, which grafts modern realities onto the ancient apparatus of tribal warriors or medieval soldiers. For example, guns and bombs feature as swords; cars and motorbikes as steeds; firefights as epic battles; jihadists as knights or lions; and the image of a knight dismounting his steed creeps in as a heroic metaphor for suicide 'martyrdom'.

The contemporary poetry is also replete with hyperbole, a literary device that was common from the earliest days of Arabic poetry. The timeless archetype of the tribal warrior and his impossibly heroic deeds is ripe for application to any contemporary 'martyr'. While jihadist hyperbole might appear to us in translation as unrealistic exaggeration, it is in fact expected in the context of inherited poetic norms. Consider the following verses from a contemporary *qaṣīda* entitled *The Epic Battle of Tarim*:

Where is the like of knights like them
Who do not accept humiliation and deferral?

The battlefield has never witnessed an act such as theirs
A wounded lion plunged into the battle

A sun shining, and stars that are never extinguished
Faces glowing like a risen half moon

My story boasted of the heroic Ḥamza
Uḥud would weep out of grief and allegiance[39]

These verses are particularly revealing of the functions behind reinventing the classical heritage because the traditional hyperbole, familiar natural imagery and glorious historical parallels mask a radically different reality. These modern-day warriors, who are enshrined in poetry as eternal heroes and set on a par with famous Islamic conquerors of old, in fact refer to a group of young jihadists shot when police stormed their 'safe house' in Tarim after a tip off. The poetry can thus re-cast a miserable defeat, such as detection and extermination or a drone strike, as a glorious epic battle.

Modern parallels with discreet segments of the pre-Islamic ode can also be identified. Typically, the classical ode would open with a section known as the *nasīb* (amatory prelude) in which the hero would cry over the traces of a desert encampment (*al-bukāʾ ʿalā al-aṭlāl*). Contemporary jihadist poets reinterpret this convention by crying over the bombed-out ruins and dead children of Palestine, Iraq and, more recently, Syria and Yemen, or by remembering bygone camaraderie with martyred 'brothers'. The pre-Islamic ode would then frequently move to the *raḥīl* (journeying) section, featuring the poet travelling in the desert. This familiar pre-Islamic theme is co-opted by today's jihadist poets into an Islamic framework to reflect the concept of *hijra* (flight) as practiced by Muḥammad when he and his early followers fled Mecca for Medina to avoid persecution and ensure the group's survival. The *raḥīl* can also be reconstructed as the journey away from the secular world towards eventual paradise through martyrdom. The following verses demonstrate both the poet's desire to separate himself from the secular world and his outrage as he laments the tragedy of fellow Muslims:

> Their [false clerics] stomachs complain of indigestion
> While children starve to death in Iraq
>
> And Chechen children freeze to death
> And people are throttled to death in Afghanistan
>
> And children in Jerusalem have had their food destroyed
> Hurling solid rocks is what they taste
>
> No! I swear by He who has accorded levels of reward for (different) deaths
> I will sell my soul to the tumult competitively
>
> The rhythms of jihad beat at my bonds
> The glinting sword will take charge of every meeting[40]

Although these verses are newly composed, the contemporary events to which they refer are lent gravitas by being imbued with the reinvented themes, metres, rhymes, form and language of the classical poetic tradition.

Claiming Authority

We now finish with a further look at the question of why al-Qāᶜida makes such liberal use of poetic tradition alongside religious and military material. The need to situate today's militant jihadist agenda inside a legitimate tradition and to bestow on it the authenticity that comes from deep cultural roots within a shared history has already been explored above. A key factor in this is the imperative of winning cultural credibility or what French sociologist Pierre Bourdieu would refer to as 'cultural capital'.[41] Like economic capital, cultural capital is a resource to be exploited in pursuit of power. This desire to amass cultural capital may well have been the motivation behind Osama bin Laden's own extensive use of poetry from the classical heritage, alongside some of his own, given that he lacked sufficient training for formal consideration as a religious authority. Bin Laden's almost ostentatious flaunting of his knowledge of the poetic heritage suggests his desire not only to move audiences but also to impress them, thereby helping to compensate for and distract attention from his lack of credentials as a religious scholar.

Poetry in Arab culture is inextricably entwined with the concept of authority. Max Weber's analysis of authority in social theory identifies three ideal types of authority: legal-rational, traditional and charismatic.[42] By charismatic authority, Weber means that a leader's credibility rests on his teaching, example, piety or heroism. The power of Arabic poetry lies in its capacity to impart authority that immediately covers two of these three ideal types, the traditional and the charismatic, thereby helping to compensate for any lack of the third type, legal-rational authority. This idea that poetry as cultural capital assisted Bin Laden's quest for power and claims to authority is borne out by Flagg Miller's research into Bin Laden's audio cassette collection. Bin Laden, who would ask visitors to bring him books on Arabic poetry, made intelligent use of what Miller aptly refers to as 'the ennobling mantle of poetry'.[43] This implies that Bin Laden, as well as likely nurturing a genuine love of poetry, also recognised its emotive power and was ambitious to make the most of this psychological weapon to bolster support for al-Qā^{c}ida's agenda.

The use of poetry might also be seen as symptomatic of a growing shift away from traditional religious authority in jihadist movements. This shift has been accelerated by modern technology that gives many more Muslims access to both primary and alternative sources of religious 'knowledge'. AQAP articulates this shift in an article entitled 'The martyrdom *^{c}ulamā$^{\supset}$*', which stresses that al-Qā^{c}ida's religious scholars draw their fatwas directly from Allah, not from the formal religious authorities. That this is part of AQAP's propaganda to counter formal religious rulings declaring suicide operations un-Islamic is clear in the rhetorical lament, 'If you could but see, O adventurous martyr, what condemnation, criticism and lament the newspapers of the secular press have scribbled using the pens of the Islamists.'[44] The jihadist article produces some 'thin' doctrinal points to counter the religious authorities, but the case is made more powerfully in the same issue of their magazine through poetry. Consider these (non-consecutive) verses:[45]

> We are the men of al-Qā^{c}ida, we are the Partisans
> We are your troops, O Osama bin Laden
>
> We hear and obey your order, come what may
> For you we sacrifice those who are lofty and exalted
>
> The Crusaders and those who are allied with them are infidels
> [Even] if he be a sheikh wearing his turban

The model is Muḥammad who lived in the darkness of a cave
And declared his jihad the day they rejected his words

The might of the umma lies in a blend of blood and dust
At Badr and al-Yarmūk and the Battle of al-Yamāma

These verses, written in the style of the classical *qaṣīda*, telescope complex doctrinal arguments into a simple matter of ignoring the formal religious authorities and claiming authority from the historical past as constructed through poetry. The effect of the poetry is to put today's jihad on a par with Islam's earliest battles, to justify suicide operations as sacrifice for the umma and to set up the Prophet Muḥammad as the prototype jihadist.

Here, the poetry offers an experience akin to what cultural theorist Julia Kristeva termed 'transgressive performance', inasmuch as it challenges legal and religious authority by portraying an alternative set of values. While Kristeva, building on the work of Mikhail Bakhtin, uses the concept of transgression to explain changed group behaviour at carnivals, the same notion might be applied to the jihadist group's attitude towards suicide bombing. This and other jihadist behaviour might equally be perceived as a transgression of logical and social codes, similarly assisted by emotive ritual and symbolism, which is performed here by the poetry.[46] In other words, poetry offers a strategy through which the illogical and illegitimate behaviour of the group (here, the group of jihadists engaging in destruction of the self to murder others) can be made to seem logical and legitimate.

Conclusion

Why do jihadists make such broad use of the classical poetic tradition? Building cultural legitimacy is essential to any jihadist propaganda project, whether it be to garner support for a resistance movement or a full-blown state-building exercise. In the battle for cultural identity, reclaiming the poetic tradition is key since its roots and resonance run so deep in Arab culture. The poetic tradition is appropriated in two ways: by reconfiguring existing poetic verses in new contexts and by injecting traditional poetic themes, forms and techniques with modern jihadist content inside new compositions. Both methods have the same effect of making the jihadist message seem a part of the authentic mainstream culture rather than a subculture or counterculture. Jihadist reclamation of the quintessentially Arab *qaṣīda* tradition also sends a strong message of differentiation from newer Arabic poetic forms that developed following contact with and influence from Western literature. At the same time, the use of the classical Arabic language, as opposed to vernaculars, erases borders both geographically and historically, thereby playing to the end goal of all jihadist movements ultimately: a global caliphate.

As we have seen from our investigation into the AQAP 'data set', jihadist poetry is almost exclusively composed in classical Arabic, and nine out of every ten instances of poetry adhere to the fundamentals of the classical *qaṣīda* model. This is not just a matter of new poetry being made to look and sound 'old' or authentic. Much of the poetry used is genuinely old and authentic. Although jihadists do not generally acknowledge sources, over half of all the poetry cited can in fact be traced back to the pre-1900 poetic heritage, with the overwhelming majority composed before the end of the Abbasid era in the mid-thirteenth century.

It is probably an exaggeration to imagine that readers/listeners would consciously recognise or be able to identify the classical *qaṣīda*s of past poets deployed in jihadist magazine articles or speeches, or even understand every word. However, the poetry might be said to operate on what one might call the 'inside' of cultural sensibilities. The Lebanese-American historian, Philip Hitti, sums it up thus:

> Modern audiences in Baghdād, Damascus and Cairo can be stirred to the highest degree by the recital of poems, only vaguely comprehended, and by the delivery of orations in the classical tongue, though it be only partially understood. The rhythm, the rhyme, the music, produce on them the effect of what they call 'lawful magic' (*siḥr ḥalāl*).[47]

The classical poetic tradition thus has the capacity to convey a message that resonates at different levels simultaneously. The centuries-old *qaṣīda* model, with its jaunty rhythms, echoing rhymes and redolent classical language, speaks to listeners/readers at a subconscious level – what cultural theorists call 'deep structure'. At the same time, the adept choice of verses featuring cultural markers (swords, horses, lions, gardens) and an easily comprehensible core theme (the binary opposition of good and evil) are recognised at a conscious level – what cultural theorists call 'surface structure'. Classical poetry therefore deftly skips the step of logical argument to convey succinctly and powerfully a sense of legitimacy, authenticity and historical precedent to modern jihadist messages and deeds.

This chapter has demonstrated how verses of poetry are comfortably inserted into articles, speeches and sermons to support arguments alongside citations of sacred texts from the hadith or indeed from the Qurʾan itself. This indicates the revered cultural status of poetry and its 'pulling power' among target Arab audiences. It can also be viewed as one of the many symptoms of the growing shift away from formal religious authority among jihadist movements. The poetry, as 'cultural capital', can be wielded as an alternative source of authority that is at once traditional and charismatic and thus helps to deflect attention away from any lack of formal religious-legal credentials. Osama bin Laden's enthusiasm for peppering his speeches with poetry might perhaps be seen in this light.

However, it is fascinating to discover that the authorities from which this poetic propaganda derives can be starkly at odds with the militant jihadists' religious ideology. Of particular note are the numerous poetic verses that can be traced back to pre-Islamic times, a period known as 'the age of ignorance'. It is ironic that non-Islamic material should be used to support radical Islamist views. This suggests that today's jihadists, particularly on the Arabian Peninsula, are motivated by indigenous tribal values and not solely focused on global Islamic values. Moreover, as has been shown above, the inclusion of verses by poets who were famously libertarian, or members of the Kharijite sect vehemently rejected by jihadists or, more recently, champions of democracy and women's rights, uncovers the expedient way in which jihadists exploit the poetic tradition for immediate propaganda gains using highly selective verses isolated from their original contexts. This idea of exploitation does not preclude the possibility that in all likelihood jihadists genuinely relate to the poetic material; after all, it is part of their heritage and runs in their veins. However, it nevertheless demonstrates that the shared cultural heritage is considered a powerful propaganda resource that can be tapped into and reconstructed in controlled contexts to generate favourable new meanings that support the jihad. This implies that local cultural material and practices play a more important and influential role in attracting primary Arab audiences to jihadist ideology than has been acknowledged.

Thus the selective redeployment of the classical poetic heritage has the effect of evoking deep cultural ties, provoking passions, clinching arguments, papering over gaps in logic, celebrating death, glorifying battle, constructing a jihadist identity, simplifying complex realities and manipulating the collective memory – all within the space of a few well-chosen verses. This is both more efficient and more effective than the kinds of discursive treatises and speeches on which Western analysts tend to focus. The ninth century Abbasid poet, Abū Tammām, whose verses feature prolifically in jihadist output, summed up the power of poetry thus: 'poetry is a glance, a glimpse of which suffices; not a sprawling long speech'. In other words, the poetic tradition offers jihadist propagandists a short-cut. It does not need to win over minds by spelling things out doctrinally. It simply needs to enable the primary Arab audience to make connections based on entrenched cultural sensibility and knowledge. This appeals to hearts, and hearts in turn win minds.

Notes

1. Thomas Hegghammer, 'Why terrorists weep: the socio-cultural practices of jihadi militants', Paul Wilkinson Memorial Lecture, University of St Andrews,

16 April 2015, 7. Hegghammer is also busy answering his own question and broader questions about the role of culture in militant jihad. See Thomas Hegghammer (ed.), *Jihadi Culture* (Cambridge and New York: Cambridge University Press, 2016).

2. Jihad essentially means 'struggle' and there are numerous different forms that this struggle 'in the path of God' can take. In fact, the 'greater jihad' is considered to be the internal struggle against sin and temptation, whereas the notion of militant 'holy war' is considered the 'lesser jihad'. In this chapter, I am referring specifically to militant jihad.
3. See Elisabeth Kendall, 'Yemen's al-Qāᵓida and poetry as a weapon of jihad', in Elisabeth Kendall and Ewan Stein (eds), *Twenty-First Century Jihad: Law, Society and Military Action* (London and New York: I. B. Tauris, 2015), 247–69.
4. Flagg Miller, *The Audacious Ascetic: What the Bin Laden Tapes Reveal About al-Qāᵓida* (London: Hurst, 2015), 252.
5. See in particular Suzanne Pinckney Stetkevych, *Poetics of Islamic Legitimacy: Myth, Gender, and Ceremony in the Classical Arabic Ode* (Bloomington: Indiana University Press, 2002) which analyses the many roles of the panegyric ode from pre-Islamic times to the end of the Arabic poetic 'golden age' in the tenth century.
6. See, for example, Richard A. Gabriel, *Muhammad: Islam's First Great General* (Norman: University of Oklahoma Press, 2011), 65.
7. Ibn Kathir, *Mawlid*, 30, http://sunnah.org/publication/mawlid.htm. See also J. C. Bürgel, 'Qaṣīda as discourse on power and its Islamization: some reflections', in Stefan Sperl and Christopher Shackle (eds), *Qaṣīda Poetry in Islamic Asia and Africa: Classical Traditions and Modern Meanings* (Leiden: Brill, 1996), 1: 451–74 (452–4).
8. Carole Hillenbrand, 'Jihad poetry in the age of the Crusades', in Thomas F. Madden, James L. Naus and Vincent Ryan (eds), *Crusades – Medieval Worlds in Conflict* (Aldershot: Ashgate, 2010), 9–24. See also Hadia Dajani-Shakeel, 'Jihad in twelfth-century Arabic poetry: a moral and religious force to counter the Crusades', *Muslim World* 66 (1976), 96–113.
9. Benedict Anderson, *Imagined Communities: Reflections on the Origin and Spread of Nationalism* (London and New York: Verso, 1983), 43–6 and ch. 5.
10. Jean-François Lyotard, *The Postmodern Condition: A Report on Knowledge*, trans. Geoff Bennington and Brian Massumi (Manchester: Manchester University Press, [1979] 1984), xxiv.
11. ᶜAbd al-ᶜAzīz al-Ṣuhaybī, 'Matā Tataḥarrakūna?' (When will you strike out?), *Ṣadā al-Malāḥim* 16 (January 2011), 22–3.
12. Laurent Bonnefoy, 'Jihadi violence in Yemen', in Jeevan Deol and Zaheer Kazmi (eds), *Contextualising Jihadi Thought* (London: Hurst, 2012), 243–58 (244–5). See also Laurent Bonnefoy, 'Violence in Contemporary Yemen: state, society and Salafis', *The Muslim World* 101 (April 2011), 324–46 (333–5).
13. Abū al-Zubayr al-ᶜUbāb, 'Duᶜā al-Inhizāmiyya wa-l-Ikhtilāṭ' (The propagandists of defeatism and confusion), *Ṣadā al-Malāḥim* 14 (June/July 2010), 14–17.

14. Translation taken from Alan Jones, *Early Arabic Poetry, Vol. 1: Marāthī and Ṣuᶜlūk Poems* (Oxford: Ithaca, 1992), 190–1.
15. See, for example, an image of an original Islamic State directive for women posted by Aymenn Jawad al-Tamimi, 'Specimen M: On women's travel and dress, Raqqa Province', http://www.aymennjawad.org/17757/the-archivist-26-unseen-islamic-state.
16. This is a verse by Khawla bint Thaᶜlaba in the 'Ḥafīdāt Umm ᶜAmmāra' section, *Ṣadā al-Malāḥim* 1 (January 2008), 18.
17. Robyn Creswell and Bernard Haykel, 'Battle lines', *The New Yorker*, 8 June 2015, http://www.newyorker.com/magazine/2015/06/08/battle-lines-jihad-creswell-and-haykel.
18. Umm ᶜAmmāra (also ᶜUmmara), born as Nusayba bint Kaᶜb, was one of the great warrior women of early Islam. Accounts relate that when she brought water to the Muslim men fighting in the Battle of Uḥud in 625 and saw some of them fleeing the battlefield, she took up arms herself and fought alongside the Prophet.
19. The various and evolving roles of women in militant jihad as conceived in the contemporary Arabic language sources produced by jihadist groups is the subject of a forthcoming article by Elisabeth Kendall and Karen Bauer.
20. Entry for 'Yemen', *The Princeton Encyclopedia of Islamic Political Thought* (Princeton: Princeton University Press, 2012), 600. See also Roel Meijer, *Global Salafism: Islam's New Religious Movement* (London: Hurst, 2009), 429–31.
21. Muhammad Qasim Zaman, *Modern Islamic Thought in a Radical Age: Religious Authority and Internal Criticism* (New York: Cambridge University Press, 2012), 266.
22. Ayman al-Ẓawāhirī, *al-Tabriʾa* (al-Saḥāb Media Organisation, 2008), 122.
23. Abū Hāshim al-Ḥudaydī, 'Ilay-ka Ayyu-hā al-Anṣārī' (To You, O Helper), *Ṣadā al-Malāḥim* 10 (July 2009), 21.
24. Muḥammad al-Murshidī, 'Yaqūlūna "inna-hum Fityā"' (They say 'they are youngsters'), *Ṣadā al-Malāḥim* 14 (June/July 2010), 11–13 (13).
25. 'Muqtaṭafat', *Ṣadā al-Malāḥim* 8 (March 2009), 41.
26. Al-Jahjāh, 'Ghurabāʾ' (Strangers/Outsiders), *Ṣadā al-Malāḥim* 6 (November 2008), 32–3 (32).
27. See Miller, *The Audacious Ascetic*, 186.
28. See, for example, Abū Hurayra al-Ṣanᶜānī, 'Sarādīb Ahl al-Sunna' (The vaults of the Sunnis), *Ṣadā al-Malāḥim* 2 (March 2008), 13–15 (13); also see line 17 of the original contemporary poem 'Qiṣṣat Mujāhid' (A jihadist's story) by Abū al-Barāʾ al-Awlaqī, *Ṣadā al-Malāḥim* 14 (June/July 2010), 66–7.
29. Perhaps the most famous early exponent of such ideas was Roland Barthes in his influential 1968 essay 'La Mort de l'Auteur' (The death of the author). Available in English in Roland Barthes, *Image, Music Text* (London: Fontana Press, 1977), 142–8.
30. Jacques Derrida, *Writing and Difference* (London: Routledge and Kegan Paul,

[1967] 1978); Michel Foucault, *Power/Knowledge: Selected Interviews and Other Writings, 1972–1977* (Brighton: Harvester, 1980).

31. This poem is from a statement released by Osama bin Laden on 26 December 2001. The verses were originally composed in a classical *qaṣīda* style by contemporary Jordanian poet and Muslim Brotherhood member, Yusuf Abū Hilāla (b. 1948). See Bruce Lawrence (ed.), *Messages to the World: The Statements of Osama bin Laden* (London and New York: Verso, 2005), 155–6.
32. See Miller, *The Audacious Ascetic*, 239, 255.
33. Al-Amīr Abī Baṣīr [Nāṣir al-Wuḥayshī], 'Sab^c Sanawāt ^calā al-Ḥurūb al-Ṣalībiyya' (Seven years of crusades), *Ṣadā al-Malāḥim* 7 (January 2009), 5–6 (6). The first verse by Ta^ɔabbata Sharran also appears in *Ṣadā al-Malāḥim* 2 (March 2008), 21, in the context of anger against corrupt and self-interested sheikhs. This is a clear indication of how corruption and disempowerment breed militant jihadism.
34. These verses are attributed to Ta^ɔabbata Sharran in al-Qāḍi al-Jurjānī, *al-Wasāṭa bayna al-Mutanabbī wa-khuṣūmi-hi* (Cairo: Dār Iḥyā^ɔ al-Kutub al-^cArabiyya, 1951), 90, available at: http://islamport.com/d/3/adb/1/137/767.html.
35. Abū Baṣīr [Nāṣir al-Wuḥayshī], 'Ilā Ahl al-Tamkīn fi al-Ṣūmāl' (To the mediators of true faith in Somalia), *Ṣadā al-Malāḥim* 8 (March 2009), 46–7.
36. For a full account of this remarkable rebellion, see Alexandre Popovic, *Revolt of African Slaves in Iraq in the Third/Ninth Century* (Princeton: Markus Wiener Publishers, 1999).
37. Hélène Cixous, *So Close*, trans. Peggy Kamuf (Cambridge: Polity, 2009; original edn 2007), 66.
38. The popular genre of the jihadist song or anthem (*nashīd*) also bears parallels with the traditional *qaṣīda*. See Behnam Said, 'Hymns (*nasheeds*): a contribution to the study of the jihadist culture', *Studies in Conflict & Terrorism*, 35:12 (2012), 863–79 (865).
39. Abū Dujāna al-Jadāwī, 'Malḥamat Tarim' (first poem), *Ṣadā al-Malāḥim* 10 (June 2009), 45–6 (45).
40. Abū Dujāna al-Jadāwī, 'Malḥamat Tarim' (second poem), *Ṣadā al-Malāḥim* 10 (June 2009), 45–6 (46).
41. Pierre Bourdieu, *The Field of Cultural Production* (Cambridge: Polity, 1993), 29–55.
42. Max Weber, *Economy and Society: An Outline of Interpretative Sociology* (Berkeley: University of California Press, 1978), 215.
43. Miller, *The Audacious Ascetic*, 253. We also know from one of Bin Laden's neighbours that he encouraged his children to read, memorise and write poetry. Michael Scheuer, *Osama bin Laden* (New York: Oxford University Press, 2011), 107.
44. 'al-^cUlamā^ɔ al-Istishhādiyyūn', *Ṣadā al-Malāḥim* 6 (November 2008), 36–7 (37). This was published a few weeks after an AQAP bomb attack on the US Embassy in Sana'a that killed twelve innocents in addition to six jihadists.

45. Abū Hājir al-Māʾribī, 'Ḥannā Junūdu-ka Yā Usāma' (We are your troops, O Osama), *Ṣadā al-Malāḥim* 6 (November 2008), 30.
46. Julia Kristeva, *The Kristeva Reader*, ed. Toril Moi (Oxford: Blackwell, 1986), 36, 41. For a full discussion of the concept of transgression, see Peter Stallybrass and Allon White, *The Politics and Poetics of Transgression* (New York: Cornell University Press, 1986).
47. Philip K. Hitti, *History of the Arabs: From the Earliest Times to the Present* (New York: Palgrave Macmillan [1937] 2002), 90.

10

Contemporary Salafi Literature on Paradise and Hell: The Case of ᶜUmar Sulaymān al-Ashqar

Christian Lange

The Palestinian ᶜUmar Sulaymān al-Ashqar (d. 2012) counts among the most prolific neo-Salafi figures writing around the turn of the century. After studying in Medina with ᶜAbd al-ᶜAzīz Ibn Bāz (d. 1999) and Muḥammad Nāṣir al-Dīn al-Albānī (d. 1999) he was, for several decades, professor of law in Kuwait and at the Faculty of Shariᶜa at Amman University. He is also one of the salient contributors to the contemporary Sunni literature on paradise and hell: he authored 'Endtime' (*al-Yawm al-ākhir*), a compilation of eschatological hadiths accompanied by occasional commentary. 'Endtime' was published in 1986 when al-Ashqar was a professor of Shariᶜa law at the University of Kuwait, a position he held until 1990. The work is a trilogy, divided into sections on the life in the grave (*al-qiyāma al-ṣughrā*), resurrection (*al-qiyāma al-kubrā*), and paradise and hell (*al-janna wa-l-nār*). It has seen several reprints, a fact that testifies to its impact on a broad contemporary readership in the Islamic world. The final third of the trilogy, which will be at the centre of attention in the following pages, was translated into both English and French and published by the Riyadh-based International Islamic Publishing House in 1999 and 2007, respectively.

Eschatology, the Imagination and Islamic Modernity

The existential relevance of works describing paradise and hell, whether in Islam or in other religious traditions, may not strike modern readers as immediately evident. By contrast, in premodern Islam, a broad consensus existed that paradise and hell were ultimately meaningful. The premodern creeds do not tire of asserting, time and again, that paradise and hell are 'real' (*ḥaqq*).[1] This sufficiently explains their broader significance as objects of historical inquiry. But why study the contemporary Muslim literature on paradise and hell? Jihadists, as tends to be emphasised in Western media,[2] might feel inspired by the promise of an immediately accessed paradise, full of sensual delights; but has the educated public in the Islamic world not moved on long ago?

To begin with, an obvious reason to study the Muslim literature on paradise and hell, and not just the contemporary one, is quite simply that it is an understudied field. One suspects the genre has not attracted much attention in Western Islamic studies because it is, particularly in the case of traditionist (that is, hadith-based) works, so plainly the product of the imagination. The imagination is a faculty of the human mind with a checkered trajectory in Western intellectual history, one that was often met with suspicion, or even derision. Thomas Hobbes, for example, considered the imagination to 'decay sense'.[3] Indeed, what one finds in traditional Islamic eschatology often appears to amount to a rather wild hodgepodge of the fantastic. Arguably, however, it is precisely its imaginative, fantastic quality that gives this literature its relevance and provides it with persuasive power. Here is not the place to show this in detail;[4] instead, an example must suffice. The paradise section contained in Ibn Qayyim al-Jawziyya's (d. 1350) long didactic poem, *al-Kāfiya al-shāfiya*, includes several pages that are dedicated to a description of the virgins of paradise, the houris.[5] 'The gaze drinks from the goblets of her beauty,' Ibn Qayyim al-Jawziyya praises one of the houris, 'you'd think you're drunk when beholding her. / Her features are perfect, her beauty is complete, / shining like the full moon on the fourteenth night.'[6] One easily pictures how the public recitation of the poem in Damascus inflamed the passions of Ibn Qayyim al-Jawziyya's traditionist followers, whom he urges, at the end of his poem, to go out and fight, even kill, their theological opponents, the Ashᶜarites.[7]

In neo-Salafi circles, Ibn Qayyim al-Jawziyya is lifted to an exemplary, iconic level. However, in respect to the passage just discussed, he is arguably an extreme case. One might observe that, on a level less charged with sensual arousal and violence, the Muslim literature on paradise and hell serves to inculcate a catechism of virtues and sins by offering vivid images of the rewards of the good and the punishments of the bad. In the compilation of hadiths about the afterlife of the Egyptian polymath al-Suyūṭī (d. 1505), this characteristic of the Islamic afterlife literature finds perhaps its clearest expression. Interspersed among the more descriptive parts, al-Suyūṭī includes information on what kind of actions (*aᶜmāl*) on earth will be punished in a certain way in hell or rewarded in paradise. For example, al-Suyūṭī relates that one of the punishments in hell consists in being dragged over the ground on the face. This, one learns as one reads on, is the punishment for those seeking martyrdom merely in order to achieve fame, for vainglorious scholars and Qurʾan readers, and for rich people who show off their generosity.[8] Likewise, following the chapters on the rejuvenated wives and the houris in paradise, readers are told in a number of hadiths that these heavenly companions are reserved for those who control their earthly angers and desires, pardon their murderers, clean mosques, fast in the month of Ramadan, perform the duty to command right and forbid wrong, pronounce supererogatory pious formulas, and in general show complete obedience to God.[9] Al-Suyūṭī's work, in other words, serves as an ethical handbook, that is, a practical guide to paradise and hell.

A third reason to study the Muslim literature on paradise and hell, particularly the contemporary one, is the issue of how the imagination that is at work in this literature relates to normative understandings of modernity. In my view, in the scholarly literature on Islam, anthropologists have articulated this point most successfully. Charles Hirschkind for example, who has studied popular Islamic media and cassette sermons in Egypt (2006), points out how uncomfortable Muslim modernists are with the traditional Muslim discourse on paradise and hell. He writes:

> Many contemporary Egyptians are … critical of the emphasis on death and the afterlife within the rhetorics of the [Islamic Revival, the] *daʿwa* movement. In their view, the plethora of sermons and books on the tortures of hell and the horrors of the grave stimulates a morbid fascination among the popular classes that distracts them from the serious issues that they, as national citizens, must confront. This unhealthy obsession, I was often told, undermines the positive orientation toward life necessary for everything from social progress to a respect for human rights.[10]

The recent study of Amira Mittermaier about dreaming and dream interpretation, again set in contemporary Egypt (2011), makes a fascinating contribution to this conversation, given that many of the dreams Mittermaier discusses are in fact dreams about the afterlife, that is, dreams that connect the dreamer with the otherworld and as such are dismissed by Muslim modernists. Mittermaier writes that the

> devaluation of the dream can be understood within a larger context of (post)colonialism and modernization … Reformist thinkers called for a this-worldly ethics by bracketing the metaphysical realm, the *barzakh*, and the afterlife, and by urging believers to focus on socio-moral reform of society instead.[11]

The modernist quest to facilitate a 'positive orientation toward life' by 'bracketing the metaphysical realm' is also foregrounded in Jane Idleman Smith's and Yvonne Yazbeck Haddad's classic study of Islamic eschatology (1981). Smith and Haddad survey a range of modern thinkers whose aim it is 'to reinstate what they understand to be the true Islamic emphasis on the importance of *al-dunyā* as well as *al-ākhira* … stressing in particular the work ethic that will help achieve material technological parity with the West.'[12] One might also think in this context of Mohammed Arkoun's (d. 2010) criticism of al-Ghazālī's (d. 1111) allegorical interpretation of the pilgrimage to Mecca as a journey toward the afterlife.[13] In Arkoun's view, the kind of attitude al-Ghazālī promotes is a *maladie à la mort*, to be rejected because it stresses death rather than affirming human creativity, freedom and life.[14]

Al-Ashqar, the End of Time and *Ambiguitätsintoleranz*

Why, however, should we turn to al-Ashqar to study contemporary Islamic eschatology? Al-Ashqar's book on paradise and hell is situated in the context of the efforts of Islamic modernism and Islamic revival movements to come to terms with and, sometimes, to oppose a (Western-style) modernity. How does 'Endtime' fit into this context, and what is its author's precise location in this ongoing negotiation?

Al-Ashqar was born in 1940 in the village of Burqa some 20 kilometres from Nāblus in northern Palestine. This is a region known for issuing a stream of Ḥanbalī scholars from as early as the sixth/twelfth century onwards, several of them achieving a certain fame in the eighteenth and nineteenth centuries.[15] The al-Ashqar family produced a number of scholars and publishers who rose to prominence in Kuwait and later, in Jordan, around the turn of the millennium. His elder brother Muḥammad Sulaymān (d. 2009), whom al-Ashqar considered one of his foremost teachers, was the general editor of the massive *al-Mawsū*ᶜ*a al-fiqhiyya*, published by the Ministry of Pious Foundations and Religious Affairs in Kuwait. In Jordan, al-Ashqar is commonly counted among the most important thinkers of the Muslim Brotherhood in the country.

Al-Ashqar's life, his trajectory from Palestine to Saudi Arabia, Kuwait and Jordan, is dotted with interesting anecdotes, as one realises when one delves into his autobiography, 'Pages from my life' (*Ṣafaḥāt min ḥayātī*). This is an entertaining read. One learns, for example, that al-Albānī, one of al-Ashqar's revered teachers, used to ride a motorcycle around Damascus, 'fearlessly but without haste' as al-Ashqar notes; that al-Ashqar was invited on occasion to ride pillion; and that both would then travel down al-Ḥāmidiyya street in Old Damascus.[16] Al-Ashqar also writes about the reasons for his expulsion from Saudi Arabia in the early sixties. Ibn Bāz, his teacher at the time, once went into the Medina market to reprimand merchants for displaying or possibly selling lewd pictures of women. A discussion in the study circles of the Medina mosque ensued as to whether the Islamic duty of 'commanding right and forbidding wrong' (*al-amr bi-l-ma*ᶜ*rūf wa-l-nahy* ᶜ*an al-munkar*) should be carried out by the tongue (*bi-l-lisān*) or by the hand (*bi-l-yad*). Al-Ashqar relates in his memoir that he took the view that one must only use the tongue and refrain from physical coercion. (This was in accordance with the Saudi state's twentieth-century officialisation of the office of *ḥisba*, which limited the authority to perform *al-amr bi-l-maʿrūf* to so-called 'Committees for Commanding Right and Forbidding Wrong';[17] it also corresponds to the moderately quietist views for which al-Ashqar was known in Jordan in later times.) However, following violent clashes between pious activists and the merchants of the Medina market, al-Ashqar was apprehended as one of the agitators, suspected of membership of Ḥizb al-Taḥrīr, put in prison for several months, and then expelled from the country.[18] In his later life in Jordan, al-Ashqar was among those Muslim Brothers who recommended peaceful collaboration with the Jordanian parliament, while others took the position that the government should be boycotted on all levels.

After departing from Saudi Arabia, al-Ashqar worked for many years at the Ministry of Education in Kuwait, in between earning a doctorate from al-Azhar University in Cairo,[19] but he was forced to leave the country after the 1990 invasion by Saddam Hussein's forces. Following this, he became a professor at the Faculty of Shariʿa at the University of Jordan in Amman in 1996, but was dismissed in 2002 by order of the Ministry. In 'Pages from my life', he states that he was quite happy to be out of work, because this gave him the time to research and write;[20] and publish he did, producing an enormous output. His autobiography lists over forty monographs and scores of articles. Among his publications is a series of eight monographs on the Islamic tenets of faiths 'in the light of the Qurʾan and the Sunna' (*Silsilat al-ʿaqīda fī ḍawʾ al-kitāb wa-l-sunna*). 'Endtime' corresponds to volumes five to seven of this series. In 1986, when the series was published, the first print-run of 5,000 copies was sold out within a couple of months, so that a second print-run of 10,000 was issued. In 1998, a Saudi-based publisher, al-Dār al-ʿĀlamiyya li-l-Kitāb al-Islāmī, agreed with al-Ashqar that the eight volumes of the series would be translated into an astonishing twenty-five languages.[21] The English translation of 'Endtime', first published in 1999, went into its fourth edition in 2003. It is difficult to know what to make of these numbers (a great number of print-runs and translations is not always proof of a large readership), but they do seem to indicate that the series has been successful and is probably al-Ashqar's most widely-read publication.

Turning to the content of 'Endtime', two questions are central. First, what propelled al-Ashqar to write this work? Indeed, why compile another collection of eschatological hadiths if plenty of traditionist handbooks on paradise and hell are available on the Arabic book market? The eschatological genre appears to be a particularly good illustration of the observation made by Kevin Reinhart that '[e]verywhere in the Islamic world, Arabic books are for sale, and these books are overwhelmingly medieval'.[22] The two most widely circulating works in the genre of traditionist eschatology, both in late-medieval and in modern times, are probably 'The memoir about the conditions of the dead' (*al-Tadhkira fī aḥwāl al-mawtā*) of al-Qurṭubī (Spain/Egypt, d. 1273) and the anonymous 'Subtle traditions' (*Daqāʾiq al-akhbār*), widely available in the Islamic world through a 1960 edition made in Cairo, with many reprints.[23] Less easily available, but presumably of greater interest to Salafi audiences, is the last volume of Ibn Kathīr's (d. 1373) universal history 'The beginning and the end' (*al-Bidāya wa-l-nihāya*), known as 'The end of the beginning' (*Nihāyat al-bidāya*) and published in separate editions. One should also mention Ibn Qayyim al-Jawziyya's 'Urging souls forward toward the lands of rejoicing' (*Ḥādī al-arwāḥ ilā bilād al-afrāḥ*), intellectually the most substantial and challenging of all. A second central question results from this list, and here this chapter connects to the broader theme of this volume: in what ways does 'Endtime' continue, reflect or subvert earlier, classical literature on paradise and hell? The two questions, as will become clear, have a lot to do with each other.

It is useful to look first at what al-Ashqar says himself about the motivations for writing his work. Again, we glean some clues from his autobiography, particularly from a passage in which al-Ashqar talks about the entire series on the Muslim creed, the *Silsilat al-ᶜaqīda*. He states that from the time he began his studies he read a lot of books on the Muslim creed (*ᶜaqīda*), more than the curriculum required of him, but that he could never fully warm to the subject. Then, he says, he came upon an important insight in the writings of Ibn Taymiyya (d. 1328) and al-Saffārīnī (d. 1774).

While we need not rehearse here basic information about the famous Ibn Taymiyya, it bears mentioning that al-Saffārīnī issued from the Ḥanbalī milieu of rural northern Palestine. Like al-Ashqar, he was born in one of the villages around Nāblus. Al-Saffārīnī wrote works on the Muslim creed, on the question of grave sins, on the ethical duty of 'commanding right and forbidding wrong', on the virtue of using the *miswāk*, and also on the afterlife.[24] The Salafi editor of al-Saffārīnī's work on eschatology, which, echoing al-Suyūṭī's compilation (*al-Budūr al-sāfira*), is called 'The swelling oceans' (*al-Buḥūr al-zākhira*), claims in his introduction that al-Saffārīnī fought against the ignorance, blind following (*taqlīd*), and moral turpitude of his time, marked as it was by the influence of the Ḥanafīs and the decline of the Ottoman Empire, preaching correct beliefs in a time of theological corruption (*al-fasād al-iᶜtiqādī*).[25]

What is this 'insight' of Ibn Taymiyya and al-Saffārīnī that stimulated al-Ashqar's renewed interest in theology in general, and eschatology in particular? In al-Ashqar's reading of the two scholars, the idea is that the traditional literature on credal matters is only of limited use. This is because this literature deals with the differences between theological opinions (*khilāf*), weighing one opinion against another. This is useful, says al-Ashqar, only in a negative sense: it helps one to understand incorrect beliefs.[26] Correct beliefs, however, can be gleaned directly from the Qur'an and the Sunna. In other words, dialectic theology or *kalām* (although al-Ashqar never uses the word) is merely a suprastructure built on top of sound belief. It serves a monitory purpose, fencing in sound belief and defining when one has crossed the line into heresy. Its use is *ultima ratio* and should be reserved for the intellectual elite. The substance of belief, however, is not found in dialectic theology, but is directly available and utterly transparent in the Qur'an and Sunna.[27]

This amounts to a strategy of eliminating ambiguity and plurality of interpretations. What we see at work here is the fundamentalist hermeneutic of the Salafis, the 'inability to tolerate ambiguity' (*Ambiguitätsintoleranz*) of Salafism, as Thomas Bauer has called it.[28] *Ambiguitätsintoleranz* also explains why al-Ashqar may have felt compelled to write his work despite the fact that Ibn Qayyim al-Jawziyya devoted a treatise to the topic – because Ibn Qayyim al-Jawziyya gives ample room to *kalām* discussions in his work, in fact so much so that ironically he comes across as a bit of a dialectic theologian himself.[29] Still, al-Ashqar continues, doubts about his own work continued to plague him. A colleague in Kuwait asked him whether he really believed that he would be able to contribute something new to the understanding of the Muslim creed. As al-Ashqar relates, 'this conversation caused me great sorrow, and I nearly stopped … but then I found confirmation in my own heart that I could not find another book written in the way that I was writing in, and so I continued.'[30] What, then, is so novel about 'Endtime'? In the following, I shall examine three aspects of the work that may provide some clues: first, the criteria for admissibility of hadith that al-Ashqar uses; second, his arrangement of chapters and choice of emphases; and third, whether or not any answers to modernist challenges to the traditional picture of paradise and hell can be found.

1. The use of hadiths in 'Endtime'

Al-Ashqar takes his hadiths from a broad range of sources. These include the canonical Six Books and Aḥmad Ibn Ḥanbal's (d. 855) *Musnad*; the less highly esteemed collections of al-Ṭabarānī (d. 971) and al-Bayhaqī (d. 1066); and late-medieval sources such as al-Qurṭubī's 'Memoir' and Ibn Rajab al-Ḥanbalī's (d. 1393) 'Causing fear of the fire' (*al-Takhwīf min al-nār*). Chains of transmission (*isnāds*) in al-Ashqar's work are reduced to a minimum; in general, only the direct source of al-Ashqar and then a Companion are named as transmitters of a tradition. Typically, a hadith is introduced by a formula such as the following: 'In the *Ṣaḥīḥayn* [i.e. the two canonical collections of al-Bukhārī and Muslim] it is related from ᶜAbd Allāh b. ᶜAbbās [a famous Companion] that the Prophet [eulogy] said … etc.'

Strikingly, not only are *isnād*s missing, but no evaluation of the level of trustworthiness of hadiths or their transmitters is provided. Earlier examples of eschatological literature, including Ibn Kathīr's 'The end of the beginning' and also al-Saffārīnī's 'Swelling oceans', regularly take care to note that a hadith is, for example, well-attested (*ḥasan*) or rare (*gharīb*). In other words, an important, classical principle of Ḥanbalī hadith criticism is not applied by al-Ashqar. There was a 'near consensus' in Sunni Islam, from the middle of the third/ninth century onwards, that it was permissible to quote weak hadiths if they served the purpose of *al-targhīb wa-l-tarhīb*, that is, 'exhortation and dissuasion' in the area of moral instruction and teachings about the afterlife.[31] Some hadith collectors, such as, for example, Abū Nuᶜaym al-Iṣfahānī (d. 1038)[32] or al-Ghazālī in the eschatological chapters of his 'Revivification of the religious sciences' (*Iḥyāʾ ᶜulūm al-dīn*), dispensed with making the weakness of *isnād*s visible. However, the more rigorous approach, the one that allows for the inclusion of 'rare' or even weak hadiths but stipulates that they be clearly identified as such, by and large remained the mainstream Sunni position.[33]

Al-Ashqar, by contrast, chooses to ignore this important principle of hadith criticism. Though quoting hadiths from authorities such as al-Ṭabarānī and al-Bayhaqī, he never addresses the issue of the trustworthiness of *isnād*s, thereby implying that all the hadiths that he quotes are sound. Al-Ashqar's teacher al-Albānī, as Jonathan Brown notes, stands for 'the most forceful and articulate rejection of using weak *ḥadīth*s for any purpose'. Al-Ashqar also espouses this stance, even though he is generous, or so it seems, in his widening of the category of 'sound' eschatological traditions.[34] The point that deserves emphasis is that the modern push toward disambiguation leaves no room in the classification of *isnād*s for categories such as 'weak' (*ḍaᶜīf*) or 'rare' (*gharīb*). Here, again, the 'inability to tolerate ambiguity' of the neo-Salafi movement becomes palpable.

2. Arrangement of topics and choice of emphases in 'Endtime'

As for the arrangement of topics in 'Endtime', it follows, *grosso modo*, that of the premodern handbooks of al-Qurṭubī, Ibn Kathīr and al-Saffārīnī. For example, in the section on paradise, al-Ashqar takes his readers through sections about the eternity of paradise, its topography, the animals that inhabit it, the human inhabitants and the pleasures they enjoy, culminating in the beatific vision, or *ruʾya*, of God.[35] Overall, his treatment is not as comprehensive as, say, that provided by al-Saffārīnī. For instance, unlike many of his predecessors in the genre, he does not relate hadiths about the question whether the inhabitants of paradise will be allowed to father children. Both Ibn Kathīr and al-Saffārīnī devote several pages to this topic.[36]

In a few places, al-Ashqar cannot resist to add some commentary. When he quotes the hadith that describes how the inhabitants of paradise visit a weekly market he observes (on the authority of the Ashᶜarite theologian and jurist al-Nawawī; d. 1277) that the word *sūq* (market) merely refers to a gathering of people, not to an actual marketplace.[37] Given al-Ashqar's own troubled experience with marketplaces, this comment may not be entirely coincidental. That the devil haunts the marketplace is an old motif in the pious literature of Islam and one that competes with the generally positive attitude of the classical jurists towards trade.[38] However, when the classical eschatological handbooks mention the market in paradise, they do not usually invoke al-Nawawī's interpretation in the way that al-Ashqar does. Nor does al-Albānī, in the short chapter on the 'market in paradise' of his collection of 'sound' eschatological traditions, make any reference to any non-literal meaning of the word *sūq*.[39] It may well be that in an age where shopping malls became ubiquitous in the countries of the Near East and the Gulf, al-Ashqar felt compelled to include the disclaimer that the blessed in paradise merely enjoy each other's company, but do not shop.

Sometimes, al-Ashqar ventures to provide a more sustained discussion, thereby emphasising certain sections and topics of his compilation. Considering his principle of avoiding secondary, theological discussions of the truth of the tenets of faith, one assumes that these sections touch on questions that al-Ashqar considers to be particularly difficult or dangerous territory, where theological argumentation is called in *ultima ratio*. When he *does* decide to delve into comparing theological arguments, he freely uses sources from different schools, in the Salafi spirit of not attaching oneself to any school (*lā madhhab*). He refers, among others, to al-Nawawī, the Ḥanafī al-Ṭaḥāwī (d. 933), the Ḥanbalī Ibn Rajab, Ibn Ḥazm of Spain (d. 1064), and Ṣiddīq Ḥasan Khān from Bhopal (d. 1890).

Al-Ashqar shows in these discussions that he is willing to reach his own conclusions. For example, he labours considerably over the hadith that there are seventy-three confessional groups (*firaq*) in Islam, of which only one goes to paradise.[40] First of all, he dismisses people like Ibn Ḥazm and Ṣiddīq Ḥasan Khān who considered this hadith to be weak (*ḍaᶜīf*).[41] Ṣiddīq Ḥasan Khān had also argued that the hadith should be rejected because it made people afraid to convert to Islam, by suggesting that only very few of those who consider themselves Muslims will enter paradise. Al-Ashqar replies that the seventy-three confessional groups should be considered of unequal size. The common people (*al-ᶜawāmm*), and the great majority of Muslims, those who simply follow the Qurʾan and Sunna, are saved. The other seventy-two confessional groups, according to al-Ashqar, are isolated extremists. Among them he counts the Muᶜtazila, the Khārijites, the Imāmī and Ismāᶜīlī Shiᶜites, the Druze and the Nuṣayrīs (that is, the Alawīs of Syria).[42] The hadith of the one saved group (*al-firqa al-nājiya*), as Josef van Ess has recently shown, has an enormously complicated reception history. Different factions have at all times claimed to be this group; neo-Salafism is only the most recent in a long line.

3. Traces of modernist challenges

How much commentary does al-Ashqar add in places where the traditional imagery of paradise and hell clashes with modern sensibilities? There is, first, the challenge of modern science. One of the eschatological hadiths that conflicts with the modern scientific worldview states that the Nile and the Euphrates spring from paradise. Al-Ashqar quotes al-Albānī to the effect that perhaps the spring (*aṣl*) of these two rivers is in paradise in the same way in which the root (*aṣl*) of humanity is in paradise; and that therefore modern geographical knowledge about the springs of the two rivers does not invalidate the hadith; that in any case the question is of the order of those things pertaining to the otherworld (*umūr al-ghayb*) that one simply has to believe in.[43] This seems to sidestep the issue. The seminal neo-Salafi writer, Rashīd Riḍā (d. 1935), in a 1921 fatwa published in his journal *al-Manār*, showed a markedly more explicit readiness to interpret the hadith figuratively. Riḍā reports that some scholars 'have suggested that the hadith construes an analogy between the sweetness, goodness and blessedness of the waters of the Nile and Euphrates and the water of paradise, by way of a figure of speech (*ᶜalā ṭarīq al-mubālagha*)', judging that 'there is nothing unnatural or constrained (*takalluf*) in this when the hadith is interpreted in this way'.[44] In this respect, al-Albānī's and al-Ashqar's position, which plays with, but does not fully embrace the figurative interpretation, is more traditional, and a step back from the kind of view expressed by Riḍā.[45] It is even further away from the kind of view held by Riḍā's teacher, Muḥammad ᶜAbduh (d. 1905). In the *Risālat al-tawḥīd*, ᶜAbduh stated that no-one is obliged to believe in the literal (*ẓāhir*) meaning of hadiths about the otherworld (*akhbār al-ghayb*), even though the rationalisation and demythologisation of these traditions should be restricted to the intellectual elite (*ᶜuqūl al-khāṣṣa*).[46]

Secondly, it seems that discussions about the emancipation of women influence some of al-Ashqar's choices in 'Endtime'. In his discussion of the hadith that states that 'most of the inhabitants of hell are women', al-Ashqar first gives a long quote from al-Qurṭubī. The passage rehearses the stock repertoire of arguments why women are less likely to enter paradise: they suffer from a deficiency in intellectual ability (*nuqṣān al-ᶜuqūl*),[47] are too attached to the ephemeral world of the here-and-now, subject to uncontrollable passions, and so forth.[48] Then al-Ashqar notes the following:

> In spite of this, many women are good and pious (*ṣāliḥāt*), respect God's laws, follow His Shariᶜa and obey Him and His messenger. A great number of them enter paradise, and among them are those who are superior to many a man in terms of the soundness of their belief and their pious actions.[49]

Although this statement indicates a certain willingness to critically engage traditionalist Muslim eschatology, the result is hardly more than lip-service to female emancipation. Note that, elsewhere, al-Ashqar opposes Rashīd Riḍā's view that the houris in paradise are the rejuvenated wives of the believers. No, says al-Ashqar, they are different, and one has plenty of them in paradise. He also relates the tradition that men's sexual potency in paradise will be a hundred times that which they enjoyed on earth.[50]

Conclusions

At first sight, then, it seems that 'Endtime' is largely deaf to modern sensibilities. Rather than using Western science as a yardstick with which to judge, and demythologise, traditional notions, it makes room for the continued belief in the paradisiacal origin of the Nile and Euphrates. The issue of gender equality is worth no more than a fleeting thought; paradise remains a male domain. Still, although occurring in peripheral fashion, 'Endtime' echoes a number of modernist challenges to the traditional Muslim picture of paradise and hell. The very fact that al-Ashqar feels compelled to respond to modernist critiques shows that he cannot escape the shadow of modernity.

In other respects, 'Endtime' can even be said to embrace a number of modern principles, parting ways with much of the premodern literature on eschatology.[51] Disambiguation of the hadith material is high on the list, as is the belief in the transparency of the sources, although the latter may be said to be characteristic of premodern Ḥanbalī thought already, which anticipated the modern Salafi anxiety about plurality in interpretation. I would also argue that 'Endtime' seeks to control and regulate the imagination. One sees this in the fact that, unlike premodern eschatological handbooks, al-Ashqar does not quote any poems about paradise and hell. Neither does he relate dream visions. He also strips his collection of hadiths that strike a more playful, dramatic or theatrical tone. One observes here what Foucault calls 'reason's subjugation of non-reason' in modern times.[52] This attempt to undermine the imagination is ironic, given that the Muslim traditionist literature on paradise and hell, as noted at the beginning of this chapter, is intrinsically connected to, and thrives on, the imagination.

In general, al-Ashqar approaches his subject with a complete lack of humour, a total seriousness, and also a certain stodginess. In the introduction, following convention, he praises the Companions and the Followers, the Salaf, but the words he chooses are telling. He characterises the Salaf as 'those who know that there is no salvation from the Fire, and no victorious entry into the Garden, except if one buckles down and gets to work with all seriousness'.[53] The words al-Ashqar uses here are *illā bi-l-tashmīr ᶜan sāᶜid al-jidd*, literally, 'except if one rolls up the sleeve of the arm of seriousness'.

One sees this irony-free attitude at work in several sections of the book. Al-Ashqar rehearses, for example, whether the stones in hell are sulphur stones or a different kind of stones.[54] The puritanical earnestness with which al-Ashqar talks about issues such as divine forgiveness also belongs in this context. He states rather matter-of-factly that Muslim sinners must reckon with punishment in hell;[55] he does not dwell at any length on the guiding principle of Sunni eschatology that God can forgive also the grave sinners, if He pleases. Al-Ashqar also reiterates Ibn Ḥazm's view that the scholarly consensus in Islam is that hell will not perish, thus distancing himself from Ibn Taymiyya and Ibn Qayyim al-Jawziyya, who entertained notions of universal salvation and the eventual 'extinction of hell' (*fanāʾ al-nār*).[56] Also al-Ashqar's section on the Prophet's power to intercede, his *shafāᶜa*, is decidedly short.

In sum, 'Endtime' is a curious mixture of old and new. It is, of course, not the only book of its kind on the contemporary Arabic book market. The glossy and sprawling *Encyclopaedia of the Otherworld* (*Mawsūᶜat al-ākhira*) of the Emirati Māhir Aḥmad al-Ṣūfī (2007), for instance, invites comparison.[57] Yet overall, 'Endtime' seems to be a representative example of contemporary eschatology written in the Salafi traditionist vein. 'Salafism,' writes Kevin Reinhart, 'in the name of an authentic Islam, prune[s] the Islamic intellectual tradition of much of the subtlety, and of course the scholasticism, of premodern Islam.'[58] Al-Ashqar's 'Endtime', on the whole, seems to confirm this observation.

Notes

1. See, for example, W. Montgomery Watt, *Islamic Creeds: A Selection* (Edinburgh: Edinburgh University Press, 1994), 44 (§17, al-Ashᶜarī), 52 (§18, al-Ṭaḥāwī), 60 (§§20–2, Wāṣiyat Abī Ḥanīfa), 66 (§21, Fiqh akbar II), 71 (§23, al-Qayrawānī), 77–8 (§§17–21, al-Ghazālī), 82 (§17, al-Nasafī), 88 (§18, al-Ījī).
2. On the 'jihadi paradigm' of paradise, with some examples from jihad poetry, see Rüdiger Lohlker and Andrea Nowak, 'Das islamische Paradies als Zeichen: Zwischen Märtyrerkult und Garten', *Wiener Zeitschrift für die Kunde des Morgenlandes* 99 (2009), 199–225 (200–3). On American media and the houris, see Nerina Rustomji, 'American visions of the *houri*', *The Muslim World* 97 (2007), 79–92.

3. Thomas Hobbes, *Leviathan* (New York: Touchstone, [1651] 1997), 23, quoted in Amira Mittermaier, *Dreams That Matter: Egyptian Landscapes of the Imagination* (Berkeley: University of California Press, 2011), 16. Cf. Wolfgang Iser, *Das Fiktive und das Imaginäre: Perspektiven literarischer Anthropologie* (Frankfurt am Maine: Suhrkamp, 1991), 296–7.
4. I refer readers to my *Paradise and Hell in Islamic Traditions* (Cambridge: Cambridge University Press, 2016), in particular to ch. 4 ('The imagination unbound', 120–62).
5. Ibn Qayyim al-Jawziyya, *Al-Kāfiya al-shāfiya fī al-intiṣār li-l-firqā al-nājiya*, eds Muḥammad b. ᶜAbd al-Raḥmān al-ᶜArīfī *et al.* (Mecca: Dār ᶜĀlam al-Fawāʾid, 1428/2007), 987–9. I owe my knowledge of this passage to Livnat Holtzman.
6. Ibid. 987, ll. 6–7. 'The fourteenth night' (*layl al-sitt baᶜda thamān*) is the night of the full moon in the Islamic lunar calendar.
7. See Livnat Holtzman, 'Insult, fury, and frustration: the martyrological narrative of Ibn Qayyim al-Jawziyya's *al-Kāfiyah al-shāfiyah*', *Mamlūk Studies Review* 17 (2013), 155–98 (191–7).
8. Jalāl al-Dīn ᶜAbd al-Raḥmān b. Abī Bakr al-Suyūṭī, *Al-Budūr al-sāfira fī aḥwāl al-ākhira*, ed. Muḥammad Ḥasan al-Shāfiᶜī (Beirut: Dār al-Kutub al-ᶜIlmiyya, 1416/1996), 463.
9. Ibid. 564–6.
10. Charles Hirschkind, *The Ethical Soundscape: Cassette Sermons and Islamic Counterpublics* (New York: Columbia University Press, 2006), 146.
11. Mittermaier, *Dreams That Matter*, 7.
12. Jane Idleman Smith and Yvonne Yazbeck Haddad, *The Islamic Understanding of Death and Resurrection* (New York: Oxford University Press, 2002), 100.
13. Abū Ḥāmid al-Ghazālī, *Iḥyāʾ ᶜulūm al-dīn*, ed. Muḥammad ᶜAbd al-Malik al-Zaghbī, 5 vols ([Cairo]: Dār al-Manār, n.d.), I: 440–2.
14. Mohammed Arkoun, *Lectures du Coran* (Paris: G.-P. Maisonneuve et Larose, 1982), 168.
15. Michael Cook, *Commanding Right and Forbidding Wrong in Islamic Thought* (Cambridge: Cambridge University Press, 2000), 163, n. 125.
16. ᶜUmar Sulaymān al-Ashqar, *Ṣafaḥāt min ḥayātī* (Amman: Dār al-Nafāʾis li-l-Nashr wa-l-Tawzīᶜ, 1430/2010), 40. My colleague at Utrecht, Joas Wagemakers, kindly provided me with a copy of this book.
17. See Cook, *Commanding Right*, 180–92.
18. Ibid. 71. Cf. Stéphane Lacroix, *Awakening Islam: The Politics of Religious Dissent in Contemporary Saudi Arabia* (Cambridge, MA: Harvard University Press, 2011), 90. I owe this reference to Ahmad Khan.
19. Al-Ashqar wrote a PhD dissertation in comparative law, which he defended in 1980 at the al-Azhar Faculty of Law and Shariᶜa (*kulliyat al-ḥuqūq wa-l-sharīᶜa*). See Ashqar, *Ṣafaḥāt*, 98.
20. Ashqar, *Ṣafaḥāt*, 114.
21. Ibid. 145.
22. Kevin Reinhart, 'Fundamentalism and the transparency of the Arabic Qurʾan',

in Carl W. Ernst and Richard C. Martin (eds), *Rethinking Islamic Studies: From Orientalism to Cosmopolitanism* (Columbia: University of South Carolina Press, 2010), 97.

23. This text is also known, in the western Islamic world, as *Shajarat al-yaqīn*, and in the eastern Islamic world, as *Ḥaqāʾiq al-Daqāʾiq*. See Lange, *Paradise and Hell*, 108–12. An English translation, by Aisha Bewley, circulates under the title *The Islamic Book of the Dead* (Norwich-San Francisco: Diwan Press, 1977).
24. On al-Saffārīnī's life and works, see Muḥammad b. ʿAbd Allāh al-Najdī, *Al-Suḥub al-wābila ʿalā ḍarāʾiḥ al-Ḥanābila*, ed. Bakr b. ʿAbd Allāh Abū Zayd (Beirut: Muʾassasat al-Risāla, 1996), II: 836–46.
25. Muḥammad b. Aḥmad al-Saffārīnī, *Al-Buḥūr al-zākhira fī ʿulūm al-ākhira*, ed. ʿAbd al-ʿAzīz Aḥmad b. Muḥammad b. Ḥammūd al-Mushayqiḥ (Riyadh: Dār al-ʿĀṣima li-l-Nashr wa-l-Tawzīʿ, 2009), 10–12.
26. Ashqar, *Ṣafaḥāt*, 143.
27. Ibid.
28. Thomas Bauer, *Die Kultur der Ambiguität. Eine andere Geschichte des Islams* (Berlin: Verlag der Weltreligionen, 2011), 58–9 and passim.
29. See, for example, the long discussion of the beatific vision (*ruʾyat Allāh*) in Ibn Qayyim al-Jawziyya, *Ḥādī al-arwāḥ ilā bilād al-afrāḥ*, ed. Zakariyyāʾ ʿUmayrāt (Beirut: Dār al-Kutub al-ʿIlmiyya, 1428/2007), 214–51.
30. Ashqar, *Ṣafaḥāt*, 145.
31. See Jonathan Brown, 'Even if it's not true it's true: using unreliable *ḥadīth* in Sunni Islam', *Islamic Law and Society* 18 (2011), 7–9.
32. See Abū Nuʿaym al-Iṣfahānī, *Ṣifat al-janna*, ed. ʿAlī Riḍā b. ʿAbd Allāh b. ʿAlī Riḍā, 3 vols in 1, 2nd edn (Beirut: Dār al-Maʾmūn li-l-Turāth, 1410/1995).
33. Brown, 'Even if it's not true', 17. Brown also notes that Ibn Taymiyya seems to have accepted the use of weak hadiths in *al-targhīb wa-l-tarhīb*, but that some scholars think that he held two different opinions, rejecting the principle on other occasions. See ibid. 26, n. 79.
34. Brown, 'Even if it's not true', 41.
35. ʿUmar Sulaymān al-Ashqar, *Al-Yawm al-ākhir, vol. III: Al-Janna wa-l-nār* (Amman: Dār al-Nafāʾis li-l-Nashr wa-l-Tawzīʿ, 1991), 117–264.
36. See Saffārīnī, *Buḥūr*, 1171–8.
37. Ashqar, *Yawm*, III: 241. Cf. Muḥyī al-Dīn Yaḥyā al-Nawawī, *Al-Minhāj fī-sharḥ ṣaḥīḥ Muslim* (Beirut: Dār al-Kitāb al-ʿArabī, 1407/1987), IX: 172.
38. For example, in the *Iḥyāʾ ʿulūm al-dīn*, al-Ghazālī relates in a chapter on the etiquette of trade that ʿAbd Allāh b. ʿAmr b. al-ʿĀṣ once said: 'Do not be the first to enter the market-place [in the morning], nor the last to leave it [in the evening], because Satan resides there and hatches offspring (*bāḍa bi-hā wa-farrakha*).' See Ghazālī, *Iḥyāʾ ʿulūm al-dīn*, II: 132, ll. 1–2. On classical *fiqh*'s relationship to trade, see Johannes Christian Wichard, *Zwischen Markt und Moschee. Wirtschaftliche Bedürfnisse und religiöse Anforderungen im frühen islamischen Vertragsrecht* (Paderborn: F. Schöningh, 1995).
39. Muḥammad Nāṣir al-Dīn al-Albānī, *Ṣaḥīḥ al-targhīb wa-l-tarhīb*, 3 vols (Riyadh:

Maktabat al-Maᶜārif li-l-Nashr wa-l-Tawzīᶜ, 2000), III: 269. This work is a selection of the 'sound' traditions (according to al-Albānī's criteria) found in the well-known work of ᶜAbd al-ᶜAẓīm b. ᶜAbd al-Qawī al-Mundhirī (d. 1258), *Kitāb al-targhīb wa-l-tarhīb.*

40. The many versions of this hadith are discussed in Josef van Ess, *Der Eine und das Andere. Beobachtungen an islamischen häresiographischen Texten*, 2 vols (Berlin-New York: de Gruyter, 2011), I: 7–64.
41. On Ibn Ḥazm's rejection of the hadith, see van Ess, *Der Eine*, II: 839.
42. Ashqar, *Yawm*, III: 61–4.
43. Ibid. 166.
44. See Rashīd Riḍā, 'Khurūj al-Nīl wa-l-Furāt min sidrat al-muntahā wa-kawnu-humā min al-janna', *Majallat al-manār* 22:4 (March 1921), 260–2 (262).
45. It is generally agreed that Riḍā, during the course of his career, gradually became more traditionalist in his views, withdrawing from (though not completely rejecting) Western-style rationalism, a break with the reformist thought of his earlier life that is supposed to have taken place some time in the early 1920s. See Ahmad Dallal, 'Appropriating the past: twentieth-century reconstruction of pre-modern Islamic thought', *Islamic Law and Society* 7:3 (2000), 325–58 (342, 357).
46. Muḥammad ᶜAbduh, *Risālat al-tawḥīd* (Beirut: Dār al-Shurūq, 1414/1994), 178 (*b. al-Taṣdīq bi-mā jāʾa bi-hi Muḥammad*).
47. Compare this with Karen Bauer's chapter in the present volume.
48. Muḥammad b. Aḥmad al-Qurṭūbī, *Al-Tadkhira fī aḥwāl al-mawtā wa-umūr al-ākhira*, ed. Yūsuf ᶜAlī Badīwī (Damascus: Dār Ibn Kathīr, 1999), III: 232–3.
49. Ashqar, *Yawm*, III: 83–4. The passage appears verbatim in Māhir Aḥmad al-Ṣūfī's *Encyclopaedia of the Otherworld* (*Mawsūᶜat al-ākhira*). See Māhir Aḥmad Ṣūfī, *Mawsūᶜat al-ākhira*, 3 vols (Beirut: al-Maktaba al-ᶜAṣriyya, 1426/2007), III: 294.
50. Ashqar, *Yawm*, III: 246–50.
51. On Islamism's 'modernity', see Bruce Lawrence, *Defenders of God: The Fundamentalist Revolt Against the Modern Age* (San Francisco: Harper & Row, 1989), ch. 1.
52. Michel Foucault, *Madness and Civilization: A History of Insanity in the Age of Reason* (*Histoire de la folie*, 1961), trans. Richard Howard (New York: Vintage Books, [1965] 1988), ix.
53. Ashqar, *Yawm*, III: 5.
54. Ibid. 32.
55. Ibid. 61ff.
56. See Jon Hoover, 'Islamic universalism: Ibn Qayyim al-Jawziyya's Salafi deliberations on the duration of Hell-Fire', *The Muslim World* 99 (2009), 181–201 (188). On the survival of the idea in the works of other contemporary Muslim authors, such as Yūsuf al-Qarāḍāwī (Egypt/Qatar, b. 1926) and Muḥammad Ḥabash (Syria, b. 1962), see Umar Ryad, 'Eschatology between reason and

revelation: death and resurrection in modern Islamic theology', in Sebastian Günther and Todd Lawson (eds), *Roads to Paradise: Eschatology and Concepts of the Hereafter in Islam* (Leiden: Brill, forthcoming); Paul Heck, 'Religious renewal in Syria: the case of Muḥammad al-Ḥabash', *Journal of Islam and Muslim-Christian Religions* 15:4 (2004), 185–207.

57. Ṣūfī, *Mawsūʿat al-ākhira*. Cf. above, note 49.
58. Reinhart, 'Fundamentalism', 98.

Index

al-ᶜAbbādī, 107
ᶜAbbāsī, Muḥammad ᶜĪd, 69–71, 73, 76
ᶜAbd Allāh Bāz, ᶜAbd al-ᶜAzīz, 66, 247, 250–1
ᶜAbd al-Nabī al-Gangūhī, 100
ᶜAbd al-Razzāq Ḥamza, Muḥammad, 68–9, 71, 73, 76
ᶜAbduh, Muḥammad, 34, 57, 108–9, 256
Abū al-Fidāᵓ, 209
Abū al-Wafāᵓ al-Afghānī, 73
Abū Bakr, 168, 179, 180–1
Abū Dāwūd, 33, 39
Abū Ghudda, ᶜAbd al-Fattāḥ, 61–2, 67, 68, 73–4, 76
Abū Ḥanīfa, 5, 54–81, 116
Abū Nuᶜaym al-Iṣfahānī, 254
Abū Nuwās, 233
Abū Tammām, 228, 242
Abū Thawr, 118
ᶜĀdil Shāh, 208
al-Afghānī, Jamāl al-Dīn, 34, 57
afterlife *see* hell; paradise
Against Extremisms (Michot), 8, 178, 183, 190–1
Ahl-i Ḥadīth reform movement, 54, 57
Aḥmad ibn Ḥanbal, 35–6, 46–7, 61, 62, 64, 66, 72, 187, 253
Aḥzān wa-Iṣrār (al-Baradūnī), 233
ᶜĀᵓisha, 111–12, 114, 116
al-Ajwiba al-fāḍila (al-Laknawī), 68
Akbar the Great, 100
Akhbār al-quḍāt (Wakīᶜ), 119
Akhbārī school, 14, 162–3
al-Ākhund al-Khurāsānī, 4, 14–15, 19–21, 22, 24–5, 26
ᶜAlasvand, Fariba, 161–4, 174–5
al-Albānī, Muḥammad Nāṣir al-Dīn, 5, 10, 33–47, 57, 60–2, 64, 69, 71–2, 73, 247, 250, 256
Algeria, 184
ᶜAlī b. Abī Ṭālib, 169, 179
ᶜAlī b. Muḥammad, 236
al-Ālūsī, 141, 142, 143, 144–5
Ambiguitätsintoleranz, 253
Amin, Kamaruddin, 43
analogy, 44, 45
Analysis of Quotations, An (Rowlandson), 206–7
Anas b. Mālik, 72, 140
al-Andalusī, Abū Ḥayyān, 36
Anderson, Benedict, 226
Anṣār al-Sunna al-Muḥammadiyya, 63, 69
al-Anṣārī, al-Shaykh Murtaḍā, 14–15
ᶜAntara Ibn Shaddād, 235
anti-Mongol fatwas, 7–8, 177, 178–85, 189, 190–1, 193–6
al-ᶜAqīda al-Ṭaḥāwiyya (al-Ṭaḥāwī), 61–2
al-ᶜAqqād, ᶜAbbās Maḥmūd, 137
Arab classical poetry, 9–10, 223–42
Arab Spring, 190–3, 229–30
al-ᶜArāqī, Ḍiyāᵓ al-Dīn, 24
Arkoun, Mohammed, 250
Arnold, Thomas, 208
Artistic Depiction in the Qurᵓan (Quṭb), 137
Asad, Talal, 52–3
al-Aṣamm, Abū Bakr, 113, 114
al-Ashqar, Muḥammad Sulaymān, 117–18, 120, 250
al-Ashqar, ᶜUmar Sulaymān, 10, 247, 250–8

Assmann, Jan, 79
authority, 10, 225, 229–30, 238–40, 241–2
al-Awlaki, Anwar, 190
Al-Azhar University, 60, 69, 73, 251
al-ᶜAziz, ᶜAbd al-Qādir b. ᶜAbd (Dr Faḍl), 181
ᶜAzzām, ᶜAbd Allāh, 186

Badāʾiᶜ al-ṣanāʾiᶜ (al-Kāsānī), 114
Baghdad, 104, 106, 107, 110, 178
Bakhtin, Mikhail, 240
Bakr Abū Zayd, 66–8, 72, 76
al-Banūrī, Muḥammad Yūsuf, 73
al-Bāqir, Muḥammad, 23
Barāʾat ahl al-sunna min al-waqīᶜa fī ᶜulamāʾ al-umma (Bakr Abū Zayd), 66–7
al-Baradūnī, ᶜAbd Allāh, 233
Basket of Fragments and Crumbs for the Children of God (Rowlandson), 207
Basra, 108, 109–10
Bāṭarfī, Khālid, 233
al-Battī, ᶜUthmān, 110, 114
Bauer, Thomas, 253
al-Bayḍāwī, 209
al-Bayhaqī, 36, 39–40, 253, 254
Bayly, Christopher, 52
Belhadj, Ali, 184
Bennett, Clinton, 212
al-Bidāya wa-l-nihāya (Ibn Kathīr), 252, 254–5
Bidāyat al-mujtahid (Ibn Rushd), 110
al-Bihbihānī, Muḥammad Bāqir, 14
Bijapur, 204, 208, 211
Bin Bayya, ᶜAbd Allāh, 189–90
Bin Laden, Osama, 181, 190, 195, 214, 223, 224, 228, 229, 233, 235, 238–9, 242
al-Biqāᶜī, 136, 140
al-Bīṭār, Muḥammad Bahjat, 71
Bonnefoy, Laurent, 230
Book of Jihad, The (Ibn al-Mubārak), 228
Bourdieu, Pierre, 238
Brown, Jonathan, 38, 57, 254
al-Buḥūr al-zākhira (al-Saffārīnī), 252, 254–5
al-Bukhārī, 34, 38–9, 40, 45, 46, 56, 67, 209
Burnell, A. C., 213
al-Burūjirdī, Ḥusayn, 24
al-Būṭī, Ramaḍān, 70

Cairo, 58, 63, 105, 251
Calder, Norman, 52–3
Caliphate, The (Muir), 212
Carlyle, Thomas, 211, 215
Catholicism, 9, 209, 211, 215; *see also* Christianity
childbirth, 163, 166, 172
Christianity, 9, 108–9, 180, 204–5, 207, 208–12, 214–16
Cixous, Hélène, 236
collective memory, 78–9, 227
colonialism, 8–9, 109, 120, 204–16, 226
conservative Qurʾanic interpretation, 160–6, 174–5
continuity, 12–13, 15, 19, 26, 226–7, 235–6
Convention of Elimination of all forms of Discrimination Against Women (CEDAW), 162
corporate Salafi publications, 71–4
Critique of CEDAW (ᶜAlasvand), 162–3
Crusades, 8, 205, 210, 214
cultural capital, 238–40, 241–2
cultural genealogy, 226–7
cultural identity, 226–7, 230, 238–42

Ḍaᶜīf Sunan *Ibn Māja* (al-Albānī), 33
Dāʾirat al-Maᶜārif al-ᶜUthmānīyya, 71
Damascus, 33, 69, 73, 105, 179, 248, 250
Dante Alighieri, 211, 216
Daqāʾiq al-akhbār (anon.), 252
al-Dār al-ᶜĀlamiyya li-l-Kitāb al-Islāmī, 251
Dār al-daᶜwa wa-l-irshād, 68–9
Darʾ al-fitna ᶜan ahl al-sunna (Bakr Abū Zayd), 66
Dār al-Ḥadīth, 69
Dār al-ᶜUlūm madrasa, Deoband, 109
De fatis linguarum orientalium (Jenisch), 210
Deoband, 109
al-Dhahabī, 36, 37, 40, 41, 76
dialectic theology, 56, 58, 253
Dickinson, Eerik, 38, 46
divorce, 103, 107, 110, 114, 163
domains of peace, 186–9
domains of war, 186–9
Dynamic *Fiqh*, 170, 173

Ebūsuᶜud Efendi, 101
Egypt, 6, 60, 62–3, 68–9, 73, 81, 100–1, 103, 105, 108–14, 118, 120, 136, 177–81, 186, 190–2, 249
Egyptian Feminist Union, 111
Eisenstein, Elizabeth, 59

emigration, 186–7, 238
Encyclopaedia of the Otherworld (al-Ṣūfī), 258
Enlightenment, 211
Epic Battle of Tarim, The, 237
eschatology, 4, 10, 247–58
evangelism, 9, 205, 207, 210, 211–12, 214–15
exegetical holism, 6, 136–51
extremism, 4, 7–8, 9–10, 177–8, 180–96, 223–42

Fadel, Mohammed, 103
al-Farāhi, Ḥamīd, 136
Faraj, ᶜAbd al-Salām, 7, 177–8, 180–1, 184, 186–8, 192, 196
al-Farīḍa al-ghāʾiba (Faraj), 7, 177–8, 180–1, 184, 186–8, 192, 196
Fatāwā ᶜĀlamgīrī, 103
Fāṭima, 168, 169
fatwas
  anti-Mongol, 7–8, 177, 178–85, 189, 190–1, 193–6
  Ibn Taymiyya's, 7–8, 177–96
  Mardin fatwa, 8, 177, 185, 186–90, 193
  Transvaal fatwa, 108–9
al-Fayyād, Muḥammad Isḥāq, 26
female poets, 230–1
Ferguson, Donald, 213
Fī ẓilāl al-Qurʾān (Quṭb), 6, 138, 142
finance, 6, 101, 102, 103, 108, 114–19, 120
Fiqh al-jihād (al-Qaraḍāwī), 181–2, 231
al-Fiqī, Muḥammad Ḥāmid, 63, 69
First Conference of Islamic Finance, Dubai, 117, 118–19
footnotes, 5, 60, 62–3, 65, 80, 81, 207, 209–10, 211, 213, 214–15
fornication, 163, 172–3
Foucault, Michel, 257

Gadahn, Adam, 190
Gaddafi, Muammar, 190, 192–3
El-Gamal, Mahmood, 119
Genghis Khan, 180
Germain, Eric, 212
gharar, 115–18, 119
al-Ghazālī, Muḥammad, 34, 108, 250, 254
Ghāzān, 178–9
al-Gīzāwī, Muḥammad Abū al-Faḍl, 112–13
gender equality, 7, 160–75, 233, 256–7
Gibbon, Edward, 211, 215
Gomaa, Ali, 118, 119–20, 121–2
grammatical analysis, 168–9
grave, life in the, 10, 247
great western transmutation, 52
Gulistān (Saᶜdī), 206–7

Haddad, Yvonne Yazbeck, 249–50
Ḥādī al-arwāḥ ilā bilād al-afrāḥ (Ibn Qayyim al-Jawziyya), 252
hadith
  Abū Ḥanīfa's approach to, 55–6, 65, 74–8
  and analogy, 44, 45
  criticism, 5, 33–47, 56, 59, 75–8, 254
  eschatological, 10, 247, 248–9, 251–8
  *isnād*s, 38–47, 143, 253–4
  and paraphrase, 45–6
  permissibility of writing, 41
  publishing of, 58–9
  renewal of study, 54
  on saluting non-Muslims, 43–4
  Six Books, 33, 39, 253
  on veiling, 39–40
  on women's deficiency in reason and religion, 7, 161, 169, 256–7
  on women's testimony, 168, 172–3
Hadith (Brown), 38
al-Ḥāʾirī, ᶜAbd al-Karīm, 24
al-Ḥakīm, Muḥsin, 25–6
al-Ḥākim al-Naysābūrī, 40
Ḥāmid, Muḥammad, 101
Ḥammūd, Sāmī Ḥasan, 114–16, 120
Ḥamza b. Bīḍ, 233
Ḥanafī school, 55–7, 60–2, 65–8, 70–1, 76–8, 101, 103, 104–5, 107, 109, 111, 112, 114, 121
Ḥanbalī school, 37, 44–5, 64, 66, 103, 107, 111–12, 250, 257
Hanson, Hamza Yusuf, 189, 190
Ḥaqāʾiq al-uṣūl (al-Ḥakīm), 25–6
al-ḥaqīqa al-lughawiyya usage, 16, 17, 20, 23
al-ḥaqīqa al-sharᶜiyya usage, 16, 17–27
al-ḥaqīqa ᶜurfiyya usage, 16–17, 18, 22
ḥaqīqa usage, 15–27
al-Ḥawālī, Safar b. ᶜAbd al-Raḥmān, 56
*ḥawza*s, 4, 12–15, 19, 24, 25, 27
Haykel, Bernard, 54
hell, 10, 247–58
heresy, 55–6

Heresy of Madhhab *Fanaticism, The* (ᶜAbbāsī), 69–71
Ḥijāb al-marʾa al-muslima (Al-Albānī), 33, 36, 39–40
ḥijra, 186–7, 238
Hinduism, 204
Hirschkind, Charles, 249
al-Hitārī, ᶜAbd al-Majīd al-Raymī, 236
Hitti, Philip, 241
Ḥizb al-Taḥrīr, 251
Hobbes, Thomas, 248
Hobson-Jobson (Yule & Burnell), 213
Hodgson, Marshall G. S., 52, 53
homosexuality, 173
al-Ḥujja al-bāligha (Shāh Walī Allāh), 55
Ḥukm al-intimāʾ ilā al-firaq wa-l-jamāᶜāt al-Islāmiyya (Bakr Abū Zayd), 66
al-Ḥurr al-ᶜĀmilī, Marjaᶜ, 162
Hussein, Saddam, 251
hyperbole, 237

Ibn ᶜAbbās, 101, 107, 108, 118, 120, 139–40, 143
Ibn ᶜAbd al-Barr, 36
Ibn ᶜAbd al-Salām, ᶜIzz al-Dīn, 104, 106
Ibn Abī al-ᶜIzz al-Ḥanafī, 60–2
Ibn Abī Jamra, Abū Muḥammad, 36
Ibn Abī Laylā, 110, 116–17
Ibn Abī Shayba, 65, 76
Ibn ᶜAdī, 56, 76
Ibn al-ᶜArabī, Abū Bakr, 109
Ibn al-Humām, Kamāl al-Dīn, 114
Ibn al-Jawzī al-Ḥanbalī, 70
Ibn al-Mubārak, 228
Ibn al-Mundhir, 110
Ibn al-Ṣalāh al-Shahrazūrī, 38, 43, 45, 106, 107, 119, 141, 143
Ibn Daqīq al-ᶜĪd, 36, 105
Ibn Ḥajar al-ᶜAsqalānī, 35, 36, 39, 40, 47, 181
Ibn Ḥajar al-Haythamī, 36
Ibn Ḥamdān, Ḥanbalī Aḥmad, 35
Ibn Ḥazm, 36, 117, 118, 255, 258
Ibn Ḥibbān al-Bustī, 56
Ibn Hubayra, 107
Ibn Isḥāq, Muḥammad, 107
Ibn Jurayj, 108
Ibn Kathīr, 36, 37, 180, 252, 254–5
Ibn Māja, 33
Ibn Masᶜūd, 36
Ibn Qayyim al-Jawziyya, 66, 67, 248, 252, 253, 258
Ibn Qudāma, 45, 110
Ibn Rajab al-Ḥanbalī, 42, 107–8, 119, 253, 255
Ibn Rushd, 36, 37, 110, 117
Ibn Shubruma, Abū al-Ṭufayl ᶜAbd Allāh, 6, 102, 109–22
Ibn Taymiyya, 7–8, 36, 37, 67, 107, 177–96, 252–3, 258
Idea of an Anthropology of Islam, The (Asad), 52–3
Iḥyāʾ ᶜulūm al-dīn (al-Ghazālī), 34, 254
ijtihād, 35, 121, 136–7
ᶜIkrima, 107
Ikhtilāf al-fuqahāʾ (al-Ṭabarī), 110, 116–17
al-ᶜ*Ilal al-kabīr* (al-Tirmidhī), 38–9
imagination, 248–9, 257
India, 8–9, 57, 58, 60, 71, 73–6, 80–1, 100, 108, 109, 136, 177, 204–16
Indian Mutiny, 212
al-Inṣāf (Shāh Walī Allāh), 55
interest, 101, 108, 115–18
International Islamic Publishing House, 10, 247
intertextual analysis, 186, 188
introductions, 5, 60, 61–2, 64, 65, 80, 81, 139–41, 208–9, 211, 213, 214
Iran, 4, 6–7, 12–27, 136, 160–75
Iraq, 4, 6, 12–13, 19, 25, 26, 100, 106, 109–10, 177, 178, 236
al-ᶜIrāqī, Zayn al-Dīn, 34
Irjāʾ, 76
al-Iṣfahānī, Muḥammad Ḥusayn, 25
al-Isfarāʾīnī, Abū Isḥaq, 141
Ishrāf (Ibn al-Mundhir), 110
Iṣlāḥī, Amīn Aḥsan, 136, 137
Islamic Jihad, 7, 177
Islamic law, 4, 5–7, 12–27, 43–5, 55–6, 59, 100–22, 160–75, 179–80, 186, 188, 215
Islamic Legal Academy, 119
Islamic reform, 5–6, 54–81, 100–2, 108–9, 177
Islamic revolution, 190–3
Islamic Salvation Front (FIS), 184
Islamic State, 223, 226, 230, 231
isnāds, 38–47, 143, 253–4
al-Itqān fī ᶜulūm al-Qurʾān (al-Suyūṭī), 142

Jād al-Ḥaqq, ᶜAlī Jād al-Ḥaqq, 181
jāhilī poetry, 224, 229–30, 235, 236, 237–8, 242
Jarīrī school, 107
Jaspers, Karl, 10

Jenisch, Bernard von, 210
jihad, 7–10, 174, 175, 177–8, 179–96, 204–16, 223–42
Jones, Sir William, 208, 210
Jordan, 33, 117, 250, 251
Judaism, 139, 149, 180
jumlatan wāḥidatan tradition, 139–40, 142–4, 149–50
al-Juwaynī, Imām al-Ḥaramayn, 106
Juynboll, Gautier, 43

Kāfī, Abū Bakr ibn Laṭīf, 46–7
al-Kāfiya al-shāfiya (Ibn Qayyim al-Jawziyya), 248
kalām, 253
Kalimāt fī kashf abāṭīl wa-iftirāʾāt (Abū Ghudda), 73
al-Kāmil fī ḍuʿafāʾ al-rijāl (Ibn ʿAdī), 56
al-Kāndahlawī, Muḥammad Zakariyyā, 73
al-Kashmīrī, Anwarshāh, 36, 37, 74
al-Kawtharī, Muḥammad Zāhid, 61–5, 67, 71–2, 73, 76, 77–8, 109, 121
'Al-Kawtharī and his attack on the classical heritage' (al-Bīṭār *et al.*), 71–2
Kerala, 204, 205, 214, 216
Khān, Ṣiddīq Ḥasan, 255
al-Khānjī, Muḥammad Amīn, 62–3
Khārijīs, 179–81, 233, 242, 256
al-Khaṭīb al-Baghdādī, 45–6, 62–5, 67, 72, 76
Khawla bint Thaʿlaba, 231
Khomeini, Ayatollah, 170
al-Khuḍarī, Muḥammad al-ʿAfīfī, 113
al-Khūʾī, Abū al-Qāsim, 4, 21, 26
al-Khumaynī, Rūḥallāh, 4, 26
Kifāyat al-uṣūl (al-Ākhund), 14–15, 19–21, 24–5, 26
Kifāyat al-uṣūl: Durūs fī masāʾil ʿilm al-uṣūl (al-Tibrīzī), 21, 24–5
Kitāb al-Futyā (Ibn al-Ṣalāḥ), 106
Kitāb al-Kāfī (al-Kulaynī), 168
Kitāb al-majrūḥīn min al-muḥaddithīn (Ibn Ḥibbān al-Bustī), 56
Kitāb al-Makāsib (al-Anṣārī), 14
al-Kitāb al-muṣannaf fī-l-aḥādīth wa-l-āthār (Ibn Abī Shayba), 65, 76
Kitāb al-thiqāt (Ibn Ḥibbān al-Bustī), 56
Kitāb rafʿ al-yadayn (al-Bukhārī), 67
Kristeva, Julia, 240
Kufa, 6, 100, 109–10, 116
al-Kulaynī, Muḥammad ibn Yaʿqūb, 168
Kurup, K. K. N., 213
Kuwait, 10, 117, 119, 247, 250, 251

al-Lā madhhabiyya akhṭar bidʿa tuhaddid al-Sharīʿa al-Islāmiyya (al-Būṭī), 70
al-Laknawī, ʿAbd al-Ḥayy, 67, 68, 74, 75–6
Lane, Edward William, 110
Lauzière, Henri, 54
Law, Edward, 210
legal theory, 4, 12–27, 59; *see also* Islamic law
legitimacy, 10, 225, 226, 235, 238–40
Libya, 190, 192–3
Life of Mahomet (Muir), 212
linguistic theory, 15–27; *see also* philology
literal meanings, 4, 15–27, 42
Lopes, David, 213
Lyotard, Jean-François, 227

Maʿālim al-dīn (al-Shaykh Ḥasan), 17–19, 22
MacIntyre, Alisdair, 53
madhhabs, 54–7, 59, 68–71, 74, 78–9, 102, 103–8, 119, 121, 255; *see also individual schools*
Madras, 204–16
Maffei, Giovanni Pietro, 209
Maḥmūd, ʿAbd al-Ḥalīm, 118
majāz usage, 15–27
Majmūʿ (al-Nawawī), 110
Majmūʿ fatāwā (Ibn Taymiyya), 179, 188–9
Makānat Abī Ḥanīfa fī-l-ḥadīth (al-Nuʿmānī), 74–5
al-Maktab al-Islāmī, 58, 69
Maktabat al-Ḥaram al-Makkī, 72
Malabar, 9, 204–16
Malik, Aftab, 189
Mālik ibn Anas, 67, 70, 72
Mālikī school, 37, 100, 103, 104–5, 107, 118
Maʿmar ibn Rāshid, 104
al-Maʾmūn, 100
al-Manār, 34, 256
Mardin Conference, 189–90
Mardin fatwa, 8, 177, 185, 186–90, 193
marjaʿiyya system, 12
marriage, 100–3, 108, 109–14, 118, 119–20, 172
marriage age, 6, 102, 109–14, 118, 119–20
martyrdom, 237, 238, 239–40, 248
al-Marzūqī, Abū Yaʿrub, 177
Maṭbaʿat al-Sunna al-Muḥammadiyya, 63
al-Māwardī, 107, 181
meat, slaughtering methods, 108–9
Mecca, 33, 56, 66, 69, 71–2, 116, 139–40, 142–3, 146–7, 149, 250

Mecelle law code, 105
Medina, 66, 69, 106, 139–40, 142–3, 147, 149, 247, 250–1
Mehmet Ali, 110
Mehrizi, Mehdi, 162, 166–70
Melchert, Christopher, 61
memory, 78–9, 227
metanarratives, 227
Michot, Yahya, 8, 178, 182–96
Miller, Flagg, 224, 239
Mir, Mustansir, 136, 137, 138
Mir-Hosseini, Ziba, 160, 173
Mittermaier, Amira, 249
Mīzān al-Kubrā (al-Shaᶜrānī), 105
Modarressi, Hossein, 13–14
modernity, 2, 3, 12, 108–9, 110, 137–8, 151, 249–50, 256–7
Mongols, 7–8, 178–85, 190–1, 194–6
monographs, 74–9
mortgages, 6, 115–16, 120
Motzki, Harald, 43
al-Muᶜallimī al-Yamānī, ᶜAbd al-Raḥmān b. Yaḥyā, 64–5, 67, 71–2
Muᶜāwiya, 179
al-Muᶜaẓẓam ᶜĪsā, al-Malik, 62–3
Mubarak, Hosni, 191–2
Mughnī (Ibn Qudāma), 110
Muir, Sir William, 207, 208, 211, 212, 215
munāsaba, 141, 142
al-Munāwī, 42, 120–1
al-Mundhirī, 42
al-Muqābala bayna al-hudā wa-l-ḍalāl (ᶜAbd al-Razzāq Ḥamza), 69, 73
al-murābaḥa li-l-āmir bi-l-shirāʾ (MAS) transactions, 115–17, 119, 120
Murjiʾa, 68, 76
Muslim Brotherhood, 73, 250, 251
Muslim ibn al-Ḥajjāj, 40, 43–4, 45, 46
Muslims under non-Muslim Rule (Michot), 8, 185, 186, 189, 193–4
Musnad (Aḥmad ibn Ḥanbal), 253
Mustanṣiriyya madrasa, Baghdad, 106
mutᶜa marriage, 100–1, 108, 118, 120
al-Mutalammis, 231–2, 235
al-Mutanabbī, Abū Ṭayyib, 228
al-Muṭīᶜī, Bakhīt, 113–14

Nafi, Basheer, 54
Nainar, Muhammad Husayn, 204, 213, 214, 216
al-Nāʾīnī, Muḥammad al-Ḥusayn, 4, 21–7
Najaf, 13, 19, 25, 26
al-Nasāʾī, 33, 76
al-Naṣr, Aḥlām, 231
natural imagery, 237
al-Nawawī, 36, 106, 110, 181, 255
Neglected Duty, The (Faraj), 7, 177–8, 180–1, 184, 186–8, 192, 196
Nejād, Zibaei, 164–5, 166
neo-Salafism, 247–58
neo-traditionalist Qurʾanic interpretation, 160, 162, 170–4
Neuwirth, Angelika, 139
non-literal meanings, 4, 15–27, 42, 256
al-Nukat al-ṭarīfa fi-l-taḥadduth ᶜan rudūd Ibn Abī Shayba ᶜalā Abī Ḥanīfa (al-Kawtharī), 65
al-Nuᶜmānī, ᶜAbd al-Rashīd, 74–5
Nūr, Zuhayr ᶜUthmān ᶜAlī, 46

Ode of Zuhayr, 229–30, 232–3
odes, 237–8
oral transmission, 227, 232, 235
Oxford movement, 211

Pakistan, 73, 74
Palestine, 238, 250, 252
Paşa, Cevdet, 105
paradise, 10, 210, 215, 247–58
paraphrase, 45–6
Pease, Allan, 164–5
Pease, Barbara, 164–5
Perry, William, 235
Peters, Ruud, 103
philology, 8, 149–50, 182; *see also* linguistic theory
plagiarism, 9, 225, 234–6
poetry, 9–10, 223–42
polygamy, 100, 110
polyvalence, 55, 56
Pomeranz, Kenneth, 52
Portuguese, 9, 204–16
post-edition polemics, 65–71, 80
postmodernism, 227, 234
Powell, Avril, 207, 212
prefaces *see* introductions
pre-Islamic poetry, 224, 229–30, 235, 236, 237–8, 242
printing, 5, 53–4, 58–9, 80; *see also* publishing
propaganda, 9, 184, 185, 193, 214, 223–42
publishing, 5, 53–4, 58–81, 251–2
Pusey, Edward, 211

al-Qādir, 107
al-Qāᶜida, 9, 181, 190, 223–42
Qalandar Sufis, 104
al-Qaraḍāwī, Yūsuf, 177, 181–2, 190, 192–3, 195, 231
al-Qarāfī, Shihāb al-Dīn, 105
qaṣīdas, 225–6, 228, 233, 234–5, 236–7, 240–1
al-Qāsimī, Jamāl al-Dīn, 55
qaṭᶜ, 14
Qaṭarī b. al-Fujāᵓa, 233
Qawāᶜid al-taḥdīth min funūn muṣṭalaḥ al-ḥadīth (al-Qāsimī), 55
Qawāᶜid fī ᶜulūm al-ḥadīth (al-Tahānawī), 67, 68
Qom, 13, 19, 24, 166–7, 170, 175
al-Qudsī, Ḥusām al-Dīn, 71
Qum *see* Qom
Qurᵓan
  aesthetic impact of, 137, 148–50
  on age of maturity (4:6), 112
  conservative interpretations, 160–6, 174–5
  holistic approaches to, 6, 136–51
  neo-traditionalist interpretations, 160, 162, 170–4
  on slaughtering of meat (5:3; 5:5), 108–9
  reformist interpretations, 160, 162, 166–70, 174–5
  on remarriage after divorce (65:4), 114
  Rowlandson's opinions on, 209–10
  on sexual relations (66:1), 112
  Sura 3, 209
  Sura 5, 141
  Sura 6, 6, 138–51
  Sura 96, 137
  on women's testimony (2:282), 7, 160–75
Qurᵓanic exegesis, 4, 6–7, 136–51, 160–75
Qurᵓanic theological instruction, 145, 147–8, 151
al-Qurṭubī, 36, 252, 253, 254, 256–7
Quṭb, Sayyid, 6, 136, 137, 138, 142, 146–50

radicalism *see* extremism
al-Rafᶜ wa-l-takmīl (al-Laknawī), 67, 68, 75–6
al-Rāfiᶜī, 36
Rahman, Fazlur, 177
Rapoport, Yossef, 103
al-Rāzī, Fakhr al-Dīn, 136, 139–40, 143–4, 146, 151
Rebuttal Against Those Who Follow Other than the Four Madhhabs (Ibn Rajab), 107–8
reformist Qurᵓanic interpretation, 160, 162, 166–70, 174–5
Reinhart, Kevin, 252, 258
resurrection, 10, 247
al-ribā, 101, 108, 115–18
Riḍā, Rashīd, 6, 57, 68–9, 136, 138, 141–5, 150–1, 256, 257
rijāl criticism, 46, 59, 75–6; *see also* hadith criticism
Risālat al-tawḥīd (ᶜAbduh), 256
Riyadh, 10, 66, 73, 117
Robinson, Francis, 80
Robson, James, 45
Rowlandson, Michael John, 8–9, 204–16
al-Rudūd (Bakr Abū Zayd), 67–8
al-Rūḥānī, Ayatallāh Muḥammad Ṣādiq, 26

Saanei, Yusuf, 7, 162, 170–4
Ṣadā al-Malāḥim, 226, 227–42
Sadat, Anwar, 7, 177, 180–1, 184, 191, 192
Saᶜdī, 206–7
al-Ṣādiq, Jaᶜfar, 23
al-Ṣadr, Muḥammad Bāqir, 4, 24
Ṣafaḥāt min ḥayātī (al-Ashqar), 250–1, 252
al-Saffārīnī, 252–3, 254–5
Ṣaḥīḥ Sunan *Ibn Māja* (al-Albānī), 33
al-Sahm al-muṣīb fī kabid al-Khaṭīb (al-Muᶜaẓẓam ᶜĪsā), 62–3
Said, Edward, 226
Salafi corporate publications, 71–4
Salafi reform movement, 54–81
Salafism, 5, 34–7, 54–81, 174, 175, 177, 231, 247–58
sales with conditions, 115–18, 119
Ṣāliḥ, ᶜAlī ᶜAbd Allāh, 229, 232
al-Ṣanᶜānī, Muḥammad al-Amīr, 231–2, 235
al-Ṣanᶜānī, Muḥammad b. Ismāᶜīl, 57
al-Sarakhsī, 114
Saudi Arabia, 5, 33, 56, 64, 66, 69, 71–2, 73, 81, 119, 177, 224, 250–1
al-Sayyid Nūh, al-Sayyid Muḥammad, 45–6
scholarly editions, 5, 53–4, 58–65, 80–1
scholars-cum-editors, 5, 53–4, 60, 65–71, 80–1
schools of law *see madhhabs*
selective reconstruction, 232–4, 242
sexuality, 104, 109–14, 163, 172–3, 257; *see also* marriage

al-Shabaab, 236
al-Shāfiᶜī, 36, 45, 67, 70, 72, 209
Shāfiᶜī school, 37, 64, 103, 105, 107
Shāh Walī Allāh, 54, 55
shakk, 14
Shaltūt, Maḥmūd, 108
al-Shanfarāᵓ, 230
al-Shaᶜranī, ᶜAbd al-Wahhāb, 105
Shaᶜrāwī, Hudā, 111
Shariᶜa, 15, 21, 23, 100–22, 179–80, 215; *see also* Islamic law
al-Shāwīsh, Zuhayr, 58, 60–1, 69, 73
al-Shawkānī, 36, 37
al-Shāyajī, ᶜAbd al-Razzāq ibn Khalīfa, 45–6
al-Shaybānī, Muḥammad b. Ḥasan, 103
al-Shaykh al-Mufīd, 172
al-Shaykh Ḥasan b. al-Shahīd al-Thānī, 17–19, 22
Shihadeh, Ayman, 144
Shiᶜism, 4, 12–27, 167–8, 179, 180, 184
Shils, Edward, 2–3
al-Shinqīṭī, Muḥammad al-Amīn, 66
al-Shīrāzī, Abū Isḥāq, 107
Shirazi, Makarim, 166
shirk, 139
Ṣiffīn, battle of, 179
simulation (of classical poetry), 9, 225, 236–8
al-Sindī, Muḥammad Ḥayāt, 54, 55
Six Books, 33, 39, 253
al-Siyāsa al-sharᶜiyya (Ibn Taymiyya), 194
Smith, Jane Idleman, 249–50
Somalia, 236
South Africa, 108–9
Specimens of 'Much Fine Gold' (Rowlandson), 207, 211
Stetkevych, Suzanne Pinckney, 225
al-Subkī, Taqī al-Dīn, 105
al-Ṣūfī, Māhir Aḥmad, 258
Sufism, 34, 56, 104, 148, 180, 190, 215
al-Suhrawardī, Abū Ḥafṣ, 104
Sunni Islam, 5, 23, 38, 54–81, 102, 105–7, 110, 118, 180, 184, 191, 247, 254, 258
Sūrat al-Anᶜām, 6, 138–51
al-Suyūṭī, Jalāl al-Dīn, 141, 142, 145, 209, 248–9
Syria, 33, 69, 73, 103, 105, 118, 177, 178–9

Taᵓabbata Sharran, 236
al-Ṭabarānī, 253, 254
al-Ṭabarī, 107, 110, 111, 116–17, 118, 139, 149
al-Ṭabāṭabāᵓī, Muḥammad Ḥusayn, 136
al-Tabriᵓa (al-Ẓawāhirī), 231–2
al-Tadhkira fī aḥwāl al-mawtā (al-Qurṭubī), 252
Tafsīr al-manār (Riḍā), 6, 136, 138, 141–5, 150–1
al-Tahānawī, Ashraf ᶜAlī, 67, 68
al-Ṭaḥāwī, Abū Jaᶜfar Aḥmad b. Muḥammad, 61–2, 70, 255
Takhrīj aḥādīth kitābi-hi Ṣifat ṣalāt al-nabī (al-Albānī), 33
Taᵓnīb al-Khaṭīb ᶜalā mā sāqa-hu fī tarjamat Abī Ḥanīfa min al-abāṭīl (al-Kawtharī), 63–4
Al-Tankīl bi-mā fī taᵓnīb al-Kawtharī min al-abāṭīl (al-Muᶜallimī), 64–5, 67, 71–2
al-Ṭanṭāwī, ᶜAlī, 118
taqlīd, 35, 70
al-Taqrīb (Ibn Ḥajar), 39, 40
al-Tārīkh al-awsaṭ (al-Bukhārī), 67
al-Tārīkh al-kabīr (al-Bukhārī), 67
Tārīkh Baghdād (al-Khaṭīb al-Baghdādī), 62–5, 76
Taylor, Jeremy, 210
temporary marriage, 100–1, 108, 118, 120
Temporary Marriage is Prohibited in Islam (Ḥāmid), 101
terrorism, 7–8, 9–10, 189–90, 223–42; *see also* extremism
testimony, 7, 160–75
'Textes spirituels' (Michot), 183–5
al-Thawrī, Sufyān, 46, 107
Thomas, David, 213–14
al-Tibrīzī, Ayatallāh Jawād, 21, 24–5
al-Tirmidhī, 33, 38–9, 41
Tohfut-Ul-Mujahideen (Rowlandson), 8–9, 204–16
tradition, defining, 2–3
transgressive perfomance, 240
Transvaal fatwa 108–9
tribal values, 224, 229–32, 236, 242
Tuḥfat al-mujāhidīn fī baᶜḍ aḥwāl al-Burtugāliyyīn (Zainuddin), 8–9, 204–16
Turkey, 8, 177, 186–9

Uljaytū, 179, 180
al-ᶜUqaylī, 62, 76
ᶜUmar, Bashīr ᶜAlī, 46–7
al-ᶜUmda (al-ᶜAzīz), 181

al-ᶜUrwa al-wuthqā, 34
al-ᶜUthmānī, Ẓafar Aḥmad, 76–7
utilitarianism, 178, 181–2, 187, 193–6

van Ess, Josef, 256
veiling, 33, 39–40, 230
Venture of Islam, The (Hodgson), 52, 53
Vilayatullah, Ahamad Ilyaas, 204, 213–14, 216
violence, 4, 7–8, 9–10, 177–86, 190–3, 194–6, 225–6, 223–42
Voll, John, 54

al-waḍᶜ, 15–24, 25
al-waḍᶜ al-taᶜayyunī, 22–3
al-waḍᶜ al-taᶜyīnī, 24
al-Wahhāb, Muḥammad b. ᶜAbd, 54
Wahhābism, 177
waqf, 101, 103
Weber, Max, 239
West, the, 52, 108–9, 110, 120, 151, 165–6, 185, 214, 216, 224, 226, 249
Woman Question, The (Mehrizi), 167
women
  attendance at mosque, 37
  as deficient in reason and religion, 7, 161, 169, 256–7
  female poets, 230–1
  and gender equality, 7, 160–75, 233, 256–7
  leading prayers, 37, 118
  marriage age, 6, 102, 109–14, 118, 119–20
  in paradise, 248–9, 257
  permission to marry, 103
  physiology, 163–5
  remarriage after divorce, 114
  representations of, 230–1
  and testimony, 7, 160–75
  use of public baths, 37
  veiling, 33, 39–40, 230
al-Wuḥayshī, Nāṣir, 233, 235–6

yāsa, 180–1
al-Yawm al-ākhir (al-Ashqar), 10, 247, 250–8
Yemen, 110, 177, 229–30, 231–2, 233
Yule, Henry, 213

al-Zabīdī, Murtaḍā, 16
Ẓāhirat al-irjāᵓ fi-l-fikr al-islāmī (al-Ḥawālī), 56
Ẓāhirī school, 107
Zainuddin Makhdum, 8–9, 204–16
zakāt, 179, 180–1
Zaman, Muhammad Qasim, 54
Zanj revolt, 236
ẓann, 14
al-Zarkashī, 120
al-Zarqāwī, Abū Muṣᶜab, 223
al-Ẓawāhirī, Ayman, 223, 231–2, 235
Zebiri, Kate, 138
zinā, 163, 172–3
Zubayr b, al-ᶜAwwām, 72, 114
Zufar, 101, 102, 103, 120
al-Zuḥaylī, Wahba, 119

EU representative:
Easy Access System Europe
Mustamäe tee 50, 10621 Tallinn, Estonia
Gpsr.requests@easproject.com

www.ingramcontent.com/pod-product-compliance
Lightning Source LLC
Chambersburg PA
CBHW061708300426
44115CB00014B/2604
9781474432160